Enforcing Shareholders' Duties

ELGAR FINANCIAL LAW

Series Editor: Takis Tridimas, *Queen Mary, University of London, UK*

This important series comprises high quality monographs on a wide range of topics in the field of financial law, hosting work by established authors of international reputation, alongside younger and more emerging authors. The series is synonymous with original thinking and new, challenging research. The subjects under consideration range from financial services law, through securities regulation, to banking law and from financial fraud, through legal aspects of European Monetary Union and the single currency, to the legal workings of international financial institutions.

Titles in the series include:

Secured Transactions Reform and Access to Credit
Edited by Frederique Dahan and John Simpson

Financial Regulation in Crisis?
The Role of the Law and the Failure of Northern Rock
Edited by Joanna Gray and Orkun Akseli

Law Reform and Financial Markets
Edited by Kern Alexander and Niamh Moloney

Regulating Credit Rating Agencies
Aline Darbellay

The Law of Securities, Commodities and Bank Accounts
The Rights of Account Holders
Marek Dubovec

Executive Compensation in Imperfect Financial Markets
Jay Cullen

Bank Funding, Liquidity, and Capital Adequacy
A Law and Finance Approach
José Gabilondo

Regulating Financial Derivatives
Clearing and Central Counterparties
Alexandra G. Balmer

Enforcing Shareholders' Duties
Edited by Hanne S. Birkmose and Konstantinos Sergakis

Enforcing Shareholders' Duties

Edited by

Hanne S. Birkmose

Professor, Department of Law, Aarhus University, Denmark

Konstantinos Sergakis

Senior Lecturer in Law, University of Glasgow, UK

ELGAR FINANCIAL LAW

Edward Elgar
PUBLISHING

Cheltenham, UK • Northampton, MA, USA

Published by
Edward Elgar Publishing Limited
The Lypiatts
15 Lansdown Road
Cheltenham
Glos GL50 2JA
UK

Edward Elgar Publishing, Inc.
William Pratt House
9 Dewey Court
Northampton
Massachusetts 01060
USA

A catalogue record for this book
is available from the British Library

Library of Congress Control Number: 2018960566

This book is available electronically in the **Elgar**online
Law subject collection
DOI 10.4337/9781788114875

Printed on elemental chlorine free (ECF)
recycled paper containing 30% Post-Consumer Waste

ISBN 978 1 78811 486 8 (cased)
ISBN 978 1 78811 487 5 (eBook)

Printed and bound in the USA

Contents

Contributors

EDITORS

Hanne S. Birkmose took her PhD in Law at the Aarhus School of Business in 2003. In 2016 she was appointed professor at the Department of Law, Aarhus University. Her research areas include company law – in particular international company law and EU company law – and corporate governance, and she has written several national and international articles within these areas. She is also the author of books on UCITS and Alternative Investment Funds in Denmark. Recently, she has mainly worked on shareholder activism and the role of institutional shareholders. In 2014 she received a three-year research grant from the Danish Independent Research Council for a project on 'Shareholders' Duties'. Hanne S. Birkmose is a member of the ECGI (European Corporate Governance Institute, Brussels), the Nordic Company Law Network and the Nordic Corporate Governance Network.

Konstantinos Sergakis is a Senior Lecturer in Commercial Law, Director of the LLM in Corporate and Financial Law and School Director of Internationalisation at the University of Glasgow. His book *The Transparency of Listed Companies in EU Law* received the prestigious prize 'Prix Solennel André Isoré' under the Presidency of the French Prime Minister as well as the 2011–2012 Special Grant from the Alexander S. Onassis Foundation. He has recently published *The Law of Capital Markets in the EU* (Palgrave Macmillan). He currently sits on the editorial board of the journals *Corporate Ownership and Control* and *Corporate Governance and Sustainability Review*. He also serves as a member of the Executive Boards of the International Association of Economic Law and of the Transnational Network in Banking and Financial Law. Konstantinos Sergakis's research interests are related to corporate law, EU capital markets law and corporate governance. He has participated in numerous international conferences and regularly publishes articles in English and French.

CONTRIBUTORS

Anita Anand is a Professor of Law and holds the J.R. Kimber Chair in Investor Protection and Corporate Governance at the University of Toronto. She served as Associate Dean at the Faculty of Law from 2007 to 2009 and since 2010 has served as the Academic Director of the Centre for the Legal Profession and its Program on Ethics in Law and Business. She is a Senior Fellow and member of the Governing Board, Massey College and is cross-appointed to the Rotman School of Management and the School of Public Policy and Governance. During the 2009–2010 academic year, Professor Anand was a Visiting Scholar at the Bank of Canada and a Herbert Smith Visitor at the University of Cambridge. In 2005–2006, she was a Canada-U.S. Fulbright Scholar and Visiting Olin Scholar in Law and Economics at Yale Law School. During the Fall 2005, she was a Visiting Lecturer in Law at Yale Law School where she taught comparative corporate governance. In Fall 2017, she was appointed Director of Policy and Research at the Capital Markets Institute, Rotman School of Management. She is a member of the Ontario Securities Commission's Securities Advisory Committee and serves on both charitable and public company boards.

Justin Borg-Barthet is a Senior Lecturer at the Centre for Private International Law, School of Law, University of Aberdeen. His research focusses on the private international law of the European Union. He has published work on a range of topics, including European company law, with a core interest in the balance between individual freedoms and the residual rights of EU Member States to govern their socio-economic affairs. His work on private international law has been cited with approval by an Advocate General of the Court of Justice of the European Union. He has acted as a consultant to the European Parliament and as an advisor on consultancy for the European Commission. He studied Law and European Studies at the University of Malta. After qualifying as an advocate in Malta, he pursued postgraduate studies at the University of Aberdeen.

Iris H-Y. Chiu is Professor of Corporate Law and Financial Regulation at the Faculty of Laws, University College London, UK. She previously taught at the School of Law, King's College London and the University of Leicester. She was a legislative draftsman and State Counsel at the Attorney-General's Chambers in Singapore prior to joining academia. Iris has published on directors' duties, shareholder stewardship and corporate governance, as well as regulatory theories and governance in the financial sector. Her key monographs are *The Foundations and Anatomy of Shareholder Activism* (Hart Publishing, 2010), *The Foundations and Future of Financial Regulation* (Routledge, 2014, co-authored with Mads Andenas) and *The Legal Framework for Internal*

Control in Banks and Financial Institutions (Hart Publishing, 2015). She is Executive Editor of the *European Business Law Review* and Co-Series Editor of the Palgrave Macmillan Corporate and Financial Law Series. She is also Director of the UCL Centre for Ethics and Law.

Matteo Gargantini works at Consob, the Italian Securities and Exchange Commission. Before joining Consob, he was Senior Research Fellow at the Max Planck Institute Luxembourg for Procedural Law. He also worked in the Capital Markets and Listed Companies Unit of Assonime, the Association of the Italian joint-stock companies. He holds a PhD in Banking and Financial Markets Law from the University of Siena, and received the Italian National Academic Qualification as Associate Professor (Law and Economics and Financial Markets Law). He teaches Financial Market Law and Regulation at Luiss Guido Carli University in Rome.

Elizabeth Howell is the Slaughter and May Lecturer in Corporate Law, and a fellow and college lecturer at Magdalene College, Cambridge. She teaches courses on contract law, company law, corporate finance, and financial regulation. Her research interests include corporate law and capital markets regulation, with particular reference to European financial market regulation. She has been a visitor to Columbia Law School, is a guest member of the Otto Hahn Group on Financial Regulation at the Max Planck Institute, and was awarded the Des Voeux Chambers Cambridge-HKU Visiting Fellowship in 2018. She is currently a member of the Consultative Working Group of the European Securities and Markets Authority (ESMA)'s Corporate Finance Standing Committee.

Corrado Malberti has been Associate Professor of Commercial Law at the University of Trento since 2015. From 2010 to 2015 he was Associate Professor of Commercial Law at the University of Luxembourg, where he was also director of the Master 1 in European Law. He graduated from the University of Milan. He completed an LLM at the University of Chicago and a PhD in Commercial Law at Bocconi University. He has published widely in the fields of company law and financial market regulation in English, Italian and French.

Mette Neville is a professor of Company Law at the Aarhus School of Business and Social Sciences, Aarhus University. Her main research areas are company law and housing law, and she is the author of numerous books and articles on these subjects. Her special interest is small and medium-sized enterprises. She is the Director of the interdisciplinary Centre for Small and Medium-sized Enterprises at Aarhus BSS, which heads several large projects on growth in SMEs, for example 'Growth Management for the Future in SMEs' (Vækstledelse for fremtiden i SMV'er) and 'The SME Board as Digital Catalyst' (SMV-bestyrelsen som digital katalysator). Mette Neville has also served on various preparatory committees on law, for instance the Danish Committee for Financial Supervisory Structure under the Danish Ministry of Economic and Business Affairs. She has also served as a Danish member of legal scholar networks in connection with EU studies.

Jennifer Payne is a professor of Corporate Finance Law at the University of Oxford and a fellow and tutor of Merton College, Oxford. She writes widely in the field of corporate law in leading journals and edited collections. Her publications include *Principles of Financial Regulation* (OUP, 2016, with John Armour et al); *The Oxford Handbook of Financial Regulation* (OUP, 2015, with Niamh Moloney and Eilis Ferran); and *Corporate Finance Law: Principles and Policy* (Hart Publishing, 2011, 3rd edition 2019, with Louise Gullifer). Jennifer is a contributor to *Palmer's Company Law*, a founder editor of the *Journal of Corporate Law Studies* and a founder editor of the Oxford Business Law Blog. She has been a visiting professor at a number of leading institutions internationally, including Melbourne Law School, the National University of Singapore and the University of Auckland. Jennifer was a member of ESMA's Securities and Markets Stakeholder Group from 2016–2018.

Christopher Puskas is entering his final year of law at the University of Toronto. Prior to entering law school, he received his Honours Bachelor of Arts (High Distinction) from the University of Toronto, where he graduated with the Gold Medal in Sociology and an award for the Best Undergraduate Research Paper. Today, he is particularly interested in private and corporate law matters. In law school, he has won a course award in Contracts and has recently won the 2018 Davies' Corporate/Securities law moot, where he also placed as the second best oralist. Prior to law school, Christopher Puskas was a competitive debater for seven years and competed nationally and internationally for the University of Toronto.

Karsten Engsig Sørensen is a professor at the Department of Law at Aarhus University. He holds a Danish law degree, a PhD (on EU Company Law), and a Danish Dr. Jur. (on joint ventures). He also has an LLM from the University of Exeter. His research is mainly focused on EU law and company law, and within these areas he has published several books and articles in both Danish and English. Additionally, he has been the editor of several books on company law, EU law and WTO law, appearing with, inter alia, Kluwer Law International and Cambridge University Press. He is a one of the two editors of the SSRN e-journal *Nordic and European Company Law* and a member of the Nordic Network for Company Law.

Christoph Teichmann is a professor of law and holds the Chair for Civil Law, German and European Company Law at the University of Würzburg, Germany. He graduated at the University of Heidelberg where he also obtained his doctoral degree. He then worked for two years in a law firm in Frankfurt, Germany, before returning to the University of Heidelberg and completing his *Habilitation* thesis (*Binnenmarktkonformes Gesellschaftsrecht*). He is co-editor of ZGR (*Zeitschrift für Unternehmens- und Gesellschaftsrecht*) and chief managing editor of ECFR (*European Company and Financial Law Review*) as well as a member of several international expert groups on company law, including the working group on the EMCA (*European Model Company Act*) and the ICLEG (*Informal Company Law Expert Group* consulting the European Commission).

Christoph Van der Elst is Professor of Business Law and Economics at Tilburg University (the Netherlands) and at Ghent University (Belgium), lecturing in the field of corporate law (and its economic analysis), corporate governance, and commercial contracts. He has also published widely on these topics. He holds both a master in law and a master in economics and has obtained a PhD in economics. He is an ECGI Research Associate, member of the Belgian Bar (Cottyn), chairman of the professional examination commission of registered auditors and member of the audit committee of the Ghent University Hospital.

Christian A. Witting is Professor of Private Law at Queen Mary University of London and an occasional Visiting Professor at the National University of Singapore. He is a Barrister and Solicitor of the High Court of Australia, formerly in service with the Commonwealth Attorney's General's Department. Christian has research interests in both company law and tort law. He is the author of two monographs – *Liability of Corporate Groups and Networks* (Cambridge University Press, 2018) and *Liability for Negligent Misstatements* (Oxford University Press, 2004). He is also the fourth and current author of the textbook *Street on Torts* (Oxford University Press, 15th edn, 2018).

Lothar Wolff is a PhD candidate at the Chair for Civil Law, German and European Company Law, University of Würzburg, Germany. He studied law at the University of Freiburg, Germany, where he obtained his law degree. His areas of expertise include company law, European law and comparative law. He is currently working on a PhD thesis on the law of corporate groups in Europe.

Foreword

In recent years, extensive attention has been paid to the role of shareholders in corporate governance. A lively discourse has developed among regulators, academics and the financial community on the role of shareholders in ensuring sustainable, long-term, corporate welfare and, more generally, the stability of the financial markets. In this context, shareholders' duties are viewed, albeit not without discord, as a driver for constructive capitalism. This volume, edited by Hanne S. Birkmose and Konstantinos Sergakis, is an important addition to this debate. It explores enforcement mechanisms of shareholder duties and is divided into four parts looking respectively at the contours and sources of shareholder duties, their enforcement, and barriers thereto. As stated by its editors, the objective of the volume is to provide an overview of the framework for the enforcement of shareholders' duties and reflect on their efficiency, adaptability to market developments, and suitability to meet the challenges of contemporary corporate and capital markets.

The contributors discuss various forms of legal and social enforcement of shareholders' duties. Whilst traditionally corporate law has relied on private enforcement, the growth of capital market regulation has introduced a host of public enforcement mechanisms. The bias in favour of public enforcement has been strengthened by the development of supranational regulatory fora, primarily the EU, which, for reasons relating to their competence, remit and nature, are better placed to introduce public rather than private law disciplines. Still, the boundaries between private and public forms of enforcement are more porous than they might appear. The contributions examine and assess various ways of enhancing private enforcement mechanisms and outline barriers to which they are subject, including jurisdictional obstacles in inter-state share ownership and obstacles posed by the lack of shareholder identification mechanisms. They also examine public law tools and, importantly, the value of social mechanisms of enforcement, which may function as the substratum for effective compliance.

The volume revisits some classic questions and addresses some new ones. Should shareholders owe fiduciary duties to the company or inter se? What explains differences among national laws in this respect? Does the rise in shareholder activism and the diversity of their interests or financial innovation justify the imposition of duties on them? Does shareholder activism lead to positive externalities for other market participants? Should EU law intervene in this area and, if so, how prescriptive should it be?

The volume examines shareholder duties in the era of fiduciary capitalism, namely the increasing participation of retail investors in corporate capital through the intermediation of institutional investors. The discourse in the various chapters is worthy and highlights perhaps three main elements: first, the need to strike the optimum balance between, on the one hand, shareholder discretion, reflecting the quasi proprietary character of shareholder rights and the character of investment decisions as individual choices made by rational economic actors, and, on the other hand, shareholder duties, demonstrating the importance of corporate activities for collective welfare; secondly, the distinction between private and public law; and thirdly, the interaction between legal and social forms of enforcement.

The publication of this volume is timely. Institutional investors are one of the market actors whose role has come under scrutiny in the aftermath of the global financial crisis of 2008 and the ensuing Eurozone crisis. In 2017, the EU adopted Directive 2017/828, due to be implemented by Member States by 10 June 2019, which seeks to encourage long-term shareholder engagement. Its objective is to increase engagement by institutional investors and asset managers and the level of monitoring of investee companies through a 'comply or explain' approach. Institutional investors and asset managers are to develop and publicly disclose an engagement policy that describes how they integrate shareholder engagement in their investment strategy. Directive 2017/828 endorses a certain idea of capitalism and fits in the wider EU policy agenda to provide for a restrained free market model. The directive views shareholders as conduits for promoting the accountability of corporates and, ultimately, as agents of good governance.

The contributors assess regulatory interventions, overall, in a positive light but there is a good degree of scepticism as to whether reliance on hard law to increase the duties of shareholders is beneficial and likely to fulfil its avowed objectives. The imposition of duties on shareholders may be rationalised by reference to various arguments but essentially forms part of a policy agenda that instrumentalises share ownership for the achievement of political objectives.

The volume brings together corporate law scholars from civil and common law jurisdictions and has a global reach. The authors offer engaging contributions from diverse perspectives, and the reader will find interdisciplinary reflections, a wealth of comparative material, original arguments, and valuable insights. This is an extremely welcome contribution to the bibliography on an important topic on which the debate is likely to remain lively for years to come.

Takis Tridimas

London, October 2018

1. Introduction

Hanne S. Birkmose and Konstantinos Sergakis

The discussion on shareholders' duties has increasingly gained momentum in the EU and has given rise to the adoption of duties in both company law and capital markets law. However, this discussion must be extended further if the duties that are increasingly imposed on shareholders are to have a genuine effect on the viability of the recent regulatory developments in this area. Enforcement mechanisms are crucial to this discussion as they are vital to preserving the credibility of markets, to ensuring compliance with regulatory objectives and with sound corporate governance practices, as well as to holding accountable persons who are supposed to fulfil the vast range of shareholders' duties. This volume presents a series of contributions touching on enforcement mechanisms that are already in place, as well as emerging or hypothetical mechanisms that will be at the centre of debate for the years to come. The overall objective of this volume is to provide a reliable overview of enforcement frameworks and to reflect on their efficiency, adaptability to market developments and suitability to the current challenges we face in company and capital markets law. This introductory chapter gives a concise presentation of the various arguments raised and focuses on the numerous rationales for enforcement and the various types of enforcement (legal and social) in the area of shareholders' duties.

I. THE SUITABILITY AND EFFICIENCY OF ENFORCEMENT

The increased emphasis on shareholders' duties has been strong at both EU and national levels. Legislators and academics have discussed which roles shareholders should have in an efficient corporate governance framework and how to ensure sensible market practices by the investor community.

In her contribution, Hanne S. Birkmose employs an analytical framework based on concepts borrowed from agency theory and economic theories of market failure to offer an understanding of why the law imposes duties on shareholders in general.[1] She argues that most often duties address the principal–agent problem that may arise between majority and minority shareholders, but also that market failure may justify imposing duties on shareholders in order to ensure the efficiency of the market. Most of the duties found in company and capital market law can be regarded as regulatory strategies[2] employed by legislators to constrain the agent's undesired behaviour. Moreover, this framework may also explain why some duties only apply to a subset of the shareholder population.[3]

However, Birkmose finds that there are exceptions as some duties can hardly be explained by the reduction of agency costs or the elimination of market failure, but seem to serve wider purposes, such as social or political objectives. This is particularly the case when it comes to the revision of the Shareholder Rights Directive[4] and the disclosure duties imposed on institutional investors. The arguments presented in the preamble of the directive in support of the imposition of special duties on institutional investors are rather vague and do not seem to be based either on the premise of agency problems or on concerns about market failure. Rather, the arguments seem to support a political agenda that has gained momentum in the wake of the financial crisis,[5] whereby legislators not only aim to constrain the actions of institutional investors in specific ways, but also to change the behaviour of institutional investors without clearly specifying what the expectations are. Consequently, enforcement becomes essential to assist this transformation. While Birkmose concludes that it is yet to be seen whether the chosen enforcement regime – which partly relies on private enforcement – will suffice, Christoph Van der Elst expresses serious concern that the European regulatory developments on institutional investors may even have counterproductive consequences for shareholder engagement. In particular, Van der Elst warns that the mandatory 'comply or explain' framework may endanger the current flexible relationship

---

1 Chapter 3, sec. II.

2 On the concepts of different legal strategies, see John Armour, Henry Hansmann and Reinier Kraakman, 'Agency Problems and Legal Strategies' in Reinier Kraakman, John Armour, Paul Davies, Luca Enriques, Henry Hansmann and Gerard Hertig (eds), *The Anatomy of Corporate Law. A Comparative and Functional Approach* (OUP 2017) 31.

3 Chapter 3, sec. III.

4 Directive 2017/828/EU of the European Parliament and of the Council of 17 May 2017 amending Directive 2007/36/EC as regards the encouragement of long-term shareholder engagement [2017] OJL132/1(Shareholder Rights Directive).

5 Hanne S. Birkmose, 'Forcing Shareholder Engagement – Theoretical Underpinning and Political Ambitions' (2018) Eur. Bus. L. Rev. 4, 639ff.

between investors and listed companies, and may result in a more rigid engagement practice by institutional investors.[6]

As discussed by Van der Elst, the changing investor landscape, while having created momentum for engagement duties for institutional investors in the EU,[7] may not be as strong a motivation for increased engagement as has been emphasised. While institutional investors have increased their ownership in European companies,[8] Van der Elst argues that not only is the actual influence of these investors in the individual companies relatively small, but the European Commission has failed to provide evidence that this group of shareholders causes the identified market failures.[9] Moreover, he finds that the prescribed duties may not necessarily be the proper remedy to solve the problems. Similar to the discussion of a fiduciary duty, the duties in the Shareholder Rights Directive may have negative side-effects in some situations. In particular, Van der Elst argues that not only may it be difficult to prove a breach of the duties in some situations, but the mandatory 'comply or explain' shareholders' duties may have a rigidifying effect on the practices of institutional investors and their relationships with investee companies.[10]

Interestingly, while the increase in institutional ownership has occurred in other jurisdictions as well – such as the US and Canada – the reliance on shareholders' duties seems to be stronger in Europe than elsewhere. Canada is particular noteworthy in this respect because Canadian markets, as well as most European markets, are characterised by a high degree of concentrated ownership. Thus, there may be more opportunities for opportunistic conduct there, and we could expect a similar development on shareholders' duties in Canada. Nonetheless, such a development is absent.

Duties can take on different forms,[11] and a well-known debate in company law is whether or not shareholders, in particular those with a controlling interest, owe fiduciary duties to other shareholders. In their contribution, Anita Anand and Christopher Puskas find that, in a Canadian context, shareholders' fiduciary duties lack a persuasive rationale despite the growing importance of shareholders in corporate governance and, moreover, that fiduciary duties are inefficient from an enforcement perspective.

---

[6] Chapter 4, sec. IV.

[7] See Chapter 4, sec. III.

[8] Chapter 4, Table 4.1.

[9] Chapter 4, sec. III.B.

[10] Chapter 4, sec. IV.

[11] Hanne S. Birkmose and Florian Möslein, 'Introduction: Mapping Shareholders' Duties' in Hanne S. Birkmose (ed), *Shareholders' Duties* (Kluwer Law International 2017) 1.

In particular, they state that a fiduciary duty may have negative effects as it may disincentivise investments by imposing costs and obligations on shareholders.[12] Furthermore, with reference to the Canadian company law and capital markets law framework, sufficient *ex ante* and *ex post* protection may, in the authors' view, provide a more efficient protection of minority shareholders than could be provided by a fiduciary duty. The different approaches to institutional ownership found in different countries offer proof that this discussion is highly politicised.

We will now turn our attention to the specific types of enforcement applicable to shareholders' duties to examine their merits and limitations in this specific area. This will in turn allow us to draw some conclusions and reflect on future regulatory steps.

II. LEGAL ENFORCEMENT

Legal enforcement can be broken down into private and public enforcement. Private enforcement has not been harmonised in an increased fashion across the EU due to national idiosyncrasies and different legal traditions. Moreover, for private enforcement mechanisms to counterbalance any violation of shareholders' duties, private parties need to exercise their rights by having the necessary information, interest, resources and time to perform such a role. These conditions are not always met, especially taking into account the ever-increasing financial intermediation in the investment chain, the communication gap between market actors and the predominant governance role exercised by funds in their day-to-day management of beneficiaries' assets. These factors have gradually disempowered beneficiaries and other affected parties from exercising their role.

Public enforcement has received much more political and legislative attention, especially in the area of administrative sanctions and measures given the increased powers awarded to regulatory bodies that are progressively being seen as more fit to exercise such powers and more adaptable to market developments and strategies. Criminal sanctions nevertheless remain largely dependent on national laws in the absence of harmonisation efforts in the area of shareholders' duties and, more generally, of capital markets law violations.[13] In the area of shareholders' duties, criminal sanctions are particularly modest or even non-existent. In his contribution, Konstantinos Sergakis explains this

---

[12] Chapter 2, sec. III.B.

[13] With the exception of a modest harmonisation effort introduced by the Market Abuse Directive: Directive 2014/57/EU of the European Parliament and of the Council of 16 April 2014 on criminal sanctions for insider dealing and market manipulation [2014] OJ L173/179.

situation in light of the traditional and long-standing predominance of private enforcement in this area since the violation of shareholders' duties is primarily seen as an internal company matter.

The two main and most common objectives of legal enforcement are the protection of minority shareholders in an intra-shareholder relationship and a wider protection of other parties potentially affected by the breach of shareholders' duties (including investors, stakeholders, etc.). The first category mainly operates within a company law spectrum, with a series of difficulties that make enforcement problematic (with proof of the damage and quantification of damage being the most notable hurdles). The second category is driven by capital markets law considerations and has attracted more attention given the ever-wider powers granted to regulatory bodies for handling breaches of shareholders' duties.[14]

In her chapter, Iris H-Y. Chiu argues that the boundaries between private and public enforcement in the area of shareholders' duties cannot be clearly identified. This can be explained in the light of the emergence of regulatory standards in an area of law that has traditionally been seen as a private matter between company constituencies (enabling company law rules) but has more recently been seen in a public interest perspective (more constraining and overarching securities regulation rules). Chiu notes that granting enforcement powers to regulatory bodies can be seen as a form of private enforcement since the regulatory intervention constitutes a form of collective action taken by an authority that is desired by market participants. At the same time, this type of enforcement can be seen as public in nature since the regulator seeks to protect the wider public interest. Most interestingly, in this respect, Chiu questions whether private and public enforcement should be 'clearly delineated in accordance with the nature of persons carrying out the enforcement, or the nature of the causes sought to be addressed'.[15] The following sections aim to highlight the various facets and trends that private and public enforcement have shown in shareholders' duties.

A. Private Enforcement

1. Types of private enforcement

Private enforcement of shareholders' duties forms an important pillar of company law regimes as it enables private parties to secure their rights against other shareholders who violate or abuse them. Nevertheless, enforcing duties

---

[14] For a more in-depth analysis of this dichotomy in the area of financial sanctions, see Chapter 9, sec. IV.

[15] Chapter 6, sec. I.

against shareholders is not always a straightforward task. Under a general scope of analysis, the enforcement mechanisms for the violation of shareholders' duties can be numerous. For example, as analysed in Corrado Malberti's chapter, these can include pecuniary sanctions and damages, invalidation of decisions taken within the company (for example, suspension of voting rights[16]), invalidation of companies' or shareholders' actions, exit options for harmed shareholders, or even exclusion of the shareholders in breach.[17]

In her chapter, Chiu notes the traditional resistance of company law to impose and enforce duties on shareholders, who are considered to hold quasi-proprietary rights in companies.[18] Christian A. Witting also acknowledges this tradition by referring, more specifically, to the well-known limited liability principle. Witting argues that shareholders hold a very important role at the top of the hierarchy in the corporate governance structures and that the 'governance function belongs to them and to no one else'.[19] He therefore proposes a residual pro rata strict shareholder liability solely in the case of unsatisfied personal injury claims from corporate wrongdoing. This new regime would, in his view, incentivise and constrain shareholders to assume their responsibilities in the governance of companies. This approach may unlock shareholders' capacity to influence corporate governance in order to avoid corporate wrongdoing that may result in personal injuries.[20] Witting also recognises that strict liability in this framework would go against the well-known limited liability principle in company law, and he therefore proposes a series of applicability criteria and conditions for such a regime to be adopted and enforced appropriately. Enforcement of such regimes may not be straightforward, hence the need to carefully design all possible ways that will make these proposals achievable. Deterrence of wrongdoing is key, according to Witting, given the hierarchical structure and formalised decision-making processes of companies that may allow them, with the input of incentivised shareholders who bear liability, to constrain behaviour and avoid wrongdoing.

Deterrence is also a central theme in the chapter on suspension of voting rights by Mette Neville and Karsten Engsig Sørensen. Suspension of voting rights was introduced at EU level through Directive 2013/50/EU[21] but it is a sanction that was already present in several Member States prior to the adoption of the directive. As some Member States have first-hand experience

---

16 Discussed in detail in Chapter 8.

17 Chapter 5, sec. III. See also Chapter 9, sec. IV.A.

18 Chapter 6, sec. II.

19 Chapter 10, sec. IX.

20 Chapter 10, sec. VII.

21 Directive 2013/50/EU amending the Transparency Directive (Directive 2004/109/EC) [2013] OJ L294/13. The amendments were to be implemented by November 2015.

with suspension and others do not, Neville and Engsig Sørensen enumerate the merits and shortfalls of the suspension of voting rights based on the available experiences. They find that suspension of voting rights may have wider potential, not only as a sanction, but also as a preventive measure, in particular in cases where the shareholders value the influence they gain through their voting rights and the shareholders have misused, or are likely to misuse, their influence within the company.[22] While they discuss the potential of suspension of voting rights in relation to duties imposed by law as well as by the private ordering of shareholders, they conclude that the greatest potential for suspension as a sanction exists in relation to the many different duties found in either the company's articles of association or in shareholders' agreements.[23] However, they also set out a number of relevant issues – including the sanctioning procedure, the duration of the sanction and which rights should be suspended[24] – that Member States and shareholders should consider if suspension is to become an efficient sanction for the infringement of duties.

Turning our attention to the various sources of private enforcement, a company's constitution may be a more feasible way to enforce duties against shareholders, mainly thanks to its contractual nature, since it binds both the company and the shareholders in a relationship. However, as Chiu notes, majority rules may prevail and impede such enforcement.[25]

Jennifer Payne and Elizabeth Howell further argue that enforcement of duties arising from the statutory contract may also be a complex task since courts perceive some issues as mere internal irregularities, potentially ratifiable by the majority, or require shareholders to bring actions in their capacity as members of the company and not in any other capacity. The authors also note the rarity of financial sanctions in this framework.[26] An alternative way to secure enforcement against majority rules can be found in the unfair prejudice petition, which aims to protect minority shareholders in an equitable fashion.[27]

Another option that may facilitate private enforcement is via a shareholders' agreement that requires the consent of all participating parties in order to bind them. Such agreements usually refer to shareholders' rights and they are less attractive in relation to shareholders' duties. As Payne and Howell note, such agreements may be more relevant in small companies and less important in larger companies with an anonymous and frequently changing

---

22 Chapter 8, sec. III.A.
23 Chapter 8, sec. IV.A.
24 Chapter 8, sec. III.B.
25 Chapter 6, sec. II.A.
26 Chapter 9, sec. III.B.
27 See Chapter 6, sec. II.B and Chapter 9, sec. III.B.

shareholder base.[28] Moreover, the award of financial remedies due to a breach of duty under a shareholders' agreement may not be straightforward. Indeed, it would be difficult to prove or quantify the losses suffered by the breach of some shareholders' duties or, more simply, the loss may have been suffered by the company and not by a shareholder, therefore barring shareholders from enforcing the breach of duties. The inclusion of agreed damage clauses in shareholders' agreements could, according to Payne and Howell, be a viable alternative in light of the above-mentioned difficulties.[29] Other means to ensure performance of shareholders' duties may also be available, such as injunctions, court orders, specific performance and equivalent enforcement.[30]

Bylaws constitute another source of enforcement of shareholders' duties. They do not require the unanimous consent of all shareholders and, as such, they may have negative effects on minority shareholders. The differences that they may have from shareholders' agreements are numerous and relate to the effects on third parties, the modalities of their adoption and modification, and their relationship with mandatory law provisions.[31] It must also be borne in mind that national laws adopt different approaches in relation to the effects of shareholders' agreements and bylaws; this further complicates enforcement features in this area of duties.

2. Barriers to enforcement

The enforcement of shareholders' duties arising from national law frequently involves a cross-border aspect as shareholders often invest in companies that are not governed by their own jurisdiction. Thus, the potential for private litigation may not be fully explored by private parties because of the litigation problems caused by jurisdictional barriers, as discussed by Justin Borg-Barthet.

The relationship between shareholders and company stakeholders that attempt to enforce shareholders' duties will be characterised by the absence of a choice-of-court agreement. This may reduce predictability, delay proceedings and increase costs of litigation.[32] There is an inherent risk that the room for jurisdictional challenge that is found in numerous situations may be abused by the stronger party in a dispute. Shareholders at risk of being sued for not fulfilling their duties will often, if not always, be large or professional investors who can take advantage of the lack of legal clarity. Consequently, Borg-Barthet argues that common classification of claims against shareholders

[28] Chapter 9, sec. II.

[29] Chapter 9, sec. II.C.

[30] For a more general discussion of these issues and further implications for affected parties, see Chapter 5, sec. IV.C.

[31] For a more general discussion of these differences, see Chapter 5, sec. IV.B.

[32] Chapter 13, sec. II.A.

by non-shareholder constituents could lead to more optimal enforcement.[33] However, due to the even greater uncertainty in cases connected to jurisdictions outside the European jurisdiction area, Borg-Barthet also argues for the need for coordination of state intervention to minimise the judicial barriers to private enforcement.[34] According to Borg-Barthet, these arguments are based on a premise that shareholders owe duties to the state, whereas the state has an interest in monitoring the activities of shareholders. This could lead to actions against shareholders by state authorities *ex officio*, or state intervention could support traditional private international mechanisms leading to a more efficient private enforcement regime.

Barriers may also flow from primary EU law, as discussed by Christoph Teichmann and Lothar Wolff, and measures regulating and enforcing shareholders' duties will have to be assessed in the light of EU primary law. Primary law is important to the feasibility of the enforcement of shareholders' duties: investors making cross-border investments may rely on the free movement of capital or on the freedom of establishment. But companies formed in accordance with the law of a Member State may also enjoy freedom of establishment in their own right, and the shareholders' position as members of the company is also protected in relation to corporate mobility.[35] If shareholders' duties prevent or deter foreign investments, e.g. by imposing fines on larger shareholders for misconduct by the investee company,[36] they may be incompatible with EU primary law as discussed by Teichmann and Wolff. Furthermore, cases of golden shares show that the obligation for states to exercise their rights in a specific manner may have a deterrent effect on investments.[37]

Teichmann and Wolff also discuss other duties imposed on shareholders that originate in the company's legal framework (membership-related duties), including the *lex societatis*. When companies exercise their freedom of establishment, it is the law of the state of incorporation that applies to shareholders' duties. However, Teichmann and Wolff argue that recent developments show that the host Member State may override the *lex societatis* by applying its own tort law and insolvency law provisions. As a result, the barriers to the enforcement of shareholders' duties flowing from EU primary law that they identify may be restricted to areas that concern the formation of a company in a given Member State or the subsequent establishment in another Member State.[38]

---

33 Chapter 13, sec. II.A.

34 Chapter 13, sec. III.

35 Chapter 12, sec. II.F.

36 See the discussion on the *Idrima Tipou* case, Case C-81/09, in Chapter 12, sec. III.A.

37 Discussed in Chapter 12, sec. III.A.

38 Chapter 12, sec. IV.C.2.

Another series of difficulties in relation to enforcement arises out of barriers to shareholder identification, as analysed by Matteo Gargantini.[39] Characteristic examples include the increased intermediation between the final account holders and the settlement system, or the use of omnibus accounts that prevents upper-tier intermediaries and issuers from identifying shareholders at lower-tier levels. These difficulties further exacerbate identification problems in a cross-border context since holding systems usually operate on a national basis. Differences in legal traditions complicate things even more since the ultimate beneficiaries will be considered mere beneficiaries in some countries, whereas intermediaries that participate in the settlement system will hold the status of shareholders.[40]

More generally, shareholder identification mechanisms exist in only about half of EU Member States and their implementation at national level remains dependent on national specificities that do not yet allow for a truly satisfactory position. The 'centralised' identification system provided in the revised Shareholder Rights Directive[41] may allow for some improvements in identifying shareholders although its features may continue to create difficulties for issuers and fellow shareholders. Gargantini analyses all these issues to demonstrate that issuers, other shareholders and regulatory bodies may find it difficult to detect violations of shareholders' duties and to react to such conduct via various enforcement mechanisms.[42]

B. Public Enforcement

Public enforcement is a traditional mechanism for dealing with violations of some well-known shareholders' duties, such as notification of major shareholdings, but is less evident for the shareholder conduct and corporate governance duties applicable to shareholders.

Interestingly, suspension of voting rights, which was introduced by Directive 2013/50 (as discussed above), may also result in a public enforcement regime as the directive requires that Member States implement rules that provide for the suspension of voting rights if shareholders fail to declare major shareholdings but leaves it up to Member States to decide on the procedure. In this and other situations, as discussed by Neville and Engsig Sørensen, national supervisory authorities are empowered to impose the suspension of voting rights.[43] According to the authors, a sanction established by EU law, but which is

---

39 Chapter 11.

40 Chapter 11, sec. II.

41 Article 3a(3) in the Shareholder Rights Directive (n 4).

42 Chapter 11, sec. VI.

43 Chapter 8, sec. III.B.1.

applied very differently on a number of parameters in different Member States, may have adverse implications for the effects of the directive.

On a more general note, securities ownership has met with unprecedented changes, notably via the massive accumulation of shares by institutions and the correlative decline in the importance of retail investors. The presence of a 'fiduciary capitalism' that gives funds the power to manage ultimate beneficiaries' savings has been regarded as means for making investment more mainstream and 'democratic' but at the same time, it is seen as a growing concern for issuers, markets and beneficiaries when their conduct fails to comply with sound corporate governance practices. Public interest concerns have been enshrined in the debate, purporting to safeguard this new age of investment. By focusing, *inter alia*, on a particular category of shareholders' duties related to shareholder conduct and corporate governance, Chiu analyses the gradual emergence of regulatory law and soft law around these duties and the implications for their enforcement. It has been said that we are witnessing a legalisation of stewardship via the introduction of a duty to demonstrate engagement, which is based on public interests that aim to re-regulate this area.[44] On the one hand, stewardship codes and, more generally, the new disclosure obligations imposed across the EU by the revised Shareholder Rights Directive are not currently subject to any type of enforcement,[45] an assumption that brings private parties back to the centre of attention as the ultimate enforcers of debatable shareholder conduct practices. On the other hand, public enforcement is beginning to take on a 'public-private' nature since it serves as a representative means for private parties that would want to enforce such duties on their own while also aiming to protect public interest considerations at large.

Chiu characterises the directive's position as 'anomalous'[46] given the current co-existence of private enforcement (as the only source of pressure) and the public interest prerogatives that are supposedly preserved under these new disclosure duties as included in the directive. Sergakis further notes that Article 14b of the directive enables Member States to provide for effective, proportionate and dissuasive measures and penalties for violations of its transposed provisions into national law. Nevertheless, this provision is very broadly formulated and can be interpreted in many different ways, raising concerns about

---

[44] Iris H-Y. Chiu and Dionysia Katelouzou, 'From Shareholder Stewardship to Shareholder Duties: Is the Time Ripe?' in Hanne S. Birkmose (ed), *Shareholders' Duties* (Kluwer Law International 2017) 143.

[45] Notwithstanding some indirect monitoring mechanisms present in some Member States. See, for example, the FRC's tiering exercise, which aims to categorise Stewardship Code signatory parties into two tiers (more or less robust adherence to the code, respectively): Chapter 6, sec. IV.

[46] Chapter 6, sec. IV.

its applicability across the EU and the future framework of public enforcement in this area. Attempting to envisage a public enforcement framework for these shareholder conduct duties, Sergakis warns against a generalised approach whereby regulators would be given extensive powers to decipher shareholder conduct statements and enforce their overall compliance with the applicable provisions. Thus, this conclusion is aligned with Van der Elst's warning that rigorous enforcement may lead to a suboptimal engagement environment.[47]

Turning our attention to the market actors who will have to fulfil such duties, Sergakis argues that the imposition of administrative sanctions and measures for these emerging duties will create an overly complex and very burdensome environment for investors, given the variety of engagement strategies already in place, by forcing them to 'reprioritize their disclosure mindset'.[48] Moreover, legal enforcement will sit uncomfortably with the very nature of these duties whose purpose is not primarily to ensure formalistic compliance with standardised regulatory objectives[49] but to enhance engagement and to fight shareholder apathy by nurturing dialogue within the investment chain.

In light of the above-mentioned limitations and complexities, Sergakis argues that, upon the transposition of the Shareholder Rights Directive, public enforcement should be solely confined to the imposition of sanctions and measures for the pure and formal compliance with disclosure duties. In other words, it is only the complete omission to produce a statement or to explain non-compliance, following the 'comply or explain' principle, that should trigger regulatory sanctions and not the content of such declarations. This stance will enable shareholders to feel constrained to produce the required statements and to continue to nurture the dialogue and engagement with other parties without further liability or exposure concerns.

Chiu adopts the view that it would be preferable for 'points of reconciliation' to be 'constantly redrawn [between private and public enforcement] as the publicisation of norms and enforcement develops in the future in relation to shareholder conduct'.[50] This position is justified, according to Chiu, in light of the regulator's role that may have to be introduced given the lack of monitoring by dispersed saver-beneficiaries. Indeed, minority shareholders and stakeholders could, according to the same author, be protected more efficiently via the standardisation of shareholder conduct rules.

---

47 Chapter 4, sec. IV.

48 Chapter 7, sec. V.

49 Such standardisation is also very unlikely to be achieved given the plethora of adopted strategies in the investment chain, of the various profiles of investors and of the different facets of shareholder engagement and conduct at large.

50 Chapter 6, sec. V.

As becomes apparent, public enforcement encompasses private and public features in shareholders' duties, and the co-existence of different sources, types and aims of enforcement makes the construction of an efficient system rather complex. As Chiu mentions, 'the merging of "private shareholder conduct" with the expectations of institutions as socially representative investors has created an ambivalent issue area whose nature remains unresolved'.[51] The difficulty in deciphering the current or future regulatory steps becomes more obvious if we take into consideration the importance of social enforcement against shareholders, to which our attention will now turn.

III. SOCIAL ENFORCEMENT

Aside from the growing reliance on duties found in company law or capital markets law, social norms may form a parallel framework that specifies legitimate or desired behaviour among shareholders or other company stakeholders. In their contribution, Anand and Puskas refer to the work of Amir N. Licht[52] and stress that social norms may act as an important driver to ensure compliance with the underlying values found in various regulations. Thus, there is a symbiotic relationship between regulation and social norms, as laws can encourage the development of social norms, but the social norms that place value on subscribing to those laws are important to ensure that the laws have an effect. The interplay between legislation and social norms is interesting in relation to corporate governance in general but also in relation to institutional shareholders in particular, where the emerging stewardship agenda can be seen as a tangible sign of social norms. Moreover, Anand and Puskas argue that even in the absence of legal constraints, these norms may have a disciplining effect on the behaviour of institutional investors.[53]

The development of social norms may not be the result of legislation alone, but also of sophisticated and indirect practices of public enforcers and market participants. In his contribution, Sergakis argues that, in order to envisage the feasibility and efficiency of enforcement in the area of shareholders' duties, a distinction must be made between traditional duties (i.e. well-known duties imposed by company and capital markets law) and emerging ones (i.e. the new disclosure duties imposed by the revised Shareholder Rights Directive related to engagement, conduct, etc.). For the former, public enforcement has served for many years as a credible means to ensure compliance and deter

---

[51] Ibid.

[52] Amir N. Licht, 'Social Norms and the Law: A Social Institutional Approach' (2005) https://papers.ssrn.com/sol3/papers.cfm?abstract_id=710621, 5.

[53] Chapter 2, sec. V.C.

violations[54] but, for the latter, the imposition of legal sanctions could have counterproductive effects in the area of shareholder engagement, which is one of the highest priorities of the corporate governance regulatory agenda at EU level. Sergakis therefore argues that for shareholder conduct duties, social enforcement[55] should be preferred since it is currently the only mechanism that can preserve their educational aspects and not transform them into liability risks for investors.

Social enforcement also presents two other advantages in relation to the role that national regulators can play in this area and their relationship with the investor community and the public at large. Sergakis underlines the importance of social enforcement so as to avoid a mechanistic reliance on regulators, which would result if market actors expected regulators to sanction such duties, thus considering themselves relieved of an ongoing engagement task. On a parallel level, he warns of the risks of regulators creating an '*ex post* certification'[56] effect for dubious or borderline investor practices in the absence of any sanctions imposed. Indeed, abstaining from sanctions could convey the message to the market that the fulfilment of these duties is presumed and that the underlying strategy is acceptable. This certification could then enable market actors to stop engaging with other parties by claiming that their policies are acceptable and that there is no scope for further engagement in the investment chain.

Notwithstanding the difficulties that arise from social enforcement, notably in light of the exclusive reliance on private parties to sanction the lack of compliance with shareholders' duties, Sergakis believes that it represents the most credible way forward, at least at this embryonic stage during which a common understanding of the content and the various facets of such duties is of utmost importance.

IV. CONCLUSION

This introductory chapter has endeavoured to gather together the various contributions in this volume on the enforcement of shareholders' duties. Well-known and emerging duties have been subject to considerable debate, with mixed views on their rationale, impact and feasibility. The enforcement of such duties is even more critical given the various rationales for the numerous

---

[54] See, for example, the analysis by Jennifer Payne and Elizabeth Howell in Chapter 9, sec. IV.B. about the merits of financial sanctions imposed by regulators in the area of shareholders' duties.

[55] The expected reputational sanctions on shareholders triggered by other private parties who will react to the idea that their conduct is not adequate, compliant with their duties or optimal.

[56] Chapter 7, sec. V.

enforcement mechanisms that come into play in this area. In the absence of market failure or agency problem considerations, the politicisation of shareholder engagement and the role that institutional investors exercise seem to be at the origin of the multiplication of duties.

The various enforcement mechanisms also reflect the difficulty in deciphering the respective rights of the parties harmed by violations of such duties and the legal instruments for their protection. Private enforcement has traditionally been seen as the preferred way of resolving issues arising from shareholders' duties but, as shown in this volume, the specificities of company law and intra-shareholder relationships may well prevent parties from achieving a satisfactory solution to their claim. The volume also highlights further barriers to private enforcement, related to primary EU law, shareholder identification issues and jurisdictional barriers against the background of the constant increase in cross-border investments and intermediation.

Public enforcement seems to be more prominent in the violation of duties related to capital markets law issues, therefore going beyond the private law agenda of companies and being associated with public interest considerations in capital markets, aiming to preserve investor confidence and market stability. National regulators are increasingly being granted enforcement powers, aiming to defend a 'private-public' role to the benefit of harmed private parties and the market at large. Notwithstanding the current regulatory trends in public enforcement, various authors have questioned the feasibility of such initiatives in the area of shareholder engagement duties, as provided in the Shareholder Rights Directive, by examining either the possibility of a constant dialogue between legal and social enforcement or by questioning legal enforcement as a whole in this area.

PART I

The contours of enforcement

2. Legal and economic rationales for shareholder duties and their enforcement

Anita Anand and Christopher Puskas

I. INTRODUCTION

As shareholder activism influences corporate decision making more and more, the question of whether shareholders, particularly those with a controlling interest, should owe fiduciary duties to other shareholders has become an increasingly conspicuous one in corporate law. The law is certain that directors and senior managers owe a duty of loyalty to the corporation but it remains unsettled regarding duties between the shareholders themselves. This chapter focuses on the duties among shareholders *inter se* and considers when, if ever, such a fiduciary duty is appropriate.

Jurisdictions reflect differing positive law on the issue of shareholder fiduciary duties. Under Canadian law, shareholders do not owe duties (fiduciary or otherwise) to consider the interests of other shareholders.[1] In light of the statutory remedies to which shareholders are entitled, it is unlikely that courts would impose an *ex ante* fiduciary duty on shareholders. By contrast, in the United States, controlling shareholders owe a general fiduciary duty to the minority.[2] In Europe, the revised Shareholder Rights Directive establishes that a duty is owed to engage with investee companies, and requires both the adoption and disclosure of an engagement policy, which includes monitoring investee companies.[3]

---

1 *Brant Investments Ltd. v KeepRite Inc. et al.*, [1991] O.J. No. 683, 1 BLR (2d) 225 [*Brant*]. See also Jeffrey G MacIntosh, Janet Holmes and Steven Thompson, 'The Puzzle of Shareholder Fiduciary Duties' (1991) 19 Can. Bus. L.J. 86.

2 *Pepper v Litton* 308 US 259 (1939).

3 Directive 2017/828/EC of 17 May 2017 amending Directive 2007/36/EC as regards the encouragement of long-term shareholder engagement [2017] OJ L132/1. See also Andrew Johnston and Paige Morrow, 'Fiduciary Duties of European Institutional Investors: Legal Analysis and Policy Recommendations' (2016) University of Oslo Faculty of Law Research Paper 2016-04, 6.

If market realities alone were examined, different outcomes might be expected. Capital markets in the United States are generally populated with widely-held corporations.[4] In contrast, Canadian markets, like those in Europe, have been and continue to be dominated by a high degree of concentration in share ownership.[5] Thus, in theory, there may be more opportunities for abusive conduct by shareholders in Canada and Europe as opposed to the United States. Nonetheless, no shareholder fiduciary duty has developed either in Canadian statute or case law, though, as other chapters in this book suggest, the law is much different in Europe.

This chapter explores the rationales for imposing fiduciary duties among shareholders *inter se*. It argues that shareholder fiduciary duties as a legal construct lack persuasive rationale, especially in the presence of a strong remedial regime. It also argues that imposing shareholder fiduciary duties is inefficient from an enforcement perspective. Section II surveys the current state of the law in Canada and other common law jurisdictions. Section III analyzes the arguments for and against shareholder duties. Section IV examines the rise of shareholder activism as a key reason that shareholder fiduciary duties are emerging as a central question in corporate law. Finally, Section V argues that the case for fiduciary duties is particularly weak in jurisdictions such as Canada where there are sufficient *ex post* remedies available to aggrieved corporate stakeholders. Additionally, there is alternative *ex ante* regulation through other administrative and judicial controls, such as securities law, which also mitigates against the need for fiduciary duties.

II. CURRENT STATE OF THE LAW IN COMMON LAW JURISDICTIONS

In law, does the concept of "fiduciary" extend to relationships between shareholders themselves? Do shareholders owe duties to each other? While common and civil law jurisdictions generally impose some type of fiduciary duty on directors and senior officers, countries differ on the issue of whether shareholders owe fiduciary duties to each other.

---

4 Accordingly, a pressing issue to be addressed within corporate law has been the entrenchment of management able to control the corporation with little oversight. See MacIntosh, Holmes and Thompson (n 1) 86–87.

5 Ibid 87.

A. Canada

Under both common law and statute, corporate directors and senior officers have long been required to act as fiduciaries without making profits for themselves, though the word "fiduciary" does not appear in the relevant legislation.[6] The duty is in fact two-fold. A duty of loyalty requires directors to act "honestly and in good faith with a view to the best interests of the corporation."[7] This duty is coupled with a duty to act with reasonable care, which is characterized as a duty "to exercise the care, diligence and skill that a reasonably prudent person would exercise in comparable circumstances."[8]

In Canada, shareholders do not owe any general fiduciary duties either to the company or to other shareholders.[9] In the limited cases where law recognizes a fiduciary duty among shareholders *inter se*, it is generally accepted that there must be some relationship of trust and confidence. In *Goldex Mines Ltd v Revill*, the Ontario Court of Appeal famously said in obiter, "the category of cases in which fiduciary duties and obligations arise is not a closed one."[10] However, later cases, such as *Brant Investments Ltd v KeepRite Inc.* and *Bell v Source Data Control Ltd*, clearly reject a general shareholder fiduciary duty, and no such duty has since been recognized.[11]

B. The United Kingdom and Australia

Canada's approach is consistent with that of the United Kingdom and Australia, which have also specified that there is no fiduciary duty owed among shareholders. In the United Kingdom, the shareholder power to alter a company's memorandum and articles of association has been limited to cases involving fraud on the minority. This includes cases where the majority expropriates the company's property or uses its power to take over shares of the minority.[12] Accordingly, courts have imposed limited obligations on con-

---

[6] *Regal (Hastings) v Gulliver* [1942] 1 All ER 378 (HL).

[7] See, e.g., Canadian Business Corporations Act (R.S.C., 1985 c. C-44) s 122(1)(a) [CBCA].

[8] Ibid s 122(1)(b). See also *Peoples Department Stores Inc. (Trustee of) v Wise*, 2004 SCC 68, [2004] 3 S.C.R. 461; *BCE Inc. v 1976 Debentureholders*, 2008 SCC 69, [2008] 3 S.C.R. 560.

[9] MacIntosh, Holmes and Thompson (n 1); *Brant* (n 1).

[10] *Goldex Mines Ltd v Revill* [1974] Carswell Ontario 871, 54 D.L.R. (3d) 672, [32].

[11] Cf. *Brant* (n 1) 16; *Bell v Source Data Control Ltd* [1986] O.J. No. 621, 39 A.C.W.S. (2d) 62, aff'd [1988] O.J. No. 1424, 12 A.C.W.S. (3d) 19.

[12] Zipora Cohen, 'Fiduciary Duties of Controlling Shareholders: A Comparative View' (1991) 12(3) U. Pa. J. Int'l L. 379.

trolling shareholders in specific circumstances. For example, in *Allen v Gold Reefs of West Africa Ltd*, the Court held that controlling shareholders may alter the company's memorandum and articles of association but only if their voting power is exercised in good faith for the benefit of the company.[13] Recently, minority interests were subsequently afforded statutory protection through the "unfair prejudice" remedy, introduced in section 994 of the Companies Act.[14]

Similarly, in Australia, there are no fiduciary duties owed among shareholders and shareholders may vote freely in their own self-interest. However, the equitable doctrine of fraud on the minority helps restrain the actions of controlling shareholders,[15] as well as a statutorily defined oppression remedy in section 232 of Australia's Corporations Act.[16]

C. The United States

In contrast to these jurisdictions, the United States has a tradition of imposing shareholder fiduciary duties. A 1919 US Supreme Court decision established a fiduciary obligation between a controlling shareholder and minority shareholders.[17] The principle was substantially strengthened in *Donahue v Rodd Electrotype Co.*, where the Court stated that "just as in a partnership, the relationship among the stockholders must be one of trust, confidence and absolute loyalty if the enterprise is to succeed."[18] The Court held that shareholders must act with "utmost good faith and loyalty."[19]

This case has been interpreted as setting out that shareholders in closely-held corporations owe a fiduciary duty to each other. But the principle appears to be broader and, in fact, US courts have recognized that controlling shareholders "owe a fiduciary duty of loyalty to minority shareholders that precludes them

---

13 *Allen v Gold Reefs of West Africa Ltd* [1900] 1 Ch 656 (CA).

14 Companies Act 2006 c. 46, s 994.

15 Pamela Hanrahan, 'The Law of Close Corporations: Australia' (2014) International Academy of Comparative Law, World Congress in Vienna 2014, https://law.unimelb.edu.au/__data/assets/pdf_file/0009/1862109/Pamela-Hanrahan-Close-Corporations-Australia.pdf, 14, 19, 23.

16 Corporations Act 2001, s 232.

17 See *Southern Pacific Co. v Bogart*, 250 US 483, 39 Sup. Ct. 533, in which Justice Brandeis argued that "the majority has the right to control; but when it does so, it occupies a fiduciary relation toward the minority, as much so as the corporation itself or its officers or directors" [487]–[488].

18 *Donahue v Rodd Electrotype Co of New England, Inc.*, 367 Mass. 578, 328 N.E.2d 505 [587].

19 Ibid.

from using their positions as controlling shareholders to extract material economic benefits from the firm at the minority's expense."[20]

Courts have applied this principle with restraint and have often limited it to cases of freeze-outs and closely-held corporations. However, just as Canadian courts have recognized that the categories of cases in which a fiduciary duty may be imposed are not closed, the same is true in the United States. For instance, where a controlling shareholder places its agent on the board or controls the board's conduct, the shareholder will be held to have indirectly acted in a managerial capacity and attract fiduciary obligations. When fiduciary obligations are imposed on controlling shareholders, courts will generally impose a strict "entire fairness" standard when reviewing an impugned transaction.[21] A transaction will satisfy the entire fairness standard only if it is the product of fair dealing and the deal is for a fair price.[22] Moreover, the entire fairness standard will apply even when the negotiations are conducted with an independent, arm's-length third party, unless the controlling shareholder crosses two procedural hurdles. First, the transaction must be recommended by a special committee; second, the transaction must be approved by a majority of the minority shareholders. If those conditions are met, the controlling shareholder will benefit from the lower, more deferential business judgment rule.[23]

---

[20] Iman Anabtawi and Lynn Stout, 'Fiduciary Duties for Activist Shareholders' (2008) 60(5) Stan. L. Rev. 1255.

[21] Webb Hecker, 'Controlling Shareholder Duty of Loyalty: Entire Fairness or Business Judgment' (2014) University of Kansas School of Law, https://law.ku.edu/sites/law.ku.edu/files/docs/recent-developments/(2)HeckerControllingShareholderDutyofLoyalty.pdf.

[22] Kerry E. Berchem, Ron E. Deutsche and Nicholas J. Houpt, 'Duties of Controlling Shareholders – Murky Waters: Tread Carefully' (2012) Akin Gump Practicing Law Institute, https://www.akingump.com/images/content/2/2/v4/22475/Duties-of-Controlling-Stockholders-PLI-Article-June-2012.pdf.

[23] Ibid 19–20. For example, in *Re MFW Shareholders Litigation*, C.A. No. 6566-CS (Del Ch. May 29, 2013) the Court held that in going private merger transactions, controlling shareholders can receive the benefit of the business judgment rule provided they create an independent committee to review the transaction and the transaction is approved by a majority of the minority shareholders who are fully informed as to the deal terms. If a lower business judgment standard is applied, significant deference will be shown to the controlling shareholder. Specifically, under the business judgment rule, the controlling shareholders must merely show that there was a legitimate business reason for their decisions and that they acted "on an informed basis, in good faith, and in the honest belief that their actions are in the best interests of the corporation." (See *Aronson v Lewis*, 473 A. 2d 805 (Del. 1984) 811). If a legitimate business purpose can be established, the minority shareholders must show that the same business objective could have been reached in a less harmful manner. This principle is similar to the business judgment rule that applies to boards of directors' decision making. See also Brian M. Lutz and Eduardo Gallardo, 'Gibson Dunn on Controlling Shareholders and

This overview reveals that the law relating to shareholder fiduciary duties is neither settled within nor uniform across jurisdictions. The question as to whether to impose such duties becomes more salient as we consider the arguments in favor of imposing shareholder fiduciary duties as well as the rise of shareholder activism.

III. PROS AND CONS OF IMPOSING FIDICIARY DUTIES

A "fiduciary" is a person who has agreed or undertaken to act in good faith for another person or entity, always placing the other person's interests above the fiduciary's own.[24] In general, legally mandated fiduciary duties exist where self-interest runs the risk of trumping one's duties to act in the interests of others. One of the primary benefits of such fiduciary duties is to address the potential for "agency costs," internal costs that arise when ownership and control are separated.

A. Fiduciary Duties of Directors

Directors and officers are agents of the corporation, which is the principal in the agency relationship. As rational self-interested actors, agents may expend less effort than they would if they were the full beneficiaries of their efforts[25] or engage in self-serving behavior to the detriment of the corporation. While agency costs may exist even when a director is ostensibly adhering to his or her fiduciary duty,[26] the imposition of this legal duty of loyalty limits the most egregious cases of self-serving behavior, such as transferring corporate assets to oneself in a non-arm's-length transaction for insufficient consideration.[27]

Fiduciary duties are especially important in light of the extensive deference afforded to directors under corporate law. Directors benefit from the business judgment rule, which is a presumption that the directors of a corporation acted on an informed basis, in good faith, and in the honest belief that the action

---

the Business Judgement Rule in going Private Merger Transactions', Columbia Law School Blog on Corporations and the Capital Markets, 3 June 2013, http://clsbluesky.law.columbia.edu/2013/06/03/gibson-dunn-on-controlling-shareholders-and-the-business-judgment-rule-in-going-private-merger-transactions/.

24 *Halsbury Laws of Canada – Business Corporations* (2018 Reissue) HBC-237 Fiduciary Defined.

25 Zohar Goshen and Richard Squire, 'Principal Costs: A New Theory for Corporate Law and Governance' (2017) Colum. L. Rev. 769–70.

26 Ibid.

27 *Aberdeen Railway Co v Blaikie Brothers* (1854) 1 All ER Rep 249, 1 Macq 461, 2 Eq Rep 1281 (UKHL).

taken was in the best interests of the company.[28] As a result of this presumption, courts defer to the decisions of directors and only intervene in cases in which it is plain and obvious that directors have acted in their own self-interest rather than in the interest of the corporation.[29] While the business judgment rule is common in many jurisdictions, some have chosen to modify the standard slightly. Delaware courts, for example, have imposed a variation on the business judgment rule by applying an "entire fairness test," which considers both procedural and substantial fairness. Delaware applies the business judgment rule only if *both* a properly functioning special committee *and* approval of a majority of the minority shareholders persist. Otherwise, it applies an "entire fairness" standard.[30]

B. The Case Against Fiduciary Duties

The traditional case against imposing a fiduciary duty on shareholders *inter se* can be broken down into three key arguments. First, shareholders, even controlling shareholders, have no legal power over corporate property or the property of other shareholders. At best, they have only indirect power to influence through the control of their shares.[31] Given the absence of direct legal power over corporate assets, it would be inappropriate to impose a fiduciary duty on shareholders.

Arguing that a fiduciary duty arises whenever one has the power to control the property of another, including the indirect control which a powerful shareholder holds, may not accurately reflect the true definition of the fiduciary duty. Such duties arise from relationships of dependence, not control. In Canada, it is the element of trust or confidence which makes a particular relationship a fiduciary one.[32] Indeed, while a fiduciary relationship may involve elements of control, this is often not the case. For example, lawyers often owe a fiduciary duty to their clients despite having no control over the actual affairs of their clients. Similarly, in the United Kingdom, a fiduciary duty arises in relationships of trust

---

[28] In the Canadian context, see *Peoples Department Stores Inc. v Wise*; *BCE* (n 8).

[29] *Unocal v Mesa Petroleum Co.*, 493 A.2d 946 (Del. 1985); *Revlon Inc. v MacAndrews & Forbes Holdings Inc.*, 506 A.2d 173 (Del. 1986); *Brant* (n 1) [75]–[76].

[30] Robert B. Little and Joseph A. Orien, 'Determining the Likely Standard of Review in Delaware M&A Transactions' (2017) Harvard Law School Forum, https://corpgov.law.harvard.edu/2017/04/28/determining-the-likely-standard-of-review-in-delaware-ma-transactions-2/.

[31] Paula J. Dalley, 'Shareholder (and Director) Fiduciary Duties and Shareholder Activism' (2008) 8 Hous. Bus. & Tax L.J. 302.

[32] *Encyclopedic Digest – Business (Ont)* (4th edn, 2010), 'Boards of Directors: Managerial Rights and Powers of Directors: Fiduciary Duties of Directors' (V.4.(f)) [703].

or confidence, particularly when an individual undertakes to "act for or on behalf of another person in a particular matter in circumstances that give rise to a relationship of trust or confidence."[33] Clearly, control is not the defining characteristic of a fiduciary relationship. Accordingly, the control wielded by controlling shareholders may be insufficient to justify a fiduciary duty among shareholders as the relationship between them is not characterized by dependence.

The second argument against recognizing the inter-shareholder fiduciary duty is that controlling shareholders have paid for their position (i.e. the so-called "control premium") and have a right to benefit from it. The principle of *caveat emptor* should govern: shareholders will act in their own self-interest,[34] and any shareholder investing in the market should be aware that controlling shareholders may have substantial influence (for better or worse) over the company. Jeffrey MacIntosh notes that it has long been argued that shareholders choose to invest their money in the company's shares and "it is part of his bargain that he will submit to the will of the majority."[35] Likewise, Robert Flannigan argues that imposing a fiduciary duty among shareholders is unwarranted since "all shareholders take the risk that they may be adversely affected by an exercise of voting rights."[36]

The third argument is that imposing a fiduciary duty may disincentivize investments by imposing additional costs and obligations on shareholders.[37] Investors typically purchase controlling interests because they believe that their ability to influence decisions will justify the price of a control premium. In the presence of shareholder fiduciary duties, "future investors will reduce the control premia they are willing to pay, and may be discouraged from making investments at all."[38] This would increase the cost of capital, reduce investment opportunities, and potentially slow business growth.[39] Thus, shareholder fiduciary duties may be a disincentive to shareholders making large investments in a company.

This is an especially potent concern in Canada, which relies on investments from large shareholders to fuel economic activity. Pension funds hold approximately 15 percent of the total assets in Canada's financial system. The eight

---

33 Lesley Anderson and Mark Harper, 'Fiduciary Duties Owed to the Excluded Shareholder' (2013) (May) Law and Financial Markets Rev. 10.

34 Robert Flannigan, 'Fiduciary Duties of Shareholders and Directors' (2004) J. Bus. L. 277.

35 Jeffrey G. MacIntosh, 'Minority Shareholder Rights in Canada and England: 1860–1987' (1989) 27(3) Osgoode Hall L.J. 603.

36 Flannigan (n 34) 286.

37 Paula J. Dalley, 'The Misguided Doctrine of Stockholder Fiduciary Duties' (2004) 33(1) Hofstra L. Rev. 175.

38 Ibid 221.

39 Ibid 222.

largest public pension funds control two-thirds of this amount, with net assets under their management amounting to over $1 trillion.[40] In terms of the breakdown of investments made by Canada's top ten largest pension funds, over $600 billion was invested across various asset classes in Canada in 2014.[41] Unsurprisingly given this level of investment, institutional investors account for over 50 percent of the market cap of the Canadian equity markets.[42] This proportion has been steadily increasing as new types of institutional investors emerge. Thus, in Canada and other jurisdictions dominated by institutional investors, consideration must be paid to the potential negative effects on the market that may flow from imposing new legal duties.

C. The Case for Fiduciary Duties

On the other side of the argument is the view that corporate governance has changed. Anabtawi and Stout argue that fiduciary duties have not historically been imposed on shareholders because shareholders were largely irrelevant to corporate governance and agency cost concerns.[43] During most of the 20th century, shareholders played a passive role in public companies because they were "rationally apathetic" to corporate governance.[44] Moreover, on the rare occasion that shareholders played an active role in the corporation, their interests were aligned with other shareholders insofar as the ultimate goal of any shareholder activity was to improve the firm's overall economic performance. The sparse shareholder activism that did occur was thus seen as beneficial to the corporation as a whole.

In making their case for the imposition of fiduciary duties on all shareholders, Anabtawi and Stout argue that these dual assumptions of disengagement and positive externalities are outdated. First, as discussed in the following section, institutional investors have replaced dormant retail investors as the dominant actors in the market. Their large holdings give them an incentive to be engaged in corporate governance and allow them to overcome collective

---

40 Guillaume Bédard-Pagé, Annick Demers, Eric Tuer, and Miville Tremblay, 'Large Canadian Public Pension Funds: A Financial System Perspective' (2016) Bank of Canada Financial System Rev.

41 Boston Consulting Group, 'The Top 10: Investing for Canada on the World Stage' (2016) https://www.otpp.com/documents/10179/20932/-/78a93e0b-29df-44d8-8152-d870628fd72a/ENG_Top_Ten_Report.pdf.

42 Howard Weston, remarks to Canadian Coalition of Good Governance, June 10, 2015.

43 Anabtawi and Stout (n 20) 1255, 1258.

44 Adolf Berle and Gardiner Means, *The Modern Corporation and Private Property* (rev. edn, Macmillan 1967).

action problems. Second, financial innovation has resulted in increased disparity of shareholders' interests.

For example, complex financial instruments have allowed for the separation of voting rights and economic interests. This has created opportunities for institutional investors to benefit by placing downward pressure on stock prices, such as in the case of hedge funds buying common stock with vote shares while simultaneously entering a derivative contract that hedges away its economic interest in the stock. Executed properly, the result of such an arrangement could be that the hedge fund takes a negative economic position in the firm by shorting its stock and profits by using its shareholder position to push for policies that lower the stock price.[45]

At its core, Anabtawi and Stout's argument can be boiled down to a concern that shareholders may influence the company to engage in economically wasteful transactions. After all, shareholders are expected to act in their own self-interest (or, in the case of a pension fund, the interests of their beneficiaries).[46] There is thus an ever-present risk that the majority's actions will result in non-productive ends rather than actions in accordance with the company's best interests. According to this logic, fiduciary duties serve to prevent shareholder actions that redistribute corporate assets and cause economic harm to both the company and other shareholders.

These arguments are most persuasive in the context of closely-held corporations. Shareholders in closely-held corporations have a relationship that has been called a "quasi-partnership."[47] Because shareholders often lack a means to exit, or at least to exit at a fair price, there are opportunities for a controlling shareholder to exploit the minority.[48] This concern has been the animating force behind the imposition of fiduciary duties among shareholders in the United States, where it has been held that a general fiduciary duty should be imposed on controlling shareholders in closely-held corporations "as if they were the partners of their non-controlling counterparts."[49]

Fiduciary duties among shareholders are useful also if the controlling shareholder has obtained its position by paying a control premium, which is the amount paid over the market price for a controlling interest in the company. The value of control varies based on the firm's performance and management, among other factors. The premium is larger for poorly managed

---

45 Anabtawi and Stout (n 20) 1280–88.

46 Cf. MacIntosh, Holmes and Thompson (n 1).

47 *Ebrahimi v Westbourne Galleries Ltd* [1973] AC 360 (UKHL).

48 Dalley (n 37) 194–95.

49 Timothy J. Storm, 'Remedies for Oppression of Non-Controlling Shareholders in Illinois Closely-Held Corporations: An Idea Whose Time has Gone' (2002) 33 Loy. U. Chi. L.J. 379, 381–82.

firms and smaller for well-managed firms. It also varies based on why a firm is performing poorly. Where poor performance is the result of poor management decisions rather than uncontrollable external factors, the control premium is higher.[50] Access to this premium is a benefit that minority shareholders do not have, by definition.

Concerns have been raised regarding whether control premiums are unfair to the remaining shareholders and to the corporation. One view of the control premium in the US is that it is "an inducement paid to the controller to breach his fiduciary duty in the specific area of the selection of his successor."[51] Following this view, it is questionable whether the premium is paid to entice the seller to overlook the interests of the company as it relinquishes its control of the company. In doing so, the seller also receives financial benefits above those received by the minority shareholders. Through this perspective, "control premium problems are, in one sense, part of the larger question of the extent of the fiduciary duties flowing from the controlling shareholders to the minority interests."[52]

IV. THE RISE OF SHAREHOLDER ACTIVISM

In order to understand fully the merits of imposing a shareholder fiduciary duty, it is necessary to identify the types of shareholders in today's capital market and the corporate governance context in which they operate. During the 20th century, Berle and Means argued that the modern corporation is one characterized by the separation of ownership and control, given that "the position of ownership has changed from that of an active to that of a passive agent."[53] For them, the main concern in corporate governance was the rise of a mana-

---

50 Aswath Damodaran, 'The Value of Control: Implications for Control Premia, Minority Discounts and Voting Share Differentials' (2005) New York University – Stern School of Business, https://papers.ssrn.com/sol3/papers.cfm?abstract_id=837405.

51 David C. Bayne, 'The Sale-of-Control Premium: The Definition' (1969) 53 Minn. L. Rev. 485, 490.

52 Thomas L. Hazen, 'Transfers of Corporate Control and Duties of Controlling Shareholders – Common law, Tender Offers, Investment Companies – and a Proposal for Reform' (1977) University of North Carolina School of Law Faculty Scholarship, http://scholarship.law.unc.edu/cgi/viewcontent.cgi?article=1116&context=faculty_publications, 1027.

53 Berle and Means (n 44) 6. For a historical analysis of Berle and Means' thesis about separation of ownership and control, see Lynn A. Stout, 'On the Rise of Shareholder Primacy, Signs of its Fall, and the Return of Managerialism (in the Closet)' (2013) Cornell Law Faculty Publications, https://scholarship.law.cornell.edu/cgi/viewcontent.cgi?referer=https://www.google.ca/&httpsredir=1&article=2310&context=facpub.

gerial superclass, who could use corporate resources to their own benefit at the expense of the companies' shareholders and who were rationally apathetic to managerial activity. Specifically, given that each individual shareholder only held a minor stake in a company, no shareholder had enough incentive to monitor management and ensure that corporate resources were being used effectively, thus leading to collective action problems and economic inefficiency. However, the rise of activist shareholders over the past 25 years undermines Berle and Means' conclusion: these shareholders are anything but passive.[54] They are sophisticated, often seeking governance changes over and above those that yield a mere return on their investment. As discussed above, a principal case for imposing shareholder fiduciary duties is based on the observation that shareholders are no longer passive agents in a corporation. This section explores the rise of shareholder activism.

Gilson and Gordon argue that the rise of shareholder activism has led to a "reconcentration of ownership in the hands of institutional investment intermediaries."[55] Yet this claim does not capture the full gamut of activist pressure. Activists may engage in one of two types of activism: offensive activism initiated by hedge funds primarily in response to poor corporate performance of potential targets, or defensive activism, involving institutional activists who take on an advocacy role when they are unhappy with the corporation in which they are invested.[56] Both offensive and defensive activists seek to participate in the governance of the corporation *ex ante*. They view shareholder participation as necessary because of the marked tendency for management to perpetuate itself in office.[57]

---

[54] "Companies of all sizes and in all industries are now the target of shareholder activism, whether initiated by a non-professional activist such as former management or by a professional activist such as an experienced hedge fund acting with the support (if not at the request) of traditional institutional investors" (Fasken Martineau LLP, 'Directors' Handbook: Shareholder Activism' (2016) https://www.fasken.com/directors-handbook-shareholder-activism/. See Ronald J. Gilson and Jeffrey N. Gordon, 'The Agency costs of Agency Capitalism: Activist Investors and the Revaluation of Government Rights' (2013) 113 Colum. L. Rev. 863; Stout (n 53) who states, "Shareholders now have more influence over boards, and executives now are more focused on share price, than at any time in business history," 1179.

[55] Cf. Gilson and Gordon (n 54) 863.

[56] Brian R. Cheffins and John Armour, 'The Past, Present and Future of Shareholder Activism by Hedge Funds' (2011) University of Cambridge Faculty of Law Research Paper 38.

[57] Committee on Securities Legislation in Ontario, *Report of the Attorney-General's Committee on Securities Legislation in Ontario* (Toronto 1965).

The foremost goal of an activist – and particularly a hedge fund activist – is to maximize investors' returns.[58] As unregulated entities, hedge funds search for and invest in high-yield products and projects on behalf of clients who have entrusted their money to the fund.[59] While hedge funds may focus on the short term to maximize their immediate returns, their focus may well coincide with the long-term interests of corporations.

Activist investors play an important monitoring role in corporations. Empirical evidence suggests that there is a positive, or at least a neutral, relationship between activists and firm value.[60] The benefits provided by the activist's monitoring flow through to minority shareholders, who are able to free-ride on the large shareholder's activism. Specifically, the presence of an activist investor is associated with improved long-term outcomes on matters ranging from executive compensation to the facilitation of takeover bids.[61] Carrothers points out that the average abnormal return at target firms in the 20 days surrounding the disclosure of activist intentions is 7.1 percent, and the average buy and hold abnormal return in the 20 months after the disclosure is 23 percent.[62] Similarly, Bebchuk et al. find a 6 percent abnormal return in stock price during the 40-day period straddling the announcement of an activist campaign.[63] This result was not offset by a subsequent long-term decrease in stock price.[64]

In short, one can argue that the market as a whole stands to benefit from hedge fund activism.[65] Imposing a fiduciary duty, however, may have the consequence of negating benefits that minority shareholders receive. The liability imposed by a fiduciary duty could have the effect of discouraging large shareholders from pursuing an active role in governance, thereby reducing minority shareholder returns.

---

58 Sham Gad, 'What Are Hedge Funds?' (2013) http://www.forbes.com/sites/investopedia/2013/10/22/what-are hedge -funds/.

59 Bennelong Funds, 'Debunking hedge fund myths' (2013) http://www.centuryprivatewealth.com.au/news/view/debunking_hedge_fund_myths.

60 Alex Edmans, 'Activists and Corp Governance' (2014) European Corporate Governance Institute Working Paper http://papers.ssrn.com/sol3/papers.cfm?abstract_id=2285781.

61 Lucian Bebchuk, 'The Law and Economics of Activist Disclosure' (2012) 2 Harv. Bus. L. Rev. 39.

62 Andrew Carrothers, 'Friends or Foes? Activist Hedge Funds and Other Institutional Investors' (2013) http://www.degroote.mcmaster.ca/articles/friends-or-foes-activist-hedge-funds-and-other-institutional-investors/.

63 L. Rev, (2015). f Hedge Fund Activism parties was 'd Holding and Other Investment Offices. Lucian A. Bebchuk, Alon Brav and Wei Jiang, 'The Long-Term Effects of Hedge Fund Activism' (2015) 115 Colum. L. Rev.

64 Ibid.

65 Ibid.

One could argue, therefore, that a shareholder fiduciary duty is unnecessary and inappropriate especially since there are already effective legal remedies to protect minority shareholders. This is the topic that the next section explores.

V. IS LEGAL CHANGE NECESSARY?

The case for the imposition of fiduciary duties for shareholders stems from the concern that shareholder opportunism needs to be managed. The majority of institutional investors are no longer passive investors and their interests may diverge from other shareholders in the corporation. Advocates for the imposition of shareholder fiduciary duties argue that such a change would prevent shareholder opportunism, which has the potential to harm other shareholders and the corporation.

While the critiques of a fiduciary duty explored above are compelling, they are incomplete. Specifically, the case for the imposition of shareholder fiduciary duties is particularly weak in Canada given the adequacy of unique *ex ante* regulation in securities law and *ex post* remedies available to minority shareholders in corporate law. In addition, and most importantly in our view, insufficient attention has been paid to the presence of norms governing institutional investors in Canada. These norms have a disciplining effect on large institutional shareholders, mitigating against a need for shareholder fiduciary duties.

A. *Ex Ante* Protection

First, the argument for imposing fiduciary duties in Canada is particularly weak given the explicit presence of *ex ante* protection for minority shareholder interests in securities law. These protections include a requirement to secure a majority of the minority approval, the creation of a special committee of independent directors, and the receipt of an independent valuation or fairness opinion.[66] For example, under Multilateral Instrument 61-101 (in force in most of Canada's biggest capital markets) during transactions which have a high potential for conflicts of interest and minority shareholder abuse, securities regulators require enhanced disclosure, independent valuations, minority approvals, and special committees of independent directors to review the transaction.[67] Although they apply only to public companies undertaking some sort of related party transaction, these measures minimize the need to impose

[66] OSC Rule 61-501 re business acquisitions among related parties. See also Anita Anand, 'Fairness at What Price? An Analysis of the regulation of Going Private Transactions in OSC Policy 9.1' (1998) 43 McGill L.J. 1.

[67] *Multilateral Instrument 61-101 Protection of Minority Security Holders in Special Transactions*, OSC 61-101. 31 O.S.C.B. 1321 (February 1, 2008) [MI 61-101].

a legal fiduciary duty among shareholders. By regulating the process, these *ex ante* protections create substantive fairness for minority shareholders.

Securities regulators also regulate change of control situations, thus providing procedural and substantive protection for minority shareholders. In 1965, William Andrews proposed that "whenever a controlling block of shares is sold, every other shareholder (of the same class) is entitled to have an equal opportunity to sell his shares, or prorate part of them, on substantially the same terms."[68] Securities regulators have adhered to this call for action and implemented legal protections for minority shareholders through an "equal opportunity rule." To purchase controlling shares, acquirers must extend the offer to minority controlling shareholders on equal terms.

Canada's "equal treatment" rule requires all holders of the same class of securities to be offered the same consideration, on a pro rata basis, for the securities in a takeover bid or issuer bid. It also forbids "collateral benefits" being offered which would give certain security holders greater consideration than others, with the exception of certain cases of employment compensation, severance and employee benefits. These rules are set out in National Instrument 62-104, which states that all shareholders in a takeover bid must be offered identical consideration and thus an equal opportunity to receive control premiums.[69]

Generally, these *ex ante* protections are efficient and provide shareholders with robust protection. Notably, Canada has one of the most cost-effective capital market regimes in the world and on the dimension of market fairness, the Organisation for Economic Co-operation and Development and the International Monetary Fund have consistently ranked Canada among the best with regard to securities regulation and investor protection.[70] In particular, the *ex ante* regulation highlighted in this section, such as the takeover bid regime in NI 62-104, has been singled out for being a significant contributor to the fairness and efficiency of Canadian capital markets.[71] Other studies on *ex ante* regulation more broadly have found that full public disclosure policies, when combined with adequate *ex*

---

[68] William D. Andrews, 'The Stockholder's Right to Equal Opportunity in the Sale of Shares' (1965) 78(3) Harv. L. Rev. 505, 515.

[69] *62-104 Take-over Bid and Issuer Bids*, 39 O.S.C.B. 4225 (May 5, 2016) at 2.23, 2.24. The one exception to this rule in NI 62-104 is the Private Agreement exception, found in s 4.2. This section allows a bidder to avoid triggering the takeover bid regime and identical consideration rules if they purchase securities from no more than five shareholders for a price that does not exceed 115 percent.

[70] Pierre Lortie, 'Securities Regulation in Canada: The Case for Effectiveness' (2011) Institute for Research on Public Policy, 7–8.

[71] Ibid 8.

post remedies (to be discussed in the next section) are more effective than public enforcement in promoting efficient capital markets.[72]

While it is true that Canada has often been criticized for its weak capital market regulation relative to other jurisdictions,[73] this has nothing to do with the efficacy of *ex ante* regulation. Those criticisms are leveled against the current structure of and resources available to securities regulators, and attempts to improve enforcement activities should focus on improving those aspects of securities regulation. A study of the Securities and Exchange Commission (SEC) in the United States, for instance, found that increasing the SEC's resources improved compliance and increased overall enforcement activity by the Commission.[74]

Thus, securities regulation can limit the need for shareholder fiduciary duties as regulators have been proactive in limiting, *ex ante*, opportunities for unfair conduct to minority shareholders. From an enforcement perspective, we are likely to see few changes to the law in this regard, especially given the existence of strong statutory remedies discussed in the next section.

B. *Ex Post* Remedies

The second reason vitiating against the need for a shareholder fiduciary duty is the presence of adequate *ex post* remedies available at corporate law, which averts any need for a shareholder fiduciary duty. The oppression remedy provides minority shareholders a remedy against oppressive conduct perpetrated by shareholders with a controlling interest. The oppression remedy is broadly drafted to cover any act or omission "that is oppressive or unfairly prejudicial to or that unfairly disregards the interests of any security holder, creditor, director or officer."[75] It has been "applied by the courts to impose duties of a fiduciary character on majority or controlling shareholders, and in a way that substantially enlarges upon comparable rights available at common law."[76]

---

[72] Rafael La Porta, Florencio Lopez-De-Silanes and Andrei Shleifer, 'What Works in Securities Laws?' (2006) 61(1) J. Finance 1, 27–28.

[73] See Barrie McKenna, 'Regulators owe it to Canadians to do better on fraud', *The Globe and Mail* (December 22, 2017) https://www.theglobeandmail.com/report-on-business/to-solve-canadas-fraud-problem-give-regulators-the-tools/article37418986/; and see Pierre Lortie, 'Securities Regulation in Canada at a Crossroads' (2010) 3(5) University of Calgary School of Public Policy, for an overview of securities regulation in Canada.

[74] Tim Lohse, Razvan Pascalau and Christian Thomann, 'Public Enforcement of Securities Market Rules: Resource-based Evidence from the Securities and Exchange Commission' (2014) 106 J. Econ. Behav. Organ. 197, 198–199.

[75] CBCA (n 7) s 241.

[76] MacIntosh (n 35) 636.

Minority shareholders are explicitly protected under the oppression remedy. Courts have used a variety of interpretive means to bring controlling shareholder conduct under the provision. For example, parent corporations that are "affiliates" are captured under the oppression remedy. Courts have drawn shareholder conduct into the oppression remedy by equating the conduct of a controlling shareholder with that of the corporation.[77] Indeed, the Ontario Court of Appeal in *Brant Investments Ltd v KeepRite Inc.* explicitly noted that "the enactment of [the oppression remedy] has rendered any argument for a broadening of the categories of fiduciary relationships in the corporate context unnecessary and, in [our] view, inappropriate."[78]

Accordingly, arguments raised by those who support the imposition of shareholder fiduciary duties are weaker in the context of a broad oppression remedy. If abusive market conduct occurs, such as a hedge fund using its controlling position to execute business practices which push for share prices to trend downward, the oppression remedy would be available to aggrieved minority shareholders to rectify this harm. Moreover, the range of remedies available under the oppression remedy is wider than that at common law,[79] thus providing courts with the discretion to deal with any type of abusive market conduct. This is especially useful in the closely-held context, where the court can order a minority shareholder to be bought out by a controlling shareholder at fair market value, prior to the oppressive conduct occurring, where no opportunities for exit exist.[80]

Additionally, the oppression remedy allows courts to look past the business judgment rule and take a contextual approach to the impugned conduct. As noted in *First Edmonton Place Ltd v 315888 Alberta Ltd*:

> The introduction of a statutory remedy against oppression and unfair prejudice is a deliberate departure from the policy of judicial non-intervention in corporate affairs. [The oppression remedy] casts the court in the role of an active arbiter of business policy … it is drawn in very broad terms and as remedial legislation should be given a liberal interpretation in favor of the complainant …[81]

Some US states have also instituted a statutory oppression remedy, though the breadth of the remedy varies from state to state. Some states use a broad definition of "oppression," with the view that the majority shareholder has

---

[77] MacIntosh, Holmes and Thompson (n 1) 130.

[78] *Brant* (n 1).

[79] See CBCA (n 7) s 241; MacIntosh, Holmes and Thompson (n 1) 133.

[80] See, e.g., *Naneff v Con-Crete Holdings Ltd*, [1995] O.J. No. 1377, 23 BLR (2d) 286.

[81] *First Edmonton Place Ltd v 315888 Alberta Ltd* [1988] A.W.L.D., 10 A.C.W.S. (3d) 268 [28].

oppressed the minority when the majority's actions violate the minority shareholder's "reasonable expectations." Other states, such as Delaware, have not explicitly addressed shareholder oppression.[82] Individual states vary in regard to the imposition of a fiduciary duty or the "reasonable expectations" standard.[83] Thus, the oppression remedy in Canada is more robust than in the US, providing adequate tools to respond to oppressive conduct by controlling or influential shareholders.

C. Normative Protection

In addition to these powerful remedies, little attention has been paid to the social norms governing institutional investors. Social norms specify behavior that is seen as desirable or legitimate in the shared view of societal members.[84] While it is now well established that, on an individual level, people behave contrary to neoclassical economic theory – such as by acting in an altruistic manner and in accordance with abstract ethical principles like fairness and equity, even if it comes at a personal cost to themselves[85] – less attention has been paid to how norms affect large institutions, and even less academic commentary has set out how social norms have a disciplining effect on large institutional investors in Canada.

This is a striking gap in the literature for if there are adequate social norms regulating institutional investors today, it begs the question: why do we need shareholder fiduciary duties in the first place? Of the sparse literature examining the interaction between social norms and law, Amir Licht's work is instructive. Licht states that laws are often only effective when they have social norms underlying them which encourage compliance with those laws.[86] In certain circumstances, laws can encourage the development of social norms but absent social norms which place value on subscribing to those laws, the laws are ineffective.[87] Accordingly, at all times, the main driver between compliance and non-compliance will be the norms that encourage or discourage adherence with the underlying values espoused in the law. Insofar as norms already encourage desirable behavior in the absence of laws, we should question why

---

82 John H. Matheson and Kevin Maler, 'A Simple Statutory Solution to Minority Oppression in the Closely-Held Business' (2007) 91 Minn. L. Rev. 657, 665.

83 Ibid 664.

84 Amir N. Licht, 'Social Norms and the Law: A Social Institutional Approach' (2005) https://papers.ssrn.com/sol3/papers.cfm?abstract_id=710621, 5.

85 Ibid 10.

86 Licht (n 84).

87 Ibid 71–74.

laws are needed at all, especially in situations where imposing new legal duties may chill the market and impose far more costs than benefits.

Our argument is straightforward: generally speaking, institutional investors do not abuse their positions of control in practice. Rather, a review of their market activity reveals a commitment by institutional investors to take on leadership roles and engage in corporate governance reforms which benefit the market as a whole and create positive externalities for minority shareholders. The reason that institutions take on this leadership role and behave in this manner, even in the absence of legal constraints, can be explained by norms that have a disciplining effect the way that large shareholder institutions are governed, organized and integrated into the Canadian market discourages them from taking positions in a company which only benefit themselves at the expense of minority shareholders.

While it is difficult to pinpoint exactly how, when and why these norms develop, academic literature has come to recognize that certain jurisdictions have different norms which materially influence institutional investor behavior. For example, Dyck et al. recently found that cultural and social norms affected how much institutional investors cared about a corporation's environmental and social performance, thus demonstrating that norms affect economic decision making.[88] Specifically, institutional investors increased a corporation's environmental and social performance when they came from countries with a strong normative commitment to those issues, but not otherwise.[89] Likewise, Cahan et al. found that institutional investors constrained by norms invested in companies with higher levels of corporate social responsibility and also influenced those corporations to increase their commitment to corporate social responsibility over time when compared to institutional investors unconstrained by norms.[90]

These studies demonstrate that social norms matter. Accordingly, perhaps norms regarding both shareholder wealth maximization and abusive behavior that harms minority shareholders need to be taken into account when considering legal reform.

---

[88] I. J. Alexander Dyck, Karl V. Lins, Lukas Roth and Hannes F. Wagner, 'Do Institutional Investors Drive Corporate Social Responsibility? International Evidence' (forthcoming J. Financial Econ.) available at https://papers.ssrn.com/sol3/papers.cfm?abstract_id=2708589, 5, 34.

[89] Ibid.

[90] Steven F. Cahan, Chen Chen and Li Chen, 'Social Norms and CSR Performance: An Examination of Positive Screening and Activism by Norm-Constrained Institutional Investors' (2013) University of Auckland Business School, https://www.business.uq.edu.au/sites/default/files/events/files/csr_and_norm-constrained_institutional_investors.pdf, 4–5.

Furthermore, institutional investor behavior reflects the presence of norms regarding acceptable corporate governance practices in the market today. Law makers should be hesitant to disrupt the status quo by imposing fiduciary obligations on shareholders *inter se*; imposing a fiduciary duty may discourage institutional investors from taking an active role in the market due to the increased risk of liability. Any proposal for reform should thus bear the burden of establishing a proof of positive effects to be gained from reforming shareholder's duties. To this date, this has not occurred and we should accordingly be skeptical about calls for reform of this sort.

Three recent examples stemming from institutional investors demonstrate the presence of social norms in this context. Prior to Bombardier Inc.'s 2017 annual meeting, the company proposed that executive chair Pierre Beaudoin stand for re-election. Major pension funds, including the Ontario Teachers' Pension Fund, Caisse de dépôt et placement du Québec, Canadian Pension Plan Investment, The Quebec Federation of Labour's Solidarity Fund and British Columbia Investment Management Corporation, stated their opposition and intention to vote against Beaudoin's re-election as executive chair.[91] The investors made public statements about their lack of support and are said to have voted against Beaudoin and a proposed executive compensation plan.[92] Beaudoin ultimately gave up his management role, though he remained part of the board.

Second, in 2017, 62 percent of shareholders voted against ExxonMobil management in favor of a resolution to disclose how climate change impacts business.[93] The vote took place at the company's annual meeting in Dallas, Texas. The same proposal received only 38 percent shareholder support the previous year. The resolution forces the company to conduct an annual "stress test" measuring how its oil assets will be affected by climate change regulation and new technology.[94] Edward Mason, head of responsible investment at Church Commissioners for England, said shareholders were showing how out of step the Trump administration had become on climate change. "Trump

---

[91] Alicja Siekierska, 'Ontario Teachers' Pension Plan withholds support for re-election of Bombardier's executive chairman,' *Financial Post* (Toronto, May 9, 2017) http://business.financialpost.com/transportation/ontario-teachers-pension-plan-votes-against-re-election-of-bombardiers-executive-chairman.

[92] Pattie Waldmier and Pan Yuk, 'Bombardier chairman forced out of executive role,' *Financial Times* (Chicago, May 11, 2017) https://www.ft.com/content/b8eb3d58-3651-11e7-bce4-9023f8c0fd2e.

[93] Ed Crooks, 'ExxonMobil bows to shareholder pressure on climate reporting,' *Financial Times* (New York, December 11, 2017) https://www.ft.com/content/8bd1f73a-dedf-11e7-a8a4-0a1e63a52f9c.

[94] Jed Kim, 'Exxon investors want a bank-style stress test for climate change,' *Marketplace* (June 29, 2017) https://www.marketplace.org/2017/06/29/sustainability/exxon-investors-want-bank-style-stress-test-for-climate-change.

is acting contrary to Wall Street and the world's largest investors," he said. "Climate change is a material financial risk and shareholders want to know how companies will manage the change to a low-carbon economy."[95] The proposal was led by pension fund of the Church of England, New York and California and supported by other large shareholders, such as Blackrock.[96]

Third, Canada's two largest banks, Toronto Dominion Bank and the Royal Bank of Canada, recently became the first major companies in Canada to adopt policies allowing shareholders to nominate directors to serve on their boards.[97] The policy change was developed with the input and support of the Canadian Coalition for Good Governance, a partnership representing Canada's largest institutional investors, which has a history of recommending similar proxy-access proposals to encourage better corporate governance.[98] The policies unveiled by the banks would allow a coalition of up to 20 shareholders, with a combined ownership of 5 percent of the company, to nominate up to 20 percent of board seats. The banks also submitted a letter to the Finance Department to amend the Bank Act, which is required to lower the combined ownership threshold to 3 percent, in accordance with the market standard in America.[99]

These are just a few of many examples which demonstrate that activist institutional shareholders routinely act in ways that benefit the corporation as a whole and create positive externalities for minority shareholders. There is no evidence of systemic abuse or a pressing need for legal reform to discipline shareholders today; rather, the evidence demonstrates that we should be encouraging shareholder activism, not erecting additional barriers. Thus, when considering whether or not to disrupt the status quo by imposing a shareholder fiduciary duty, we should be very cautious about altering the current equilibrium: imposing such a duty may have a chilling effect on investments and discourage institutional investors from playing an active leadership role in corporate governance due to the increased constraints on action and increased risk of liability. If that occurs, minority shareholders would be harmed much more than would be justified by the negligible increase in protection which a shareholder fiduciary duty would provide.

---

[95] Dominic Rushe, 'Shareholders force ExxonMobil to come clean on cost of climate change,' *The Guardian* (New York, May 31, 2017) https://www.theguardian.com/business/2017/may/31/exxonmobil-climate-change-cost-shareholders.

[96] Ibid.

[97] Janet McFarland and James Bradshaw, 'TD, RBC to allow certain shareholders to nominate board directors,' *The Globe and Mail* (Toronto, September 29, 2017) https://beta.theglobeandmail.com/report-on-business/td-royal-bank-to-allow-shareholders-to-nominate-board-directors/article36442345/?ref= .

[98] Ibid.

[99] Ibid.

VI. CONCLUSION

This chapter has argued that the rationale for imposing a duty of loyalty among shareholders *inter se* is strongest in capital markets with a preponderance of controlling shareholders. Yet even in such markets, an inter-shareholder fiduciary duty appears to be necessary in the presence of a strong remedial regime. Moreover, in markets like Canada where there are norms that encourage institutional investors to exercise their influence for the betterment of the corporation as a whole, we should be skeptical about disrupting the status quo with haphazard legal obligations.

A key unanswered question is whether fiduciary duties among shareholders should exist in the private or closely-held corporation. The argument is stronger in such cases but the problems identified above, including a lack of a relationship of trust between shareholders, may be a vitiating factor.

3. Duties imposed on specific shareholders only, and enforcement implications

Hanne S. Birkmose

I. INTRODUCTION

Duties imposed on shareholders are no longer a rare and exotic phenomenon in European company and capital market law.[1] Rather, they should be seen as a trend that has gained momentum since the financial crisis. Shareholders' duties typically apply to all shareholders. However, *the nature of the situation* sometimes requires that duties be imposed on one or more shareholders.[2] These duties apply to all shareholders in principle but it is a given situation that leads to imposing duties on some shareholders. In other situations, *the nature of the shareholder* gives rise to the imposition of shareholder duties. That is, these duties apply only to the subset of shareholders who fulfil certain criteria, such as size or categorization. From an economic perspective we would expect duties to be imposed on shareholders if the situation raises concerns regarding the interests of the company, the market or company constituents, or if a shareholder's attribute leads to concerns that such a shareholder might pose a risk to those interests protected by company law or capital market law. The latter is the main focus of this chapter. It is not obvious why the presence of certain shareholders or groups of shareholders *per se* imposes a risk to interests protected by law, and it is particularly interesting that specific categories of shareholders, such as institutional investors versus retail investors, have given rise to such concerns.

[1] For an overview of shareholders' duties found in European company and capital market law, see Hanne S. Birkmose and Florian Möslein: 'Introduction: Mapping Shareholders' Duties' in Hanne S. Birkmose (ed), *Shareholders' Duties* (Kluwer Law International 2017) 1.

[2] An example is the duty to pay up outstanding share capital when asked to by the company, or disclosure duties relating to voluntary or mandatory bids. See Melanie Döge, 'The Financial Obligations of the Shareholder', p. 287, and Karsten Engsig Sørensen, 'Shareholders' Duty to Disclose', p. 310, both in Birkmose (ed) (n 1).

To develop this argument, I employ an analytical framework based on concepts borrowed from agency theory and economic theories of market failure. This framework, presented in Section II, offers an initial understanding of why the law imposes duties on shareholders in general, as well as additional duties on particular shareholders when *the nature of the shareholder* motivates the imposition of certain responsibilities. In Section III, I identify a number of duties imposed on shareholders who share certain characteristics or classifications. The duties identified in Section III are then discussed in Section IV in order to highlight the purposes of imposing the duties and to determine whether the duties can be explained by the analytical framework. The fit with the analytical framework is important: if we can explain the duties through the framework, then we will have identified an economic theoretical basis for the imposition of specific duties on a specific subset of shareholders and the duties we find in company law and capital market law. If not, then the duties can be seen as a political instrument rather than a necessary legal measure to protect the interests of company constituents or capital markets. Both situations have implications for the enforcement of these duties, which is the focus of Section V. The enforcement implications may differ among the different duties and not all will be reviewed in detail; the aim is to stress some fundamental enforcement implications that follow from duties being imposed on some shareholders only. Section VI concludes.

II. THE AIM OF REGULATING SHAREHOLDERS AND LEGAL STRATEGIES: A LAW AND ECONOMICS APPROACH

In general, company law is intended to reduce the costs of transactions taking place by means of a business form with certain characteristics.[3] In this respect, company law can be considered a substitute for the private ordering in companies.[4] While pursuing this goal, the regulatory framework seeks to constrain value-reducing forms of opportunism and to control conflicts of interest, in particular among company constituents[5] – including shareholders, the board of

---

[3] See John Armour, Henry Hansmann, Reinier Kraakman and Mariana Pargendler, 'What Is Corporate Law?' in Reinier Kraakman, John Armour, Paul Davies, Luca Enriques, Henry Hansmann and Gerard Hertig (eds), *The Anatomy of Corporate Law. A Comparative and Functional Approach* (Oxford University Press 2017) 1f., 22f.

[4] This is a point of view clearly articulated in the nexus of contracts theory. See the seminal paper by Michael Jensen and William Meckling, 'Theory of the Firm: Managerial Behavior, Agency Costs and Ownership Structure' (1976) 3 *Journal of Financial Economics* 305–360.

[5] See Armour et al. (n 3) 1f., 22f.

directors, creditors, employees and even society. Conflicts of interest can have a debilitating effect on a company, particularly when one opposing interest has an information advantage over another. Such a context has been deeply considered by agency theory,[6] and company law in particular plays an important role in reducing asymmetric information and facilitating the monitoring of an agent.

Principal–agent theory most commonly focuses on relationships between the information-rich board of directors and the company's shareholders whose interests they ostensibly serve.[7] By contrast, this chapter seeks to understand the asymmetric information and power relations in other agency relationships relevant to company law. In particular, the agency relationship between majority and minority shareholders is relevant to the discussion on shareholders' duties. An additional conflict that may be relevant for the understanding of shareholder duties involves the relationships between shareholders and the company's other contractual parties, such as creditors and employees.[8] In all of these contexts, information asymmetries may lead to suboptimal outcomes. However, conflicts of interest and asymmetric information may also occur outside the agency relationships in companies. Such conflicts of interest may occur between the company and non-contractual parties, so-called externalities.

Armour et al. argue that legislators turn to a basic set of legal strategies when addressing agency problems in limited liability companies. Legal strategies is used as a term to mean a generic method of deploying law in a functional way.[9] They argue furthermore that legal strategies for controlling agency costs can be largely divided into two categories: 'governance strategies' and 'regulatory strategies'.[10] Governance strategies seek to facilitate the principal's own efforts to control the agent's behaviour, while regulatory strategies tend to constrain the agent's behaviour, that is, regulatory strategies are prescriptive and dictate substantive terms that govern the content of the agency relationship. However, regulatory strategies and governance strategies may also be interrelated. Disclosure provisions are often part of a regulatory strategy, but also serve as an important auxiliary mechanism to the governance strategies pursued by company law. While disclosure requirements will have a positive effect on the ability of the principal to control the agent, the full effect of the disclosure depends partly on the efficiency of the adjacent governance strate-

---

6 John Armour, Henry Hansmann and Reinier Kraakman, 'Agency Problems and Legal Strategies' in Reinier Kraakman et al. (eds), *The Anatomy of Corporate Law. A Comparative and Functional Approach* (Oxford University Press 2017) 29.

7 Ibid 29f., who define three different agency problems in a company.

8 Ibid 30.

9 For an extensive discussion, see ibid 31ff.

10 Ibid 31.

gies.[11] Moving beyond Armour et al., I argue that the concepts of governance strategies and regulatory strategies can also broaden our understanding of shareholders' duties found in capital market law.[12] Here, the function of the law is to mitigate any negative effects that actions of market participants may have on the efficiency of the capital market.

Theories that build on fundamental economic concepts may deepen our understanding of governance and regulation. Agency costs occur partly because of market failures of many kinds,[13] and legal intervention may be needed to correct these failures.[14] To the extent that legal intervention makes it possible for a company's constituents to arrange their affairs *inter partes* to maximize their individual welfare, a governance strategy may be preferred. For instance, shareholders' control rights may enable the principal to control the agent's behaviour. However, a regulatory strategy may be preferable if the bargaining power of the parties is unequal. This could be because of market failure that follows from an agent having more or better information than the principal. Here, substantive terms of the law may be intended to increase the level of information of the under-informed party and level out the imbalance of power in transactions. Outside the agency relationship, externalities, which describe the cost or benefit that affects a party who did not choose to incur that cost or benefit, may also be the result of market failure.[15] Here, legal intervention may seek to 'internalise' an externality, so that costs and benefits will affect mainly parties to the transaction. As non-contractual third parties typically have limited influence over the company or its shareholders, situations where their interests might otherwise not be protected are likely best served through regulatory rather than governance strategies.

Consequently, even when we assume that the overall aim of company law is to enable economic actors to transact easily by means of a business form with certain characteristics, and the choice of legal strategy should take into consideration the private ordering of the parties, it seems that governance strat-

---

[11] See Erik P. M. Vermeulen, 'Beneficial Ownership and Control. A Comparative Study – Disclosure, Information and Enforcement', OECD Corporate Governance Working Papers No. 7 (OECD Publishing) 11, http:dx.doi.org/10.1787/5k4dkhwckbzv-en.

[12] Armour et al. (n 3) 32 also note that the strategies can be deployed to protect nearly any vulnerable principal–agent relationship.

[13] Market failure may be defined as situations where the market equilibrium cannot be obtained because the assumptions underlying perfectly competitive markets are not fulfilled. See among others Robert Cooter and Thomas Ulen, *Law & Economics* (Berkeley Law Books 2016) 38ff. and Anthony Ogus, *Regulation. Legal Form and Economic Theory* (Hart Publishing 1994) 29.

[14] See among others Ogus (n 13) 29ff.

[15] See Armour et al. (n 6) 30. See also Ogus (n 13) 35ff.

egies are of limited relevance in relation to shareholders' duties. Governance strategies mainly focus on the principal as they rely on the principal's ability to control the agent's behaviour.[16] Duties, including shareholders' duties, are relevant to regulatory strategies that aim to constrain the agent, when some shareholders are understood to act as the agents of other shareholders. Moreover, the efficiency of governance strategies depends on the ability of the principal (e.g. minority shareholders) to exercise their control rights.[17] However, if control rights are to have any effect on the control of the agent, the minority must be able to exercise their rights at a low cost. Because of collective action problems, this also indicates that it is more likely that regulatory strategies may be preferred in company law to control agency costs involving shareholders as agents.

While company law most often deals with conflicts of interest between various groups of company constituents, it is debated whether company law should regulate externalities as well.[18] Still, we see that company law also serves ends other than to enable company constituents to transact easily. Some legal initiatives that go beyond the maximization of the value of the firm may be due to the presence of externalities, but other initiatives seem to serve wider purposes, such as social or political objectives.[19] If such legal initiatives involve duties being imposed on the shareholders, then a regulatory strategy will be preferred by legislators as well because the aims of the regulation are unlikely to be met without legal provisions that dictate the required courses of action.[20]

Capital market law's aims are different from those of company law. The contractual relationship between market participants is of less importance here as a primary aim is to ensure the existence of efficient capital markets. Moreover, capital market law also serves an important public interest function, in the sense that the state has a clear interest in the well-being of capital markets, which goes beyond advancing the private interests of individual market participants. Thus, elimination of market failures, including those caused by asymmetric information, is a main focus in capital market law. This supports the idea that regulatory strategies will be preferred in capital market law.

16 See Armour et al. (n 6) 31ff.

17 Ibid.

18 See Armour et al. (n 3) 23.

19 Ibid 24.

20 See for an introduction to the public interest theory, Ogus (n 13) 29ff.

III. DUTIES IMPOSED ON DIFFERENT SHAREHOLDER CATEGORIES

The existence of agency problems and resulting market failures in limited liability companies may explain why both company law and capital market law impose duties on shareholders, and why we should expect a preference for regulatory strategies. In this section, I identify some of the actual shareholders' duties we find in company law and capital market law, with emphasis on duties that are limited to shareholders that possess certain characteristics or are classified in a certain way.

Shareholders can differ in many respects, such as age, gender or nationality, but these differences do not appear to have an impact on their duties.[21] Rather, company law responds to the potential of some types of shareholders to negatively impact governance issues. Likewise, capital market law seems to focus on the potentially negative impact on the market that a subset of a company's shareholders might be in a position to cause.

Not surprisingly, size seems to be the dominant feature that triggers duties, and shareholders' duties may vary in accordance with the size of their shareholdings.[22] For instance, in both company law and capital market law, disclosure duties can be triggered when certain thresholds relating to the size of shareholdings have been crossed. These duties might include disclosure of shareholders' identities and the proportion of voting rights held, when that proportion reaches, exceeds or falls below certain thresholds.[23] Moreover, national company law may obligate shareholders to disclose their intentions upon acquisition of a certain proportion of the voting rights,[24] or a majority shareholder to purchase a minority shareholder's shares on request, when the proportion of shares owned by the former reaches a certain threshold.[25]

While duties that are contingent on size most often are constructed around thresholds, other duties, such as fiduciary duties and the duty not to abuse rights,[26] are applied increasingly intensively as holdings increase. Additional sets of duties may be assigned to large shareholders who have a specific,

[21] See Birkmose and Möslein (n 1) 18.

[22] Ibid 19–20.

[23] See Sørensen (n 2) 309ff.

[24] See the German Securities Act para 27(a)(1).

[25] See, e.g., the Danish Companies Act para 73.

[26] See Andreas Cahn, 'The Shareholders' Fiduciary Duty in German Company Law', and Pierre-Henri Conac, 'The Shareholders' Duty Not to Abuse Rights', both in Birkmose (ed) (n 1).

defined relationship to the company.[27] 'Related parties' may be required to disclose relevant information to the market or the company on transactions with the company or gain the approval of disinterested shareholders before the transaction. Another special case is that of parent companies, which may be subject to specific duties with respect to liability (piercing the corporate veil)[28] or disclosure (consolidated accounts).[29]

Looking at the classification of shareholders and shareholders' duties, one particular type of shareholder stands out: institutional investors.[30] This classification is not new[31] but it seems to have become more important with the adoption of the amended Shareholder Rights Directive (SRD II). The directive requires a subset of institutional investors to publicly present an engagement policy and also record how they have cast their votes. In addition, they must work to implement their engagement policy and report on progress in this regard.[32] A variety of meanings have been ascribed to 'institutional investors', which is why Art. 2 of SRD II clearly defines the term for the purposes of the directive. In broad terms, the provisions in SRD II only apply to undertakings carrying out activities of life assurance or institutions for occupational retirement provision and asset managers. Thus, other categories of institutional investors are not covered by the provisions.

Besides duties on institutional investors, we find only few duties imposed on subsets of shareholders based on classification. These mainly relate to the

---

27 Until the adoption of the amended Shareholder Rights Directive (SRD II), related party transactions was an unharmonized area of EU company law, and national rules varied widely. SRD II includes rules on related party transactions in Art. 9c. Even though the duty to ensure a due process is imposed on the company, the process relies on the identification and relative influence of the shareholder.

28 See Blanaid Clarke, 'The Duties of Parent Companies' in Birkmose (ed) (n 1) 229–54.

29 Sørensen (n 2) 314f.

30 For other classifications, see Jennifer G. Hill, 'Images of the Shareholder – Shareholder Power and Shareholder Powerlessness' in Jennifer G. Hill and Randal S. Thomas (eds), *Research Handbook on Shareholder Power* (Edward Elgar Publishing 2015); E. Isaac Mostovics, Nada K. Kakabadse and Andrew Kakabadse, 'Corporate Governance: Quo Vadis?' (2011) 11(5) *Corporate Governance* 613–26; Mathias M. Siems, 'With Great Power Comes Great Responsibility: Ideal and Real Types of Shareholders', and Marina Bitsch Madsen, 'A New Approach to Shareholder Heterogeneity', both in Birkmose (ed) (n 1).

31 Institutional investors have been subject to special regulation in hard law, including the AIFM Directive and the UCITS Directive, Directives 2011/61/EC and 2009/65/EC.

32 The duties are subject to the comply-or-explain principle, see Art. 3g.

obligations of states in their capacity as shareholders and concern so-called 'golden shares'.[33]

IV. THE PURPOSE OF IMPOSING DUTIES ON DIFFERENT CATEGORIES OF SHAREHOLDERS

The overall aims of company law and capital market law were briefly discussed in Section II. Consequently, we expect that the purpose of company law's imposition of duties on shareholders is to protect the interests of company constituents, in particular other shareholders, creditors and employees, who have an immediate contractual interest in the company. However, as mentioned, company law may include provisions that aim to protect the interests of non-contractual parties affected by externalities or other interests such as the societal interest in companies. In capital market law, we expect that the overall purpose of imposing duties on shareholders is to ensure the financial interests of the market and the market as an institution; that is, market transparency, efficiency and integrity.

A. Duties Depending on Shareholder Characteristics

A closer look at shareholders' duties found in company law yields the expectation that the duties imposed on subsets of shareholders mainly address agency problems, in order to protect the interests of the minority shareholders and to a lesser extent other contractual constituents. The possibility of a majority shareholder having an information advantage over minority shareholders is a key problem in the principal–agent relationship, which is why it is not surprising that we find various disclosure requirements in company law. Absent regulation, the biggest piece of secret information possessed by the majority shareholder is the knowledge that the shareholder is the majority shareholder. Minority shareholders are worried about power but also about intentions; simply knowing who the majority shareholder is goes some distance towards letting the minority holders know whether or not they should be worried.

Disclosure duties may protect the interests of minority shareholders or other company constituents, either because the disclosure is expected to constrain the behaviour of the large shareholder directly, or because the disclosure is seen as a tool to transform the behaviour of the agent. In general, the disclosed information allows minority shareholders or others to incorporate the infor-

[33] See Thomas Papadoupoulos, 'Shareholders' Duties in Case of State Ownership' in Birkmose (ed) (n 1) 255–79.

mation when making decisions.[34] When shareholders are required to publish information, for example on the size of their holding, it is not the information in itself that protects other shareholders, but the elimination of asymmetric information and thereby the increased opportunity for the principal to incorporate the information when making decisions. This change in the power balance between the agent and the principal may constrain or transform the behaviour of the disclosing shareholder. An example is disclosure of related party transactions, involving a shareholder who is in a position to extract value from the company due to his position.[35] Disclosure of information on the transaction will allow other shareholders to incorporate the information in their decision-making process, whether or not they are to approve the transaction at the general meeting. Thus, it is also likely that a related party will refrain from entering into some transactions, such as those that would transfer value from the company to the shareholder, when this would not be well received or not approved by the shareholders.

The correlation between the size of the shareholding and the existence or intensity of specific shareholders' duties is linked to shareholder power and the ability to affect corporate governance.[36] A large or controlling stake in a company obviously translates into corresponding voting power at the general meeting and, consequently, the possession of private power can be a legitimate argument for its regulation, and for the imposition of duties in particular, if the purpose is to protect the minority shareholders or other company constituents.[37] Thus, the law may define uniform thresholds for sizes of shareholdings that should trigger the application of specific shareholders' duties. This fits well with the theoretical framework discussed above as shareholders' duties may be applied to protect the interests of the principal. These considerations may also explain other duties that serve to protect the interests of minority shareholders, such as a majority's duty to purchase a minority's shares, or its duty not to abuse rights.[38]

Turning to shareholder duties found in capital market law and following the analytical framework presented in Section II, we expect to find duties that deal

---

[34] Armour et al. (n 6) 38f.

[35] See Luca Enriques, Gerard Gerig, Hideki Kanda and Mariana Pargendler, 'Related Party Transactions' in Kraakman et al. (eds) (n 3) 147ff.

[36] For an extensive account of shareholder power, see Hill and Thomas (eds), *Research Handbook on Shareholder Power* (n 30). See also Birkmose and Möslein (n 1) 19.

[37] However, shareholder power is not a clear-cut, absolute category for imposing duties as other stakeholders, in particular minority shareholders, may also be in a position to affect corporate decisions, see Birkmose and Möslein (n 1) 19.

[38] See Jan Andersson, 'Exit in Private Companies: An Overview' in Birkmose (ed) (n 1); Cahn (n 26); and Conac (n 26).

with situations where the risk of market failure endangers the overall aim of ensuring market transparency, efficiency and integrity. Consistent with these expectations, we find that the duties here mainly consist of disclosure duties aimed at shareholders of a certain size. Such disclosure requirements in capital market law can largely be explained by the analytical framework as disclosure is an important remedy for overcoming inefficiencies in the market due to lack of transparency and market failure. However, we also find disclosure duties that aim to ensure good corporate governance. Corporate governance considerations have not traditionally been an integrated part of capital market law but this seems to be changing.[39] Disclosure and transparency are fundamental to the regulation of capital markets as well as to insuring good corporate governance, which is why such duties found in capital market law may prevent market failure as well as furthering the goal of good corporate governance: other shareholders as well as market participants more generally may benefit from the knowledge of ownership and control structures, or the intentions of large shareholders.[40] Consequently, in some situations disclosure duties may serve private as well as public interests.

B. Duties Specifically for Institutional Investors

Turning to shareholder categories, it is difficult to identify in company law situations where some types of shareholders are understood to act as agents on behalf of other company law constituents. Still, we find duties imposed on certain categories of shareholders, especially institutional investors, regardless of the size of their holdings. Consequently, we would expect that the justification for legal intervention aimed at a certain category of shareholders would be based on market failure. However, this argument seems to carry weight only in situations where there are concerns that a specific category of shareholders might have a negative impact on the company or the market. In the absence of agency relationships or market failure, the analytical framework presented in Section II cannot explain such duties.

Therefore, it is surprising that we find duties imposed on certain categories of shareholders in company law. However, the duties imposed on institutional investors only apply to listed companies. This raises the question of whether we can explain these duties with theories on market failure and the need for public intervention to restore market efficiency.

---

39 See in particular the discussion in Sørensen (n 2) 311ff.

40 Ibid 312ff.

The arguments given by the European Commission for imposing duties on institutional investors suggest that SRD II aims to protect several interests. As stated in Recital 16 of the Preamble to the directive:

> Public disclosure of such information could have a positive impact on investor awareness, enable ultimate beneficiaries such as future pensioners to optimise their investment decisions, facilitate the dialogue between companies and their shareholders, encourage shareholder engagement and strengthen their accountability to stakeholders and civil society.

First, the disclosure duty is expected to have a derived positive effect on investor awareness. While awareness is not explained, it is likely that the Commission has in mind the ability of investors to react to the disclosed information.[41] It is unclear, though, how the information will help investors in their investment or corporate governance decisions. The disclosure requirements only ensure that the investor community becomes aware of the institutional investor's policy on active ownership and how they have been active historically, including how they have exercised their voting rights. This information will mainly be of value to investors if they know in which companies the institutional investors currently have shares but such information is not always publicly available.[42] If the purpose is to increase investor awareness in order to support investors' decisions on investment or corporate governance issues, then it could be relevant to disclose the information by all larger shareholders that potentially could affect the corporate governance of listed companies, and not only institutional investors.

A second purpose is to 'enable ultimate beneficiaries such as future pensioners to optimise investment decisions'. Disclosing information on the policy on active ownership and on how the policy has been implemented and the results thereof, including how the voting right has been exercised, allows beneficiaries such as future pensioners to make an informed decision on to which institutional investor to entrust the management of their pension funds. While institutional investors act as the beneficiaries' agents, this relationship is traditionally considered to be outside the company law context and therefore not regulated by company law. However, the actions of the institutional investors in the company may result in externalities in relation to the beneficiaries. Still, this argument does not explain why disclosure duties are imposed on only

---

[41] The Danish translation reads *investorers informationsniveau* (the level of information of investors).

[42] Ownership information will be available in Sweden, while in Denmark it will only be available for shareholders with a 5% share or more, who are required to disclose their ownership under the Companies Act para 55.

a subset of institutional investors[43] as the beneficiary argument extends to all institutional investors.

Third, it is said that the disclosure duty will facilitate dialogue between the board of directors of a company and the shareholders. This argument, along with the argument that disclosure may encourage shareholder engagement, seems to be based on traditional corporate governance arguments and agency theory. The Commission has emphasized on several occasions that effective control by shareholders is an essential element of the European corporate governance model.[44] Moreover, increased engagement by one group of shareholders may have a positive effect on other shareholders as it might help mitigate the collective action problem. However, the agency argument does not explain why solely institutional investors are targeted, and not all larger shareholders. Institutional investors are not *per se* better at controlling the boards of listed companies, nor should they be expected to have a larger impact on corporate governance problems such as collective action than any other shareholder with comparably sized holdings. Interestingly, these new duties seem not to aim to constrain the behaviour of institutional investors with regard to the company in which they have invested, but rather to transform their behaviour into conformance with current understandings of best practices in relation to shareholder engagement.

On the whole, the particular focus on institutional investors regardless of size seems to indicate that the fourth purpose, to 'strengthen their accountability to civil society', is of importance. Arguably, however, this purpose is not fully clear. Undoubtedly, civil society has an interest in the financial well-being of companies but the extent of any accountability to civil society is arguable.[45] It follows from the traditional division of powers in limited liability companies that the board of directors will be responsible for ensuring that companies fulfil these duties, and the shareholders' role will be limited to controlling the board. From a corporate governance perspective, all shareholders, not only institutional investors, have an interest in monitoring the board and it should not be a duty in particular of the institutional investors. Emphasizing a duty for institutional investors to include in their engagement policy how they monitor investee companies on issues such as non-financial performance

---

[43] The amended Art. 2 of SRD II defines institutional investors. In broad terms, the provisions in SRD II cover only undertakings carrying out activities of life assurance or institutions for occupational retirement provision.

[44] See, among others, Action Plan: European company law and corporate governance – a modern legal framework for more engaged shareholders and sustainable companies, section III (COM (2012) 740 final).

[45] See Hanne S. Birkmose, 'Forcing Shareholder Engagement – Theoretical Underpinning and Political Ambitions' (2018) 29(4) Eur. Bus. L. Rev. 613–642.

and social and environmental impact suggests that institutional investors are expected to be watchdogs of civil society's interests in listed companies. Such a paradigm shift is arguably inconsistent with other principles of corporate governance.[46] While participation in corporate governance traditionally has been left to shareholders to choose, the recent amendment to the Shareholder Rights Directive has taken a stronger stand on the involvement of a certain subset of the institutional investor population in corporate governance.

In short, several arguments are presented in support of SRD II's imposition of special duties on institutional investors. While the emphasis on monitoring the boards of investee companies can be justified with reference to traditional agency arguments, these arguments stress the importance of monitoring by all shareholders, and not only one group. And, while it is also generally acknowledged that, due to their size, large shareholders may be well positioned to overcome barriers to collective shareholder engagement, corporate governance arguments cannot explain why only some institutional investors are targets, and not large shareholders in general. Moreover, in this agency context the shareholders are the principal vis-à-vis the directors, and duties being imposed on the principal can hardly be explained by agency theory. Rather it seems that more vague arguments are used to justify the new disclosure duties imposed on institutional investors, and that these are based neither on the premise of agency problems nor on concerns about market failure.[47] Moreover, contrary to most other duties imposed as components of regulatory strategies, these duties not only aim to constrain the actions of the institutional investors in specific ways, but also to change the behaviour of the institutional investors without specifying clearly what their expectations are.

The fact that we find duties aimed at certain groups of shareholders, and these obligations cannot be explained by theories of agency or market failure, raises some questions in relation to efficiency of these duties and their enforcement.

V. ENFORCEMENT CHALLENGES

So far, we can conclude that duties that are imposed only on a subset of shareholders can largely be explained with reference to a law and economics analytical framework: a subset of shareholders' acts (and thus should be regulated) as an agent for other shareholders (primarily majority vs. minority shareholders) or because some shareholders are capable of taking advantage of the potential for market failure, an outcome that legislators ought proactively

---

46 Ibid.

47 As mentioned in Section II, company law may be employed by regulators for other objectives than wealth maximization.

to hinder. Thus, duties imposed in company law may be regarded as necessary interventions in the private ordering of companies to protect the interests of other shareholders or company constituents, or to eliminate market failure that may harm a wider group of non-contractual stakeholders. Likewise, duties imposed in capital market law may be necessary to eliminate market failure and consequently protect the integrity of the market. However, to ensure that the aim of such regulatory intervention is achieved, it is necessary that we ensure that shareholders comply with their duties[48] and that we are able efficiently to enforce these duties.

A. Who Will Enforce Duties Aimed at Groups of Shareholders?

Largely, it has been confirmed that regulatory strategies dominate when imposing duties on specific categories of shareholders. The efficiency of regulatory strategies relies on effective disclosure mechanisms that enable an external authority, such as a court or a regulatory body, to determine whether or not the shareholder complied with a particular prescription.[49]

Duties that are imposed on a subset of shareholders in company law most often aim to address agency problems and thus protect the interests of a principal. However, the legal nature of the duties differs and some are not well defined, such as fiduciary duties or the duty not to abuse rights. In situations where duties are based on principles rather than statutory law, or where the statutory provisions are less well defined, enforcement relies on private initiative: the parties are referred to courts unless other remedies such as arbitration have been agreed.[50] Even though principals have a direct interest in the enforcement of duties aiming at protecting their interests, the reliance on private initiation of enforcement may render enforcement less efficient where the duty is less well defined as the outcome of such litigation is more difficult to predict. For one thing, it may be difficult for principals to prove that the duty has been breached, and second, free-riding and other collective action problems, or jurisdictional rules, may hinder any of the minority shareholders from initiating the litigation process. Thus, shareholders are less likely to perform the duties diligently if it is up to weaker principals to enforce them.[51]

Other statutory duties may be more concise and thus easier to enforce. Examples are disclosure duties. Even in these situations, litigation costs, collective action problems or jurisdictional rules may hinder effective enforce-

[48] See Armour et al. (n 6) 32.
[49] Ibid
[50] See Chapters 5 and 9.
[51] Ibid.

ment. However, we also find a few duties in company law that are enforced by public authorities. This seems to be the case when the interests the duty aims to protect are not pure private interests, but also public interests. One example is the duty to disclose major shareholdings in non-listed companies, which is found in many Member States and which was discussed in Section IV.A. Another example is the recent amendment to the Shareholder Rights Directive and the disclosure duties imposed on institutional investors in Art. 3g. Here, Member States are required to ensure that institutional investors and asset managers either comply with the requirements set out in the provisions or publicly disclose a clear and reasoned explanation as to why they have chosen not to comply with one or more of the requirements.

Moving from company law to capital market law, the preferred approach to regulation has changed from the private law sphere to the public law sphere in most cases. Consequently, enforcement no longer relies on private initiative by shareholders or contractual stakeholders, but in most cases on a public authority, such as a national financial supervisory authority, or a quasi-regulatory authority, such as a national stock exchange. Since enforcement of capital market duties does not rely on private initiative, it may be assumed that enforcement in general is more effective. However, as discussed by Iris H-Y. Chiu and Konstantinos Sergakis in this volume,[52] public enforcement may also be suboptimal.

B. Additional Challenges Related to Duties Imposed on a Subset of Shareholders

When duties are limited to a subset of shareholders, it is essential that we are able to delimit which shareholders or which group of shareholders have to comply with a given duty. When duties are imposed on a subset of shareholders, these shareholders incur compliance and other costs.[53] In case of conflicts of interest or market failure, the cost imposed on either company constituents or third parties as a consequence of the shareholders' actions may justify the duties. However, the duties should not go further than necessary to secure the interests at risk, nor should they be imposed on others than those acting as agents or causing market failure.

---

[52] See Chapters 6 and 7.

[53] See also Daniëlle Melis, Leen Paape and Mijntje Lückerath-Rovers, who warn against loading institutional investors with too many burdens in 'Enforceability of Institutional Investors' Responsibilities in Corporate Governance Through the Dutch Corporate Governance Code: Are Regulators and Practitioners on the Same Page (and to Who Are Institutional Investors Accountable)?' Working Paper 2017, 21, https://papers.ssrn.com/sol3/papers.cfm?abstract_id=1975763.

It was argued in Section III that the duties imposed on a group of shareholders depend either on size or on a specific categorization of the shareholders. In the first situation, the duties aim to counterbalance the power of significant shareholders, which are considered agents of other company constituents or which may cause market failure. This correlation between the size of shareholding and the application of specific shareholders' duties is linked to shareholder power and the ability to affect corporate governance.[54] However, shareholder power may depend on factors other than the size of a shareholding, such as the legal and socio-economic framework provided by the company law rules on internal decision-making[55] or the degree of concentrated or dispersed ownership. Thus, even though the law defines uniform thresholds for sizes of shareholdings that should trigger the application of specific shareholders' duties, it may be difficult to determine the precise threshold. Despite the difficulties in defining absolute thresholds, we find duties that rely on defined thresholds. An example is transparency requirements that specify when a shareholding is significant and how a shareholder with such a holding must make this fact public. This is particularly the case in capital market law, for example in relation to the disclosure of significant shareholdings in the Transparency Directive.[56] Absolute thresholds may simplify enforcement but they might still be problematic as, depending on the situation, not only direct holdings, but also indirect holdings and different forms of control structures can be relevant for determining the size of a shareholding. However, if the duty depends on a shareholder's relative influence,[57] it will create uncertainty for the shareholder(s) that might be affected because rather than a specific threshold, several factors could influence when the duty is triggered. This may also weaken enforcement as it may be more difficult to determine whether a duty applies or if it has been violated. Still, we also find duties that intensify with size, such as a duty not to abuse rights, fiduciary duties or duties in relation to related party transactions that depend on the ability to influence the company.

---

[54] For an extensive account of shareholder power, see Hill and Thomas (eds) (n 30). See also Birkmose and Möslein (n 1) 19.

[55] See Florian Möslein (ed.), *Private Macht* (Mohr Siebeck 2015); with respect to shareholder (majority) power, see in particular Christian Hoffmann, 'Private Macht im Gesellschaftsrecht – Die Macht der Mehrheit', in ibid 353.

[56] Directive 2004/109/EC of the European Parliament and of the Council of 15 December 2004 on the harmonisation of transparency requirements in relation to information about issuers whose securities are admitted to trading on a regulated market and amending Directive 2001/34/EC [2004] OJ L390/33.

[57] In relation to the agency conflict between subsets of shareholders, see also Armour et al. (n 6) 30.

A further complication in the enforcement of duties that relates to shareholder power is that the notion of a shareholder is not well defined.[58] Some duties might be imposed on the owner of the shares, while others might be imposed on the persons or entities that exercise the voting right, or those that own relevant financial instruments.[59]

Duties that relate to specific categories of shareholders only partially seem to aim at addressing agency problems or market failure, as discussed above in Section IV.B. Rather, the duties set out in the SRD II seem to be imposed on a subset of shareholders as a transformative tool capable of changing the behaviour of this group for several purposes. While the clear delimitation of institutional investors found in Art. 2 may ease enforcement, it has other implications. When duties are imposed on a subset of shareholders, these shareholders incur cost, including compliance costs, which may result in a competitive disadvantage for this group of shareholders vis-à-vis shareholders who face no special obligations. Moreover, jurisdictional barriers may hinder enforcement, as when shareholders are of different nationalities.[60] Consequently, the duties in SRD II are restricted to a subset of EU institutional investors. This may severely reduce the impact of the duties.

C. Can Enforcement Ensure Compliance?

It is relevant to consider the nature of the duty that is imposed on certain shareholders in order to discuss the extent to which enforcement can ensure compliance with the prescribed duty. In most situations, we would expect that it is possible to determine whether or not shareholders complied with a particular prescription, regardless of whether compliance has to be determined by the courts or a public or quasi-public entity, because regulatory duties are prescriptive and dictate substantive terms.[61] This is in particular the case for rules, but also standards or principles where compliance has to be verified *ex post* and confirmation may require more scrutiny, typically by courts.[62]

However, disclosure duties, which are an important group of shareholders' duties in company law as well as in capital market law, give rise to particular enforcement challenges. Enforcement of disclosure duties only ensures com-

---

58 See the discussion in Sørensen (n 2) 322 in relation to disclosure duties, and Melis et al. (n 53).

59 Voting rights relating to financial instruments have been added to the Transparency Directive Art. 13(1)(a)–(b) with Directive 2013/50/EU in relation to the notification requirements laid down in Arts 9, 10 and 13.

60 See Chapter 13 and also Sørensen (n 2) 322f. and Melis et al. (n 53).

61 See Armour et al. (n 6) 31.

62 For the distinction between rules and standards, see ibid 32f.

pliance with the disclosure duty itself. While disclosure in itself may offset the information advantage which some shareholders have, and to some extent have a disciplining effect on the disclosing shareholder,[63] in most agency contexts the disclosure is a means to the end. For instance, disclosures that include information on the identity of the shareholder, the number of shares held and voting rights theoretically allow other company constituents to act upon the disclosure to safeguard their own interests.[64] Or in relation to market failure, the disclosure will allow the market to include the information in the assessment of the shareholders' potential impact on the market and ensure an efficient market. In these situations, enforcement of the disclosure duty itself may not ensure that the underlying aim of the duty is fulfilled.

D. Realizing the Underlying Goals

As far as duties that aim to improve asymmetric information in the agency relationship are concerned, the disclosure is the aim of the regulation as it enables the shareholders to include the information in their governance decisions and must therefore be enforced vigorously. However, because of the private ordering of the internal affairs of the company, minority shareholders or other company constituents are entrusted with the task of reacting on the information, and it is presumed that no further external involvement is needed. In this respect, disclosure duties are an important auxiliary mechanism to the governance strategies pursued by company law, as discussed in Section II.[65]

The disclosure duties in SRD II are different from those otherwise required by other EU or national law in relation to shareholders. As described above, Member States are responsible for ensuring that the institutional investors covered by the provisions in Art. 3g(1)(a) either comply with the requirements set out in the provisions in an engagement policy or publicly disclose a clear and reasoned explanation as to why they have not done so. However, there is no requirement as to the specific content of the policy. Thus, a parallel may be drawn with the disclosure duty found in the European corporate governance framework. Soft law in the form of recommendations or codes has been the predominant instrument. Soft law itself need not be enforced, as the normative element (best practice) in the recommendation or code may motivate interested parties to react to non-acceptable behaviour. However, disclosure on

[63] For instance, if a related party has to disclose a transaction with the company then he might refrain from entering into transactions if he predicts that the disclosure of the transaction will receive a negative response from others.

[64] See Armour et al. (n 6) 38f.

[65] 'Governance strategies seek to facilitate the principal's control over the agent's behaviour', ibid 31. This includes shareholder rights, such as the voting right.

compliance is essential[66] as it provides stakeholders with easily accessible key information about the practices applied and allows stakeholders to integrate the information in their decision-making process.[67] Consequently, since the adoption of Directive 2006/46/EC, listed companies have had to publish an annual corporate governance statement according to the comply-or-explain principle.[68]

However, it is generally acknowledged that corporate governance disclosure based on comply-or-explain may be suboptimal.[69] The problems are numerous, including free-riding and collective action problems. These problems may be even more distinct in relation to the disclosure requirements laid down by the SRD II. As discussed in Section IV.B, the purposes of the disclosure seem to be numerous. In particular, these duties seem to be imposed on shareholders as a transformative tool capable of changing the behaviour of shareholders. Here the purpose is to incentivize shareholders to behave in a certain manner, in which some had not done before the requirement was formalized. In this case, the motivation is not a value reduction encountered by other company constituents if the duties are not imposed, but rather that the constituents may experience a relatively higher value increase as a consequence of the change in behaviour by some shareholders.

As mentioned above, Member States are required to ensure that institutional investors and asset managers either comply with the disclosure requirements or explain why they have not done so. However, the disclosure will only ensure compliance with the formal requirements; it will not in itself improve corporate governance in investee companies. Engagement by institutional investors can only have an impact on corporate governance if the individual institutional investor adopts a meaningful engagement policy that reflects the resources and the ability of the investor to engage. Likewise, the implementation of the engagement policy and the actual engagement in investee companies must reflect not only the engagement policy, but also the fact that any decision to engage or refrain from engagement is taken on a considered basis, where the actual situation of the individual investee company is taken into consideration. Member States are not required to assess the value of the

---

66 In the case of periodical disclosure, where the disclosure is expected, the compliance issue is not so much whether it happens, but its quality, see Armour et al. (n 6) 39.

67 See RiskMetrics, 'Study on Monitoring and Enforcement Practices in Corporate Governance in the Member States', 23 September 2009, 59ff.

68 Directive 2006/46/EC of the European Parliament and of the Council of 14 June 2006 amending Council Directives 78/660/EEC on the annual accounts of certain types of companies, 83/349/EEC on consolidated accounts, 86/635/EEC on the annual accounts and consolidated accounts of banks and other financial institutions and 91/674/EEC on the annual accounts and consolidated accounts of insurance undertakings.

69 RiskMetrics (n 67) 70ff.

engagement of institutional investors or the value of information disclosed. The question then is, who is to ensure that institutional investors do not just carry out a box-ticking exercise, but rather engage in a meaningful way and disclose on their engagement in an equally meaningful way?

In traditional corporate governance disclosure, the market is expected to include the quality of the disclosed corporate governance statements in the pricing of a listed company's shares. Consequently, if the market is disappointed with the disclosed report it will be reflected in a lower market value. Thus, the board of a listed company has a strong incentive to ensure quality in the corporate governance reporting. Applied to the disclosure of institutional investors, it is questionable whether market pressure will sanction poor disclosure practices. First, it is not clear who 'the market' is. Institutional investors need not be listed on a stock exchange, even though it is stated in the Preamble of SRD II, as discussed above, that disclosure could have a positive impact on investor awareness. Moreover, it is not a given that investor awareness refers to the institutional investors' investors, but could equally well be other investors that invest in the same companies as the institutional investors. If so they have no immediate means to put pressure on the institutional investors. Market pressure could also come from the institutional investors' beneficiaries as the Preamble states that disclosure should enable ultimate beneficiaries, such as future pensioners, to optimize investment decisions. But even beneficiaries may not always have the right means to put pressure on the institutional investors.[70] The dialogue between institutional investors and investee companies is also mentioned, and even though the boards in listed companies may have an interest in their investors' preferences, they also lack the means to put pressure on the institutional investors. Finally, accountability to society is mentioned but society has been given no rights which allow sanctioning beyond the formal enforcement of disclosure.

Regulators could have imposed a model on institutional investors that required the institutional investors to implement an engagement policy with a certain content and at the same time have given financial supervisory authorities, for instance, the power to enforce and sanction non-compliance.[71] However, a self-regulatory model has been chosen that relies on the institutional investors to fulfil the aim of the provisions, which is consistent with the 'one size does not fit all' rationale behind the chosen flexible approach. The incentive for institutional investors to engage in activities which traditionally have been considered voluntary seems limited though, and engagement can

---

[70] See Melis et al. (n 53).

[71] Discussion of the implications of such a model is outside the limits of this chapter.

only be expected to the extent that the return on investment is expected to be positively impacted.[72] However, there is always a risk that regulators will intervene later, which is why it can be argued that investors may have to choose between more engagement and more regulation.[73]

VI. CONCLUCION

While most of the duties found in company law and capital market law today can be explained by the analytical framework introduced in Section II, the recent duties imposed by SRD II seem to take shareholders' duties to a new level. While most duties depend on certain shareholder characteristics, the duties in SRD II depend on a certain categorization of shareholders. Moreover, while other duties seem to regulate the potential (negative) impact of some shareholders due to their relative influence, the duties in SRD II seem to seek to transform the behaviour of the shareholders. Thus, rather than restricting their behaviour, the aim is to incentivize institutional investors to behave in a manner in which they had not done otherwise. Consequently, enforcement becomes essential to assist this transformation. The model chosen relies largely on private enforcement as company stakeholders are expected to hold institutional investors accountable for the quality of their engagement disclosure. In most situations, enforcement by private parties is motivated by a potential value reduction encountered by other company constituents. However, in this situation the argument seems to be that enforcement is motivated by a potential increase in value, experienced by the constituents as a consequence of the change in behaviour of some shareholders. Such an increase is shared by all shareholders but the costs are borne only by the shareholders on whom the duties are imposed. As has been discussed, the chosen model may not ensure efficient enforcement, and the impact of SRD II may therefore be weakened.

---

72 Melis et al. (n 53).

73 Ibid 8.

4. Shareholder engagement duties: the European move beyond stewardship

Christoph Van der Elst

I. INTRODUCTION

For a long period of time it was a common belief that shareholders had no duties vis-à-vis the company. As Hoffman put it for the US, 'shareholders owe the corporation no legal duties' and are 'uniquely blessed by the freedom to do what they will with their capital'.[1] Shareholders' obligations were limited to the fiduciary duties in close companies 'akin to the duties partners owe to one another'[2] and to a prohibition on self-dealing by majority shareholders.[3] Similarly, in the UK Flannigan notes that neither the shareholder nor the company owes fiduciary duties to one other.[4] The Italian view resembles the UK approach: 'Italian company law does not expressly foresee any general obligation or duty for shareholders vis-à-vis each other, or between majority and minority shareholders, or towards the company as a whole. The only exception is given by the shareholder's conflict of interest rules.'[5] For France,

[1] David A. Hoffman, 'The "Duty" to Be a Rational Shareholder' (2006) 90 Minn. L. Rev. 537.

[2] Roberta S. Karmel, 'Should a Duty to the Corporation Be Imposed on Institutional Shareholders?' (2004) 60 Business Lawyer 2.

[3] Iman Anabtawi and Lynn Stout, 'Fiduciary Duties for Activist Shareholders' (2010) 60(5) Stan. L. Rev. 1255; Jeffrey Baumann, A Palmiter and E Weiss, *Corporations: Law and Policy* (6th edn, Thomson 2007) 36. For a comparative overview see Zipora Cohen, 'Fiduciary Duties of Controlling Shareholders: A Comparative Approach' (1991) 12 U. Pa. J. Int'l Bus. L. 379.

[4] Robert Flannigan, 'Fiduciary Duties of Directors and Shareholders' (2004) J. Bus. L. 285. Premium-listed companies on the London Stock Exchange must enter into an agreement with their controlling shareholder ensuring a number of governance requirements (Listing Rule 6.5.4).

[5] Sabrina Bruno and Eugenio Ruggiero, 'Italy', in Sabrina Bruno and Eugenio Ruggiero (eds), *Public Companies and the Role of Shareholders* (Kluwer 2011) 85.

Gainet found that the limited rights to act against controlling shareholders mitigate the higher level of obligations of the shareholders than in the US.[6]

Following the financial crisis the (European) focus shifted from rights that shareholders should have or can claim towards the duties of the shareholders. Commissioner Michel Barnier announced in March 2010 that the 'costs of the difficulties [of financial institutions] are borne by shareholders and by unsecured creditors'.[7] He had also noted that shareholder rights had been discussed for years: 'it is time to also talk about shareholder's obligations'.[8] In her recent book *Shareholders' Duties*, Birkmose, together with Möslein, maps the different kinds of shareholders' duties.[9] Some duties are derived from the contractual relationships between the shareholders, which can be laid down both in the articles of association and in shareholder agreements. Further, statutory law can impose specific duties on shareholders such as the duty for the general meeting of shareholders of Danish companies not to 'pass a resolution if it is clear that the resolution is likely to give certain shareholders or others an undue advantage over other shareholders or the limited liability company' and the duty to disclose major shareholdings which results from the Transparency Directive.[10] More generally, in many countries there is a general principle that an abusive use of any kind of right is forbidden. Therefore, shareholders, too, whether majority or minority shareholders, should not make abusive use of their rights, in particular of their voting right and their right to information.[11] In specific circumstances, the shareholders have had other duties imposed on them. This is the case for shareholders of financial institutions. Shareholders

---

[6] Celine Gainet, 'Controlling Shareholders' Fiduciary Duties Owed to Minority Shareholders – A Comparative Approach: The United States and France' in Robert Cressy, Douglas Cumming and Chris Mallin (eds), *Entrepreneurship, Finance, Governance and Ethics* (Springer 2013) 137–74.

[7] M Barnier, 'Laying the foundations for crisis prevention and management in Europe', Speech 10 March 2010, http://europa.eu/rapid/press-release_SPEECH-10-112_en.htm.

[8] Michel Barnier quoted in Hanne S. Birmose, 'Shareholders' Duties in European Company Law' (2016) 13 Eur. Comp. L. 1, 5.

[9] Hanne S. Birkmose and Florian Möslein, 'Introduction: Mapping Shareholders' Duties' in Birkmose Hanne S. Birkmose (ed), *Shareholders' Duties* (Kluwer Law International 2017) 1–25.

[10] See https://www.esma.europa.eu/regulation/corporate-disclosure/transparency-directive.

[11] For a more extensive analysis of the abusive use of shareholder rights, see Pierre-Henri Conac, 'The Shareholders' Duty Not to Abuse Rights' in Hanne S. Birkmose (ed), *Shareholders' Duties* (Kluwer Law International 2017) 363–76.

that acquire an interest in the financial institution that is likely to be influential must prove that they have a good reputation and should be financially sound.[12]

Commissioner Barnier kept his promise to provide more shareholders' duties. According to the European Shareholder Rights Directive, institutional investors and asset managers must develop an engagement policy and make sure there is a follow-up of the implementation of the policy. I am of the opinion that these mandatory European rules are too far reaching as they intervene in the internal relationship of one particular class of shareholders with the company whereas it is not proven that it always serves the interests of the beneficiaries of these investors and neither is it clear whether it can reach the aspired-to goals of less short-termist behaviour. Best practice recommendations can better serve these purposes.

In the next section, I start with a brief overview of the importance of the different types of shareholders, their investment behaviour and their relative importance in different countries, providing insights into the relative position of the Directive's envisaged institutional investors in the shareholder community. Next I discuss a number of means of shareholder engagement and its different use by different shareholder types in different European Member States. In Section III, I briefly study the different engagement duties which have been developed in a number of corporate governance codes and the European Shareholder Rights Directive. Section IV addresses the monitoring and enforcement effects of the European shareholders' engagement duties for institutional investors and asset managers and criticizes the shift from a voluntary comply-or-explain stewardship to the stiffening mandatory engagement system. I show in this section that the mandatory duties endanger the current flexible relationships between investees and investors. Section V provides a conclusion.

II. OWNERSHIP STRUCTURES AND SHAREHOLDER ENGAGEMENT

A. Ownership Structures

The role and position of shareholders have changed in recent times. While before the 1990s shareholders were not identified and acted behind the scenes,

[12] Art. 23 of Directive 2013/36/EU of the European Parliament and of the Council of 26 June 2013 on access to the activity of credit institutions and the prudential supervision of credit institutions and investment firms, amending Directive 2002/87/EC and repealing Directives 2006/48/EC and 2006/49/EC [2013] OJ L176/338.

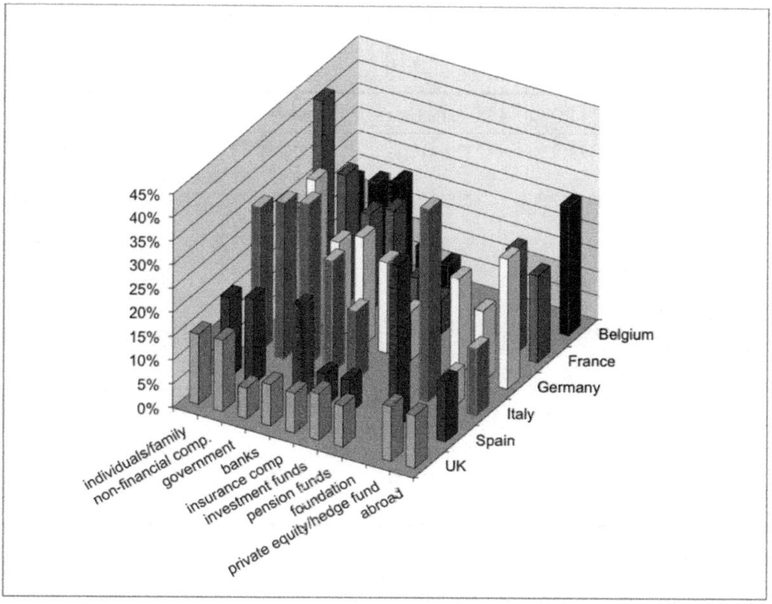

Source: Christoph Van der Elst, 'The Influence of Shareholder Rights on Shareholder Behavior' (2010) Corp. Fin. & Cap. Mark. L. Rev, Figure 8b, 57.

Figure 4.1 Average voting block of different types of shareholders in different European countries

today many, if not all, shareholders are known to the company and in many countries the company is equipped with tools to identify its shareholders' base.[13] These data show that different types of shareholders hold different kinds of voting blocks in different countries, as shown in Figure 4.1. First, due to the different economic structure of countries, some types of shareholders are more common in some countries than in others. This is the case for pension funds that hold voting blocks in many UK companies, whereas this type of shareholder is as good as absent in many other countries. There is a similar finding for foundations, prominently present in some countries, while absent in other countries.

Next, the average voting block of individuals, non-financial companies and the government is larger than that of insurance companies, investment funds and pension funds. Also, some types of shareholders prefer the acqui-

---

[13] See, e.g., in France, the procedure provided for in Art. L.128 Commercial Code. The Shareholder Rights Directive requires that companies can identify their shareholders (Art. 3*bis*).

Table 4.1 *Share ownership structure in the EU and its major economies in 2012 (1990)*

	EU	France	Germany	Italy*	UK
Individuals/family	11% (22%)	11% (19%)	9% (20%)	37% (56%)	11% (26%)
Non-financial comp.	17% (22%)	21% (33%)	38% (38%)	25% (22%)	2% (3%)
Government	4% (4%)	6% (7%)	2% (4%)	6% (8%)	3% (2%)
Banks	3% (6%)	4% (9%)	5% (14%)	11% (2%)	1% (0%)
Insurance comp. and pension funds	8% (25%)	4% (7%)	10% (8%)	4% (-)	10% (49%)
Investment funds and other fin. intermediaries	21% (8%)	12% (9%)	8% (2%)	4% (-)	24% (9%)
Foreign	38% (14%)	42% (17%)	28% (17%)	12% (6%)	48% (12%)
	100%	100%	100%	100%	100%

Note: * Including unquoted shares and other equity.
Source: Observatoire De L'Epargne Européenne and Insead OEE Data Services, *Who Owns the European Economy? Evolution of the Ownership of EU-Listed Companies Between 1970 and 2012*, 85–90.

sition of a controlling voting block, while others prefer liquid stakes. French families, Italian foundations (which often have families as beneficial parties) and the Italian government belong to the former class. German and Italian non-financial companies acting as shareholders also prefer to hold de facto controlling voting blocks. Investment funds never hold controlling voting blocks. This does not come as a surprise as European Undertakings for Collective Investment in Transferable Securities (UCITS) are not allowed to acquire 'any shares carrying voting rights which would enable [them] to exercise significant influence over the management of an issuing body'.[14] Over the years the shareholder base has become more international in all countries.

The acquisition strategy of the different types of shareholders resulted in different ownership patterns in these countries, as can be seen in Table 4.1. The most significant investment policy developments can be found in the shareholder classes of insurance companies and pension funds, investment funds and overseas shareholders. First, UK insurance companies and pension funds, which controlled over half of the shares of UK companies in 1990,

[14] Art. 56, para 1 of Directive 2009/65/EC of the European Parliament and of the Council of 13 July 2009 on the coordination of laws, regulations and administrative provisions relating to undertakings for collective investment in transferable securities (UCITS) [2009] OJ L302/32.

diversified to other assets and as a class only controlled 10 per cent of all UK listed shares by 2012. Due to a significantly different social security system, the importance of this type of shareholder has always been modest in many continental European countries, such as France, Italy and Germany. The role of investment funds and other financial intermediaries is soaring. In the UK this class of shareholders accounts for almost one-quarter of all shares, while it has quadrupled in Germany. Although the trend is similar in all countries, the absolute importance of this class of investors is still different. Finally, the investment community is now a worldwide community. With the exception of the Italian market,[15] foreign investors have become the most important investor class for stock exchange listed companies in many European companies, holding as much as almost half of the shares of UK companies.

B. Shareholder Engagement

1. Participation in the general meeting of shareholders

The differences in and the development of the ownership structures raises the question of how they affect the engagement of the shareholders vis-à-vis their investees, especially as the Shareholder Rights Directive introduced specific rules addressing the relationship between some types of investors and their investees.[16]

It is difficult to measure the engagement of shareholders directly. The most typical engagement technique is a meeting with the (major) shareholders (outside the shareholders' meeting) but data of this kind of engagement is not readily available. However, there are a number of indirect techniques that provide a reliable insight into how shareholders engage with companies. First, the attendance at meetings signals the willingness of shareholders to vote, second, (larger) shareholders have the right to add a shareholder proposal to the agenda items of the meeting; and third, shareholders have the right to interrogate the board of directors. I have collected data in relation to all three engagement means, which can be found in Tables 4.2 and 4.4 and Figure 4.2.

Table 4.2 shows the development of the participation of shareholders in general meetings of index listed companies in nine European countries between 2007 and 2017. These numbers include all voting mechanisms, such as attending in person, voting by mail, proxy voting or any other instrument. Until 2010 companies experienced a low willingness of shareholders to be actively involved in Belgium, the Netherlands and Switzerland where fewer than half of shareholders voted. In Italy, Germany and the UK over 60 per cent

[15] The numbers for Italy include non-listed companies, which could negatively affect the total percentage of foreign investments.

[16] Shareholder Rights Directive, Art. 3g.

Table 4.2 *Average AGM attendance rates of companies of the national major index (2008–2017) (per cent)*

	Belgium	Denmark	France	Germany	Italy	Netherlands	Spain	Switzerland	UK
2008	45.4		58.9	60.0	61.2	47.5	71.7	48.3	61.8
2009	48.6		63.7	57.7	59.6	47.9	72.6	51.0	64.5
2010	46.6	36.2	61.5	56.1	58.8	48.9	69.1	53.1	67.2
2011	46.9		64.7	56.5		58.1	72.2	55.4	69.0
2012	53.5	41.9	65.4	53.7	64.6	63.7	68.3	57.6	70.9
2013	57.0	43.6	65.7	49.9	65.2	62.7	66.2	60.5	71.0
2014	59.4	54.1	64.5	55.1	66.6	68.4	67.6	58.0	70.3
2015	62.7	61.5	65.3	54.9	65.1	70.4	67.8	64.2	71.8
2016	59.2	63.4	65.8	59.9	66.6	70.5	68.2	63.0	72.9
2017	65.7	61.7	65.4	60.0	66.5	72.1	71.7	66.7	73.4

Sources: Georgeson, *Georgeson's 2017 Proxy Season Rev.*, 2017; Georgeson, *Georgeson's 2016 Proxy Season Rev.*, 2016; *Georgeson, Georgeson's 2014 Proxy Season Rev.*, 2014; Belgium: own research; the Netherlands 2007–09: Eumedion, Evaluatie AVA-seizoen 2010; Italy, Denmark and Switzerland 2008–10: ISS, *Voting Results Report Europe 2010.*

of shareholders voted. By 2017 the average level of voter turnout passed 60 per cent in all the countries and in the Netherlands, Spain and the UK even 70 per cent. These average voter turnouts hide three significant differences in (the modes of) attendance. First, there is a significant spread between companies. In many countries companies can be found with attendance rates lower than 20 or even 10 per cent.[17] Second, the participation rates of small shareholders owning less than 5 per cent of the shares differ. According to a study by Lafarre – similar to the development of overall attendance levels – small shareholder attendance increases over time but in Belgium and Austria it only reached 30 per cent in 2013, up from 10 per cent in Belgium and 28 per cent in Austria in 2010, and approaching 65 per cent in the UK.[18] Third, the means of participation shifted from attendance in person to voting by mail.[19] It raises the question whether 'attending the meeting by mail' is sufficient for being considered as an 'engaged' shareholder.

[17] See for a number of examples ISS, *Voting Results Report 2011 Europe*, 6.

[18] Anne Lafarre, *Theory and Practice of Shareholder Behavior* (Emerald 2017) 105.

[19] At Atos voting by mail represented 70 per cent of the voter turnout in 2012. By 2016 this voting mechanism represented over 95 per cent of all votes. See Christoph Van der Elst and Anne Lafarre, 'Blockchain and the Annual General Meeting' (2017) 14(4) Eur. Comp. L. 171.

These attendance levels do not provide information on the participation readiness of the different types of shareholders. American research shows that retail investors only vote 30 per cent of their shares while over 90 per cent of the institutional investors' shares are voted.[20] I am unaware of European data of voting readiness of different classes of shareholders. However an analysis of more than 400,000 retail investors of a German blue-chip company shows that those 'with better resources, i.e., particularly well-educated or rather sophisticated and more experienced retail investors, are more likely to use their corporate voting right.'[21] Further, institutional investors make predominantly use of electronic voting and sending the votes by mail and seldom physically attend the meeting.[22]

In many civil law countries the general meeting of shareholders can only validly take decisions if a sufficient number of shareholders attend the meeting. This is the case in Belgium, France, Spain and Italy (Table 4.3). In the latter three countries, every ordinary general meeting must be attended by shareholders holding 20 to 50 per cent of the shares, whereas in all these countries 25 per cent to 50 per cent of the shares must be (re)present(ed) for extraordinary meetings (EGMs). When this threshold is not passed, the company must re-call the meeting. Consequently, only (vainly) attending shareholders and the company suffer from the absenteeism of the other shareholders.

In particular, companies with a widely dispersed ownership structure are the 'victims' of this mandatory requirement in these countries. Nyrstar, a leading Belgian zinc and lead smelting company, organized between December 2015 and May 2017 no fewer than nine EGMs. With attendance rates varying between 2.4 per cent and 37 per cent, each EGM had to be called a second time because the quorum was not reached at the first EGM. Finally, at the EGM of May 2017 the agenda items were unanimous approved by all attending shareholders representing only 2.4 per cent of all shares.

Often, companies can limit the discomfort for the engaged shareholders by announcing shortly before the meeting that due to the low enrolment of shareholders the general meeting of shareholders will be adjourned.

---

[20] Broadridge & PriceWaterhouseCoopers, *Proxy Season Rev.* 2 (Sept. 2017), https://www.broadridge.com/_assets/pdf/broadridge-2017- proxy-season-review.pdf (last accessed 15 January 2018).

[21] André Schmidt, 'Determinants of Corporate Voting – Evidence from a Large Survey of German Retail Investors' (2017) 18 Schmalenbach Bus. Rev. 1, 71–103.

[22] Association française de la gestion financière, *Exercice des droits de vote par les sociétés de gestion en 2012* (March 2013 Service Economie Recherche), 8.

Table 4.3 Quorum requirements for general meetings of shareholders

General meeting		Belgium	France	Italy	Spain
Ordinary (AGM)	Quorum	No	20% voting shares first call	50% share capital first call	Voting shares representing 25% subscribed capital first call
Extraordinary (EGM)	Quorum	50% share capital first call	25% share capital first call; 20% second call	50% share capital first call; 1/3 second call; 1/5 later calls	Voting shares representing 50% subscribed capital first call, 25% second call
Special	Quorum		33.1% voting shares envisaged capital first call; 20% second call		
Law		Art. 558 CC	Art. L. 225-98, 225-96 and 225-99 CC	Arts 2368–2369 CC	Arts 193–194 LSC

Source: Author's own research of Companies Acts in Belgium, France, Italy and Spain.

2. Shareholder proposals

Shareholders have the right to add proposals to the agenda of the meeting. According to the Shareholder Rights Directive, Member States must provide (large) shareholders the right 'to put items on the agenda of the general meeting, provided that each such item is accompanied by a justification or a draft resolution to be adopted in the general meeting' and the right 'to table draft resolutions for items included or to be included on the agenda of a general meeting'.[23] Member States can require shareholders to 'hold a minimum stake in the company, such minimum stake shall not exceed 5 per cent of the share capital'.[24] Table 4.4 provides an overview of the number of tabled shareholder proposals in nine European countries. In some countries, like Belgium and the

[23] Art. 6, para 1 of Directive 2007/36/EC of the European Parliament and of the Council of 11 July 2007 on the exercise of certain rights of shareholders in listed companies [2007] OJ L184/17 (Shareholder Rights Directive).

[24] Shareholder Rights Directive, Art. 6, para 2.

Table 4.4 *Number of shareholder proposals*

	2006	2007	2008	2009	2010	2011	2012	2013	2014	2015	2016	2017
Belgium				5		2	1	11	3	2	1	
Denmark			3	4	43	13	8	18	71	16	24	59
France			11	8	15	6	27	16	11	39	24	18
Germany	1	38	26	9	17	4	18	43	18	21	28	32
Italy			1	2	2	11	128	149	116	183	206	126
Netherlands		5			3	1	2	1	3	2		1
Spain							17	10	6	15	23	2
Switzerland	3		1	1		30	7	27	15	20	18	15
UK	12	5	7	2	13	13	20	81	22	24	20	15

Sources: 2006–09: Luc Renneboog and Peter Szilagyi, 'Shareholder Engagement at European General Meetings' in Massimo Belcredi and Guido Ferrarini (eds), *Boards and Shareholders in European Listed Companies* (Cambridge University Press 2013) 315–64; 2010–17: data from ProxyInvest (collected 5 January 2018).

Netherlands, shareholders make seldom use of their right to put items on the agenda. In other countries, like Italy, it is common practice that shareholders make use of general meetings to voice their concerns via shareholder proposals. However, the Italian case is rather specific. Minority shareholders have a right to have a minority nominee elected in the general meeting of shareholders. It resulted in the practice of presenting slates ahead of the general meeting.[25] More than 56 per cent of all the Italian shareholder proposals relate to the approval of the (re)election of a director. A further 13 per cent of the proposals are the approval of the (re)election of a member of the internal boards of auditors (collegio sindacale). In all other countries shareholders make thrifty use of this shareholder right. Overall the number of proposals has been higher since the turn of the decade but this could be due to the different database that was used. Moreover, since 2010 the number of proposals has fluctuated in most countries but no trends can be distinguished.

3. Shareholder questions

Finally, shareholders have the right to ask questions during the general meeting of shareholders. The European Shareholder Rights Directive explicitly provides this right: 'Every shareholder shall have the right to ask questions

---

[25] For an empirical analysis of the use of this system of slate voting see Massimo Belcredi, Stefano Bozzi and Carmine Di Noia, 'Board elections and shareholder activism: The Italian experiment', in Massimo Belcredi and Guido Ferrarini (eds), *Boards and Shareholders in European Listed Companies* (Cambridge University Press 2013) 365–422.

related to items on the agenda of the general meeting.'[26] The company must provide an answer and only exceptionally can refuse not to:

> the right to ask questions and the obligation to answer are subject to the measures which Member States may take, or allow companies to take, to ensure the identification of shareholders, the good order of general meetings and their preparation and the protection of confidentiality and business interests of companies.[27]

Making use of the question right shows another (part of the) engagement of the shareholder.

In the Netherlands, many Dutch companies provide the minutes of the general meetings of shareholders *in extenso*, including the questions raised. This provides insights into the different shareholder types that raise questions and how often the shareholders make use of this right. In a recent study, Anne Lafarre and I study the questions raised in the AEX and AMX companies.[28] At every meeting an average of 39 questions were raised (Figure 4.2). The average is influenced by 1 per cent of the general meetings of only three companies during which over 100 questions were raised, with an absolute maximum of 192 questions. The median number of questions is 36.

An overwhelming majority of all questions are raised by individual shareholders and small shareholders' associations, and more particularly the Dutch Vereniging voor Effecten Bezitters (VEB), which has more than 40,000 members,[29] and the Association of Investors for Sustainable Development (VBDO).[30] Every year the individual shareholders and their representative organizations ask between 80 to 90 per cent of this average of 39 questions. Of this 80 to 90 per cent, the representatives of the shareholders' associations raise the highest number of questions.

All other types of shareholders, predominantly the institutional investors, raise less than 20 per cent of the questions. In absolute numbers the institutional investors account for close to 5 questions at every general meeting, with one outlier of 52 questions at the meeting of Ahold in 2008. The average number of questions of other shareholders, such as non-financial companies, the government, labour unions and foreign shareholders, varies between 1 and 2.5 questions per meeting per year.

---

[26] Shareholder Rights Directive, Art. 9, para 1.

[27] Shareholder Rights Directive, Art. 9, para 2.

[28] Anne Lafarre and Christoph Van der Elst, 'Corporate Sustainability and Shareholder Activism in the Netherlands', Working Paper 2018, 23.

[29] For more information see https://www.veb.net (last accessed 15 January 2018).

[30] For more information see https://www.vbdo.nl (last accessed 15 January 2018).

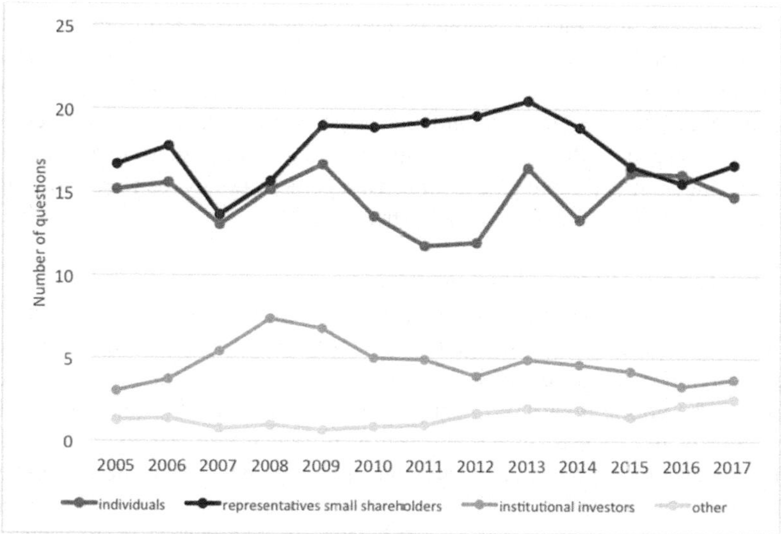

Source: Anne Lafarre and Christoph Van der Elst, *Corporate Sustainability and Shareholder Activism in the Netherlands* (14 May 2018) European Corporate Governance Institute (ECGI) – Law Working Paper No. 396/2018. Available at SSRN: https://ssrn.com/abstract=3156614.

Figure 4.2 Average number of questions different shareholder types raise at AGMs of AEX and AMX companies

The number of questions that the different classes of shareholder types raise is relatively stable over time. Individual shareholders are more active in asking questions in some years than in others and this compensates for the different number of questions of shareholders' associations. Overall both groups raise together every year between 27 and 35 questions.

Institutional investors showed an increased interest in questioning the board during the financial crisis. Afterwards this type of investor limited its number to 3 to 5 questions. The number of questions of all other kinds of investors is much lower and only recently exceeded an average of 2 questions per year per company.

These numbers do not correlate with the ownership structure of Dutch companies. Over 70 per cent of the shares of AEX companies belong to foreign shareholders, many of them being foreign institutional investors.[31] The remainder is divided between Dutch institutional investors (12 per cent),

---

[31] Aegon, an AEX company, estimates that around 78 per cent of all the shares belong to institutional investors, https://www.aegon.com/investors/shareholders/major-shareholders/ (last accessed 3 November 2018).

Dutch non-financial companies (10 per cent) and families and individuals (6 per cent).[32] Consequently, it can be concluded that a small minority of all shareholders, individuals and their representatives raise a very large proportion of the questions, while other types of shareholders make hardly any use of this shareholder engagement technique. In particular, this raises the question of how dialogue with investee companies that institutional investors and asset managers must make part of their engagement policy, as required in the Shareholder Rights Directive, will be structured.[33]

4. Intermediate conclusion

From the evidence presented above it can be concluded that more shareholders are willing to participate in the general meeting of shareholders than a decade ago. Companies in most countries experience an increase in their voter turnout. However the voting means of different classes seem to differ. An overwhelming majority of the investors make use of an electronic voting facility, not being present or represented during the meeting, which questions whether engagement is limited to voting and whether other means of shareholder engagement are used. At the meeting only individuals and their representatives raise many questions. Some shareholders make use of shareholder proposals although the use of this instrument is very limited for agenda items other than the election of Italian board members.

Institutions seem to employ low-cost means of voting and it appears that they consider the annual gathering of the board and the shareholders in the AGM not to be a suitable means for shareholder engagement other than for presenting the results of their electronic votes. Depending on the nature of the shareholder and the size of its voting block, these investors seem to prefer, if any, private negotiations, testimonials from the CEO, the chairman or other top executives, public letter-writing or lawsuits.[34] As the Shareholder Rights Directive requires that institutional investors and asset managers develop an engagement policy, these investors will have to show which engagement mechanisms are being used and how they are used. I discuss and assess this novel requirement next.

---

32 These numbers are taken from Eumedion, *Evaluatie AVA-seizoen 2010*, 16.

33 See Section III.B.

34 For an overview of the use of these techniques, see Skadden and Activist Insight, *Activist Investing in Europe – A Special Report* (September 2016); Eddy Wymeersch, 'Shareholders in Action' (2017) 4 Eur. Comp. Law 50–57.

III. SHAREHOLDER ENGAGEMENT DUTIES

Above it was shown that ownership structures still differ significantly from country to country, and even within countries, between different companies. Further, many shareholders are aware of their role in the company and actively engage with the company through participating in the general meeting of shareholders, sometimes putting items on the agenda of the meeting and regularly asking questions in these meetings. However, regulators and more recently legislators, were of the opinion that this relationship between the (institutional) investors and their investees should be further developed. In particular, the European Commission considered that the shareholder engagement of institutional investors and asset managers was inadequate: 'there is clear evidence that the current level of "monitoring" of investee companies and engagement by institutional investors and asset managers is often inadequate and focuses too much on short-term returns, which may lead to suboptimal corporate governance and performance' [35] Therefore, regulators and legislators took action and introduced more stringent engagement requirements.

A. Engagement Policy and Reporting in Some European Member States

The boards of directors of UK companies must address a significant proportion of no-votes in the directors' remuneration report[36] and, more generally, explain what actions they intend to take when a significant proportion of votes have been cast against a resolution.[37] Further, the UK Stewardship Code[38] directly requires that firms authorized to manage funds, other than private capital funds, explain their commitment vis-à-vis the investees. These firms must disclose an engagement policy, monitor and explain when they will actively intervene in investee companies, and have a policy on voting and the disclosure of this activity.[39]

The 2016 edition of the Dutch Corporate Governance Code requires that institutional investors post annually 'their policy on the exercise of the voting

---

[35] Shareholder Rights Directive, Recital 2.

[36] Large and Medium-sized Companies and Groups (Accounts and Reports) (Amendment) Regulations 2013, reg. 23(c).

[37] UK Corporate Governance Code, September 2014, provision E.2.2, currently under revision (Financial Reporting Council, *Proposed Revisions to the UK Corporate Governance Code* (December 2017), Provision 5, 4).

[38] Financial Reporting Council, *The UK Stewardship Code* (September 2012).

[39] The Code contains six principles in total.

rights for shares they hold in listed companies'[40] and report annually 'on how they implemented their policy on the exercise of the voting rights in the relevant financial year'. However, reporting on the compliance of this best practice remains the company's responsibility.

In December 2017 the Belgian Corporate Governance Committee launched a consultation to amend the Belgian Corporate Governance Code.[41] The proposed changes to the Code contain a request for institutional investors and voting agencies to explain their voting behaviour. Similar to the Dutch Code, the Belgian Code requires investees to comply but provides no guidance as to what should be done in the event that the shareholders do not communicate with the company or institutional investors and voting agencies do not explain their voting behaviour.

B. Engagement Policy and Reporting in the Shareholder Rights Directive

In the Shareholder Rights Directive, the European Commission has taken this shareholder involvement approach one step further and turned shareholder engagement into a legislative requirement for institutional investors and asset managers. Only institutional investors and asset managers are subjected to this engagement requirement of having and disclosing an engagement policy and disclosing how the policy is implemented.[42]

It might be expected that this requirement flowed from the legislative objective to align the interests of the management bodies of the institutional investors with the beneficiaries of these investors. However, according to Recital 15 of the Shareholder Rights Directive it is unlikely that this alignment was the European legislator's major concern. This recital simply starts from the premise that institutional investors and asset managers do not engage with companies and that there is undue influence from the 'capital markets' to perform in the short term. It is the belief of the European legislator that the requirement for establishing an engagement policy and reporting its implementation, with particular emphasis on the use of the voting rights, will overcome this problem. The interests of the beneficiaries of the institutional investors are referred to only indirectly.

---

40 Monitoring Commission, *The Dutch Corporate Governance Code* (The Hague, 8 December 2016) https://www.mccg.nl, Best Practice Provision 4.3.5.

41 See https://www.corporategovernancecommittee.be/en/about-2009-code/start-public-consultation.

42 For a detailed specification of the different institutional investors and asset managers see Shareholder Rights Directive, Art. 2(e) and (f).

I doubt that the development, disclosure and reporting on the implementation of an engagement policy of institutional investors and asset managers will reach the goal of less short-termism.

First, the position of these classes of shareholders is important but they are seldom the largest shareholder class in continental European companies. From Table 4.1 it follows that insurance companies, pension funds and investment firms and companies account for 29 per cent of total ownership of European companies, varying from 8 per cent in Italy, over 16 to 18 per cent in France and Germany, to 34 per cent in the UK, down from 58 per cent. There is a growing importance of investment firms and investment companies in all countries but due to the significant shift of investment by pension funds and insurance companies from listed shares to other assets the relative importance of these classes of investors decreased significantly in the UK.[43] The European Commission does not provide evidence that it is those investor classes that are causing the identified short-termism present in the capital market.

Second, the average voting block of these types of shareholders is of a non-controlling and mostly non-influential nature as Figure 4.1 illustrates, not the least because some of the institutional investors are forbidden to acquire voting blocks that could provide significant influence in the investee.[44] For many institutional investors diversification and index investing is their main strategy.

Third, many European listed companies have a controlling shareholder. Consequently, to the extent that it could be up to the shareholders to determine the investment strategy and take decisions that could jeopardize the long-term performance of the investee, institutional investors and asset managers can only signal their discontent with this strategy and the decisions taken but cannot have a decisive or final say. In fact, the most effective technique could be applying the 'Wall Street Rule' or voting with one's feet, which negatively affects the stock price and warns the board of dissatisfied shareholders.[45] Voting with one's feet is at odds with an 'engagement' policy.

Fourth, the division of powers between the board of directors and the general meeting of shareholders is of such a nature that (developing the) investment strategy and the decision-taking in the long-term interest of the

---

[43] I acknowledge that the total number of shares in the hands of these types of shareholders is higher as the investor class 'abroad' also comprises foreign institutional investors. However, information on the size of these relative holdings is not available.

[44] Art. 56, para 1 of Directive 2009/65/EC of the European Parliament and of the Council of 13 July 2009 on the coordination of laws, regulations and administrative provisions relating to undertakings for collective investment in transferable securities (UCITS) [2009] OJ L302/32.

[45] Anat Admati and Paul Pfleiderer, 'The "Wall Street Walk" and Shareholder Activism: Exit as a Form of Voice' (2009) 22 Rev. Fin. Stud. 2645–85.

company belongs to the board of directors and can only indirectly be influenced by the shareholders. Some of the most important tools that shareholders can use to challenge the strategy are to (a) vote for or against the (re)election of directors who (insufficiently) strive for the long-term interest of the company, (b) vote against the decision to issue new shares for investment purposes of the investee, or (c) vote for the (dis)approval of the remuneration package of the directors who should contribute to the long-term performance of the company.

Furthermore, institutional investors can have conflicting interests in this corporate decision-taking process. Goranova and Ryan illustrate this finding with the acquisition of Merrill Lynch by Bank of America:

> 471 institutional investors held shares in both firms, constituting 46.9 per cent of BofA's and 53.5 per cent of Merrill Lynch's outstanding equity (Thomson 13F). While many singular shareholders of BofA (those who did not hold stock in Merrill Lynch) saw the deal as a dilutive and wasteful acquisition of toxic assets and 'massive unknown risks' ..., those with interests on both sides were likely also concerned with the fate of Merrill Lynch and their impending terminal losses if the deal did not go through.[46]

Also, even for less disruptive decisions, shared views of all institutional investors, let alone all shareholders, are not to be expected.[47]

Finally, if the goal of the European legislator is the development of an engagement policy of shareholders serving the long-term interests of the investee, it is remarkable that only institutional investors and asset management have to develop an engagement policy. Holding companies and some other non-financial companies, the government and banks are also types of important shareholders that must act in the interest of their beneficiaries, but they are excluded from the Shareholder Rights Directive engagement policy requirements.[48] I agree that it is common practice of some of these investors to disclose their engagement with their investees.[49] However, not all shareholders of these

---

[46] Maria Goranova and Lori Verstegen Ryan, 'Shareholder Empowerment: An Introduction' in Maria Goranova and Lori Verstegen Ryan (eds), *Shareholder Empowerment* (Palgrave 2015) 15 (reference omitted).

[47] An assessment of the voting practices of 27 UK institutional investors shows that for eight significantly opposed voting items of six major UK companies, only one voting item was unanimously voted *against* by 24 investors (the other three investors did not participate) (ShareAction, *Asset Managers Voting Practices: in Whose Interests?* (London, May 2015) 13.

[48] The competence of the European legislator for issuing rules for these types of investors is outside the scope of this study.

[49] See, for good examples, the Belgian holding company engagement policy, Ackermans & van Haaren, http://en.avh2016.be/ackermans-van-haaren/missie-historiek.aspx (last accessed 15 January 2018) and the Swedish Wallenberg family, https://www

classes are so transparent. It is hard to see why different shareholder classes are treated differently with respect to their engagement duties vis-à-vis investees.

IV. MONITORING AND ENFORCING SHAREHOLDER ENGAGEMENT DUTIES

This new engagement requirement also raises questions related to the supervision of these duties as well as to the legal consequences when the institutional investors and asset managers fail to comply with the requirements. Corporate and capital markets law is familiar with two different methods of monitoring and addressing failures of compliance: private monitoring and enforcement varying from open letters over proxy contest and filing complaints, to suing the company and public enforcement, including public warnings over suspension of voting rights and sometimes even criminal sanctions.

The current existing private monitoring and enforcement systems[50] related to corporate governance can be summarized as follows.

First, it has already been shown that in those countries where companies depend upon the participation of sufficient shareholders for a valid general meeting of shareholders to take place, it is the responsibility of the company to adjourn the meeting and call a new meeting for which commonly lower quorum levels are applicable.

Second, it is the company that needs to report the non-compliance with the corporate governance code. For example, in the UK it is up to the company to provide an explanation for the significant number of no-votes it encountered for the remuneration items at the general meeting. In addition it needs to explain what actions it has taken to consult the shareholders. Whereas shareholders must show their engagement (in a comply-or-explain voting policy), they can remain passive and wait for the investee's actions to be contacted.

When companies fail to comply or explain the non-compliance with the best practice to have their shareholders respond to the request to provide reasons for voting against the agenda item, they can be held accountable in two different ways.

First, the capital market will respond and take appropriate action, which includes all activist steps available. 'The linchpin of the "comply or explain" mechanism is the expectation that investors will use the disclosures in relation to non-compliance to question whether instances of noncompliance are justified' but, as Ahern continues, 'the relative apathy of institutional investors is

---

.wallenberg.com/sites/default/files/files/pdf/wallenberg_onepager_fickformat_9juni_final.pdf (last accessed 1 March 2018).

[50] Konstantinos Sergakis addresses the public enforcement question in Chapter 7.

notorious'.[51] Obviously, it is even more unlikely that any 'market action' will take place when shareholders, including institutional investors, fail in their shareholder engagement to comply, resulting in the investee's incompliant behaviour. Passive shareholders do not respond to this failure, whereas active shareholders that point at the investee for failing to comply with the shareholder engagement duty incriminate themselves.

Second, the bodies responsible for national corporate governance codes (should) provide monitoring and enforcement. According to an EcoDa study, different monitoring systems co-exist in the European Union, and in many countries the bodies responsible for the development of the code also perform the monitoring.[52] In some countries like France and the Netherlands a separate body provides monitoring. However, in the majority of the cases these monitoring agencies are voluntary initiatives.[53] Even in those countries where the monitoring agencies are installed by law the role is commonly limited to establishing a report based upon the disclosed corporate governance information of the listed companies.[54] Some monitoring agencies address the companies when shortcomings are identified.[55]

The Shareholder Rights Directive introduced a *mandatory* comply-or-explain regime for developing and implementing an engagement policy but it is not accompanied by any kind of specific monitoring or enforcement mechanism. The Directive left it to the Member States to provide 'measures and penalties applicable to infringements of national provisions adopted pursuant to this Directive and ... [to] take all measures necessary to ensure that they are imple-

---

[51] Deirdre Ahern, *Replacing 'Comply or Explain' with Legally Binding Corporate Governance Codes: An Appropriate Regulatory Response?* (working paper, 17 June 2010), http://regulation.upf.edu/dublin-10-papers/5A3.pdf.

[52] EcoDa, *Corporate Governance Compliance and Monitoring Systems Across the EU* (Brussels 2015) 19–21.

[53] Ibid.

[54] See, e.g., for France Art. L121-18-3 of the Monetary and Financial Code, obliging the financial supervisor, AMF, to render every year a report based on the disclosed corporate governance statements and authorizing it to publish every recommendation it considers useful (see for these reports, http://www.amf-france.org/Publications/Rapports-etudes-et-analyses/Gouvernement-d-entreprise?, last accessed 8 February 2018). These recommendations aim to improve the disclosure practices of companies, such as the recommendation to improve the transparency of the information presented at general meetings and shareholder voting. The Portuguese supervisor also published compliance reports (see http://www.cmvm.pt/pt/EstatisticasEstudosEPublicacoes/Publicacoes/governosociedadescotadas/Pages/Relatorios_GovernoSociedades_Home.aspx?pg, last accessed 10 February 2018).

[55] According to its 2017 report the French Haut Comité de gouvernement d'entreprise has sent approximately 30 letters to the chairmen of listed companies pointing, inter alia, at major governance shortcomings (*Rapport* (Paris 2017) 11).

mented',[56] thus supporting a more formal, less flexible relationship. Those enforcement mechanisms must be effective, proportionate and dissuasive. In its 2014 Recommendation, the European Commission supports efficient monitoring 'to be carried out at national level, within the framework of the existing monitoring arrangements'[57] but the recommendation falls short in the measures to ensure the Directive's implementation.

The Directive's mandatory comply-or-explain regime fits the far-reaching 'disclosure' type of Leyens' typology of binding mechanisms.[58] According to this typology, the engagement policy disclosure should be considered as a binding 'form of revocable self-commitment. Revocation is possible in the future. As long as such a revocation is made properly, any binding effect that might have existed previously ceases to exist.' Institutional investors and asset managers can provide in a clear and reasoned explanation why they have chosen not to comply with the development and disclosure of an engagement policy and the disclosure of its implementation but they must be considered self-committed if a policy is disclosed and implemented. The Directive does not provide a term during which the engagement policy must remain unaltered in force. It follows from the Directive that these investors can change their policy at will but it needs to be properly disclosed and afterwards the investors are committed to the altered policy. Consequently, it can complicate the reporting in the year the policy has been changed.

This commitment to the *mandatory* comply-or-explain policy also raises the question whether the investees and the beneficiaries of institutional investors or asset management can act against the presumed breach of a shareholder engagement duty. More than likely, it will often be hard for both the beneficiaries and the investees to prove whether a breach took place or how the breach caused damage, but it is not impossible. A number of situations can be differentiated. First the institutional investor can be in breach for developing or disclosing the engagement policy and its implementation and not providing a reasonable explanation. While this breach can be proved relatively easily, the damage that can be caused to investees or beneficiaries is difficult to demonstrate. Hence, for these cases, it seems more logical that administrative agencies act against this breach, meanwhile considering the negative effects its sanctioning mechanism can have for the beneficiaries of the institutional

---

56 Shareholder Rights Directive, Art. 14b.

57 Art. 11 of the Commission Recommendation of 9 April 2014 on the quality of corporate governance reporting ('comply or explain') [2014] OJ L109/43.

58 Patrick Leyens, 'Self-commitments and the Binding Force of Self-regulation with Respect to Third Parties in Germany' in Harald Baum, Moritz Bälz and Marc Dernauer (eds), *Self-regulation in Private Law in Japan and Germany* (Carl Heymanns Verlag 2018), in press.

investor. Currently, in a number of Member States a supervisory agency monitors compliance with corporate governance codes. This monitoring can be broadened and include the (disclosure of) an engagement policy requirement of investors. A failure of this disclosure of the policy or of the explanation why this disclosure did not take place can be adequately sanctioned A sanctioning system can make the management body of the institutional investor and/or asset manager (personally) liable based on a breach in the disclosure requirements. Support for this approach can be found in Article L 233-7, VII of the French Commercial Code. When a shareholder of a French listed company passes the threshold of 10, 15, 20 and 25 per cent of the capital or the voting rights she must disclose the goals she intends to pursue for the six months to come, if she wants to take control over the company and intends to nominate one or more members of the (supervisory) board. If during this period of six months the intentions of the shareholders changes, a new disclosure must be made. According to Germain and Magnier a false statement could lead to civil responsibility of the board members.[59] A similar reasoning can be applied for the situations where the institutional investor's engagement policy is incomplete or only partially disclosed as well as situations where the policy has been changed but the disclosure is late.

The situation is more complex when the institutional investor does not comply with its engagement policy. Different situations can (co)exist: the investor does not vote its shares or does not monitor the investees, the investor deviates from its engagement policy or discloses incorrect information as to the implementation of its engagement policy, among others.[60] Obviously, in these situations it can occur that the investee or the beneficiary is caused harm. When the investee can assume that the institutional investors participate in general meetings, it can expect that the threshold for organizing the meeting will be reached. When those institutional investors decline to attend the meeting, the company can be forced to adjourn the meeting, incurring unex-

[59] Michel Germain and Véronique Magnier, *Les Sociétés Commerciales* (LGDJ, Lextenso 2014) 992–93.The law provides for the suspension of the voting rights as sanctioning mechanism (Art. L 233-14 Commercial Code). However the approach of Germain and Magnier can be more appropriate for sanctioning the shortcoming of institutional investors and asset managers in the disclosure of their engagement policy. In the Netherlands there is a specific procedure of the Enterprise Chamber to investigate the affairs of the company. The court can also take into account the conduct of the shareholders: Anne Lafarre, Britt Schippers, Steffie van den Bosch, Christoph Van der Elst, Ger van der Sangen, *Doelbereiking en effectiviteit van de wet aanpassing enquêterecht in de praktijk* (WODC-rapport 2791, Tilburg University, Departement of Business Law 2018) 235.

[60] Like the use of a proxy voting advisor when the policy requested the institutional investor to be actively and independently involved in voting.

pected additional costs. Further, if a beneficiary of an investment company selected this company for its specific engagement guidelines, such as negotiating and voting for the implementation of specific corporate social responsibility or other measures, the investment company's perceived shortcoming could result in claims for specific damages by beneficiaries and other parties based on an implementation of the policy that could be read adversely to the engagement policy. I illustrate this as follows. At BAE Systems, the board of directors proposed that the general meeting of 10 May 2017, like all general meetings since 2011, should provide it with the authority to incur political expenditure. The board motivated its request for authorization as follows:

> It remains the policy of the Company not to make political donations or incur political expenditure as those expressions are normally understood. However, the Directors consider that it is in the best interests of shareholders for the Company to participate in public debate and opinion-forming on matters which affect its business. To avoid inadvertent infringement of the Companies Act 2006, the Directors are seeking shareholders' authority for the Company and its subsidiaries to make political donations and to incur political expenditure during the period from the date of the Annual General Meeting to the conclusion of next year's Annual General Meeting or close of business on 30 June 2018, whichever is earlier, up to a maximum aggregate amount of £100.000.[61]

Whether this amount will be used and for what exact purposes is not precisely identified in the notice of the meeting documentation. The voting policy of Royal London Asset Management (RLAM) states that

> RLAM will normally vote against any authority that would allow directors to make donations to political parties. RLAM would choose to support such an authority only in exceptional circumstances where there was a pressing business case in favor of the authority and where the authority would not have an unduly negative impact upon the company's reputation.[62]

However RLAM has voted *for* this agenda item since 2011.[63] It could be that BAE Systems demonstrated to RLAM's satisfaction the existence of such exceptional circumstances in private discussions or debated this issue during

---

[61] BAE Systems, *Notice of Annual General Meeting 2017*, https://investors.baesystems.com/~/media/Files/B/Bae-Systems-Investor-Relations-V3/Annual%20Reports/notice-of-meeting-2017.pdf.

[62] Royal London Asset Management, *Voting Policy 2017*, https://www.rlam.co.uk/Documents-RLAM/Sustainable%20Investing/2017%20RLAM%20Voting%20Policy.pdf, 15.

[63] Royal London Asset Management, *Proxy Voting: Our Record*, http://www.rlam-voting.co.uk/voting/search.php?CoName=BAE+Systems+plc&_searchType=5.

the general meeting, but this information is not available.[64] A beneficiary of RLAM could consider this vote *for* to be in breach of RLAM's voting policy.

I have already mentioned that many institutional investors of Bank of America voted for the acquisition of Merrill Lynch, albeit it was dilutive and risky, because they also had an important voting block in the latter. This vote can be in conflict with the engagement policy but beneficial to the beneficiaries of the institutional investors and (some of the) investees.

These are just two examples whereby the *mandatory* comply-or-explain shareholder engagement duties can endanger the current flexible stewardship relationship between investors and investees. While in both situations there can be good (undisclosed) arguments for the ways the institutional investors and asset managers voted, beneficiaries and third parties could be triggered to act against any deviation of the (implemented) engagement policy, stiffening an open and cooperative engagement between these types of shareholders and companies. Therefore, and taking into account the goals that the engagement duty should achieve according to the Shareholder Rights Directive, the instrument of Article 3g of the Directive, I challenge the *mandatory* duty to establish an engagement policy and the disclosure of its implementation, at least to the extent it can complicate the relationship between beneficiary, investor and investee. I am of the opinion that a voluntary stewardship code is a more appropriate means to this end. It would allow use to be made, in a more flexible way, of the different engagement mechanisms such as private negotiations, testimonials from the CEO, the chairman or other top executives, and public letter-writing, all commonly used instruments.[65]

V. CONCLUSION

Recently, regulators, but also the European legislator, have introduced engagement duties for some classes of shareholders. In this chapter I study the development of shareholder ownership over time as well as different kinds of engagement activities. I found that the classes the European legislators are addressing are important but seldom the most important shareholder classes. Further, the instruments that different shareholders' classes use to engage with their investees are different too. Many shareholders vote, although, according to some studies, individual investors are less keen to make use of their voting rights, and differences between companies can be significant. Individual inves-

---

[64] The political donations agenda items were approved during all general meetings of BAE Systems with 95.7 per cent (2014) to 98.9 per cent (2016) of the votes. If RLAM had voted differently the approval of these agenda items would not have been endangered.

[65] Cf. n 34.

tors often use their question rights at general meetings, some investors make use of the agenda right, while institutional investors are keen to have private meetings with their investees' representatives. Therefore I question the mandatory duty for institutional investors and asset managers to make use of the instrument of the engagement policy and the disclosure of its implementation. It is far from proven that these legislative measures are suitable, reasonable and necessary to reach the goals of Recital 15 of the Shareholder Rights Directive,[66] in particular less short-termism in the capital market. Furthermore, it is unclear whether the duties can be appropriately monitored, taking into account the specific relationships between companies, (institutional) investors, asset management, beneficiaries and other corporate incumbents. The mandatory requirements can stiffen these relationships. I am of the opinion that these duties should be or have stayed embedded in a stewardship code.

---

[66] See, for a similar finding based on a different approach, European Company Law Experts, *Shareholder engagement and identification* (2015) https://ssrn.com/abstract=2568741.

PART II

The sources of enforcement

5. Contractual enforcement of shareholders' duties

Corrado Malberti

I. INTRODUCTION

To understand the scope and nature of the enforcement of shareholders' duties, it is necessary to compare this type of enforcement with that of contracts and agreements shareholders may have concluded with companies or third parties. In some cases, contractual arrangements may reinforce shareholders' duties by providing more effective remedies. In other circumstances, contracts may clarify what other shareholders or companies expect from a shareholder or introduce obligations in addition to those mandated by law. However, sometimes, contractual obligations may also conflict with shareholders' duties and jeopardize the performance of such duties.

After discussing the distinctive features of contractual and non-contractual enforcement, and the different types of enforcement mechanisms available in company law, I investigate the respective scopes of corporate and contractual arrangements. More precisely, I examine the possible effects of shareholders' agreements on companies and third parties, the legal principles applicable to their adoption and modification, the relationship between party autonomy and mandatory law, and the role of disclosure and confidentiality. Afterwards, I analyze the remedies available in cases of breaches of shareholders' duties. Then, I discuss the role of damages, injunctions, court orders, specific performance, and equivalent performance in the contractual enforcement of shareholders' duties. I conclude by examining some alternative enforcement mechanisms.

This chapter is organized as follows: Section II provides a general definition of contractual enforcement, explaining how it can be distinguished from non-contractual enforcement. In this section, I also discuss some enforcement mechanisms that are not necessarily contractual. Section III examines the various contractual enforcement mechanisms that are available in company law. Section IV discusses the nature of the enforcement mechanisms, based on whether they are included in shareholders' agreements or in bylaws. This section also presents some practical implications of this distinction and examines the available remedies in cases of a breach. Section V concludes the chapter.

II. DEFINING CONTRACTUAL ENFORCEMENT OF SHAREHOLDERS' DUTIES

A. Distinguishing Between Contractual and Non-Contractual Enforcement

To analyze the contractual enforcement of shareholders' duties, it is essential to define the nature of contractual enforcement in company law and to examine how that enforcement may become relevant when shareholders are in breach. To that purpose, it is important to distinguish between the enforcement mechanisms that have a contractual nature and those that do not.

Contractual shareholders' duties may originate from both shareholders' agreements and bylaws,[1] while other duties are imposed on shareholders directly by law.[2] In fact, the duties imposed by shareholders' agreements and bylaws are normally introduced with the consent of all shareholder, or at least of a majority of them and, generally, for their mutual interest.[3] Yet, shareholders' duties may also derive from other contractual sources, such as from default rules.[4] Normally, the contractual enforcement mechanisms provided by company law also reflect the mutual interest of the parties on whom they are imposed and who have agreed on their introduction.

Therefore, as a working definition, we can describe the contractual enforcement of shareholders' duties as those enforcement mechanisms based on contractual arrangements. This working definition gives emphasis to the shareholders' decision to subject themselves to some enforcement mechanisms, and, as explained in the following pages,[5] it also implies that these mechanisms are not necessarily laid out in bylaws or shareholders' agreements.

1. Shareholders' agreements

The contractual enforcement of shareholders' duties may rely on shareholders' agreements. In this case, such mechanisms are introduced following

---

1 For the purposes of this chapter, the word 'bylaws' refers to the instrument of incorporation or the statutes in the terms provided by Directive 2017/1132/EU.

2 Jennifer Payne, 'Contractual Aspects of Shareholders' Duties' in Hanne Søndergaard Birkmose (ed), *Shareholders' Duties* (Kluwer Law International 2017) 107, 128.

3 Ibid.

4 Cf. ibid 119ff.

5 See Section II.A.3–5.

a decision by the shareholders that have agreed to be parties to the agreement. Shareholders' agreements have some important features. First, these arrangements are normally binding only on the persons that concluded them and not necessarily on other present and future shareholders, nor on the company itself. Secondly, to take effect, shareholders' agreements usually require approval from all the parties involved, even though – after the agreement is established – the participants may also decide to take decisions by a majority vote. Thirdly, considering that these arrangements are essentially contracts, the freedom shareholders enjoy in concluding such agreements may be greater than that available in drafting bylaws.[6]

2. Bylaws

Shareholders may also decide to adopt mechanisms to support the enforcement of their duties in bylaws. In principle, the introduction of these arrangements does not require the unanimous consent of all shareholders since, normally, these decisions are taken by a majority vote. In addition, even though national company laws usually require that modifications to bylaws should be decided by a general meeting, it cannot be ruled out that certain legal systems would also allow the introduction of enforcement mechanisms in bylaws by means of a decision by a corporate body other than the general meeting.

Since bylaws modifications do not normally require unanimous consent, enforcement mechanisms may also be introduced to the detriment of minority shareholders. Clearly, in these cases, the most evident abuses will be addressed by the rules and principles existing in each jurisdiction to avoid the abuses of majority. Finally, it is also important to highlight that, when introduced in bylaws, the scope of these enforcement mechanisms is normally broader than that of ordinary contractual arrangements, since these clauses will also bind future shareholders.

3. Default rules

In addition to the enforcement mechanisms that are established entirely by party autonomy, other mechanisms provided by company law can also be contractual in nature. A first example is those enforcement mechanisms that, although provided by law, may still be opted out of. If default company law is deemed to reflect the hypothetical bargain between the parties, who remain free to opt out of legal rules by contract,[7] it follows that legal enforcement

---

[6] For a more detailed analysis of these problems, see Section IV.B.

[7] As explained in John Armour, Henry Hansmann, Reinier Kraakman and Mariana Pargendler, 'What Is Corporate Law' in Reinier Kraakman, John Armour, Paul Davies, Luca Enriques, Henry Hansmann, Gerard Hertig, Klaus Hopt, Hideki Kanda, Mariana Pargendler, Wolf-Georg Ringe and Edward Rock (eds), *The Anatomy of Corporate*

mechanisms frequently reflect no more than an implied contractual choice. This is not to say, however, that all enforcement mechanisms that may be opted out of also are necessarily contractual in nature. In fact, default company law may also serve functions that are different from that of reflecting the hypothetical bargain between the parties.[8]

4. Enabling rules

Closely related to the enforcement mechanisms that rely on default rules to mimic the hypothetical bargain are those legal provisions that enable shareholders to implement additional enforcement mechanisms by adopting predefined sets of rules. Since the enforcement mechanisms that rely on enabling company law are freely adopted by shareholders, they might appear similar to the clauses introduced in bylaws or in shareholders' agreements by virtue of party autonomy. However, these mechanisms also share traits in common with default rules since these enabling rules are outlined in company law provisions that may be 'opted in' by shareholders. Therefore, in this case, the autonomy granted to the parties is limited to the choice of whether or not to take advantage of predefined sets of rules.

5. Mandatory law

The enforcement of shareholders' duties may also be ensured by mandatory law. When an enforcement mechanism is based on mandatory law it is not contractual in nature since, in principle, it does not depend on a choice taken by shareholders or companies. It should also be highlighted that, frequently,

---

Law (3rd edn, Oxford University Press 2017) 1, 18: '[a] significant part of corporate law … consists of default provisions. To this extent, corporate law simply offers a standard form contract that the parties can adopt, at their option, in whole or in part. A familiar advantage of such a legally provided standard form is that it saves costs – specifically, it simplifies contracting among the parties involved by requiring that they specify only those elements of their relationship that deviate from the standard terms'; on this point, see also Payne (n 2) 119ff.

[8] E.g., that of a 'penalty default': see John Armour, Henry Hansmann and Reinier Kraakman, 'What Is Corporate Law' in Reinier Kraakman, John Armour, Paul Davies, Luca Enriques, Henry Hansmann, Gerard Hertig, Klaus Hopt, Hideki Kanda and Edward Rock (eds), *The Anatomy of Corporate Law* (2nd edn, Oxford University Press 2009) 1, 20f. In the end, the cost of contracting bylaws justifies the adoption of default rules that tend towards the hypothetical bargain between the parties. However, a legal system, for political purposes, may also decide to use default rules to promote solutions that would not reflect the hypothetical bargain, placing on the parties the cost of contracting them out.

enforcement mechanisms are based on procedural rules that, by their very nature, tend to be mandatory.[9]

Nevertheless, it should also be acknowledged that, in the end, the creation of a legal entity is an exercise of party autonomy. In this sense, it has been argued that the adoption of a company form governed by a set of mandatory provisions shares some traits in common with the adoption of an enabling set of rules.[10] This approach is correct, especially in those legal systems in which some sort of regulatory competition between company forms exists.[11] In this perspective, in the context of European company law, to the extent that competition among the Member States of the European Union exists, the enforcement mechanisms that are completely independent from the exercise of party autonomy are those mandated by the harmonized European company law. Obviously, this does not imply that the choice of a company law form in a given jurisdiction, from among the many forms available in the European Union, is always driven by the selection of a given set of enforcement mechanisms. Nor can that possibility be ruled out completely. In brief, in the presence of some sort of regulatory competition, the boundaries between mandatory and default law become less well defined.

Finally, it should also be admitted that national law can add another layer of complexity to this already intricate framework. In fact, national company laws may allow companies to adopt bylaws clauses on a 'contract procedure' or 'party rulemaking',[12] namely, those clauses that may have an influence on the way company law is enforced, for example, by selecting a specific forum or by altering the rules on the allocation of litigation fees.[13] These clauses may also provide for alternative dispute resolution methods.[14] All these clauses use contractual arrangements to modify the procedural enforcement mechanisms and may therefore fall into the definition of contractual enforcement, although in some cases – as in that of forum selection clauses – the only contractual element of the enforcement would be the simple selection among the non-contractual mechanisms provided by the jurisdictions that may adjudicate a case.[15]

---

[9] Cf. e.g., Jeffrey Neil Gordon, 'The Mandatory Structure of Corporate Law' (1989) 89 Colum. L. Rev. 1549, 1591.

[10] Armour et al. (n 8) 19.

[11] Ibid 19, 21f.

[12] Verity Winship, 'Shareholder Litigation by Contract' (2016) 96 B.U. L. Rev. 485, 486ff.

[13] Ibid, in particular 507ff.

[14] Ibid, in particular 500ff.

[15] On international company litigation and arbitration, see Marco Ventoruzzo, Pierre-Henri Conac, Gen Goto, Sebastian Mock, Mario Notari and Arad Reisberg, *Comparative Corporate Law* (West Academic 2015) 625ff.

B. Enforcement Mechanisms that are Not Necessarily Contractual

Apart from the cases in which enforcement mechanisms are essentially contractual in nature, and those in which, when some conditions are satisfied, this nature may be recognized, it is also important to clarify that contractual enforcement should be distinguished from other forms of enforcement that are not necessarily contractual. Two kinds of enforcement mechanisms that should not be confused with contractual enforcement are: the enforcement of contractual shareholders' duties, and the private enforcement of shareholders' duties.

Starting with the enforcement of contractual duties, it should be noted that the fact that a shareholder's duty is contractual in nature does not necessarily imply that it should also be enforced by means of contractual mechanisms. In this sense, the introduction of contractual duties in bylaws and shareholders' agreements is something different from the introduction of contractual enforcement mechanisms. In truth, contractual duties may certainly be enforced by means of non-contractual enforcement mechanisms,[16] and contractual enforcement mechanisms may be devised to ensure the performance of duties that are not contractual in nature.[17]

With regard to private enforcement, the fact that the law grants the initiative of the enforcement to private persons plays little or no role in determining the contractual or non-contractual nature of an enforcement mechanism. Therefore, given that contractual enforcement is based on contractual arrangements, the simple fact that an enforcement mechanism is activated by a private person does not mean that this type of enforcement is contractual. Furthermore, private enforcement mechanisms are frequently provided for and governed by mandatory law.

III. TYPES OF ENFORCEMENT MECHANISMS

A. Pecuniary Sanctions and Damages

The sanctions for a violation of shareholders' duties may take different forms. Certainly, shareholders' agreements and bylaws may provide for pecuniary sanctions. With regard to these sanctions two issues deserve attention: (a) the amount of the penalty or damages that may be awarded for the breach of the duty, and (b) the interplay between pecuniary sanctions and other enforcement mechanisms.

---

[16] For example, a violation of contractual duties provided in the bylaws may trigger an action for damages or for the invalidation of companies' actions or decisions, as would a violation of the duties provided by law.

[17] This could happen, for example, when a specific penalty or other sanctions, such as exclusion from the company, are provided by the bylaws in case of non-compliance with a duty imposed by law.

Starting with the first issue, penalties and damages for a violation of a duty may be determined in different ways. For example, they may just cover the compensation of the loss caused by the breach, possibly including the expected gains that would have derived from the performance of the duty. Alternatively, the law may impose the restitution or disgorgement of the profits earned by the shareholder in default, or even impose an award of punitive damages.

In addition, it is also possible that the parties determine – especially in shareholders' agreements – such damages by providing clauses on liquidated damages or on termination fees. Moreover, legal systems may also allow the introduction of so-called private penalties in shareholders' agreements and bylaws.[18]

Importantly, not all jurisdictions are equally inclined to award each of these pecuniary sanctions; this is particularly true for punitive damages. In general, the different approaches to this issue reflect the different function damages play in a given legal system. For example, in some jurisdictions emphasis is given to the compensation of the loss suffered, while in other legal systems, attention is also given to the deterrent effect of these sanctions.[19]

With regard to the second issue, it is important to stress that, while in some countries damages are the primary relief, other jurisdictions prefer to first resort to remedies that ensure the performance of obligations.[20] Certainly, also in the latter jurisdictions, damages and penalties may play a role, but in these legal systems shareholders retain the possibility of obtaining the very performance of the duties undertaken by the shareholder in default.

B. Invalidity of Company's Decisions

Violations of shareholders' duties may also result in the invalidation of decisions taken within the company. In fact, bylaws – and in some cases even the law[21] – may impose on shareholders the duty to disclose some information, for

---

[18] Private penalties are punitive sanctions (e.g. a fine), provided, for example, in contractual arrangements that are not meant to compensate for the loss suffered by the innocent party. For instance, depending on the jurisdiction examined, penalty and liquidated damages clauses may have a punitive nature, a compensatory nature or a mixed nature (see Bénédicte Fauvarque-Cosson and Denis Mazeaud (eds), *European Contract Law* (Sellier 2008) 313, describing the different nuances between liquidated damages in English and American law, the *Vertragsstrafe* in German law, the *clausola penale* in Italian law, and the approaches to these penalties in Belgian and French law).

[19] Ibid.

[20] See Section IV.C.

[21] In European law, see, e.g., Directive 2004/109/EC, which, in art. 9, imposes the notification of the acquisition or disposal of major holdings, and which, in art. 10, in imposing the notification of the acquisition or disposal of major proportions of voting rights, also refers to some agreements concerning the exercise of voting rights. With

example, participation in shareholders' agreements or purchase of shareholdings. In the absence of this disclosure, the voting rights of the shareholder in breach may be suspended, and decisions approved with the decisive vote of that shareholder may be declared invalid.[22]

More generally, the voting rights of shareholders and, therefore, also the validity of the resolutions of the general meeting, may be subject to the performance of shareholders' duties. This enforcement mechanism is different from the award of damages or penalties, and it normally ensures a better protection of performance.

In any case, even the contractual enforcement mechanisms based on the suspension of voting rights and the invalidation of a company's decisions do not always ensure the performance of shareholders' duties. In fact, the enforcement of these duties will need to rely on the rules and procedures that govern the corporate bodies and challenges to the validity of a company's decisions. These rules may provide for short delays for filing the action or they may limit the grounds on which resolutions can be challenged, or even entirely exclude the possibility of an action. In addition, even in the event of a successful challenge to the validity of a company's decision, it is possible that the law provides for some protection for the innocent third parties that relied on the resolutions taken in violation of the bylaws. Furthermore, if these enforcement mechanisms are not provided in bylaws, but in shareholders' agreements, depending on the relevant jurisdiction, their effects may be even more limited.[23]

C. Invalidation of a Company's Actions

In addition to invalidating companies' decisions, the violation of shareholders' duties may also result in the invalidation of companies' actions. Examining

---

regard to shareholders' agreements, several jurisdictions impose such disclosure: see Marie-Agnes Arlt, 'Austria' in Sebastian Mock, Kristian Csach and Bohumil Havel (eds), *International Handbook on Shareholders' Agreements* (Walter de Gruyter GmbH 2018) 141, 148f, with reference to the shareholders' agreements concerning the shares of listed companies; Corrado Malberti, 'Italy' in Mock, Csach and Havel (eds) 413, 424f and 428f, with reference to the shareholders' agreements concerning the shares of both listed companies and companies that resort to capital markets; David Pérez Millán, 'Spain' in Mock, Csach and Havel (eds) 567, 585f, with reference to shareholders' agreements concerning the shares of listed companies; Rafal Zakrzewski, 'England and Wales' in Mock, Csach and Havel (eds) 247, 255f and 259f, with reference to agreements concerning the shares of publicly traded companies and to some other peculiar situations.

22 For further details on the suspension of voting rights, see Chapter 8.

23 As will be explained in the following pages, many jurisdictions exclude the possibility for shareholders' agreements to bind the companies whose shares are concerned with those agreements (see Section IV.A).

in particular the rules governing limited liability companies in the European Union, this conclusion derives from art. 9 of Directive 2017/1132/EU of 14 June 2017 relating to certain aspects of company law.

According to the first sentence of the first paragraph of that provision, the '[a]cts done by the organs of the company shall be binding upon it … unless such acts exceed the powers that the law confers or allows to be conferred on those organs'. Therefore, from that provision, it follows that if the national law gives the shareholders the power to take certain decisions, a violation of this competence may result in the invalidation of the company's actions. However, unless contractual enforcement is understood in a broad sense, so as to consider even the choice of a jurisdiction for the incorporation of a legal entity a contractual one, this enforcement mechanism displays few contractual characteristics.

Nevertheless, at least to some extent, contractual mechanisms that rely on limits on powers to represent the company may also be designed to ensure the performance of shareholders' duties. Apparently, there is little room to use art. 9 of Directive 2017/1132/EU as a tool to ensure contractual enforcement, since the second paragraph of that article provides that '[t]he limits on the powers of the organs of the company, arising under the statutes or from a decision of the competent organs, may not be relied on as against third parties, even if they have been disclosed'. Therefore, the limits on the powers of directors provided in bylaws are without effects vis-à-vis third parties. Similarly, art. 9(1) of Directive 2017/1132/EU states that the '[a]cts done by the organs of the company shall be binding upon it even if those acts are not within the objects of the company', arguably excluding the possibility of the object clause being used, with effects on third parties, to limit the powers of companies' legal representatives.

In reality, art. 9(2) of Directive 2017/1132/EU is interpreted to allow Member States to make the limits on the powers of legal representatives provided in bylaws applicable vis-à-vis third parties, at least in cases of collusion or abuse of power of the directors, or when the third party acted intentionally to the detriment of the company.[24] Furthermore, with regard to the object clause, after stating that the object is irrelevant for third parties, art. 9(1) of Directive 2017/1132/EU also states:

> However, Member States may provide that the company shall not be bound where such acts are outside the objects of the company, if it proves that the third party

---

[24] As Eric Stein, *Harmonization of European Company Laws* (The Bobbs-Merrill Company Inc. 1971) 294, correctly points out: '[i]n a declaration, adopted by the Council of Ministers, it was made clear that the provision in the directive will be interpreted … so as to exclude fraud'.

> knew that the act was outside those objects or could not in view of the circumstances have been unaware of it.

Therefore, in the jurisdictions that take advantage of that possibility, object clauses may be drafted with the aim of limiting the scope of the activities performed by the company, arguably, also in the interest of some shareholders, so as to ensure that a company is not allowed to carry out transactions without following the procedure required to modify the object clause.[25]

D. Exit and Exclusion

The enforcement of shareholders' duties may also be ensured by providing an exit right to the innocent shareholders that have been harmed by a breach. Alternatively, it is also possible to devise contractual mechanisms to exclude the shareholder in breach. In some cases, these mechanisms are provided by law, but it is also possible to draft bylaws and shareholders' agreements to achieve the same results.[26]

Depending on the national company law, when included in bylaws, exit rights may take different forms, such as a right of withdrawal, an appraisal right or, more simply, a sell-out right that may be activated upon occurrence of specific events. The most relevant issues raised by these clauses concern the calculation of the value of the shares for which the exit right is granted and the identification of the persons who will have to pay for these shares. This obligation, for example, may be imposed on the shareholder in breach, on all the other shareholders, or on the company itself.

These same problems are also delicate when the exit right is laid out in shareholders' agreements. Obviously, in these cases, given that in many jurisdictions shareholders' agreements and bylaws have different effects, it may be difficult to qualify that exit right as a right of withdrawal or as an appraisal right and to impose on companies the obligation to pay for and receive the shares.

In a similar vein, it is also possible that bylaws or shareholders' agreements provide for the exclusion or the cash-out of the shares owned by shareholders that are in breach of their duties. In these situations as well, the calculation of the value of the shares that are cashed out and the identification of the persons

---

25 It is also possible that some limitations on the powers to represent companies are included in shareholders' agreements. Depending on the relevant legal system, these clauses may be irrelevant or have some implications for companies' actions. Certainly, in the European Union, art. 9(2) Directive 2017/1132/EU is also applicable to these clauses.

26 For further details on the use of exit rights in company law, see Jan Andersson, 'Exit in Private Companies: An Overview' in (ed), (n 2).

who will pay and receive the shares may give rise to some problems. Certainly, also in these cases, national company laws may provide for different legal mechanisms to achieve the exclusion or the cash-out, depending on whether that possibility is granted in the bylaws or in a shareholders' agreement.[27]

E. Invalidation of Shareholders' Actions

The invalidation of shareholders' actions is another contractual enforcement mechanism that may be laid out in bylaws and shareholders' agreements. For example, in some cases, shareholders' duties may take the form of an obligation to inform the other shareholders and/or one or more corporate bodies of the intention to transfer shares. These arrangements are particularly common in the clauses that set limits to the right to transfer shares, like in the case of pre-emption clauses, or when the transfer of shares is made conditional upon the approval of a corporate body or of other shareholders. More generally, these clauses aim at safeguarding the shareholding structure of companies and, beyond the duty of disclosing the intention to transfer shares, they may also impose other obligations on shareholders with a view to achieving that goal. In some cases, national company laws may directly provide these mechanisms as default or mandatory rules. However, these arrangements may also be adopted in shareholders' agreements or bylaws.

The duties imposed on shareholders by clauses that limit the right to transfer shares may have different effects if included in bylaws or in shareholders' agreements. In the legal systems that limit the effect of shareholders' agreements on companies, the breach of a clause that imposes limitations on the right to transfer shares would probably result in a simple award of damages. However, if a country admits that shareholders' agreements may also have effects on the interested company, a transfer of shares made in violation of these limitations could probably be considered void or without effects. Finally, with regard to the limitations on the right to transfer shares included in bylaws, if compared with the limitations included in shareholders' agreements, national company laws are probably more willing to recognize that their violation can make a transfer of shares invalid also for the company.

[27] For example, bylaws may provide for redeemable shares while shareholders' agreements frequently rely on contractual mechanisms such as options rights.

IV. CONTRACTUAL ENFORCEMENT IN SHAREHOLDERS' AGREEMENTS AND BYLAWS

A. Possible Approaches

The analysis of the different contractual enforcement mechanisms of shareholders' duties reveals that one key element for determining their effectiveness can be found in national laws' different approaches to the respective effects of shareholders' agreements and bylaws. In fact, while shareholders' agreements are essentially contracts, bylaws have a corporate nature, and many countries give emphasis to the fact that the arrangements included in these two documents should be treated differently.

The distinction between bylaws and shareholders' agreements may be based on the so-called principle of separation, which imposes a distinct separation between corporate clauses and contractual arrangements.[28] In addition to that principle, the principle of privity or relativity of contracts, which states that normally contracts bind only those persons that concluded them, may play an important role.[29] By giving relevance to the different nature of shareholders' agreements and bylaws, the jurisdictions that rely on one of these two principles may limit the scope of the enforcement of shareholders' duties included in shareholders' agreements, especially if compared with the enforcement of the shareholders' duties provided in bylaws.

The legal effects shareholders' agreements may have on companies and third parties is therefore an important aspect for evaluating the different strategies to ensure the contractual enforcement of shareholders' duties. The majority of jurisdictions recognize that a clear distinction should be made between bylaws and shareholders' agreements and that these two documents have different effects.[30] In addition, in the European Union, normally Member

---

[28] The *Trennungsprinzip*, or principle of separation, plays a role, for example, in Austria (n 21) (161f), Italy (Malberti (n 21) 414ff and 430f), Sweden (Rolf Dotevall, 'Sweden' in Mock, Csach and Havel (eds) (n 21) 595, 598f and 601f), Greece (Georgios Psaroudakis, 'Greece' in Mock, Csach and Havel (eds) (n 21) 305, 311), and Switzerland (Michael A. Meer, 'Switzerland' in Mock, Csach and Havel (eds) (n 21) 605, 606 and 616).

[29] See, e.g., in Spanish law, Pérez Millán (n 21) 575 and 582ff.

[30] On this problem, in general, see Sebastian Mock, Kristian Csach and Bohumil Havel, 'Shareholders' Agreements between Corporate and Contract Law' in Mock, Csach and Havel (eds) (n 21) 3, 15f; for Austria, see Arlt (n 21) 161f; for Belgium, see Tom Matthijs, 'Belgium' in Mock, Csach and Havel (eds) (n 21) 167, 182; for the UK, see Zakrzewski (n 21) 271; for Israel, see Omer Kimhi, Achiad Harel and Yve Binestock, 'Israel' in Mock, Csach and Havel (eds) (n 21) 389, 406; and for Brazil, see Ivens Henrique Hübert, 'Brazil' in Mock, Csach and Havel (eds) (n 21) 187, 200.

States make a clear distinction between shareholders' agreements and bylaws and give different effects to the provisions included in these two documents.

In some countries, such as Russia,[31] this distinction is even made clear in the law. In fact, art. 32.1 of Federal Law No. 208-FZ of December 26, 1995 on Joint Stock Companies states:

> A corporate agreement shall be only mandatory for the parties thereto. A contract made by a party to a corporate agreement in defiance of the corporate agreement may be only declared invalid by court upon a suit of either party to the corporate agreement concerned, if it is proved that the other party to the contract has known or certainly has had to know about the restrictions provided for by the corporate agreement.

A clear-cut distinction between shareholders' agreements and bylaws does not necessarily mean that the former are completely irrelevant for companies. Even if a legal system follows the principle of separation between shareholders' agreements and bylaws, it is still possible that shareholders' agreements may be relevant, at least for the interpretation of bylaws: the more a jurisdiction admits the subjective interpretation of bylaws, the more it will take into account the intentions the parties expressed in shareholders' agreements.[32] In these legal systems, a connection between bylaws and shareholders' agreements is ensured at least on the grounds of interpretation, so as to coordinate the content of these two documents.

In other jurisdictions, on the contrary, it is clearly admitted that shareholders' agreements may also have effects on bylaws provisions. A prominent example of this approach is found in Brazilian company law,[33] which, accord-

---

31 See Giuseppe Benedetto Portale, 'Patti parasociali con «efficacia corporative» nelle società di capitali' (2015) Riv. Soc. 1, 6f.

32 In general, on this issue, see Mock, Csach and Havel (n 30) 20ff; in favour of an objective interpretation are Austria (Arlt (n 21) 161), Greece (Psaroudakis (n 28) 325f), Italy (Malberti (n 21) 434), Sweden (Dotevall (n 28) 601f); in favour of an objective interpretation, but with some exceptions, are Denmark (Mette Neville, 'Denmark' in Mock, Csach and Havel (eds) (n 21) 221, 238), Germany (Sebastian Mock, 'Germany' in Mock, Csach and Havel (eds) (n 21) 277, 295f), Spain (Pérez Millán (n 21) 582), Switzerland (Meer (n 28) 616); for a mixed approach, see the Czech Republic (Bohumil Havel, 'Czech Republic' in Mock, Csach and Havel (eds) (n 21) 207, 217f); finally, for the direct influence of shareholders' agreements on bylaws, see Brazil (Henrique Hübert (n 30) 200).

33 For a description of the rules and principles governing shareholders' agreements in Brazil, see Henrique Hübert (n 30) 187ff.

ing to art. 118 of Law No. 6.404 of 15 December 1976 as modified, states that, when certain conditions are satisfied:

> Shareholder agreements regulating the purchase and sale of shares, preference to acquire shares, the exercise of voting rights, or the exercise of control must be observed by the corporation when filed in its head office.

A similar approach is also followed in Colombia by the *Sociedad por acciones simplificada* (SAS), since, according to art. 24 of Law 1258/2008:

> The shareholders' agreements on the purchase or sale of shares, the preference to acquire them, the restrictions to transfer them, the exercise of voting rights, the person who will represent the shares in the general meeting and any other allowed matter, must be complied with by the company when they have been deposited in the offices where the administration of the company operates, provided that their term does not exceed ten (10) years, renewable by the unanimous will of their subscribers for periods not exceeding ten (10) years.[34]

B. Practical Implications

1. Effects on third parties

Bylaws and shareholders' agreements may also have different effects from the perspective of the enforcement of shareholders' duties. Since bylaws' provisions are binding on both companies and present and future shareholders, when compared with shareholders' agreements, they are more likely to ensure an effective enforcement of shareholders' duties. However, as indicated above, some jurisdictions admit that even shareholders' agreements have effects beyond the parties that concluded them. Furthermore, the fact that shareholders' agreements do not have effects on companies does not necessarily imply that only damages or penalties would be available as a remedy for the innocent parties.

2. Adoption and modification

An important difference between contractual enforcement mechanisms provided in shareholders' agreements and bylaws concerns the different rules applicable in case of their adoption and modification. In fact, unless agreed otherwise, shareholders' agreements can be modified only with the unanimous consent of all shareholders, while, for amending their content, bylaws normally only require the approval of a majority of the shareholders. In principle,

---

[34] On shareholders' agreements in the Colombian SAS, see, e.g., Andrea Guaccero, 'Patti parasociali e regole statutarie: una prospettiva comparata' in Giuseppe Carcano, Chiara Mosca and Marco Ventoruzzo (eds), *Regole del mercato e mercato delle regole* (Giuffrè 2016) 283, 301ff.

it is therefore easier to adopt and modify bylaws' provisions than to conclude and amend shareholders' agreements.[35]

3. Role of mandatory law

In several legal systems the scope of mandatory law in company law is broader than that of default rules.[36] In addition, contract law frequently admits broader contractual freedom than company law. Therefore, the interplay between the different scopes of mandatory law in company and contract law may favour the adoption of contractual enforcement mechanisms in shareholders' agreements instead of in bylaws.

Furthermore, some contractual enforcement mechanisms of shareholders' duties may be allowed by contract law and prohibited by company law. This could occur, for example, for the arrangements that require shareholders to cast their vote at the general meeting in a given direction and provide for a penalty in the event that they fail to do so. In fact, in these cases, company law might have an unfavourable view of the disenfranchisement of shareholders, who should be left free to exercise their voting rights in the general meeting. However, that same arrangement, which is invalid if included in the bylaws, could be considered valid if included in a shareholders' agreement. In these situations, shareholders' agreements may be used to escape the application of certain mandatory law principles laid out in company law.

However, it should also be admitted that enforcement mechanisms laid out in shareholders' agreements frequently have different effects from those they would have if included in bylaws. Given these differences, some legal systems may decide to recognize the validity of shareholders' agreements exactly because these arrangements have different – and normally more limited – effects than bylaws provisions.[37]

4. Disclosure

Another important difference between shareholders' agreements and bylaws may be found in the different rules that govern the disclosure of these various documents. For example, European company law requires that all limited liabil-

---

[35] Obviously, shareholders' agreements may also be concluded by some shareholders and not necessarily by all shareholders.

[36] E.g., for public companies, in Greece and Sweden, company law has mainly a mandatory nature (see respectively Psaroudakis (n 28) 307, and Dotevall (n 28) 595), while, in Switzerland, company law has mainly a default nature (see Meer (n 28) 605). In general, on the problem of the relationship between mandatory and default rules, see Klaus Jürgen Hopt, 'Directors' Duties and Shareholders' Rights in the European Union: Mandatory and/or Default Rules?' in Carcano, Mosca and Ventoruzzo (eds) (n 34) 35ff.

[37] For example, this is the case for Italy; see, e.g., Malberti (n 21) 414ff and 433ff.

ity companies disclose their bylaws, while no general obligations are imposed for shareholders' agreements, even if in some cases national laws impose such disclosure.[38] Therefore, if shareholders value confidentiality, they may prefer to adopt enforcement mechanisms in shareholders' agreements and not in bylaws, even if that could result in a limitation of the effects of these mechanisms.

C. Remedies

1. Damages and pecuniary sanctions

The different scope and effects of bylaws and shareholders' agreements may also be relevant for determining the remedies available in cases of a breach of shareholders' duties. Starting with damages and pecuniary sanctions, both bylaws and shareholders' agreements may provide for penalties and be the basis for an award of damages. However, as mentioned above, in some cases contractual penalties may be considered invalid if included in bylaws, but valid if included in shareholders' agreements.[39]

Normally, shareholders' agreements allow more freedom in drafting clauses on penalties than bylaws do, since, given their contractual nature, they may affect only the parties that concluded them and not the company. Thus, the shareholders' choice of providing pecuniary sanctions in shareholders' agreements and not in bylaws may be driven by the different scope of mandatory law in company and contract law, which, in turn, may grant shareholders more freedom in drafting shareholders' agreements instead of bylaws provisions.

2. Injunctions, court orders, specific performance, and equivalent enforcement

Injunctions, court orders, and specific performance are frequently available in national company law to ensure the performance of shareholders' obligations. When these enforcement mechanisms are granted by a court's decision, they are not entirely contractual since they rely, at least for their activation, on the intervention of public authorities. However, if the working definition of contractual enforcement proposed in the previous pages[40] is correct, i.e. an enforcement mechanism based on contractual arrangements, it can also be concluded that shareholders' agreements and bylaws may be drafted so as to give the innocent parties the possibility to take advantage of at least some of these reliefs.[41]

---

38 See n 21 above.

39 See Section IV.B.3.

40 See Section II.A.

41 Interestingly, in Brazil, art. 118 para 3 of Law No. 6.404 of December 15, 1976, as modified, states that shareholders' agreements 'may make provision for the specific

Injunctions and court orders are probably more useful in cases where shareholders' duties are laid out in shareholders' agreements, at least as long as these agreements are not binding on companies. For example, if a shareholders' agreement sets limits on the voting rights of the shares acquired above a certain threshold, the company may not be bound to take that arrangement into account. As a result, a resolution of the general meeting taken in violation of that obligation will be valid according to company law, even if it is in breach of shareholders' agreements.

For those reasons, these remedies may play an important role, in particular when the performance of shareholders' obligations is simply at risk, and not yet consummated. In fact, in these situations, courts are more willing, for example, to order shareholders, as agreed in shareholders' agreements, to cast their vote in a given direction or to offer their shares to certain specific acquirers. Injunctions and court orders granted before the consummation of the breach may also be available in the countries that rely on the principle of separation between shareholders' agreements and bylaws. In reality, for those legal systems, in the case of shareholders' agreements, the award of injunctions, court orders, or specific performance raises fewer problems before the consummation of the breach since the innocent parties to shareholders' agreements are just asking for the performance of the contractual obligations before any company law principle comes into play. In this sense, if an injunction, a court order, or specific performance is requested, for example, before the vote is cast at the general meeting or before the shares are transferred to third parties, courts may be more willing to accept that request.

However, once the breach is consummated (e.g. after a resolution of the general meeting has been taken or some shares have been transferred to third parties), it is harder to challenge the validity of an approved resolution or of an effected transfer of shares on the grounds of company law. In these situations, the request for an injunction, a court order, or specific performance may have direct implications for the rules and principles that govern company law, and many legal systems may be reluctant to recognize the binding effect of shareholders' agreements on companies.[42]

In any case, although a legal system relies on the principle of separation, and although a breach has been consummated, courts in some jurisdictions can still order some sort of performance of shareholders' agreements, by granting an equivalent performance. For example, a court could require shareholders

performance of the commitments undertaken', cf. n 49 below and the accompanying text.

[42] Obviously, for the jurisdictions that admit an interplay between shareholders' agreements and bylaws, the award of specific performance raises fewer problems, even when granted after the breach.

to vote in favour of revoking a resolution of the general meeting or to buy back the shares transferred to third parties.[43] This remedy is different from that of specific performance since it endeavours, after a breach is already consummated, to achieve the same results that would have been achieved by the performance of the obligations undertaken by the shareholder in breach.

To assess injunctions, court orders, and specific performance, another element to take into account is their general availability in a jurisdiction in cases of breaches of contract. It is well known that national laws have different approaches toward remedies and that several jurisdictions favour execution and specific performance over the award of damages. These different approaches may also become relevant in the performance of shareholders' duties since specific performance may be more difficult to obtain in legal systems that consider damages the primary remedy in case of breach.

However, it should also be admitted that, in some cases, a legal system's general approach to remedies might give little guidance on the availability of injunctions, court orders, and specific performance for the enforcement of shareholders' duties. An interesting example of this is provided by US law, which considers damages the primary relief in case of breach.[44] Yet, in spite of the preference for the award of damages, Section 7.31.(b) of the Revised Model Business Corporation Act (RMBCA) provides that even voting agreements are specifically enforceable.[45] Conversely, in Italian law, which considers specific performance a primary remedy, the recourse to injunctions, court orders, and specific performance is normally not allowed in cases of a breach of shareholders' agreements.[46]

The solutions adopted in these two countries with regard to the reliefs in cases of a breach of shareholders' agreements are hardly reconcilable with their general approach to damages and specific performance. However, it should also be acknowledged that these two countries have different approaches to the principle of separation, which is a cornerstone of Italian company law,[47] while, according to the RMBCA, shareholders' agreements may, under certain conditions, also have effects on companies.[48] In that perspective, the reluctance

---

[43] See, e.g., Guaccero (n 34) 298ff, and Portale (n 31), 7f, n 24, who both refer to some peculiar French decisions.

[44] See, e.g., Joseph Perillo, *Contracts* (7th edn, West Academic 2014) 511 and 581f.

[45] See Wulf Kaal, 'National Report of the United States of America' in Mock, Csach and Havel (eds) (n 21) 645, 653f and 665f.

[46] See Malberti (n 21) 433ff, who also discusses some exceptions to that principle.

[47] For further details, see ibid 416ff and 432f.

[48] See RMBCA, s 7.32.(a).

of Italian law to grant remedies based on specific performance can probably be understood as a corollary of the principle of separation.[49]

3. Self-enforcing arrangements

In some cases, the breach of shareholders' duties does not exclusively depend on the intentions of shareholders since an act that may result in a shareholders' breach will need to be acknowledged as valid and effective by the company. For example, if a provision of the bylaws states that the voting rights of the shares acquired by a shareholder above a given threshold may not be exercised at the general meeting, and if this clause also provides for the suspension of voting rights, the shares in question will not be counted for approving a resolution. In addition, although a resolution is taken with the approval of the shares whose voting rights have been suspended, its validity may be challenged, at least as long as a legal system recognizes this possibility. Similarly, if the shares of a company are registered, and if the exercise of shareholders' rights is made conditional on the entry of the acquisition of those shares in the company's register, directors and company officers may be bound not to allow that entry, at least so long as the rules provided by law and the bylaws have not been complied with.

In both cases, the directors and officers of the company may face liability for their actions in violation of the law or the bylaws, and also the validity of their actions may be challenged. Therefore, imposing on directors and officers the duty – and giving them the power – to avoid the breach may strengthen the effectiveness of shareholders' duties. This is also true when the director or officer who is required to give full effect to the act that would consummate the breach is the very shareholder bound by the duty. In fact, in this case, the shareholder will not only be liable for his breach as a shareholder, but also for the breach of the fiduciary duties that, as director or officer, he owes to the company. Hence, in many cases, shareholders' duties are, in some way, self-enforcing since their violation would also require directors and officers to breach the duties imposed on them by the law or the bylaws.

These mechanisms are common when shareholders' duties are included in bylaws. However, the incorporation of shareholders' duties in bylaws is not in itself sufficient to curb any risk of breach since, in many cases, the breach

---

[49] In this same perspective, it is also not surprising that Brazilian law, which allows shareholders' agreements to have effects on companies, also grants the remedy of specific performance for the commitments undertaken in those agreements: see art. 118 para. 3 of Law No. 6.404 of December 15, 1976 as modified, and cf. n 41 above. In addition, as Henrique Hübert (n 30) 203 also emphasizes, 'specific performance is considered the general rule on enforcement in Brazil, while damages should only be claimed when specific performance is not possible'.

of shareholders' duties does not require the cooperation of the company. This occurs when the performance of shareholders' duties included in bylaws is not mediated by the company's directors or officers. For example, if a provision of the bylaws requires shareholders to disclose the acquisition of shares above a certain threshold, the performance or breach of this obligation does not depend on the companies' directors or officers.

Self-enforcing mechanisms may also be available for shareholders' duties included in shareholders' agreements. This possibility exists in the legal systems that do not strictly apply the principle of separation and that admit that shareholders' agreements may also have effects on companies since, in these jurisdictions, companies' directors and officers may also be bound by shareholders' agreements. However, in the countries that do not allow shareholders' agreements to have direct effects on companies it is unlikely that the enforcement of shareholders' duties could be reinforced by relying on directors' and officers' duties.

D. Alternative Enforcement Mechanisms

Even in the countries that rely on the principle of separation, in spite of the fact that the enforcement of shareholders' duties may not be granted by relying on directors' and officers' duties, it is still possible to devise some arrangements to strengthen the performance of the shareholders' duties incorporated in shareholders' agreements. Some of these mechanisms rely on third parties, while others may be directly activated by the innocent parties.

A first example of these alternative enforcement mechanisms consists of the creation of separate legal entities to which shareholders contribute their shares. These structures, for example, may be used to ensure the stability of a coalition of shareholders that controls a company. In these arrangements, the enforcement of shareholders' duties in the subsidiary will be indirectly granted by the bylaws and the directors of the parent. These mechanisms, however, are not without burdens since they imply the creation of another legal entity and a transfer of the shares to that entity, with all the consequences that derive from that transaction. In addition, it should also be said that that mechanism cannot be used to reinforce the performance of those shareholders' duties that are not mediated by the exercise of the rights attached to the shares.[50]

As an alternative, to reinforce the performance of shareholders' duties, it is also possible to rely on the creation of voting trusts, fiduciary arrangements, or the appointment of irrevocable agents. Each of these mechanisms may be more

[50] For example, this could happen when the duty imposed on the shareholder simply requires him or her to disclose any acquisition of new shares.

or less available depending on the legislation in force in each jurisdiction. All these arrangements would limit the possibility of a breach by the shareholders involved since the rights attached to the shares will be exercised by a trustee, a fiduciary or an agent. Normally, these mechanisms are also less burdensome than the creation of a new legal entity since, in principle, they do not imply the transfer of full title on the shares.[51] However, also in this case, these arrangements may not be used to ensure the performance of any kind of shareholders' duty.

Another legal strategy that may be used to strengthen the performance of shareholders' duties consists of granting to the innocent shareholder, in a shareholders' agreement, the possibility to sell his or her shares or to buy the shares of the shareholder in breach. For their effectiveness, these mechanisms do not necessarily rely on third parties. However, depending on the way these clauses are drafted and on the applicable company law, they may still require some cooperation from the shareholder in breach.[52]

V. CONCLUSION

This chapter investigated the scope and nature of the enforcement of shareholders' duties, comparing the contractual enforcement mechanisms provided by bylaws and shareholders' agreements. This analysis showed that, in many jurisdictions, company and contractual arrangements have different scopes, and national laws still attach a different value to the obligations undertaken in bylaws and shareholders' agreements. This distinction plays an important role in drafting contractual mechanisms aimed at ensuring the performance of shareholders' duties.

After having examined the nature of the contractual enforcement of shareholders' duties, I presented the tools provided by both company and contract law to ensure the enforcement of these duties. The analysis of these tools made clear the different effects of bylaws and shareholders' agreements and the rules and principles applicable to them. In addition, I have also analysed the remedies available in cases of a breach of shareholders' duties and discussed the role of damages, injunctions, court orders, specific performance, and equivalent performance. Finally, I have highlighted that the enforcement of shareholders' duties may also be facilitated by some mechanisms that, by relying on the cooperation of companies' directors or officers, or even of third parties, could limit the risk of breaches.

---

[51] In a similar vein, another strategy could be that of creating joint ownership on the relevant shares and to appoint an agent that acts on behalf of the co-owners.

[52] In fact, the lack of cooperation from the shareholder in breach may prevent the transfer of the shares from or to the innocent shareholder, jeopardizing the effectiveness of this alternative enforcement mechanism.

6. Private vs public enforcement of shareholder duties

Iris H-Y. Chiu

I. INTRODUCTION

This chapter focuses on the nature of 'private' and 'public' enforcement against shareholders in order to critically tease out the differences in terms of their rationales and broad characteristics. The chapter will raise the question whether the boundaries between the two are clear, and the implications for considering the suitable loci for enforcement. It is not a comprehensive study of the sources of law for enforcement but key examples will be raised.

'Private' enforcement relates to civil actions taken against shareholders, generally for the purpose of addressing rights and remedies between shareholders *inter se*, or between shareholders and the company. These actions are generally found in company law. As Member States in the EU maintain key differences in their corporate law systems as a matter of differences in political economy, company law is not heavily harmonised in the EU. The private enforcement actions discussed herein are taken from UK company law. 'Public' enforcement relates to enforcement action undertaken by an authority with powers designed to secure compliance, and in relation to shareholders, we look to regulatory bodies for securities markets where shareholders participate as investors in corporate equity. Such regulatory bodies include the securities regulator and/or Listing Authority. The UK's Financial Conduct Authority (FCA), which is the securities regulator-cum-Listing Authority, is referenced herein as an example.

The boundaries between private and public enforcement is not crystal clear. For example, we increasingly see regulatory standards being established in relation to shareholder conduct and in corporate governance relations. This is an area that would be regarded as falling within the 'private' sphere of company–shareholder relations or shareholder relations *inter se*. We can regard such enforcement as 'private' because the taking of a collective action by the regulator is an efficient aggregation of enforcement that market participants would have wanted. However, the regulatory standards can also be explained on the basis of certain public/collective interest in the types and impact of shareholder conduct, thus justifying regulatory enforcement. The centralisation of discretion upon a regulator to exercise a power of enforcement achieves the effect of maintaining a certain collective order or upholding certain expectations in the wider public interest. Hence the nature of this enforcement should not merely be regarded as a 'delegated' form of collective private enforcement, but as 'public' enforcement.

The uncertain boundaries between private and public enforcement against shareholders are a reflection of the broader issue surrounding increased expansion of the regulatory scope of corporate governance. Should private and public enforcement be clearly delineated in accordance with the nature of persons carrying out the enforcement, or the nature of the causes sought to be addressed? Neither criterion can be fully determinate as 'private' securities litigation can serve a public purpose of market discipline[1] and regulatory enforcement of corporate governance standards can be pursuant to the protection of certain groups of constituents.[2] At a wider level the examination of the nature of private and public enforcement against shareholders raises the issue of the evolution of company law and securities regulation, and the changing relationship between these two bodies of law.

II. PRIVATE ENFORCEMENT UNDER COMPANY LAW

We turn first to 'private' enforcement against shareholders. Typically, such enforcement relates to enforcement in order to redress certain rights or to obtain certain remedies. In UK company law, shareholders are owed various duties by the company[3] and sometimes directly by

---

1 Rafael La Porta, Florencio Lopez-de-Silanes and Andrei Shleifer, 'What Works in Securities Laws' (2006) 71 J. Finance 1.

2 To be discussed in Section IV.

3 Such as in relation to the conduct of general meetings, see ss 301ff, UK Companies Act 2006, facilitating shareholders' right to vote and to exercise exclusive approval over certain transactions reserved to them. These include the right to amend the constitution, s 21; the right to ratify irregularities in directors' conduct, s 239; the right to appoint or remove directors, s 168; the right to overturn board decisions by a special majority, Art. 4 of the Model Articles for Private and Public Companies 2008; the right to approve loans, guarantees made in favour of directors, transactions with directors above certain thresholds, ss 190ff; the right to approve directors' remuneration packages, s 439A; the right to make changes to capital structure such as reduction of capital or buybacks, ss 641, 694ff; and the right to determine if a takeover offer should be accepted, see *Hogg v Cramphorn Ltd* [1967] Ch 254, and more recently the Kraft takeover of Cadbury plc in the UK; see discussion in Georgina Tsagas, 'A Long-Term

directors.[4] However the converse is not the case, i.e. shareholders do not owe duties to the company, or to each other *within the company law context.* Shareholders are free to enter into shareholder agreements whereby they may be bound to contractual duties *vis-a-vis* each other[5] but company law does not normally impose on shareholders duties to each other or to the company, due to the quasi-proprietary framing of their rights.[6] UK company law regards shareholders as having rights based on an amorphous notion of 'property', tied to their decision rights in voting derived from their contribution to capital. This 'quasi-proprietary' right is not exercisable over corporate assets as such, but the 'proprietary' framing entails a treatment of shareholders as enjoying rights and freedoms and refrains from imposing curtailments to freedom, i.e. duties owed to others.

The resistance in company law against imposing duties upon shareholders can be illustrated by a recent UK Supreme Court decision. In *Eclairs Group Ltd and Glengary Overseas Ltd v JKX Oil & Gas plc*,[7] the company JKX Oil plc suspected that a couple of shareholders were increasing their stakes stealthily in order to launch a surprise takeover bid for the company. Two trust vehicles Eclairs and Glengary raised their stakes in the company and it is suspected that they were holding the company's shares on trust for a couple of known associates. The company wished to pass some resolutions with regard to reappointing several directors and to approve directors' remuneration packages, so called a general meeting to do so. It was expected that the resolutions would be contested. The company then served requests upon the two trust vehicles, which were registered members, to require the furnishing of information on the beneficial shareholdings of the company's shares and the intentions of such owners, under section 793 of the Companies Act. Eclairs and Glengary initially refused to provide the relevant information but subsequently furnished what the company considered to be inadequate information. Under the company's constitution, the failure to furnish information required under section 793 of the Act triggers the application of the company's sanctions, which in this case related to the suspension of shareholder voting rights. Eclairs and Glengary

---

Vision for UK Firms? Revisiting the Target Director's Advisory Role Since the Takeover of Cadbury's Plc.' (2014) 14 J. Corp. L. Stud. 241.

4 Where directors have undertaken personal responsibility to advise shareholders for example, see *Allen v Hyatt* (1914) 30 TLR 444; *Kieth Platt v Colin Platt and Anor* [1999] 2 BCLC 745 (Ch).

5 *Russell v Northern Bank Development Corp Ltd* [1992] 1 WLR 588; *Halton International Inc. v Guernroy* [2005] EWHC 1968 (Ch).

6 *Her Majesty's Commissioners of Inland Revenue (Respondents) v Laird Group plc (Appellants)* [2003] UKHL 54.

7 [2015] UKSC 71.

challenged the company's decision on the basis that the power exercised was pursuant to an improper purpose, in order to prevent the shareholders from frustrating the passing of the relevant resolutions at the general meeting and from carrying out a surprise takeover of the company. The first instance court agreed with Eclairs and Glengary but the Court of Appeal disagreed, finding for the company on the basis that the company could impose conditions on shareholders in relation to the exercise of their rights, and those rights could be suspended when conditions were not met.[8] The Court of Appeal's holding was overturned in the Supreme Court, which held that the company's exercise of power to impose conditions on the two shareholders and then proceeding to invoke the conditions was an exercise of power partly pursuant to the objective of preventing the shareholders from being able to launch a surprise takeover bid. Such a move on the part of the shareholders would be within the scope of their quasi-proprietary shareholder rights and not illegal. To pre-empt this would be an improper exercise of directors' powers and the directors were held to be in breach of their duties for invoking the suspension of Eclairs' and Glengary's voting rights. The case illustrates the wide berth accorded to shareholder rights, particularly voting rights, and that these are not to be circumscribed by even legitimate conditions that the company can impose. The case reflects the entrenched tradition in the UK that resists the imposition of *duties* on shareholders *vis-a-vis* the company.

However, enforcement against shareholders by the company or by other shareholders is possible within the context of the company's constitution. This is an area that straddles both company and contract law, discussed below.[9] Private enforcement against particular shareholders or groups of shareholders may also be pursued to obtain remedies for 'unfairly prejudicial' treatment[10] but such remedies are awarded in equity, and are not based on duties or expectations imposed on shareholders as to their conduct.

A. Enforcement under the Company's Constitution

Shareholders derive their rights under company law and under the constitution of the company. Where the former set of rights is usually actionable against the company, the right to enforce constitutional provisions can be directed at the company or to other shareholders.[11] It is to be noted that such enforcement is on an *inter se* basis, i.e. the company and shareholders can enforce the constitution

---

[8] *Eclairs Group Ltd and Glengary Overseas Ltd v JKX Oil & Gas plc* [2014] EWCA Civ 640.

[9] UK Companies Act 2006, s 33.

[10] Ibid s 994.

[11] *Borland's Trustee v Steel* [1901] 1 Ch 279.

against each other, and shareholders can also do so *inter se*. In *Hickman v Kent & Romney Marsh Sheep-Breeders' Association*[12] the company's constitution contained a clause that required members and the company to submit to arbitration where disputes needed to be resolved formally. The member concerned filed a suit in the High Court instead, and the company asked for proceedings to be stayed in favour of enforcing the arbitration clause in the company's constitution. The court granted the stay and allowed the constitutional provision to be enforced by the company against the member. This may seem to be an exception to the almost exclusively 'rights-based' framing of the position of shareholders in UK company law. However, such enforcement can be explained on the basis of the contractual nature of the company's constitution.

The company's constitution binds the company and shareholders to a contractual relationship, and hence the company's enforcement against the member in the case above can be regarded as a form of contractual enforcement recognised in company law. However, the contractual analysis is circumscribed by the company law context as a member's attempt to enforce his/her right under the constitution may sometimes fail. In *Pender v Lushington*[13] a shareholder whose votes were not counted in accordance with his constitutional right was able to obtain an order requiring the company to adhere to the constitution and therefore realise his rights. However, in *MacDougall v Gardiner*[14] a member's attempt to enforce a constitutional right to demand a poll at a general meeting was not upheld as the majority of the general meeting had voted to ratify the irregularity of not conducting a poll. It seems that rights that are not 'specific' to an individual shareholder could be subsumed under the general position of 'majority rules' in company law, i.e. in relation to decision-making by the organs of the company (the board or the general meeting, whichever is applicable).

In sum, the enforcement of constitutional rights against shareholders individually or as a collective body is well established as a form of private enforcement in UK company law. However, such enforcement rights may be moderated by the general tenets of majority decision-making in company law. In such a case, it is possible for an aggrieved member to carry out a form of equitable enforcement in the form of the 'unfair prejudice' petition discussed below.

B. Enforcement under the Unfair Prejudice Petition

Where a member is of the view that 'the company's affairs are being or have been conducted in a manner that is unfairly prejudicial to the interests of

---

12 [1915] 1 Ch 881.

13 (1877) 6 Ch D 70.

14 (1875) 1 Ch D 13.

members generally or of some part of its members', s/he may petition to the court for an appropriate remedy to address the 'unfair prejudice'.[15] This provision allows enforcement against shareholders, usually majority or controlling shareholders by minority shareholders.

The scope of unfair prejudice is fairly wide and includes breach of agreements or inequitable behaviour in the context of companies that are highly structured around personal relations, making them quasi-partnerships.[16] The court may grant a wide range of remedies[17] if an unfair prejudice petition is successful, including remedies for the company in an appropriate case.[18] The unfair prejudice petition has been utilised largely in contexts where inequitable behaviour has been alleged in privately held companies featuring majority and minority shareholders in close relational dynamics.[19] In *Croly v Good*[20] a long-time employee became a minority shareholder in a small private company and worked closely with the controlling shareholder-cum-executive in growing the business. Unfortunately they fell out and the minority shareholder was expelled from the company and offered a pittance in terms of the buy-out of his shares. In an unfair prejudice petition brought against the controlling shareholder, the court upheld the petitioner's complaint that he had been treated unfairly, and in the context of the men's close working relations, the court ordered the minority shares to be bought out not on a commercial basis (namely with discount for minority stakes) in order to achieve a fair redress of the grievance.

The unfair prejudice petition is a form of enforcement that is based on equitable considerations in terms of the relational dynamics between parties and also in relation to the remedy to be sought. Although the court can make orders of remedy as to how a particular shareholder should conduct him- or herself, such as in *Re H R Harmer*,[21] where the overbearing patriarch of the family company was ordered not to dominate board decision-making, the most common remedy is for the termination of relations between the parties who have fallen out in the company whereby the minority is bought out at a fair

---

[15] UK Companies Act, s 994.

[16] *O'Neill and Anor v Phillips and Others* [1999] BCC 600; *Ebrahimi v Westbourne Galleries Ltd and Others* [1972] 2 All ER 491.

[17] UK Companies Act 2006, s 996.

[18] *Lowe v Fahey* [1996] 1 BCLC 262; *Clark v Cutland* [2004] 1 WLR 783.

[19] E.g., *Croly v Good* [2010] EWHC 1 (Ch); *Shepherd v Williams* [2010] EWHC 2375 (Ch), both companies featuring only two shareholders each, and disagreements resulting in the ousting of one party by the other from the board could amount to behaviour of unfair prejudice.

[20] [2010] EWHC 1 (Ch).

[21] [1958] 3 All ER 689.

price.[22] This type of enforcement provides an 'escape route' for shareholders as the default 'majority rules' model of decision-making in company law can entail injustice at times. Hence, this type of enforcement cannot be seen to be providing a form of regulation of shareholder conduct within company law as it is not based on *ex ante* duties or standards of conduct imposed on shareholders. Further, the use of minority buy-out as the common remedy in successful cases shows that this regime cannot be used to promote 'voice' in the company in terms of the minority's dissent regarding the conduct of company affairs.

C. Conclusion on the Typical Nature of Private Enforcement

Overall, private enforcement in company law against shareholders is usually on the basis of enforcing agreed rights, such as under the constitution (with the caveats raised earlier), or for obtaining a remedy on an equitable basis. There is very little in terms of norms or standards that govern shareholder conduct in a company due to the 'proprietary' framing of shareholder rights in UK company law, which puts excessive emphasis on their freedom of conduct. Such enforcement can thus be characterised as 'individualistic' in nature and for 'compensatory' purposes. We will contrast these characteristics with typical enforcement of a public character that is more 'collective' and for 'regulatory' purposes shortly.

III. PUBLIC ENFORCEMENT UNDER SECURITIES REGULATION

Public enforcement against shareholders typically relates to their position as investors in the securities market and not in relation to shareholder conduct in a company, although this notion is undergoing change. Investors in the securities market may have imposed on them regulatory duties for the purpose of maintaining the public interest of an efficient market. This position is more harmonised in EU regulation as EU regulation has achieved a high level of convergence in regulating securities offerings, markets, and issuers' as well as shareholders' conduct in publicly traded markets. The convergence has been achieved in the policy interest of creating a single capital market.[23]

Securities market regulation addresses the primary market, where corporate issuers directly offer their securities for the first time, or offer new issues, and the secondary market, where existing securities may be bought or sold

---

[22] *Re Apollo Cleaning Services Ltd* [1999] BCC 786.

[23] Eilis Ferran, *Building an EU Securities Market* (Cambridge University Press 2004) generally.

by anyone. On both markets, mandatory disclosure regulation is imposed on issuers in order to overcome information asymmetries which affect both the price efficiency of securities[24] as well as the level of investor protection. Mandatory disclosure is often justified to ensure that optimal amounts of accurate information are released in order to foster an efficient securities market[25] in which the market prices efficiently reflect all information underlying the securities at any given time. Price efficiency promotes fairness and certainty and supports investor participation in the markets. At first blush, imposing regulatory duties on investors as a matter of securities regulation looks contrary to the erstwhile approach that imposes duties on issuers *vis-a-vis* their investors. However, I point out that just as mandatory disclosure obligations apply to issuers for the purposes of maintaining a price-efficient market, duties of transparency for investors are increasingly important in achieving the same goal.

In the UK an investor acquiring shares in a publicly traded company must inform the issuer and the Listing Authority of her holdings if she crosses a 3 per cent threshold and every 1 per cent thereafter.[26] Further, EU regulation compels net short sellers in equities to disclose to the relevant regulator short positions from 0.2 per cent of the company's equity onwards with every increase of 0.1 per cent.[27] Where short positions reach 0.5 per cent of the company's equity, public disclosure needs to be made by the net short seller.[28]

---

[24] Eugene Fama, 'Efficient Capital Markets: A Review of Theory and Empirical Work' (1970) 25 J. Finance 383; Ronald J. Gilson and Reiner H. Kraakman, 'Mechanisms of Market Efficiency (1984) Va. L. Rev. 549 on the 'Efficient Capital Markets Hypothesis'. See also Jeffrey N. Gordon and Lewis A. Kornhauser, 'Efficient Markets, Costly Information and Securities Research' (1985) 60 N.Y.U. L. Rev. 761 where it is pointed out that it is uncertain whether the efficiency of any given market can be satisfactorily tested. But the thesis of information affecting price can be defended by looking at a variety of mechanisms affecting trading behaviour and concluding that the distribution of information into the market ultimately translates into stock price. Durnev et al. have also developed a model to test the relationship between securities disclosure and price efficiency in the market and have concluded that disclosure improves efficient capital allocation, see Art Durnev, Merritt Fox, Randall Morck and Bernard Yeung, 'Law, Share Price Accuracy, and Economic Performance: The New Evidence' (2003) 102 Mich. L. Rev. 331–86.

[25] John C. Coffee Jr., 'Market Failure and the Economic Case for a Mandatory Disclosure System' (1984) 70 Va. L Rev. 717; Merritt B. Fox, 'Rethinking Disclosure Liability in the Modern Era' (1997) 75 Wash. U. L.Q. 903; Joel D. Seligman, 'The Historical Need for a Mandatory Corporate Disclosure System' (1983) 9 J. Corp. L. 1.

[26] FCA Listing Rules DTR 5.1, 5.9. This is transposed from Art. 13, EU Transparency Directive 2004, which starts the disclosure threshold at 5 per cent. The UK transposition is therefore stricter.

[27] EU Short Selling Regulation 2012, Art. 5.

[28] Ibid Art. 6.

In some jurisdictions, it is not only investor holdings/interests and identities that may be price-sensitive information in the marketplace. As investors are asked and expected to engage with companies,[29] engagement agendas and behaviour may also become important signals in the marketplace for other investors. The disclosure of investment objectives is increasingly being viewed as a price-sensitive signal to the market as signals of shareholder activism intentions will likely affect share price. In the US, institutions that acquire 5 per cent or more of a publicly traded company's equity as beneficial owners must disclose the stake and the purpose of the investment.[30] In the EU, the Transparency Directive is silent on the issue of intentions-related disclosure, but some EU Member States, including France and Germany, impose additional disclosure obligations for large investors in relation to the objectives pursued by their investment.[31]

Regulatory enforcement against non-compliance would be for the purposes of maintaining the collective and public interest in a transparent and efficient market, distinguishing typical public enforcement from private enforcement, discussed above.

The securities regulation regime envisages that private securities litigation is available in some instances. A private suit can be maintained for compensation purposes if loss is suffered as a result of breach of securities regulation requirements such as mandatory disclosure.[32] Although such an action may ride on a regulatory enforcement action and is permitted under legislation, it is private in nature and seeks to redress the loss suffered by an individual. The pursuit of such an action is thus pursuant to compensatory and not regulatory purposes. However, as section 150 of the Financial Services and Markets Act 2000 only permits private securities litigation to lie against 'an authorised person', i.e. a person regulated by the FCA, and in the case of the securities markets, the issuer, no private action can lie for compensation between an investor and another investor alleged to have breached disclosure requirements, discussed above. The enforcement mechanism for investors' mandatory disclosure as discussed above is exclusively *regulatory* in nature.

It is observed that the typical rationale and nature of public enforcement against shareholders in the realm of securities regulation is changing. There is a rise in regulatory law and soft law in terms of governing investors' conduct as shareholders in companies, in order to meet certain public interest needs and objectives. In the section below, I examine this new phenomenon and its

---

[29] Discussed in relation to the EU Shareholder Rights Directive below.

[30] Securities Exchange Act 1934, Schedule 13D.

[31] Discussed in Dionysia Katelouzou, 'Myths and Realities of Hedge Fund Activism: Some Empirical Evidence' (2013) 7 Va. L. & Bus. Rev. 459.

[32] Financial Services and Markets Act 2000, s 150.

mixed 'public-private' nature. I believe this phenomenon raises broader issues regarding the role of securities regulation in the hitherto private sphere of corporate governance.

IV. PUBLIC ENFORCEMENT OF SHAREHOLDER CONDUCT NORMS?

A. The Growing Importance of Institutional Shareholders

The changing nature of shareholder conduct norms from exclusively 'private' under company law to at least 'quasi-public' under securities regulation can be attributed to changes in the nature of securities ownership.[33] Securities ownership is now largely held by institutions, whether domestic or foreign, and individual ownership now accounts for a very small footprint. With the rise in pensions saving and other forms of private saving by the working population, such savings are increasingly managed as collective pools of funds by institutions, whether as pension funds, retail investment funds or alternative investment funds. Collective pooling of savings into investment funds ensures sufficiently affordable access to investment due to economies of scale. The rise of the collective investment management phenomenon is widely supported in the face of the retreat of state welfarism in individual financial provision.[34] The institutions that manage such collective pools of investment capital have increasingly become dominant investors in corporate equity.

The ownership by institutional investors of global equity, whether in the US or EU, has been on the rise.[35] As owners of corporate equity, funds and their asset managers become shareholders of companies. Not only do they assume legal rights under company law, but institutional ownership of corporate equity has been an important driving factor for the adoption of the centricity of shareholder value as a corporate objective.[36]

---

[33] See Chapter 4.

[34] See, e.g., Gordon L. Clark, *Pension Fund Capitalism* (Oxford University Press 2000).

[35] John K. Thompson and Sang-Mok Choi, 'Governance Systems for Collective Investment Schemes in OECD Countries', OECD Occasional Paper (April 2001); PwC, *Asset Management 2020: A Brave New World* (2013) http://www.pwc.com/gx/en/asset-management/publications/asset-management-2020-a-brave-new-world.jhtml.

[36] Engelbert Stockhammer, 'Financialization and the Slowdown of Accumulation' in Ismail Erturk, Julie Froud, Sukhdev Johal, Adam Leaver and Karel Williams (eds), *Financialization At Work: Key Tests and Commentary* (Routledge 2008); Paddy Ireland, 'The Financialization of Corporate Governance' (2009) 60 N. I. L.Q. 1.

As institutions became the dominant group of corporate shareholders, Hawley and Williams[37] envisioned that the ownership of corporate equity by institutional funds would usher in an age of 'fiduciary capitalism'. Institutions would act in their corporate governance roles in a representative capacity for myriad savers, democratising the corporate governance process and bringing about the promising prospects of long-term and responsible forms of capitalism under such 'universal ownership'. Although subsequent observations are sceptical as to whether institutions indeed conduct a form of 'fiduciary capitalism' in their capacity as shareholders, as their corporate governance roles often reflect their own short-term interests rather than their beneficiaries' interests,[38] the 'representative' capacity and scale of institutions as shareholders raise questions of public interest in terms of their shareholder conduct. The corporate governance roles of institutions not only impact upon their crucial roles in intermediating savers' capital (and meeting essential long-term needs such as retirement provision), but also impact upon the long-term wealth-creating capacity and role of the corporate sector.[39]

In widely held, publicly listed corporations, institutional shareholders, who are minority shareholders, are not incentivised to carry out their corporate governance roles of monitoring management.[40] Agency problems[41] can result in poorly managed companies, poor corporate performance and investment returns, not to mention corporate failure.[42] The sidelining of governance rights by institutional investors in publicly traded equity is preferred due to the relative ease of exit in a liquid market like the London Stock Exchange. Moreover, such ease of trading also means that institutional investors would focus on

---

37 James P. Hawley and Andrew T. Williams, *The Rise of Fiduciary Capitalism: How Institutional Investors Can Make Corporate America More Democratic* (University of Pennsylvania Press 2000).

38 See Larry Randall Wray, 'Money Manager Capitalism and the Global Financial Crisis' (2009) http://ssrn.com/abstract=1478508; Ronald J. Gilson and Jeffrey N. Gordon, 'Agency Capitalism: Further Implications of Equity Intermediation' (2014) http://ssrn.com/abstract=2359690; Roger M. Barker and Iris H-Y. Chiu, *Corporate Governance and Investment Management* (Edward Elgar Publishing 2017) 10–197.

39 BIS, *The Kay Review of UK Equity Markets and Long-Term Decision Making* (Final Report, 23 July 2012).

40 Institutions may have too many portfolio companies to monitor and, being minorities, they would not likely be incentivised to dedicate cost and effort to monitoring individual companies.

41 Michael Jensen and William H. Meckling, 'Theory of the Firm: Managerial Behavior, Agency Costs and Ownership Structure' (1976) 3 J. Financial Econ. 305.

42 See Iris H-Y. Chiu, *The Foundations and Anatomy of Shareholder Activism* (Hart Publishing 2010) 16–70.

trading gains in order to realise investment returns,[43] rather than deriving such returns from a long-term commitment to the company and its productivity growth.[44] The commoditisation of the company as a tradeable asset in an institution's portfolio has two ramifications for public interest – one is the failure of a market mechanism for 'monitoring' the corporate sector[45] and the other is the prioritisation of short-term financial performance by companies as reflected in their share price returns. The latter phenomenon, known as 'short-termism', has an undesirable long-term impact on the health of the corporate sector and may undermine the likelihood of institutions meeting their investment promises to ultimate savers.

Although policy-makers have encouraged and nudged[46] institutional investors to become more engaged in corporate governance to overcome the market failure of their monitoring roles, we are observing new tendencies in relation to how institutions use their shareholder rights. In particular, Barker and Chiu observe a rise in 'instrumental' use of corporate governance rights by a variety of different institutions, i.e. pension funds, mutual funds, hedge funds, private equity funds and sovereign wealth funds, in different ways in order to further their own objectives and interests.[47]

Such an instrumental approach to corporate governance has been observed in contemporary shareholder activism since the 1990s, as shareholder activism began to arise in corporate America led by public sector pension funds such as CalPERS.[48] Shareholders have started to become engaged with their governance rights as the exploitation of these could relate to financial outcomes and improved investment gains. Such forms of shareholder activism, known as 'defensive activism', culminate in episodes of challenge by shareholders against management in relation to corporate underperformance so that corporations can take necessary steps, such as changing management, strategy etc. in order to address this.[49] Commentators have observed defensive activism at play as institutions agitated for CEO turnover in light of poor corporate perfor-

---

43 Dalia Tsuk, 'From Pluralism to Individualism: Berle and Means and 20th-Century American Legal Thought: The Modern Corporation and Private Property by Adolf A. Berle and Gardiner C. Means Review' (2005) 30 Law and Social Inquiry 179.

44 An alternative way as put forward by Colin Mayer, *Firm Commitment* (Oxford University Press 2013).

45 Paul Myners, *Institutional Investment in the UK: A Review* (HM Treasury 2001).

46 Via soft law, such as section E of the UK Corporate Governance Code, which applies on a 'comply or explain' basis, and the EU Shareholder Rights Directive 2007, which facilitates the exercising of voting rights.

47 See Barker and Chiu (n 38) 122–97.

48 See Chiu (n 42) 1–15.

49 Ibid 16–70.

mance.[50] Another area where defensive activism has been observed, especially in the UK, relates to shareholder discontent over high executive pay[51] where the performance of the company may not warrant such levels of pay. In 2012 a 'shareholder spring' over executive pay took place in the UK.[52] Although defensive activism may be important to protecting institutions' investment objectives and hence their beneficiary savers' interests, it has to be borne in mind that such activism is ultimately for the purposes of securing investors' expectations of corporate performance. If short-termism is pursued, the impact of such activism need not be socially desirable in the long term.

Empirical research carried out by Buchanan et al.[53] finds, very interestingly, that shareholders in the UK who enjoy more rights under the company law framework than those in the US find it less forbidding to engage in occasional episodes of engagement such as fielding shareholder proposals. However, such shareholders are largely conflicted, and the post-engagement impact on the company is markedly more negative than results in the US. That said, contrary research shows that the desire to please short-termist shareholders forces companies to be innovative, to grow and to undertake frequent strategic reviews such as diversification in order to be profitable, and this is often beneficial in the long term too.[54]

Hedge fund activism, a more recent phenomenon, is a more extreme example of the instrumental approach. This brand of activism is described as 'offensive activism' by Armour and Cheffins. Offensive activism involves taking an equity stake in a company in order to assume corporate governance interventions.[55] The corporate governance interventions are made in the hope of pursuing share price gains, and this has become an important investment

---

50 Mike Strivens, Susanne Espenlaub and Martin Walker, 'The Influence of Institutional Investors over CEO Turnover in the UK' (2008) http://ssrn.com/abstract=991595.

51 Ibid. This is not to say that such shareholder activism is based on sophisticated research or information processing, as some commentators found that much of shareholder activism against high pay is responsive to top-line figures only. This possibly reveals the superficiality of such shareholder engagement and also the desire on the part of institutions to minimise cost in demonstrating engagement. See Carsten Gerner-Buerle and Tom Kirschmaier, 'Say on Pay: Do Shareholders Care?' (2016) http://papers.ssrn.com/sol3/papers.cfm?abstract_id=2720481.

52 'Boards wake up to a shareholder spring', *Financial Times* (4 May 2012).

53 Bonnie G. Buchanan, Jeffrey M. Netter, Annette B. Poulsen and Tina Yang, 'Shareholder Proposal Rules and Practice: Evidence from a Comparison of the United States and United Kingdom' (2012) 49 Am. Bus. L.J. 739.

54 Mariassunta Gianetti and Xiaoyun Yu, 'The Corporate Finance Benefits of Short Horizon Investors' (ECGI Working Paper 2016).

55 John Armour and Brian Cheffins, 'The Rise and Fall (?) of Shareholder Activism by Hedge Funds' (2012) 14 J. Alternative Investments 17.

management strategy for activist hedge funds such as Carl Icahn's investment funds, Pershing Square and Ceviar Capital for example.

Hedge fund activism is based on an instrumental exploitation of shareholder rights in company law, whether the right to vote, influence or participate in decision-making at general meetings or to exercise voice in more informal ways. Partnoy and Thomas[56] refer to hedge fund activism as a form of 'financial innovation' in investment strategy that is mediated through its corporate governance role. Hedge funds have shown special interest in merger arbitrage, capital issues such as buybacks and dividends, and exploitation of short-term information asymmetries, all for the purposes of exploiting for financial gain. Further extreme forms of commoditisation of proprietary rights in relation to shareholding have been observed where hedge funds engage in empty voting, i.e. exercising the right of voting although they have hedged their interest in the shares away.[57] Although empty voting has not been observed to be on the rise or have caused deleterious effects generally, the perverse incentives in empty voting are of concern to policy-makers.[58]

A number of commentators[59] call such activists essential 'governance entrepreneurs' who provide a much-needed role in the market to monitor investee companies where institutional funds have been passive. Hedge fund activism, especially of the American brand,[60] could produce a wider effect upon corporate culture. Some commentators find qualitative changes in terms of better corporate governance and management accountability after an episode of hedge fund activism.[61] There seems to be a significant body of consistent[62] empirical evidence on positive operating performance for companies subject to

---

56 Frank S. Partnoy and Randall S. Thomas, 'Gap Filling, Hedge Funds, and Financial Innovation' (2006) http://ssrn.com/abstract=931254.

57 Henry T. C. Hu and Bernard B. S. Black, 'The New Vote Buying: Empty Voting and Hidden (Morphable) Ownership' (2006) 76 S. Cal. L. Rev. 811.

58 Wolf-Georg Ringe, 'Hedge Funds and Risk Decoupling: The Empty Voting Problem in the European Union' (2013) 36 Seattle U. L. Rev. 1027.

59 Paul Rose and Bernard Sharfman, 'Shareholder Activism as a Corrective Mechanism in Corporate Governance (2014) 5 B.Y.U. L. Rev. 1015; Bernard Sharfman, 'A Theory of Shareholder Activism and its Place in Corporate Law' (2015) 82 Tenn. L. Rev. 101.

60 Katelouzou (n 31) 459.

61 Shane Goodwin, Akshay Singh, Walter Slipetz and Ramesh Rao, 'Myopic Investor Myth Debunked: The Long-term Efficacy of Shareholder Advocacy in the Boardroom' (2014) http://ssrn.com/abstract=2555701.

62 But see evidence to the contrary, John C. Coffee and Darius Palia, 'The Impact of Hedge Fund Activism: Evidence and Implications' (2014) http://ssrn.com/abstract=2496518; Frank Partnoy, 'U.S. Hedge Fund Activism' (2015) http://ssrn.com/abstract=2585290.

activist campaigns five to ten years after the campaign has concluded and the hedge fund has exited.[63] There is, however, also contrary empirical evidence.[64]

Other commentators[65] are of the view that hedge fund activism only brings disruption to the management role that mediates all stakeholders' needs in relation to the corporation and causes imbalance and board capture to shareholder demands. Empirical research[66] shows that only the most disruptive forms of shareholder activism, such as agitating for the merger, sale or sale of part of a company achieve significant share price reactions. Such disruptive behaviour could be deleterious to stakeholder interests.[67]

In sum, the dominance of institutional shareholders and their assumption of corporate governance roles (or assumed by asset managers as their delegates) have raised issues of public interest. Their broad footprint raises their corporate governance roles to a social scale of importance, and the nature of their engagement with shareholder rights impacts upon the corporate sector as a whole. We see regulatory law gradually arising to address issues of shareholder conduct and I turn to three examples below.

B. Prohibition Against Private Equity Funds from Asset Stripping

Private equity buy-out funds take controlling stakes in mature businesses, whether to assist a management buy-out, or to take a publicly listed company

---

[63] Lucian Bebchuk, Alon Brav and Wei Jiang, 'The Long-Term Effects of Hedge Fund Activism' (2015) 115 Colum. L. Rev. 2085; Marco Becht, Julian Franks, Jeremy Grant and Hannes Wagner, 'The Returns to Hedge Fund Activism: An International Study' (2014) http://ssrn.com/abstract=2376271; Alon Brav, Wei Jiang and Hyunseob Kim, 'The Real Effects of Hedge Fund Activism: Productivity, Asset Allocation, and Labor Outcomes' (2015) http://ssrn.com/abstract=1551953. On medium-term value creation, see Nick W. A. Stokman, 'Influences of Hedge Fund Activism on the Medium Term Target Value' (2007) http://ssrn.com/abstract=1019968.

[64] Coffee and Palia (n 62); Partnoy (n 62).

[65] David J. Berger and Kenneth M. Murray, 'As the Market Turns: Corporate Governance Litigation in an Age of Stockholder Activism' (2009) 5 N.Y.U. J.L. & Bus. 207; Dan Bernhardt and Ed Nosal, 'Gambling for Dollars: Strategic Hedge Fund Manager Investment' (2013) http://ssrn.com/abstract=2367475; William W. Bratton, 'Hedge Funds and Governance Targets' (2007) 95 Geo. L.J. 1375. But see Katelouzou (n 31) 459.

[66] 'Activist hedge funds not so good for shareholders', *Financial Times* (20 May 2015); Marco Becht, Julian Franks, Jeremy Grant and Hannes Wagner, 'The Returns to Hedge Fund Activism: An International Study' (2014) http://ssrn.com/abstract=2376271.

[67] Robby Heuben and Gert Straetmans, 'Shareholder Rights and Responsibilities in the Context of Corporate Social Responsibility' (2016) 27 Eur. Bus. L. Rev. 615 argue that some forms of offensive activism raise the risk profile of the company, having implications for its cost of raising capital and its longer-term prospects.

private. Although they may change the company's strategy and improve efficiencies and operating performance, they are controversial for their extractive behaviour in relation to portfolio companies. Buy-out funds often favour short-term structuring such as selling off freeholds,[68] selling off ancillary (though viable) businesses for a short-term gain,[69] or cutting costs, such as by reduction of workforce and investment, in order to extract investment gains quickly.

The relative opacity and unaccountability of buy-out funds' roles in their portfolio companies, as well as allegations of wealth transfer, have caused concern. In 2007 Sir David Walker recommended that buy-out-owned portfolio companies with a market capitalisation exceeding £300 million, with over 1,000 full-time equivalent UK employees and generating at least 50 per cent of revenues in the UK, should make yearly enhanced disclosures to the public in addition to yearly financial information filing.

The Alternative Investment Fund Managers Directive (AIFM Directive), transposed into Regulations in the UK,[70] now provides for regulatory scrutiny by compelling disclosure by fund managers leading up to the buy-out, as well as post buy-out. Where a buy-out fund has obtained control of the non-listed portfolio company, disclosures have to be made to the company (in particular its employees), shareholders and the FCA in relation to the identity of the fund managers and funds that have acquired control; their policies in managing conflicts of interest between the funds, managers and portfolio company; and their policies relating to employees and employment in the portfolio company.[71] The AIFM Directive also requires yearly annual reporting that the portfolio company makes to shareholders to be made available to employees.[72] The AIFM Directive's most robust and direct attack upon buy-out funds' extractive behaviour is found in Article 30, which prohibits fund managers for a period of 24 months after the buy-out from supporting in any way asset stripping of the portfolio company by way of capital reductions, distributions, redemption of shares or acquisition of own shares. Fund managers are prevented from voting in favour of such resolutions and are held to a duty to use best efforts to prevent asset stripping from taking place.[73]

---

[68] Jules Domenichini, 'Public to Private Transactions, Private Equity Ownership and IPOs: A Case Study of Debenhams' (2012) http://ssrn.com/abstract=1516293.

[69] Jonathan Ford, 'Private equity, not the mobile, killed Phones 4U', *Financial Times* (21 September 2014).

[70] Financial Services and Markets (The Alternative Fund Managers) Regulations 2013, Part 5, regs 34ff.

[71] AIFMD, Art. 28; Financial Services and Markets (The Alternative Fund Managers) Regulations 2013, reg 39.

[72] AIFMD, Art. 29.

[73] Ibid Art. 30.

These measures regulate the conduct of private equity funds as controlling shareholders of portfolio companies, intervening into the 'private freedoms' of shareholder rights. Presumably, the investment regulator in each Member State, such as the UK FCA, can take enforcement action against private equity funds that are in breach of Article 30 or disclosure obligations. Such enforcement can be by way of fines or censure.[74] These measures are aimed at meeting the public interest in ensuring that portfolio companies of a certain social footprint are not exploited to the disadvantage of stakeholders such as employees, but in doing so, the balances in private law are recalibrated in favour of public or social interest.

C. Enhanced Listing Regime

Listing rules were introduced to subject controlling shareholders of UK Premium-listed companies on the London Stock Exchange to certain standards of conduct, in order to address possible exploitation of minority shareholders and poor corporate governance.[75]

The first key component of the Enhanced Listing Regime is that, if a Premium-listed company has a controlling shareholder,[76] the controlling shareholder must enter into a mandatory agreement[77] with the company. This agreement is intended to regulate the blockholder's influence over the company, ensure that the company's constitution does not undermine the position of minority shareholders and preserve the 'independence' of the business. The aim is to limit the extent of private benefit that can be extracted by controlling shareholders as well as mitigating the lack of accountability to minority shareholders.

Business 'independence' is defined in broad terms, meaning that the company is not overly reliant on conducting business with the controlling shareholder or on access to the controlling shareholder for financing. All commercial transactions and arrangements conducted with the controlling shareholder have to be at arm's length and on normal commercial terms. If a Premium-listed company fails to put in place a mandatory agreement, or

---

[74] There is no enforcement to report to date.

[75] The scandals involving Bumi plc and ENRC, which have now delisted, culminated in these reforms, see discussion in Roger M. Barker and Iris H-Y. Chiu, 'Protecting Minority Shareholders in Blockholder-Controlled Companies – Evaluating the UK's Enhanced Listing Regime in Comparison with Investor Protection Regimes in New York and Hong Kong' (2015) 10 Cap. Markets L.J. 98.

[76] Defined as a shareholder with control of at least 30 per cent of the voting shares.

[77] Listing Rules 6.1.4ff. It is not necessary that every controlling shareholder enters into a separate agreement.

fails to comply with the independence terms, or if an independent director on the board is of the view that the agreement is not complied with, then minority independent shareholders are given extra monitoring powers to veto all related-party transactions.[78]

A second key aspect of the Enhanced Listing Regime introduces a re-ordering of voting rights under certain circumstances. This aims to give more weight to minority shareholders' voice than would ordinarily be the case in the general meeting. In particular, independent minority shareholders are provided with additional voice when appointing independent directors or when a cancellation of the Premium listing is proposed. Their approval by majority is sought as a class instead of being subsumed under the general meeting, although in the case of electing independent directors, a protest vote of independent shareholders can only temporarily delay the majority decision for a period of 90 days.

Minority shareholder protection may be regarded as a 'private matter' for company law enforcement. Hence the nature of enforcement set out above is a regulatory-assisted form of enforcement by minority shareholders and independent directors. The nature of enforcement reflects an interesting hybrid of maintaining the 'privateness' of shareholder relations *inter se* yet recognising that regulatory assistance is required in view of the inequalities in power. We can even regard the elevated status of minority protection standards as an exercise of transaction cost reduction by regulatory standardisation. By imposing regulatory standards, an even level of protection desired by the market is provided without the need for costly individual bargaining. The 'regulatory' aspect of such enforcement is accounted for based on the public interest in minority protection in these companies, which have a larger social footprint than in the case of private companies. Further, the London Stock Exchange has an interest in maintaining its reputable global brand as a marketplace for well-governed companies that inspire investor participation. This regime meets a mixture of private and public interest and incorporates both private and regulatory-led aspects in enforcement.

D. Stewardship Norms

An area of soft law worth noting is the development of 'stewardship norms' in the UK and EU, as best practices in shareholder conduct. Whether we are concerned about shareholder apathy or instrumental forms of shareholder activism, these best practices seem to chart a blueprint for optimal and constructive forms of engagement, focused on the medium to long term and avoiding only the pursuit of selfish interests. As shareholder conduct is essentially a private

---

[78] With no minimum size threshold.

matter under company law, the Code's inroad into governing shareholder conduct is subtle and based on 'nudge' and soft law.

The UK Stewardship Code was developed in 2010[79] by the investment industry and the Financial Reporting Council (FRC) to require institutions to develop stewardship policies to integrate corporate governance roles into their investment management, engage in informal engagement (including escalations where justified), voting, public disclosure and the management of conflicts of interest. It remains uncertain whether stewardship meets institutions' private investment objectives and improves upon their fiduciary accountability to beneficiaries, or it is purposed to meet public interest in terms of becoming a constructive force for shaping corporate behaviour and performance for the long term.[80] However these provide a conduct template whether for passive and disinterested institutions or for activist ones that approach their corporate governance roles instrumentally. The EU has adopted similar stewardship notions in the recent Shareholder Rights Directive 2017,[81] also purposing them as soft law subject to a comply-or-explain basis, but more overtly connecting the norms of institutional shareholder conduct to social expectations.[82] The Directive sets out expectations of constructive engagement with a view to companies' long-term performance and mandates public disclosure of various aspects of investment management and how they affect institutions' corporate governance roles.

Stewardship norms are fashioned as soft law but their quasi-public interest nature can be discerned in the FRC's oversight role of the Code and practice of stewardship.

E. Stewardship as Quasi-public Standards for Shareholder Conduct?

The Stewardship Code is overseen by the FRC, which is a body responsible for setting accounting standards, overseeing financial reporting by companies and disciplining auditors. The Code is open to voluntary signatories and therefore has no universal binding force as public standards of conduct for institutional shareholders. However, the Code principles set a bar in terms of the constructive and balanced manner of shareholder engagement expected on the part of institutions.

---

79 Version now as of 2016, https://www.frc.org.uk/investors/uk-stewardship-code.

80 Iris H-Y. Chiu, 'Institutional Shareholders as Stewards: Towards a New Conception of Corporate Governance?' (2012) 6 Brook. J. Corp. Fin. & Com. L. 387.

81 Directive 2017/828/EU of the European Parliament and of the Council of 17 May 2017 amending Directive 2007/36/EC as regards the encouragement of long-term shareholder engagement, Art. 3g–3i.

82 Preamble, Recitals 14–16.

In theory, the conduct of stewardship would be primarily scrutinised by institutions' beneficiaries whose savings are pooled in institutions' funds. Beneficiaries have, under trust or contract law, the right even to instruct their funds to exercise corporate governance rights.[83] Further, the Code explicitly reinforces beneficiaries' right under trust or contract law to demand institutions to provide yearly accounts of how stewardship has been conducted.[84] However, beneficiaries' actions and scrutiny are likely to be limited. Savers are too dispersed and apathetic, and are unlikely to amount to a force to be reckoned with.

Code signatories have taken to rhetorical adoption of the Code in order to make positive impressions for themselves without really putting the Code into practice. Hence, the FRC has taken it upon itself to exert pressure on signatory institutions to adhere to the Code in a spirited manner. The FRC has introduced a tiering system in order to place Code signatories into two tiers, the top tier representing robust adherence to the Code and the lower tier representing more cosmetic alignment.[85] This also means that the FRC has assumed implicit responsibility for monitoring the conduct of stewardship in accordance with Code standards and has made quasi-regulatory judgements.

The EU Shareholder Rights Directive has also adopted shareholder engagement as a best practice for institutions subject to comply-or-explain.[86] Institutions and their investment chain, including asset managers and proxy advisers, are subject to extensive disclosure obligations about how management of assets would deliver the long-term interests of beneficiaries and how exercising corporate governance roles in their equity investments would play a part towards that.[87] The Directive has moved one step further by connecting shareholder engagement with both the private interest of meeting beneficiaries' long-term objectives as well as the public interest of collectively meeting savers' financial interests in the future. It remains uncertain whether any public enforcement can take place on the basis of the mandatory disclosures required or institutions' (perhaps sub-optimal) shareholder conduct. Institutions and proxy advisers are required to make public disclosures of their engagement policy and code of conduct respectively[88] but asset managers report to their institutional clients, not publicly.[89] There is no enforcement authority for the

---

[83] Ewan McGaughey, 'Does Corporate Governance Exclude the Ultimate Investor?' (2015) 16 J. Corp. L. Stud. 221.

[84] Principle 7.

[85] FRC, 'Tiering of Stewardship Code Signatories', https://www.frc.org.uk/investors/uk-stewardship-code/uk-stewardship-code-statements.

[86] Art. 3g.

[87] Art. 3g–3j.

[88] Art. 3h, 3j.

[89] Art. 3i.

public disclosures as this is not framed as securities regulation.[90] In the UK, the FRC may by extension of its oversight of the Stewardship Code oversee the relevant disclosures but there is no formal enforcement power that can be exercised. Without a clear means of public enforcement, beneficiaries' private demands for accountability or enforcement rights would remain the only means of enforcement. This default position characterises the Directive's provisions as facilitating largely private enforcement, an anomalous position given the public-interest underpinnings of the provisions.[91] This is an area that ambivalently straddles private law, where shareholder conduct is not regulated by *ex ante* norms, and securities regulation, where standards consistent with market expectations *should* be imposed. The merging of 'private shareholder conduct' with the expectations of institutions as socially representative investors has created an ambivalent issue area whose nature remains unresolved.

V. CONCLUSION

Although we are able to distil the typical characteristics of private and public enforcement against shareholders, the dividing line is blurring in the case of securities regulation being extended to regulate shareholder conduct in certain instances. Dynamics in corporate governance have long been recognised in company law as a private matter and it is inherently difficult for regulators to provide *ex ante* standards or to judge shareholder conduct *ex post.* Even directors' duties which are subject to *ex ante* standards remain privately enforced under company law.[92] However, protections of disadvantaged groups, such as minority shareholders and stakeholders, may perhaps be most efficiently secured through standardisation of conduct rules in relation to intractable and established problems. Katelouzou and I have argued a case for regulating institutions' corporate governance conduct more generally as meeting aspects of public interest[93] so that regulatory enforcement can become more formalised and empowered. The regulators' role is important in light of the lack of monitoring by dispersed saver-beneficiaries. The regulator's public-interest-based perspectives can also be important in moderating the social externalities of 'private' corporate governance, where neither corporate behaviour nor the

---

[90] See discussion in Chapter 7.

[91] Iris H-Y. Chiu and Dionysia Katelouzou, 'Making a Case for Regulating Institutional Shareholders' Corporate Governance Roles' [2018] J. Bus. L. 67.

[92] Companies Act 2006, ss 170–177.

[93] Iris H-Y. Chiu and Dionysia Katelouzou, 'From Shareholder Stewardship to Shareholder Duties: Is the Time Ripe?' in Hanne S. Birkmose (ed), *Shareholder Duties in the EU* (Wolters Kluwer International 2017).

corporate governance roles of investors are aligned with public interest.[94] The 'private' dimension remains important for individual entities to seek compensatory redress where relevant and I do not envisage the eclipse of private enforcement by public enforcement. However, points of reconciliation would need to be constantly redrawn as the publicisation of norms and enforcement develops in the future in relation to shareholder conduct.

[94] See, e.g., the discussion in relation to bank corporate governance leading up to the global financial crisis, in Mads Andenas and Iris H-Y. Chiu, *The Foundations and Future of Financial Regulation* (Routledge 2014) chapter 13, and citations therein.

7. Legal vs social enforcement of shareholder duties

Konstantinos Sergakis

I. INTRODUCTION

Enforcement mechanisms are crucial to the viability of businesses and capital markets at large, as they purport to hold accountable legal and natural persons who violate applicable rules, as well as to inculcate a sound compliance culture and sensible market practices into such persons. On the one hand, legal (public and private) enforcement constitutes the core element of a wider EU and international trend towards deterrence, dissuasion and compensation. Academic literature has not conclusively determined which enforcement means are preferable. On the other hand, social enforcement (for example, 'name and shame') is based on softer tools that inform interested parties of a violation so as to trigger cascading effects on investors, third parties and stakeholders at large. The reputational effects upon persons that have breached duties therefore becomes the main enforcement mechanism of social sanctions. Such social approaches have traditionally been used for companies, and can also be extended to some shareholder duties, since they offer a less interventionist approach to an emerging area.

This chapter aims to decipher the adaptability and efficiency of both legal and social enforcement mechanisms in the area of shareholder duties. It covers both traditional[1] and emerging (namely governance and engagement)[2] share-

[1] 'Traditional shareholder duties' is a term used in this chapter to denote the well-known shareholder duties that have been introduced in the history of company and capital markets law. See Section II for a brief introduction.

[2] 'Emerging shareholder duties' is used for all the new duties introduced by the revised Shareholder Rights Directive: Directive 2017/828/EU of the European Parliament and of the Council of 17 May 2017 amending Directive 2007/36/EC as regards the encouragement of long-term shareholder engagement [2017] OJ L132/1. See Section II for a brief introduction.

holder duties in an overarching and policy-oriented approach.[3] It critically challenges the general orientation of legal systems towards desirable levels of efficiency within a mixture of soft law and hard law norms. I endeavour to contribute to the emerging debate about the range and feasibility of enforcement mechanisms in the area of shareholder duties by advocating that both legal and social enforcement mechanisms must be combined to achieve optimal impact on shareholder practices without deterring investment and capital-raising operations. Furthermore, I argue that although legal enforcement has a clear and well-established *raison d'être* in the area of the traditional shareholder duties, it currently sits uncomfortably with the conceptual and operational spectrum of emerging duties. Indeed, social enforcement has significant merits in the area of the emerging duties and should stand as a viable alternative to legal enforcement, at least at the current stage.

The chapter will conclude with a series of proposals that could be taken into consideration for any future reform of enforcement mechanisms in the area of shareholder duties. In parallel, it proposes the need to rethink current legislative initiatives in this area and to strike a new balance between legal and social enforcement in order to shape a more meaningful and efficient enforcement landscape.

II. BACKGROUND OF SHAREHOLDER DUTIES AND THEIR ENFORCEMENT

Traditional shareholder duties vary considerably depending on their sources (contractual arrangements, statutory provisions and general legal principles), purpose (protection of the investee company, shareholders, stakeholders, market integrity and other constituencies), the types of companies or business situations within which they apply, and the types of shareholders (retail and institutional) that are supposed to fulfil them.[4] Although their presence within the company law and capital markets law frameworks has been solidly established, their interpretation, characterization and applicability have not always been viewed as a straightforward exercise.

This is due to the fact that the shareholders who are supposed to exercise such duties may not be directly identifiable, or the duties themselves may not be applied across different jurisdictions in the same way on account of variable

---

[3] A more in-depth analysis of some enforcement aspects is offered by Jennifer Payne and Elizabeth Howell (Chapter 9) Iris H-Y. Chiu (Chapter 6) and Corrado Malberti (Chapter 5).

[4] For a complete overview, see Hanne S. Birkmose and Florian Möslein, 'Mapping Shareholders' Duties' in Hanne S. Birkmose (ed), *Shareholders' Duties* (Kluwer Law International 2017).

cultural, political and legal traditions.[5] Notwithstanding some inevitable obstacles in their application, legal (private and public) enforcement mechanisms of these duties are laid out and are used, with various nuances, at the national and EU levels. Indeed, legislators have traditionally opted for legal enforcement to ensure a minimum respect for shareholder duties across different situations and market actors. Social enforcement in this framework has not yet acquired significant importance, notwithstanding some recent laudable efforts,[6] mainly due to shareholder apathy towards violations of shareholder duties or a tendency for such violations to be rapidly 'forgotten'.

In parallel to the traditional shareholder duties, the emergence of new shareholder duties, based on the stewardship and shareholder engagement concepts, has recently gained momentum across the EU,[7] and the Commission proceeded to an amendment of the Shareholder Rights Directive with the aim of encouraging long-term shareholder engagement.[8] Aiming to increase transparency in financial intermediation, Article 3g of the amended Shareholder Rights Directive requires Member States to ensure that institutional investors and asset managers will develop an 'engagement policy' that defines the general way they will exercise their activities with regard to the integration of shareholder engagement into their strategy, the monitoring of and dialogue with investee companies, the exercise of voting rights, the use of proxy advisory services and cooperation with other shareholders.[9] Most importantly, this engagement policy must describe how they manage actual or potential conflicts of interest that may arise in this framework. They are also expected to describe in this policy how they monitor investee companies with regard to non-financial performance and social and environmental impact, as well as how they communicate with relevant stakeholders of these companies.

The enlargement of the engagement spectrum is – in theory – welcome, but it may prove to be problematic in practice since non-financial elements and stakeholders may be difficult to evaluate, disclose and describe in a meaning-

---

5 Some jurisdictions may be more open to the imposition of such duties than others. National courts may also adopt different stances as to the recognition and enforcement of such duties.

6 See Section IV.

7 Blanaid Clarke, 'The EU's Shareholder Empowerment Model in the Context of the Sustainable Companies Agenda' (2014) 11(2) European Company Law 103; Florian Möslein and Karsten Engsig Sørensen, 'Nudging for Corporate Long-Termism and Sustainability? Regulatory Instruments from a Comparative and Functional Perspective' (2017) https://ssrn.com/abstract=2987734.

8 Directive 2017/828/EU.

9 Ibid art. 3g.

ful way.[10] EU law has undoubtedly taken this into account, which is why such disclosure obligations will function in accordance with the 'comply or explain' principle;[11] institutional investors and asset managers will either declare compliance with these requirements or publicly disclose an explanation as to why they have chosen not to comply with one or more requirements. The flexibility given to investors in this framework is considerable since they can disregard certain or all requirements, while nevertheless being expected to explain their stance in a clear and reasoned way. Experience gained from the application of this same principle in the corporate governance statements issued by companies in various jurisdictions has shown that the explanatory part is not meaningful most of the time;[12] such reservations with regard to the efficiency of this principle in this new emerging area thus still hold true.

From the above-mentioned disclosure obligations, we can observe a shift of attention from a purely private company law agenda (with enabling rules among shareholders and companies) towards a top-down capital markets law agenda (with stricter requirements based on increased disclosure obligations for all market actors in the investment chain).[13] Institutional investors and asset managers are now expected to make public various facets of their engagement with companies, shareholders and stakeholders. Such widely applicable disclosure obligations reflect EU law's vision about the future role that such investors are expected to play with regard to a wider range of actors in capital markets. Chiu and Katelouzou have opined that we are witnessing a legaliza-

---

[10] Ibid, art. 3h also aims to frame the investment strategy of institutional investors and their arrangements with asset managers by introducing a series of disclosure obligations. Institutional investors must publicly disclose, among other things, how the investment strategy they adopt is in line with the profile and duration of their liabilities and how it contributes to the medium- to long-term performance of their assets. Asset managers are also expected to disclose on an annual basis to institutional investors, with which they have arrangements, how their investment strategy complies with such arrangements and contributes to the medium- and long-term performance of the assets of the institutional investor: ibid, art. 3i.

[11] On the various aspects of this principle in this area, see Iain MacNeil and Xiao Li, 'Comply or Explain: Market Discipline and Non-Compliance with the Combined Code' (2006) 14(5) Corporate Governance: An International Review 486; Andrew Keay, 'Comply or Explain in Corporate Governance Codes: In Need of Greater Regulatory Oversight?' (2014) 34(2) Legal Studies 279; Konstantinos Sergakis, 'Deconstruction and Reconstruction of the "Comply or Explain" Principle in EU Capital Markets' (2015) 5(3) Accounting, Economics and Law: A Convivium 233.

[12] Marc T. Moore, '"Whispering Sweet Nothings": The Limitations of Informal Conformance in UK Corporate Governance' (2009) 9 J. Corp. L. Stud. 95.

[13] On the more general distinction between the private or facilitative law and public or regulatory law, see Marc T. Moore, *Corporate Governance in the Shadow of the State* (Hart Publishing 2013).

tion of stewardship via the introduction of a duty to demonstrate engagement, which is based on public interests that aim to re-regulate this area.[14]

Yet is disclosure enough on its own to ensure engagement and long-termism in capital markets? Indeed, these new obligations may be viewed in a more critical light; Birkmose has noted that disclosure in this area will not necessarily increase the low levels of engagement since it does not create any financial incentives for investors towards the accomplishment of such role. At a parallel level, it may increase the costs of engagement if the ultimate beneficiaries start exerting pressure upon institutional investors for more engagement.[15]

Questions therefore arise regarding the enforcement methods for these shareholder duties as it will prove particularly difficult to achieve meaningful compliance with these broadly formulated provisions, which are also based on the 'comply or explain' principle. Moreover, legal sanctions potentially imposed in this area, given the legalization of stewardship as previously mentioned, may raise doubts about their legitimacy given the lack of clarity of the duties themselves, the difficulty in deciphering the expected outcome of such duties, and the embryonic stage of their understanding by courts and national competent authorities (NCAs). A role for social enforcement is therefore a legitimate step forward, as will be shown later in this chapter, and will allow such duties to evolve within a framework of increased dialogue, higher standards for common understanding by the parties concerned and – ultimately – their applicability.

Having provided a background of both traditional and emerging shareholder duties, as well as an initial look at the important role that various enforcement mechanisms could play in both frameworks, the analysis will now focus on the specific elements of both legal and social enforcement so as to examine their usefulness and efficiency in this framework.

III. LEGAL ENFORCEMENT

Legal enforcement strategies in corporate and capital markets law have traditionally relied on two main operational pillars: public enforcement, which refers to criminal or administrative proceedings, and private enforcement, which consists of civil claims by harmed parties due to violations of the applicable legal rules. The analysis will aim to highlight the merits and shortfalls

---

[14] Iris H-Y. Chiu and Dionysia Katelouzou, 'From Shareholder Stewardship to Shareholder Duties: Is the Time Ripe?' in Hanne S. Birkmose (ed), *Shareholders' Duties* (Kluwer Law International 2017) 143.

[15] Hanne S. Birkmose, 'European Challenges for Institutional Investor Engagement – Is Mandatory Disclosure the Way Forward' (2014) 2 Eur. Company & Fin. L. Rev. 214, 236.

of both enforcement systems in capital markets law in general and in relation to imposing duties on various market actors (for example, issuers). It will then apply *mutatis mutandis* these elements in the area of shareholder duties to test their adaptability and efficiency in the specific framework of this chapter.

Driven by the ramifications of the global financial crisis, national laws have considerably strengthened – at least on paper – their formal sanction mechanisms to increase deterrence and punish various types of violations more severely. Nevertheless, the imposition of sanctions has, in practice, proven to be a particularly complex task. Historically, legislation in various countries has treated several violations differently, undoubtedly reflecting countries' cultural, political and legal traditions, and related, among other factors, to the political determination to tackle illegal behaviour efficiently; to the regulators' sophistication with regard to deciphering complex market practices; and to 'regulatory capture' issues. Choosing enforcement practices that are commensurate with and efficiently targeted to the distinctive features of each rule-breaking incident can prove to be quite arduous. This is due not only to the particulars of each case of reprehensible behaviour, which inevitably vary across different types of market actors and different markets at large, but also to the different symbolic connotations conveyed by each enforcement mechanism.

The creation of the EU internal market and the risks associated with national legal practices have triggered a series of initiatives aimed at harmonizing enforcement measures at the EU level. Overall, these initiatives show some accomplishments. For example, a common understanding has gradually emerged that similar breaches of legal rules in different jurisdictions must be sanctioned with equal severity at the EU level. Nevertheless, considerable differences persist at the national level, creating discrepancies between national laws and opening space for regulatory competition. Sanction strategies in various legal systems have therefore failed to demonstrate their effectiveness in terms of punishment and dissuasion, either because the applicable framework is not stringent enough or because its implementation lacks consistency, frequency and rigour.

The distinctive merits of such mechanisms in ensuring accountability, restoring justice and shifting social norms make them worthy of more extensive research and greater attention from policymakers to ensure their efficiency and their impact on various market actors.

Public and private enforcement approaches currently coexist as part of a wider EU and international trend towards deterrence, dissuasion and compensation. Academic literature has not conclusively determined which enforcement means is preferable; various authors have offered different views on the importance and usefulness of various types of enforcement mechanisms.[16] On the one hand, there is a doctrinal trend favouring the efficiency of 'private enforcement', based on the argument that private parties have more incentives to bring a civil claim against non-compliant behaviour.[17] On the other hand, a more holistic conception of enforcement mechanisms has been advanced, which can secure the protection of capital markets from defective strategies, namely that 'public enforcement' has an important role to play.[18] The EU legislature has aimed to reinforce harmonization trends in various areas of capital markets law with regard to enforcement mechanisms but the steps taken are perfectible since they leave considerable space for the persistence of national idiosyncrasies. Indeed, the difference between national legal provisions is striking despite these harmonization trends.

A. Private Enforcement

Starting with general considerations of the merits and problematic aspects of private enforcement, civil liability is admittedly a characteristic example of an enforcement scheme that has not yet made a convincing case for its own merits for two main reasons:

a. civil liability mechanisms rely on the motivation of private parties, and
b. they have not been harmonized across the EU so as to provide such parties with facilitated cross-border access to compensation.

Private enforcement presents, in theory, the advantage of motivating private parties to take action so as to defend their interests against a violation and seek compensation for the loss suffered. Nevertheless, one of the most common problems in this area is that reliance upon such parties depends on their incentives to initiate litigation and seek compensation. Indeed, shifting the debate to the area of shareholder duties, shareholder apathy may be particularly damaging in this context, resulting in a theoretically efficient framework rarely being used and losing significance. The uncertainty that derives from this observa-

---

[16] On the coexistence of public and private enforcement in the area of shareholder duties, see Chapter 6.

[17] Rafael La Porta, Florencio Lopez-de-Silanes and Andrei Shleifer, 'What Works in Securities Laws?' (2006) 61 J. Finance 1.

[18] Bernard S. Black, 'The Legal and Institutional Preconditions for Strong Securities Markets' (2001) 48 UCLA L. Rev. 781; Michelle Welsh and Vince Morabito, 'Public vs Private Enforcement of Securities Laws: An Australian Empirical Study' (2014) 14(1) J. Corp. L. Stud. 39. On the coexistence and the distinctive features of private and public enforcement, see Guido Ferrarini and Paolo Giudici, 'Financial Scandals and the Role of Private Enforcement: The Parmalat Case' (2005) ECGI – Law Working Paper No. 40/2005, 42, http://ssrn.com/abstract=730403.

tion makes the prospects of private enforcement less promising. Shareholders may feel less interested in pursuing litigation against other shareholders, and the same phenomenon may prove to be true in the case of companies that may be reluctant to initiate litigation against their majority shareholders.

Moreover, the discrepancies among national laws in private enforcement mechanisms are striking. Some Member States have traditionally been more receptive to the implementation of civil liability regimes, unlike others that continue to have very complex or less protective civil liability provisions. Moreover, there are continuous obstacles to the establishment of individual responsibility across the EU,[19] and some jurisdictions' current efforts to accentuate individual responsibility lack efficiency due to ambiguous wording or the absence of a common understanding of the contours of such responsibility.

Going beyond the mere existence of different civil liability provisions across the EU, national courts also apply civil liability rules in different ways, depending on their legal traditions; the discrepancies in terms of both the content of the provisions and the applicability by the courts result in diverging levels of investor protection across the EU. The persistent uncertainty around this issue does not favour the creation of a rigorous accountability framework for shareholders as the risks of liability arbitrage among different jurisdictions will certainly continue to play a major role for issuers or market actors when choosing capital markets for their activities in the EU.

In some (but very few) areas of capital markets law, related to issuers and not to shareholders,[20] the EU has attempted to provide a common framework that establishes an obligation for national laws to include civil liability provisions, while leaving it up to Member States to determine the *modus operandi* of such provisions. Consequently, it has not yet offered a convincing liability

---

[19] See, e.g., civil liability rules in the area of issuer periodic disclosure obligations, which provide that 'responsibility for information prepared and disclosed … should lie at least with the issuer *or* its own administrative, management or supervisory bodies' (emphasis added): art. 7 of Directive 2013/50/EU of the European Parliament and of the Council of 22 October 2013 amending Directive 2004/109/EC of the European Parliament and of the Council on the harmonisation of transparency requirements in relation to information about issuers whose securities are admitted to trading on a regulated market, Directive 2003/71/EC of the European Parliament and of the Council on the prospectus to be published when securities are offered to the public or admitted to trading, and Commission Directive 2007/14/EC laying down detailed rules for the implementation of certain provisions of Directive 2004/109/EC [2013] OJ L294/13.

[20] See, e.g., civil liability for infringements related to prospectus disclosure obligations: art. 11 of Regulation (EU) 2017/1129 of the European Parliament and of the Council of 14 June 2017 on the prospectus to be published when securities are offered to the public or admitted to trading on a regulated market, and repealing Directive 2003/71/EC [2017] OJ L168/12.

regime at the EU level but has only shown, in an experimental way, the first steps towards a broader and more harmonized future civil liability regime provided that political determination allows such developments to take place.

Adding to these concerns, investors across the EU do not benefit from a facilitated procedural framework that would allow them to bring an action to court without being forced to face dissuasive cost, resource and time constraints. As a result, they feel less incentivized to perform this role and to seek compensation for the harm suffered. It also seems surprising that EU law has shown a timid move towards the acceptance of private enforcement in some areas – therefore asking indirectly for market actors to assume a sanctioning role in capital markets[21] – while at the same time refraining from convincing national laws to ease the exercise of civil claims.

Although legal transplants of US-style class actions to the EU would not necessarily be the preferred way forward,[22] given the numerous market, legal and cultural specificities and constraints of EU Member States, the question remains open: do investors deserve a facilitated path to launching a civil action given the interconnectivity of capital markets and the need to offer the same level of protection across the EU? If the answer is yes and if EU law is not yet in a position to harmonize this field further given the above-mentioned constraints, then national laws need to offer concrete and convincing solutions for an efficient and facilitated access to civil procedures.

Harmonization of civil liability regimes in capital markets law not only corresponds to a legitimate need for protection and compensation, but also goes hand in hand with an ever-growing cross-border operational framework for shareholders, whose violations of their duties may impact various actors in different jurisdictions. It therefore remains to be seen whether the political willingness at the EU level will in the future be decisive in overcoming the barriers of different legal traditions.

I argue that, notwithstanding these difficulties, private enforcement remains, to a great extent, the most appropriate spectrum of action for dealing with violations of shareholder duties within the scope of company law. Violations of shareholder duties have primarily been conceived as a company law matter, directly related to the private aspects of relationships arising between shareholders and companies. Market actors harmed by infringements committed by natural or legal persons need to receive appropriate compensation for their

---

21 Indeed, although compensation should be distinguished from deterrence, as private enforcement serves primarily the first function, compensatory schemes should also be seen as indirect deterrence mechanisms given their dissuasive function for the repetition of infringements by defendants.

22 Rüdiger Veil (ed), *European Capital Markets Law* (2nd edn, Hart Publishing 2017) 178.

loss; the compensatory function also serves as a deterrent to prevent similar infringements from recurring in the future, as well as accountability at large for the persons concerned. Nevertheless, civil claims related to the breach of shareholder duties have not always been successful, and – as we have seen – various obstacles remain.[23]

As capital market law violations have gradually gained importance, the visibility of private enforcement has declined since public enforcement has taken on a more prominent role in the defence of public interests (such as market integrity) that go beyond the purely private (company and shareholder) interests potentially affected by a breach of shareholder duties.

B. Public Enforcement

Public enforcement lies within the sphere of administrative and criminal sanctions. Beginning our analysis with a general view of the rules laid out in capital markets law (whose features also apply – already or prospectively, as we will see later in this chapter, to violations of shareholder duties), administrative sanctions and measures have probably been the only sanctions framework that has been promoted with such certainty at the EU level. The reason behind this legislative choice is undoubtedly NCA status and structure; NCAs are nowadays the focal point in capital markets regulation given their 'know-how' and their ongoing contact with markets and market actors. They are considered to be the most suitable sources for sanctions also because they are considerably faster than civil or criminal courts in investigating and imposition sanctions. Various EU legislative texts provide for both sanctions and measures, the former being mainly handled through pecuniary sanctions that are now subject to minimum harmonization rules[24] and the latter aiming to serve other objectives, such as the safeguarding of market integrity and investor protection.[25] Minimum harmonization in this area is welcome but more is undoubtedly

---

[23] For a complete overview of such issues, see Chapter 9.

[24] National laws are expected to provide for 'minimum maximums' so as to increase their maximum sanctions and accentuate their dissuasiveness. Of course, an even more efficient solution would be for EU law to reach an agreement among national laws and introduce 'minimums' for all infringements; such a revolution would improve the efficiency of sanctions since no trivial minimums would be allowed for the sanctioning of infringements.

[25] Measures typically include, among others, the issuance of a public statement indicating the nature of the infringement and the identity of the (legal or natural) person concerned, as well as the publication of an order requiring the persons concerned to cease the conduct constituting an infringement and to avoid repetition of similar activities. They may also refer to the withdrawal or suspension of the authorization of an institution (for example, an investment firm, market operator or regulated market) or

needed for national rules to achieve the same levels of deterrence. The current EU efforts to bring national laws closer should be seen as the first phase of a long-term strategy that will aim to achieve higher levels of harmonization.

A new regulatory trend in the area of administrative sanctions is related to the provision of a useful guide for NCAs covering the elements that they must take into account when determining the type and level of such sanctions.[26] These factors continue to multiply in various EU legislative texts,[27] showing a clear preference for harmonizing the regulatory reaction in an indirect way. Administrative sanctions are thus expected to converge, namely to go beyond the minimum and maximum of each national legal framework (these will continue to vary) and to reach similar levels of efficiency, while operating within their own national contexts. This is definitely an encouraging step towards gradual convergence of the *modus operandi* of NCAs. It may prove even more useful than formal harmonization measures that deal with minimal penalties insofar as it could accustom authorities to a new way of thinking about and calculating the severity of sanctions, prompting them to adopt a much more holistic approach that may not necessarily coincide with traditional approaches.

The crucial question that therefore needs to be asked is whether administrative sanctions and measures can constitute a reliable enforcement spectrum for shareholder duties – both the traditional and emerging ones. As far as the traditional shareholder duties are concerned, NCAs have already shown an increased degree of familiarity and sophistication, which, factored into the ongoing harmonization efforts mentioned above, could convey positive signs as to the adaptability and efficiency of such an enforcement framework.[28]

Nevertheless, concerns may be raised with regard to the suitability of such sanctions and measures in the area of the emerging shareholder duties. Indeed, the lack of familiarity with and sophistication of the broadly formulated, evolving and novel intellectual mindset of these duties may create major challenges to efficient enforcement by NCAs. As a first assessment of the overall presence of administrative sanctions on measures in this area, I support the argument

---

the temporary or permanent ban of investment firms or any member of their management body.

[26] The gravity of the duration of the breach, the degree of responsibility and the financial strength of the natural or legal person, the magnitude of profits and losses suffered by third parties due to the breach, the level of cooperation with the competent authority, any eventual former breaches and any measures taken to prevent the breach from recurring.

[27] See, e.g., art. 39 of the Prospectus Regulation (n 20) and art. 28c of the Transparency Directive (n 19).

[28] See, e.g., the administrative sanctions and measures applicable to violations of the notification of major holdings duties provided by art. 28 of the Transparency Directive (n 19) and transposed into national law.

that such enforcement tools should be constrained in the area of traditional shareholder duties and should not yet be developed in the area of emerging shareholder duties. As will be shown later in this chapter,[29] Article 14b of the Shareholder Rights Directive, which lays out the possibility of imposing such sanctions and measures for the emerging shareholder duties, may create more harm than good in the overall efficiency of such enforcement tools.

Criminal proceedings have largely been marginalized across the EU. Criminal courts have traditionally shown a certain degree of reluctance in imposing criminal sanctions due to the high level of proof required in this framework. Their rarity has regrettably acted as a weakening factor for their presence in EU legislative texts. Moreover, the lack of harmonization among national frameworks has not helped in trusting these types of sanctions to create an efficient counterbalance to violations in capital markets. The various discrepancies among national frameworks for the duration of imprisonment, the maximum pecuniary sanctions and the rules surrounding criminal provisions are notable problems that require further reflection and reforms.

EU law is considerate of such discrepancies, as well as the difficulty in achieving a commonly accepted framework among Member States; this is why, for almost all infringements in capital markets law, EU legislative texts leave it up to the Member States to provide for such sanctions and to define their features. The three criteria that EU law requires within this flexible framework are effectiveness, dissuasiveness and proportionality. Although these criteria are pertinent and useful for national developments, it is also true that they largely depend on national mentalities and legal traditions; they cannot, therefore, on their own, function as a reliable guide for further harmonization. The inevitable result is that criminal provisions remain an unexplored field of public intervention in capital markets, notwithstanding their potential contribution to combating illegal practices.

Nevertheless, new criminal provisions, especially in the area of market abuse,[30] are emerging to denote a political determination either to tackle illegal behaviour efficiently or to convey a stronger message to the public about governmental responsiveness to socially unacceptable market practices. Criminal courts have been particularly reluctant to impose criminal sanctions due to the requirement of intent, which makes these enforcement mechanisms very difficult – if not impossible – to apply. The latest EU reforms in the area of market abuse have thus not managed to clarify the contours of criminal provisions

---

[29] See Sections V and VI.

[30] Directive 2014/57/EU of the European Parliament and of the Council of 16 April 2014 on criminal sanctions for insider dealing and market manipulation [2014] OJ L173/179.

to ensure their efficiency; these reforms convey a message about EU-level harmonization that is more symbolic than realistic.[31]

As far as the specific area of shareholder duties is concerned, criminal provisions are too modest or non-existent. Moreover, a distinction must be made between duties that are dealt with under a company law spectrum and a capital markets law spectrum. The first category has considerably less important and dissuasive provisions for the breach of shareholder duties and the ensuing criminal sanctions. The second category, being predominantly characterized by market integrity concerns, provides for much higher sanctions.

The criminal provisions applicable in the area of violations of notifications of major shareholdings in French law are characteristic in that respect. According to traditional company law rules, such violations risk the imposition of penalties of €18,000,[32] a particularly modest amount if the potential gains from non-compliance with notification of major shareholding rules are taken into account. According to the capital market law provisions, such violations can also be seen as misleading statements in the market and they can therefore trigger substantially higher criminal sanctions, namely five years' imprisonment and €100 million in fines.[33] It therefore becomes evident that criminal sanctions in the area of shareholder duties mainly reflect the prevalence of private enforcement since the 'internal affairs of the company' regulatory approach is much less important due to the presence of criminal sanctions. The law considers civil liability in this respect to be much more appropriate, and the criminal provisions in place cannot be considered dissuasive or even proportionate to the illegal gains potentially made. The presence of capital market law-driven criminal provisions is undoubtedly much more important but these provisions do not relate to the notification of major shareholdings (i.e. to the violation of shareholder duties) since they aim to target and sanction any violation that can destabilize informational equality in the market. The rationale for specific criminal provisions for the sanctioning of shareholder duties is therefore of limited importance, notwithstanding the overall dissuasiveness and symbolic message that such sanctions could convey to shareholders and other market actors.

[31] Michiel Luchtman and John Vervaele, 'Enforcing the Market Abuse Regime: Towards an Integrated Model of Criminal and Administrative Law Enforcement in the European Union?' (2014) 5(2) New. J. Eur. Crim. L. 192.

[32] Art. L. 247-2-I, *Code de commerce*.

[33] Art. L. 465-1, *Code monétaire et financier*.

IV. SOCIAL ENFORCEMENT

In parallel to legal enforcement tools, social sanctions also play an important role, at least in theory; these refer to the reaction stemming from market actors with regard to the infringement of applicable rules. Such reaction may have a considerable effect on the reputation of the persons concerned (both natural and legal), as well as clear financial implications for their activities.

Along with more formal enforcement mechanisms, EU law appears to be opting for an approximation of legal sanctions to informal enforcement strategies, such as 'naming and shaming', via the disclosure not only of the violations themselves (e.g. public warning instead of the imposition of pecuniary sanctions), but also of formal sanctions imposed (e.g. pecuniary sanctions).[34] This particular focus on enhancing the dynamics of social sanctions, based on the unpredictable cascading effects on investors, third parties and stakeholders at large, is entering an entirely new phase given the current discrepancies across jurisdictions, with some regulators currently adopting these practices with positive results and others who are reluctant to do so, citing concerns about disproportionality and unpredictable market reactions.

The discreet reinforcement of social sanctions through the use of disclosure as an exposure tool towards other market actors is a welcome revolution in EU law, but its ultimate efficiency will depend on the behavioural patterns of these actors. For social sanctions to take on a meaningful dimension and to act as a counterbalance to various infringements, market actors already need to have the necessary education and evaluation skills to act responsibly when they receive any information related to infringements. Education is the key here as it will prove critical for market actors that must reprioritize their strategies and not focus exclusively on the financial implications of infringements.

Empirical evidence on the efficiency of social enforcement in the area of issuer disclosure of compliance with corporate governance code provisions can be particularly useful in this context. Indeed, taking as a case study the use by issuers of the 'comply or explain' principle, investors who receive the related information tend to remain apathetic even if the company does not provide sufficient explanation for non-compliance with a code, especially in the case

---

[34] See, e.g., art. 42(1) of the Prospectus Regulation (n 20) and art. 29 of the Transparency Directive (n 19). Such provisions form part of legal enforcement tools since they are imposed by NCAs and they purport to sanction the persons concerned by disclosing either the penalty itself or a public warning. I therefore refer to such measures as social sanctions, paying attention to their meta-regulatory function, namely the expected reputational effects of such actions upon the shareholders concerned and their ramifications for other market actors.

where its operations are profitable.[35] This apathy towards 'non-compliance' – which only transforms itself into interest when corporate strategies create losses – is an alarming message for the usefulness and the overall impact of social enforcement, based on the example of the perception of the 'comply or explain' principle.

Applying this empirical evidence to the emerging shareholder duties, analysed in Section II and based on the 'comply or explain' principle, we could argue that if potentially harmed investors are solely concerned with avoiding the losses arising from infringements of such duties, and sanction at the social level the shareholders concerned (by withdrawing from agreements, selling securities, etc.), it is only when they are financially harmed that social enforcement loses its importance in this context; indeed, harmed actors will be unlikely to react when they are not themselves financially affected, notwithstanding the presence of an event that should in theory trigger a negative reaction. The reprioritization of investor strategies therefore lies in understanding the need to react to all infringements, even when investors themselves are not directly harmed, and to avoid adopting a single-minded vision of such violations. It is therefore hoped that these new disclosure tools will, together with educational efforts, inculcate market actors with a different mentality so as to enhance the functioning of social sanctions.

Additionally, social enforcement mechanisms can be seen as a first experimental approach to enforcement strategies in emerging legal norms that will allow a gradual and steady transition towards legal enforcement, once these norms have been interpreted and used consistently at both national and EU levels. For example, the emerging governance/engagement shareholder duties could justify the option of social enforcement, as will be explained in the next section, due to their novel character, which is still relatively unknown both to NCAs and to market actors.

V. ENFORCEMENT TRENDS IN THE AREA OF EMERGING SHAREHOLDER DUTIES

The revised Shareholder Rights Directive currently attests to an ever-strengthening trend moving from enabling company law to overarching and more constraining capital markets law rules. The 'publicization of the relationship between companies and their equity financiers'[36] shows the emergence of

---

[35] Sridhar Arcot, Valentina Bruno and Antoine Faure Grimaud, 'Corporate Governance in the UK: Is the Comply or Explain Approach Working?' (2010) 30(2) Int'l. Rev. L. & Econ. 99.

[36] Chiu and Katelouzou (n 14).

semi-hard law provisions in the area of stewardship, which raises the question of the adaptability of legal enforcement in the area of the emerging shareholder duties. Indeed, stewardship elements have traditionally been dealt with via soft law measures and social enforcement, but Article 14b of the Shareholder Rights Directive enables Member States to provide for effective, proportionate and dissuasive measures and penalties for violations of its transposed provisions into national law. Indeed, the wording of this article is very broad and can be interpreted in many different ways, raising concerns about its applicability across the EU and the ensuing consequences for the reliability of legal enforcement actions in this context.

Therefore, the political preference for legal enforcement requires further reflection as it becomes apparent that EU law paves the way for a more interventionist approach and marginalizes social enforcement mechanisms that have been present so far. Although it is true that NCAs may gradually be able to gain familiarity with this new normative spectrum and exercise their enforcement powers accordingly, it is highly doubtful if such a statement can hold true at this stage. It is preferable to opt for a differentiated approach depending on the range of potential violations of Article 3g (engagement policy) and Article 3h (alignment of investment strategy and arrangements with asset managers) of the Shareholder Rights Directive so as to determine the ensuing enforcement mechanisms.

On the one hand, administrative measures and sanctions could be envisaged for the simple and straightforward lack of disclosure (namely without any associated explanation statement as required in such cases) of either the institutional investor engagement policy[37] or the annual disclosure related to the implementation of such policy[38] or the arrangements with asset managers.[39] The same argument could be applied to the lack of disclosure of the alignment of investment strategy with investor liabilities.[40] NCAs should be able to simply verify if such disclosure (or the explanation required according to Article 3g) has been published, and could be in a position to proceed with the imposition of sanctions or measures if this is not the case. The NCA's examination should be based solely on the mere compliance with a pure disclosure obligation (or publication of explanation where applicable).

On the other hand, when it comes down to deciphering the informational content of disclosure related to the engagement policy (or of the explanation of non-compliance) and to the alignment of the investment strategy, NCAs will

37 Directive 2017/828/EU, art. 3g(1a).

38 Ibid art. 3g(1b).

39 Ibid art. 3h(2).

40 Ibid art. 3h.

find it particularly difficult to delineate the contours of overall compliance due to the inevitably variable circumstances within which engagement and investment strategies constantly evolve. These circumstances also affect the content of emerging shareholder duties and the overall understanding of whether such duties are effectively fulfilled. Indeed, it is this vast range of information that cannot be sanctioned with legal enforcement mechanisms as it will be particularly challenging to draw the line between violations of disclosure (or explanation)[41] duties and simple borderline cases that cannot and should not be sanctioned given their specificities and the perils of bluntly adopting legal enforcement. Social enforcement should therefore be preferred in such cases.

The *de facto* strengthening of administrative sanctions and measures may be a sign of interventionism and regulatory visibility in the eyes of the public but NCAs should also be able to perform this role efficiently so as to make these powers meaningful. Since it is currently debatable if regulators are already familiar with these duties to the extent that the exercise of their powers would be satisfactory and convincing, it would be preferable to examine the merits of maintaining social enforcement mechanisms in this area. This should not preclude any future discussions or reforms towards the enhancement of legal enforcement but, given the premature character of the latter in the area of emerging shareholder duties, I argue that social enforcement remains the most realistic option for the time being. Other arguments could be advanced in favour of maintaining social enforcement mechanisms in shareholder duties.

Imposing legal enforcement tools in the new governance/engagement duties risks creating an operational environment that is overly regulated, dissuading shareholders from conducting their activities in capital markets with flexibility as far as these emerging duties are concerned. Creating unreasonably burdensome conditions for market actors may impede business entrepreneurship and the development of innovative solutions since various actors will be primarily concerned with compliance with a series of legal requirements and not with the effectiveness of their strategies. Moreover, the risk of creating an overly complex and costly legal framework is also present since the shareholders concerned will need to invest in additional resources and costs so as to comply with the new legal requirements. Such costs may be reduced given the degree of sophistication that shareholders have acquired all these years, while disclos-

---

41 For example, art. 3g(1) requires a clear and reasoned explanation in case of lack of disclosure of the engagement policy. Although clarity and reasoning may be two criteria that can be broadly conceived as reliable, it will be particularly difficult for enforcement purposes to award sanctioning powers to NCAs. This is due to the fact that both criteria can be particularly difficult to apply consistently across cases within the national context but also across NCAs in the EU given the degree of subjectivity that they entail.

ing information upon the same issues within a soft law framework, but it is also expected that additional resources will be needed when legal enforcement can take place. The eventuality of sanctions being imposed will force shareholders to reprioritize their disclosure mindset.

Another major concern about the perils of legal enforcement at this stage, which merits particular attention, is that it does not fit harmoniously with the conceptual premise of the new shareholder duties that relate to the engagement and interaction with other market actors. I strongly believe that the main benefit of these new duties is to trigger further engagement in the markets, increase the educational benefits or disclosure in this area and gradually fight against shareholder apathy. Imposing legal enforcement thus risks weakening the educational benefits that can be derived from increased disclosure in this area. The parties concerned will inevitably focus on the liability factor of compliance and might be deterred from disclosing further information. Legal enforcement might therefore transform educational tools into liability risks and severely undermine one of the fundamental objectives of the Shareholder Rights Directive, namely the 'proper alignment of interests between the final beneficiaries of institutional investors, the asset managers and the investee companies' and the 'development of longer-term investment strategies and longer-term relationships with investee companies involving shareholder engagement'.[42] Administrative sanctions and measures, as currently included in Article 14b, sit uncomfortably with the Directive's overall aims.

Additionally, the recipients of disclosure in this context risk relying mechanistically upon NCAs in the presence of legal enforcement instead of engaging with shareholders. This is due to the fact that they will most probably perceive administrative measures and sanctions as an adequate safeguard against non-compliance risks and they will not be as motivated to interact with shareholders to challenge their strategies in a fruitful way and seek to obtain more information that is relevant to their priorities. The inclusion of legal enforcement at this stage will therefore legitimize investor disengagement and will make shareholder apathy more justified in the eyes of the public. The presence of administrative sanctions and measures should therefore be completely dissociated by any connotation of regulatory assurance that these duties are complied with.

Another major risk of legal enforcement in this area, following on from the educational challenges mentioned above, is the legitimization of certain borderline shareholder practices in the absence of actions taken by NCAs. Indeed, if NCAs fail to investigate non-compliance elements and, subsequently, to sanction them, the new shareholder duties will be perceived by the market

---

42 Directive 2017/828/EU, Recital 19.

as complied with and not raising any further concerns. An inactive regulatory stance can therefore be seen as an *ex post* certification of dubious practices. If the market relies mechanistically on NCAs for the sanctioning of these duties and the NCAs do not detect any violation or decide, after investigation, not to pursue any further action, the shareholders concerned will be encouraged to argue that their activities in the market raise no further concern. This will also enable them to stop engaging with other parties that may want to challenge their activities and further engage in dialogue with them. The overall risk will therefore be a mutually neutralizing effect of engagement and further apathy, from the perspectives of both the shareholders concerned and the recipients of information.

VI. REFLECTIONS ON FUTURE DEVELOPMENTS

The analysis of the above-mentioned difficulties in efficiently enforcing the breach of shareholder duties brings us to the conclusion that a new regulatory mindset can be proposed so as to ensure that future regulatory steps will not only be credible in theory, but also adaptable to the real dimension of the various company and shareholder features and challenges.

In this chapter I therefore propose a reprioritization of the regulatory agenda for the shaping of enforcement systems around shareholder duties. The regulatory efforts towards reforms should therefore be based on:

a. an increased and selective focus on the private enforcement agenda,
b. a meticulous consideration of the overall implications of increased enforcement mechanisms in capital markets,
c. a proper reform debate of NCAs and, lastly,
d. more educational efforts in the area of the new shareholder duties.

The first element of consideration relies upon the assumption that the private enforcement agenda has its own unquestionable merits in the area of shareholder duties. The presence of certain imperfections mentioned above, such as apathy and litigation obstacles in the area of civil liability, should not be seen as rationales for the marginalization of private enforcement. On the contrary, these challenges should justify enhanced fine-tuning of the private enforcement agenda so as to enable potential claimants to use this means of legal protection efficiently. Therefore, instead of awarding an increasing reliance on public enforcement mechanisms, considering that these would ensure a better system of protection for parties affected by the breach of shareholder duties, a more productive approach to the current shortcomings of private enforcement would be to find new incentives for claimants to use civil liability regimes.

The second element of consideration is the potentially undue burden of stringent enforcement mechanisms in emerging shareholder duties upon the attractiveness of capital markets. As mentioned above, while the emerging duties currently seem to attract an interventionist approach from the legal order, the educational benefits of a measured (and less interventionist) approach are far greater at this embryonic stage than the mere imposition of sanctions. This is due to the fact that the legal sanctions-only approach would risk changing the quintessence of the core nature of capital markets law – which has traditionally struck a balance between flexible and constraining legal norms – by transforming it into an 'enforcement-only'-driven framework. This transformation could prove counterproductive and gradually discourage market actors from being part of capital markets and satisfying their engagement duties.

The third element of consideration relates to the fact that NCAs have not yet been subject to a proper reform debate. Nevertheless, the Shareholder Rights Directive gives them a broad range of enforcement powers in a field that has not yet been fully understood.[43] The risk of accentuating enforcement in this area therefore risks driving NCAs to a more formalistic and less substantial approach when it comes to deciding borderline cases that may be seen as entailing some elements of non-compliance with shareholder duties but would not on the whole justify any formal enforcement action. The formalistic approach would also be accompanied by a lack of convergence in the exercise of the regulatory know-how among NCAs. These concerns therefore justify the need for a proper reform debate of NCAs at the national and EU level in the area of the enforcement of shareholder duties.

The fourth element of consideration relates to the need to invest more resources in educational efforts to enable the parties concerned to prepare themselves for more meaningful compliance while aiming to understand the benefits of more engagement with other constituencies in the market. At the same time, educational efforts need to be dedicated to all recipients of such disclosure so as to clarify the variety of expectations that they should have in respect of these new duties, the content of the new requirements, and the informational contours of the information disclosed. This will enable all parties to converge their understanding of these new duties and better understand their respective rights and responsibilities. Intervening directly with legal enforcement without passing through this educational stage will ultimately impede greater convergence in the understanding, application and optimal use of these duties at the expense of clarity, engagement and stewardship.

---

43 See ibid, art. 14b, mentioned above.

VII. CONCLUSION

This chapter aimed to highlight the various merits and shortfalls of social and legal enforcement in the area of shareholder duties. The coexistence of hard law and soft law measures in company law and capital markets law has offered opportunities for legal norms to impose various duties upon shareholders. The analysis focused on traditional and emerging shareholder duties. It further described, under a general approach and then one more targeted to shareholder duties, the current regulatory trends in legal (private and public) enforcement, the ongoing efforts at more harmonization across the EU, and the persisting obstacles to a facilitated and converged framework. Social enforcement was also analysed and its merits developed, along with the need to educate market actors so as to unblock shareholder apathy and to allow social sanctions to be perceived as equally convincing and to have an effect upon the market.

I argued that although legal enforcement has shown convincing rationales in the area of traditional shareholder duties, the perspectives of its introduction in the area of emerging shareholder duties needs further examination. Legal enforcement may indeed compromise the promising features of such new duties – in terms of engagement, educational efforts and increased dialogue among market actors – by transforming them into sources of liability and risk for shareholders. The chapter also provided some considerations for future reflection, related to the perils of expanding legal enforcement without an *ex ante* clear prioritization of regulatory aims and attempted to draw a first conceptual framework for any future reform in enforcement mechanisms.

I therefore sustained the opinion that, for the time being, social enforcement mechanisms should be maintained while investing resources and time to increase the familiarity of legal enforcers (NCAs being the most appropriate example) with these new duties so as to gradually prepare them for the imposition of enforcement tools in the future. A balanced approach needs to be maintained so as to allow the market to evolve harmoniously with the legalization of shareholder duties and to benefit from their introduction into the legal landscape without regarding them as onerous requirements with liability risks. Enforcement has a clear role to play in this area but it will only achieve desirable levels of efficiency when used meticulously and wisely by the legal order.

PART III

Sanctioning shareholders' duties

8. Enforcing shareholder duties through suspension of the exercise of voting rights

Mette Neville and Karsten Engsig Sørensen

I. INTRODUCTION

Recently, suspension of voting rights has been introduced in the European Union through Directive 2013/50/EU.[1] According to the amended Transparency Directive, this sanction should be available to the relevant authorities in the Member States in case of infringements of the duty to notify major shareholdings. The reason for introducing this sanction is that it is considered a particularly effective sanction by the Commission.[2] This raises the question why, and for which type of infringements, this sanction is effective. These questions will be analysed further in this chapter. We discuss the potential use of suspension of the exercise of voting rights as a sanction for different types of infringements, and the potential limits and challenges in using this sanction. We start by focusing on the use of this sanction regarding infringements of duties introduced by law, either capital markets law or company law. Subsequently, we discuss whether suspension of voting rights has potential as a sanction in the private ordering of shareholders such as the articles of association or shareholder agreements.

II. THE USE OF SUSPENSION OF THE EXERCISE OF VOTING RIGHTS AS A SANCTION

Suspension of the exercise of voting rights may be a sanction used to enforce shareholder duties. However, suspension of the exercise of voting rights is

[1] Directive 2013/50/EU amending the Transparency Directive (Directive 2004/109/EC). The amendments were to be implemented by November 2015.

[2] See the Impact Assessment prepared by the Commission for the Directive, SEC (2011) 1279 final/2, 41.

more often used for regulatory purposes rather than sanctioning, and before examining in more detail the use of suspension as a sanction, it is worth briefly outlining and contemplating these alternative uses of suspension of the exercise of voting rights.

A. Suspension of the Exercise of Voting Rights as a Regulatory Tool

A suspension of the exercise of voting rights may serve to limit the influence of a shareholder either in specific decisions or more generally, even in situations where it does not serve as a sanction. An example of the former is a situation where shareholders are not allowed to vote on a certain decision because they have a special interest in the issue. According to the law in some countries, a shareholder will not be allowed to vote when the general meeting must decide whether or not the company should take legal action against the shareholder.[3] Also, some countries have rules which suspend the voting rights of shareholders when the company must decide whether to enter into a contract with the shareholder or someone closely related to the shareholder. This includes rules on related-party transactions, which may require the approval of the shareholders, but without the participation of the shareholder that is a party to the transaction.[4] Following the adoption of the revised Shareholder Rights Directive, such rules may be introduced in more countries.[5]

In the aforementioned examples, the suspension rules serve the purpose of avoiding shareholders exercising influence over decisions where they have a special interest that may conflict with the interest of the company and/or the interests of the other shareholders. Other company law rules seek to suspend voting rights for some shareholders more generally. This includes voting ceilings according to which no shareholder may exercise voting rights above a certain number of votes, where consequently the voting rights will be suspended on those shares that are in excess of the stipulated number.[6] Another

---

[3] See for instance the Danish Companies Act § 86 and the German Public Companies Act, § 136.

[4] It is only one of several strategies for regulating related-party transactions, see Reinier H. Kraakmann, John Armour, Paul Davies, Luca Enriques, Henry Hansmann, Gerard Hertig, Klaus Hopt, Hideki Kanda, Mariana Pargendler, Wolf-Georg Ringe, and Edward Rock, *The Anatomy of Corporate Law* (3rd edn, Oxford University Press 2017) 156–58.

[5] See Directive 2017/828/EU, Art. 9c(4).

[6] Normally a voting ceiling will be imposed by the company's articles of association but occasionally it may also be imposed by law. This could be the case when state enterprises are privatised, see for instance the VW Law § 2(1), which was one of the contested provisions in the golden share case against Germany, Case C-112/05, *Commission v Germany*.

example of a general suspension of voting rights occurs for shares held by the company that issued the shares or held by its subsidiaries. According to the Codified Company Law Directive, the voting rights on these shares should be suspended until such time as they are sold off again.[7] The purpose is to avoid management, by exercising voting rights on these shares, being able to safeguard their own interests at the expense of the interest of the company.

It has been suggested that other shareholders should have their voting rights suspended due to similar concerns that they cannot be trusted to exercise their voting right in the interest of the company. Thus, it has been suggested in legal literature that voting rights should be suspended for certain sovereign wealth funds[8] or for those having a negative interest in the company effected by risk-decoupling through so-called 'empty voting and short-selling'.[9] So far, none of these proposals has been adopted.

Thus, it is clear that the suspension of voting rights may not only be a sanction, but may also be imposed without there being any breach of duty. In these cases, suspension will often serve as a preventive measure, namely preventing a shareholder from exercising voting rights in situations where it is likely that the shareholders will not act in the interest of the company, but will act to preserve their own interests at the expense of the company's interests (as, for instance, with related-party transactions) or they will serve non-relevant interests (management) or may even have an interest in acting against the interests of the company (empty voting, short-sellers). As we will see below in Section II.B, this is a different aim from the one that the current rules using suspension as a sanction serve, and we may make use of this insight once we later contemplate where there may be additional uses for the sanction.

---

7 See Directive 2017/1132/EU, Art. 63(1)(a). An additional example is the suspension which takes place after a bidder has acquired control over a company after a public bid and lasts until the Commission has given its approval under the Merger Control Regulation, see Art. 7(2).

8 See Ronald J. Gilson and Curtis J. Milhaupt, 'Sovereign Wealth Funds and Corporate Governance: A Minimalist Response to the New Mercantilism' (2008) 60 Stan. L. Rev. 1345ff.

9 See Henry T. C. Hu and Bernard S. Black, 'Empty Voting and Hidden (Morphable) Ownership: Taxonomy, Implications, and Reforms' (2006) 61 Bus. Law. 1011ff. See also Carl Clottens, 'Empty Voting: A European Perspective' (2012) 9 Eur. Co. & Fin. L. Rev. 446ff.; and Wolf-George Ringe, 'Hedge Funds and Risk-decoupling: The Empty Voting Problem in the European Union' (2012–13) 36 Seattle U. L. Rev. 1027ff. On a similar discussion in relation to short-selling, see Konstantinos Sergakis, 'The Duties of a Short Seller' in Hanne S. Birkmose (ed), *Shareholders' Duties* (Kluwer Law International 2017) 170–72.

B. Suspension of Voting Rights as a Sanction

Suspension of voting rights as a sanction has most often been introduced in national law in connection with breach of duties linked to shareholders obtaining control in a company.

With the adoption of Directive 2013/50/EU amending the Transparency Directive, the Commission's suspension of voting rights was introduced for the first time as a sanction in the EU.[10] If shareholders fail to declare major shareholdings according to the national rules implementing the Transparency Directive (Directive 2004/109/EC), the new Directive requires that Member States ensure that the suspension of voting rights is available as a sanction. The Directive stipulates only a few criteria that the national implementation must comply with, but leaves it to the Member States to decide on most of the details. As will also be clear from Section III.B, the Member States have implemented the Directive very differently.

Another example of suspension being used as a sanction is national legislation implementing the Fourth EU Anti-Money Laundering Directive[11] and the new Regulation on information accompanying transfer of funds.[12] The Directive introduced a central public register which identifies the ultimate beneficial owners of companies and trusts. Companies are required to keep information about their beneficial owners but the Directive does not explicitly require the Member States to impose a disclosure duty on shareholders. However, the UK, for example, has imposed a duty for companies to investigate and obtain information about beneficial owners, as well as a duty to supply information on registrable persons.[13] The Directive has also left the question of sanctions to the Member States. Some Member States have introduced suspension of voting rights as a sanction when the shareholder fails to declare a beneficial ownership or does not react to a notice from the company seeking

---

[10] Regarding credit institutions, the Member States were encouraged to introduce the sanction for persons or companies that did not comply with the duty to declare qualifying holdings. The rule is now included in Directive 2013/36/EU requiring the Member State in such cases to allow 'either for exercise of the corresponding voting rights to be suspended, or for the nullity of votes cast or for the possibility of their annulment', see Art. 26(1). Here suspension is just one of several alternatives.

[11] Directive 2015/849/EU on preventing the use of the financial system for money laundering or terrorist financing (4AMLD).

[12] Regulation 2015/847/EU of the European Parliament and of the Council of 20 May 2015 on information accompanying transfers of funds and repealing Regulation (EC) No. 1781/2006.

[13] By comparison, the Danish rules implementing the new Directive do not impose a duty on beneficial owners, but rather only on the company that has to register and report on beneficial owners.

information about such persons.[14] In the UK, the rules of the new disclosure regime were implemented in 2017 through the Small Business, Enterprise and Employment Act 2015, which amended the Companies Act 2006. A failure to respond to a notice from the company seeking information about the beneficial owners (termed 'people with significant control') is a criminal offence. The company (board of directors) may issue a warning notice and if the information is not forthcoming by the end of a one-month period, a restriction notice may be issued. If a restriction notice is served, any transfer of the relevant interest is void and no rights may be exercised nor any shares issued in respect of that interest.

Yet another example of disclosure rules where non-compliance can lead to suspension are the rules in s 793 of the UK Companies Act. According to the rules, the directors of a public company can serve a notice upon persons suspected of being interested in its voting shares seeking information about the interest. If the person fails to comply with the obligations in s 793, s 794 permits the company to apply to the court for, inter alia, restrictions.[15] The court order may result in the withdrawal of voting rights, the withholding of capital and income payments, and the invalidation of any transfer of shares, cf. s 797.

The Takeover Directive, Directive 2004/25/EC, requires that any party, acting alone or in concert with others, directly or indirectly, that acquires a controlling interest in a listed company, must launch a public offer for all outstanding shares. In several Member States, for example Germany[16] and

[14] According to the Swiss Code of Obligations, an acquiring entity that does not comply with its disclosure obligation regarding beneficial owners, will have its voting rights in the Swiss company suspended until notification is made, cf. § 697m(3) (inserted by No. I 2 of the Federal Act of 12 December 2014 on the Implementation of the revised recommendations 2012 of the Financial Action Task Force, in force since 1 July 2015 (AS 2015 1389; BBl 2014 605). Further, the acquiring entity's right to dividends (and repayment of capital) is irrevocably forfeited for the period until disclosure is made. The company could reclaim any dividends paid out prior to a notification. Failure to comply with the notification obligations will not prevent a valid transfer of ownership of the relevant shares. While the shareholder's rights may be suspended or even forfeited, such failure does not prevent the acquirer from becoming owner of the shares.

[15] See Paul L. Davies and Sarah Worthington, *Gower's Principles of Modern Company Law* (10th edn, Sweet & Maxwell 2016) paras 28–51.

[16] In Germany, there is a triple system of sanctions against a controlling shareholder who has breached the duty to make a bid cf., § 35 of the German Takeover Act (WpÜG). According to § 60, a controlling shareholder may be subject to an administrative fine up to the amount of EUR 1 million, according to § 59.

Sweden,[17] a controlling shareholder who fails to make a mandatory bid within the deadline will have, or can have, his or her voting rights suspended.

The final example is from Danish company law. According to § 33 of the Danish Public Companies Act, at least 25 per cent of the share capital, and at least DKK 50,000, must always be paid upon the company's establishment. This payment must be made in proportion to each equity interest. If a premium is determined, the premium in public limited companies must be paid in full, regardless of the fact that part of the share capital is not paid. If the remaining capital is not paid at the request of the company's board of directors, it follows from § 34, subsection 3 of the Danish Companies Act that the shareholder cannot exercise his or her right to vote at the general meeting for any part of his or her shareholding in the company, and the relevant shareholding is not considered to be represented at the general meeting until the amount has been paid and registered in the share capital.

III. A WIDER USE OF SUSPENSION AS A SANCTION FOR INFRINGEMENT OF LAW?

As appears from the above, the present use of the sanction is mainly linked to infringements of duties related to the acquisition of substantial shareholdings and, thus, influence. Except for the regulation of the mandatory bid duty, the suspension of voting rights is used solely as a sanction for a breach of shareholders' reporting obligations. If the Commission is assuming that the suspension of voting rights is an effective sanction, it may be considered whether it would be appropriate to apply it as a sanction in other areas. After contemplating in which situation the sanction may be used (Section III.A), it is discussed how best to frame the sanction to ensure its effectiveness (Section III.B).

A. Additional Situations in Which Suspension May Be Used

It is natural to consider using the sanction in relation to other duties that are linked to the exercise of voting rights, thus keeping the natural link between the infringement and the sanction. Also, based on the conclusion in Section

---

17 In Sweden, there is a double system of sanctions. When a controlling shareholder fails to make a mandatory bid, the financial authorities can decide that the bidder should pay an administrative fine amounting to at least SEK 50,000 and a maximum of SEK 100 million, cf. ch. 7, 7 § of the Financial Securities Act. According to the provisions, the financial authorities *can* decide that the controlling shareholder may not represent the shares held by him or her. Regarding sanctions, see SOU 2005:058 *Ny reglering av offentliga uppköpserbjudanden (takeover utredningen)* and Rolf Skog, Erik Sjönan, Göran Nyström and Robert Ohlsson, *The Swedish Takeover Code* (Informa Law 2016).

II.A, it may be worth considering using the sanction, in particular in situations where the infringements indicate that the shareholder can no longer be expected to act in the interest of the company.

These two prerequisites may, for example, be present in the case where a shareholder abuses his or her influence in the company. Many jurisdictions have provisions that forbid the conduct of company affairs, typically through the exercise of influence at the general meeting, that are 'unfairly prejudicial' to the interest of members generally or to a part of the company's members, or in breach of a duty of loyalty.[18] In some cases, such abuse will lead to the invalidity of the decision but in serious cases of abuse of influence, various judicial remedies aimed at the offender are typically prompted. Often the courts are given the possibility of winding up a company in the event of serious abuse of majority powers, or the possibility of requiring that a shareholder who has caused damage to the other shareholders, deliberately or by gross negligence, redeems the shares of the injured shareholders, or the possibility of granting a right to exclude the offender.[19] Sanctions in the form of dissolution of a company, redemption of shares or exclusion must be seen as *ultimo ratio*, and therefore one could raise the question whether suspension of voting rights could be a less intrusive sanction. This might be the case in public companies where shareholders are only investors and where the company is managed by a professional board of directors. However, abuse of influence in large companies is rare since ownership is typically spread between several minor shareholders. The problem of abuse of influence will often be much more relevant in SMEs. Here, the ownership and control structure often more closely resembles that of a partnership. SMEs are typically characterised by having few owners, with overlap between ownership and management. A sanction in the form of suspension of voting rights constitutes a very serious sanction as the ability to influence the company's management is essential for the share-

---

[18] S 994 of the UK Companies Act 2006. In Germany, the duty of loyalty (*Treuepflicht*) is based on case law of the Federal Court of Justice [BGH] and the general good faith requirement in the Civil Code [BGB].

[19] § 61 of the German Limited Liability Companies Act [*GmBH Gesetz*] gives the authority to terminate cooperation, having the effect that the company is dissolved. There must be *Verhältnissen der gesellschaft liegende, wichtigem Grund* [weighty grounds]. Moreover, the courts have established that there is a right to redemption even though the legislation only refers to dissolution by operation of law. The background in this respect is that dissolution can be an inappropriate solution. In the UK, the remedy for unfair or prejudicial conduct does not authorise the courts to dissolve a company. Nevertheless, there is a separate procedure which a minority shareholder may seek to use to have the company wound up. A company may be wound up by the court if the court is of the opinion that it is just and equitable to do so (see s 122(1) of the Insolvency Act 1986).

holders in these companies. Additionally, given the fact that SMEs are based on the shareholders working closely together, a suspension of voting rights for a period of time is not a realistic solution. If a conflict has led to oppression, for example, a suspension of one shareholder's voting rights, it would only fuel the conflict at a later stage.

In addition to closed corporations, misuse of influence in groups of companies may occur. In groups of companies the parent company may wish to optimise the financial transactions and business activities in the group. Here, there is an obvious risk of the parent company using its controlling influence to implement decisions that are in the parent company's interest, but not necessarily in the interest of the subsidiary. This is particularly problematic if the subsidiary is not wholly owned, as a minority shareholder would have an independent interest in receiving the maximum return from the subsidiary. If the parent company abuses its influence in the subsidiary, the suspension of voting rights would be effective if it is required that the resolution should be taken at the general meeting. However, many decisions are made at board level and if the parent company is still able to influence the board of the subsidiary through informal contact, the suspension would have limited impact. Only if the board of the subsidiary is elected by the general meeting without the votes of the parent company would the suspension effectively undermine the influence of the parent company. But even if it is possible to use suspension as an effective sanction, it is also clear that there is a reluctance to do so as the integration of corporate groups is normally either accepted or even encouraged.[20] As a consequence, the governance of corporate groups is often under-regulated and it seems less likely that the suspension of a parent company's voting rights will be introduced as a sanction.[21]

Finally, it may be worth considering whether the sanction may also be useful in situations in which the breached duty is not linked to the acquisition of control or the exercise of influence. In these situations, there is no natural link between the infringement and the sanction, but if the sanction is effective, this may not be a problem. However, if the link is missing, it may be less likely that the exercise of voting rights is important to the shareholder, and therefore the suspension may not be an effective sanction. If, for instance, the suspension of voting rights were to be introduced for infringements of the insider trading regime, it would

---

[20] See, for instance, the ongoing discussion in the EU as to whether to legitimise group interests and thereby facilitate group governance; see Informal Company Law Expert Group (ICLEG), *Report on the recognition of the interest of the group* (October 2016).

[21] That is not to say that there is no regulation of corporate groups. To our knowledge, even in those countries that have an extensive regulation of groups, the sanction of suspension of voting rights is not used.

likely not prove effective as a sanction since the exercise of voting rights is not important to most insiders. For the same reason, it may not be effective for infringement of the market abuse regime or rules regulating short-selling.

B. Framing the Sanction

If suspension of the exercise of voting rights is used as a sanction for the infringement of a wider range of shareholder duties, the imposition of the sanction should be regulated, including how it should take effect and how suspension should be ended. Looking at the examples where this sanction is already used, it is clear that these issues can be regulated very differently, and consequently the sanction may work very differently. It is also clear that these details are very important to how the sanction will work and consequently how effective the sanction will be. The purpose of the following is to point to some of the most important questions in relation to the implementation of suspension as a sanction for infringement of duties imposed in law and present the pros and cons of the different solutions.

1. Procedure for imposing the sanction

The procedure laid down for imposing the suspension of voting rights is very important for how the sanction works in practice. There are fundamentally different ways of doing this which can be illustrated by the way that the Member States have implemented Article 28b(2) of the Transparency Directive (Directive 2013/50/EU), which requires that the Member States implement rules that provide for the suspension of voting rights if they fail to declare major shareholdings (and some types of financial instruments). Here Member States have chosen very different procedures for suspending the voting rights.[22] One is imposing the sanction automatically *ex lege* and thus without the need for a decision by the supervisory authorities or a court order. This is the solution chosen in Germany, where the suspension of rights is triggered automatically by a breach of the notification rules.[23] In other Member States, the suspension of voting rights requires a decision by either the financial supervisory authorities or the courts. In the Nordic region (Sweden,[24]

---

[22] See our analysis of how the Member States have implemented the sanction for infringement of the duty to declare major shareholdings in Karsten Engsig Sørensen and Mette Neville, 'Suspension of the Exercise of Voting Rights – A Step Towards Deterrent and Consistent Sanctioning of EU Transparency Requirements?' (2017) 14(4) Eur. Comp. L. 150–61.

[23] Cf. § 28(1) of the German Securities Trading Act (WpHG).

[24] The Swedish Securities Act, ch. 6, 3o §.

Finland[25] and Denmark[26]) it is the national supervisory authorities that are empowered to decide suspension of voting rights. In the UK, the decision is left to the courts.[27]

As mentioned above, suspension of voting rights is only used at EU level in connection with the notification rules but at national level suspension has also been used as a sanction in the takeover legislation in some countries, and again different procedures for imposing the sanction have been used. In Germany, if a controlling shareholder fails to put forward a mandatory bid within the prescribed four-week deadline after gaining control, the shareholder will automatically *ex lege* have his or her voting right suspended. If one looks to the Swedish takeover legislation, suspension is not imposed automatically, but only after a decision made by the supervisory authorities.[28]

Finally, there are examples where the board of directors plays an important role in the enforcement of the sanction. As explained in Section II.B, this is the case in the UK, where the board in some cases has the power to apply to the court for a suspension of voting rights in the case of violation of a notification duty. In other cases, for example if a person fails to respond to a notice from the company seeking information about the beneficial owners, the board of directors may even invoke the sanction on its own.

As the examples above indicate, there seem to be different traditions as to how to impose suspension of voting rights as a sanction. If a wider use of suspension of voting rights as a sanction is considered, it is important to consider the pros and cons against the different procedures for imposing suspension as a sanction.

The choice between imposing suspension as a sanction *ex lege* or on the basis of a decision by a public authority, the court or the board of directors must reflect a balanced consideration of the effectiveness of the suspension as a sanction, legal certainty and predictability.

Regarding the efficiency of the suspension, the optimal solution depends on what one wants to obtain. If suspension is considered a sanction to prevent influence at an upcoming general meeting, the suspension is in many cases only effective if the suspension is imposed *ex lege* as the ban then enters into force as soon as the rules are violated and thus the shareholder cannot vote on any decision after this time. If the imposition of the suspension as a sanction requires a decision by a competent authority or, even worse, the courts, there is a risk that the offender will vote at a general meeting held after the violation

---

25 Cf. the Finnish Securities Act, ch. 17, 1a §.

26 The Danish Securities Act, § 29 a.

27 Cf. the transparency Regulations 2015 (SI 2015/1755) amending the Financial Services and Markets Act (FSMA) by introducing s 89NA.

28 *Lag (2006:451) om offentliga uppköpserbjudanden på aktiemarknaden* (Financial Securities Act), Ch 7, 7 §.

of the notification rules but before the decision on the suspension is taken. This makes it a less effective sanction in these cases as it will typically not be possible to roll back major transactions like M&As. Leaving the decision to the board may allow for a faster decision but it still requires that the board should be aware of the problem and have some time to investigate and react.

So, it seems that an enforcement *ex lege* may be preferable. However, an *ex lege* solution requires that it should be fairly clear whether or not there is an infringement. The more complicated the rules are, the harder it will be for the shareholders to know whether or not they have complied with their obligations, and it would be contrary to basic principles of legal certainty to use an *ex lege* solution. Even though it may often be fairly easy to decide whether the rules on notification of major shareholdings have been breached, it may not be so simple when, for example, some types of derivatives are involved, or in cases involving concerted practices among several shareholders. When deciding whether or not a shareholder is a beneficial owner it may be even more complex. If the sanction is extended to other types of infringement – such as abuses – it is clear that it may be very difficult to decide whether or not there is a breach. The more complicated it is to establish whether a shareholder has breached the rules that triggers the suspension, the less appropriate it is to impose the sanction of suspension of voting rights *ex lege*.[29]

There are also other concerns linked to the automatic imposition of the sanction. One is whether reliance on a legal presumption of liability, whereby the burden of proof is placed on the shareholder whose voting right is suspended, is compatible with the principle of effective judicial protection. Another question is whether an *ex lege* approach will violate the principle of respect for the rights of the defence, as entrenched in Article 47 of the EU Charter of Fundamental Rights and in Article 6(2) of the European Convention on Human Rights. Both questions were addressed more directly in Case C-418/11, *Texdata Software GmbH*. After careful scrutiny of the *ex lege* sanction imposed in Austria, the Court accepted that none of the fundamental principles were infringed.

However, the arguments adopted by the Court may indicate that an *ex lege* approach may require rules that make it possible to object to the sanction and that sufficient time must be given to file the objection.

---

[29] Cf. Christoph H. Seibt, 'Der (Stimm-)Rechtsverlust als sanktion für die Nichterfüllung kapitalmarktrechtlicher Mitteilungspflichten im Lichte des Vorslags der Europäisher Kommission zur Reform der Transparenzrichtlinie' (2012) 33(17) ZIP 797, 801.

2. The effect of suspension

If a suspension is imposed either after a procedure or *ex lege*, it has to be decided how the sanction will take effect. This raises a number of issues, including the question of which rights to suspend and the timeframe within which the suspension should take effect.

a. Which rights should be suspended?

It seems rather straightforward how suspension of the exercise of voting rights should work, but in fact there are many possible nuances of how the suspension can be imposed. First, it needs to be decided which shares are affected by the suspension. Normally, it will only affect the shares owned by the shareholder who has breached a duty. However, in some situations it may be appropriate to extend the sanction to other shareholders. This may be the case where a group of shareholders is acting in concert and this group fails to fulfil its obligation to either declare a major shareholding or its duty to make a mandatory bid.[30] Also, suspension is often extended to shares owned by other companies in a group, if the offender is part of a corporate group.[31]

Next, it will have to be decided whether the offending shareholder will lose voting rights on all or only a part of his or her shareholding. For most infringements, it will probably be most appropriate to apply the sanction for the complete shareholding. However, upon failure to declare a major shareholding, several states have chosen a solution whereby the suspension only affects the shares that exceed the threshold that has not been declared correctly.[32] This implies that only a small fraction of the voting rights may be affected and thus the effectiveness of the sanction can be called into question.

---

[30] This is the situation in Germany where the duty to declare a major shareholding will be extended to a group acting in concert. The German rules on suspension when the duty to offer a mandatory bid is not fulfilled will also be extended to others acting in concert with the offeror and to other companies in the same group as the shareholder who have triggered the duty, see the German Takeover Act (WpÜG) § 59. According to the Swedish Takeover Act, an offeror for companies listed on a Swedish Exchange is under a duty to undertake to the relevant Swedish Exchange to comply with the Takeover Rules and to submit to the sanctions that may be imposed by the relevant Swedish Exchange. The SFSA's powers as the competent authority under the Takeover Act include the prohibition of public offers and the suspension of voting rights attached to target shares held by an offeror.

[31] Thus, the German rules sanctioning infringement of the rules on notification of major shareholdings extend the suspension to shares owned by other companies in the same group, see MüKoAktG/Bayer, WpHG § 28, para 17.

[32] This is the case in the implementation of the sanction in Finland and Sweden. See the Finnish Securities Act, ch. 17, 1a § and the Swedish Securities Act, ch. 6, 3o §.

Furthermore, it needs to be decided whether voting rights are suspended for all or only some of the decisions taken by the general meeting.[33] In the suspension regimes in operation, so far it seems that they apply to all decisions voted on in the period of suspension. When designing future sanction regimes, it may be more appropriate to allow the shareholders to vote on some issues and not on others, depending on the nature of the duty infringed. It is not easy to find good examples where it may be appropriate to differentiate between different types of decision but if, for instance, suspension is introduced as a sanction due to an abuse of influence, voting rights may only need to be suspended in votes on issues where there is a risk of repeating the abuse.

Finally, it should be considered whether a suspension of the exercise of voting rights is enough for the sanction to be effective. The exercise of voting rights will most likely be important for shareholders that have a substantial amount of votes or even control. Therefore, suspending all voting rights will be effective when regulating substantive shareholders, as is presently done with the rules on notification of major shareholdings and takeover rules. Enforcing a broader suspension of shareholders' rights, for instance economic rights such as the right to dividend or the right to attend the general meeting, can be considered too. This solution has been adopted in Germany, where the suspension of rights under both the takeover regime and the regime on major shareholdings affects all shareholder rights.[34] This obviously makes it a much stronger sanction as it will also have an impact on shareholders that do not intend to use their voting rights. But if the idea of the sanction is to make a link to the violation of duties related to influence, it may be less logical to extend the sanction to suspension of economic rights.[35]

b. Duration of the suspension

The first important issue to solve when it comes to the duration of the suspension is to establish when the suspension enters into force. If the sanction is imposed *ex lege*, it is possible to implement the suspension from the moment the law has been violated. If, however, the suspension is imposed by a court

---

[33] In addition, it is worth considering whether special rights allotted to shareholders who hold a fraction of the total voting rights should be affected. For example, in some countries only shareholders who hold 5% or 10% of the voting rights may call a general meeting, and if voting rights are suspended, it would be logical that they lose this right.

[34] Another example is found in the UK where, if a shareholder fails to provide information when notified under the Companies Act 2006, Pt 22, the courts can order suspension of the voting rights, suspension of the right to dividend and other return of capital and restriction on transfer of shares, see Companies Act 2006, s 797(1).

[35] See also Rüdiger Veil, 'Wie viel "Enforcement" ist notwendig?' (2011) Heft 1 ZHR 83, 101.

order or by a decision made by another national authority, the date will often be specified in that order or decision. Since such an order or decision must be made after the infringement has taken place, there is likely to be a period after the offence where the suspension may not be in place, which makes the sanction less effective.

Subsequently, it must be decided how long the suspension should last. A commonly chosen solution is that the suspension should last until the offender has corrected his or her offence by either declaring a shareholding or executing a mandatory bid. Even though such a system seems fair at first glance, it also seems that such a system may be abused by an offender who decides to buy time and correct an offence just before the time he or she needs to exercise his or her voting rights. Therefore, there may be a need to allow for an extension of the suspension. If suspension is used as a sanction against certain types of abuse, it does not make sense to let the suspension last until the abuse has been remedied. In this case, it is necessary to stipulate either a specific period of time or let a competent court or authority decide on the issue when the suspension order or decision is taken.

Since the suspension is a sanction imposed on a shareholder who has committed an offence, it seems logical that the suspension should be lifted on the shares when they are sold to a different (independent) shareholder.

IV. SUSPENSION AS A PRIVATE ORDERING SANCTION

Many shareholder duties are stipulated in either the articles of association of a company or in a shareholder agreement. Our impression is that the suspension of voting rights is not used extensively as a sanction for such duties, but at least there is precedence in some countries.[36] But even if it is not a sanction often used, it is worth contemplating when it may be used and how the sanction should be constructed if applied. These two issues are discussed further below.

A. The Potential for Using Suspension as a Sanction in Private Ordering

In listed companies the possibility of suspension has already been introduced as a sanction for infringements of the duty to declare major shareholdings and in some countries for infringements of the takeover regime. However, as

[36] Thus, in the UK it seems to be common that the directors are permitted by the company's articles to impose suspension in different situations, see Davies and Worthington (n 15) paras 28–51.

pointed out in Section III.B.1, it will not always be a sanction readily used by the authorities as in some countries it requires a qualified infringement and that the authorities take action. In these countries, the companies may adopt supplementary rules allowing for a wider application of the sanction in situations where there is a breach of duty imposed by law, such as, for instance, notification requirements or duties under the takeover regime.[37] It may also be possible for listed companies to decide that shareholders who have engaged in market abuse or insider dealings should as a consequence have their votes suspended.

However, it will most likely be in unlisted and especially small and medium-sized companies where it will be most relevant to consider introducing the suspension of the exercise of voting rights as a sanction for a breach of duty. It is in these companies that we find a number of different duties imposed on shareholders either in the company's articles or in a shareholder agreement. As mentioned in Section III.A, it would be logical to use the sanction when a shareholder infringes a duty that relates to the exercise of voting rights. This may include situations where a shareholder has abused his or her voting rights or has voted contrary to what has been agreed, for instance in the shareholder agreement. But also, it may include other types of infringement where it would be desirable to cancel the influence of a shareholder because there is doubt whether the voting rights will be exercised in the interest of the company. This would be the case, for instance, where the shareholder has breached a non-competition clause, and since he or she is competing with the company, he or she may no longer be assumed to have the best interest of the company in mind. Another example would be where a shareholder is excluded from the company for a breach of either the law, the articles or a shareholder's agreement, and it takes some time before the exclusion can be effected. In this situation, it would also seem prudent to allow for a suspension of the voting rights belonging to the excluded shareholder to ensure that the voting right is not used to cause havoc in the transition period.

But even if suspension of voting rights may be used as a sanction, it may not necessarily be the most effective sanction. There are many other sanctions available for infringements of duties laid down in a company's articles or a shareholder agreement, including conventional fines, compensation or the exclusion of the shareholder. Thus, it should be considered whether suspension

---

[37] Thus, it appears that in the UK it is common that the company's articles give the directors the power to impose a suspension on those shareholders who do not disclose their interest in shares after having served a notice according to Pt 22 of the Companies Act 2006, see Davies and Worthington (n 15) paras 28–51. For the sake of completeness, it should be mentioned that voting rights above a certain ceiling are often suspended in articles or agreements, but in this case the suspension is not operating as a sanction.

of voting rights is the most appropriate or effective sanction compared to these alternatives. Compared to conventional fines and compensation, the sanction of suspension will take effect for some time after the infringement has taken place and may therefore benefit the running of the company for a period, for instance by ensuring that decision making in the company is not affected by biased shareholder influence. A conventional fine or compensation may have a preventive effect in making it less likely that a shareholder will repeat the mistake but a suspension may work even better if it effectively prevents a shareholder from exercising voting rights upon breach of the shareholder duties. However, suspension will normally be limited in time and therefore the shareholder will be able to exercise influence once again. If suspension is imposed on a controlling shareholder or a shareholder with substantive veto rights, the revival of the influence may cause disruption in the company. The shareholder may want to overturn the decision taken without the shareholder. Therefore, suspension may only be a way of temporarily suppressing a problem. For this reason, it will often be necessary to find a more permanent solution if the shareholder has serious problems cooperating on the running of the company.[38]

B. The Implementation of the Suspension of Voting Rights as a Sanction in the Articles of Association or Shareholder Agreements

Even though there may be situations where it makes sense to use suspension of voting rights as a sanction, careful consideration is needed to construct the suspension regime to optimise it as a sanction. This raises a number of questions, including whether it is possible to adopt such rules as part of the articles of association or a shareholder agreement (Section IV.B.1) and, if so, how the sanction should be formulated in these situations (Sections IV.B.2 and IV.B.3). Each of these questions will briefly be discussed in the following.

1. National rules on private ordering – freedom of contract or mandatory provisions?

The possibility of suspending voting rights can only be introduced in the articles of association or a shareholder agreement if national law allows for supplementing the legislation. Most countries have a certain degree of freedom of contract that allows shareholders to make private ordering in the

[38] See, e.g., Harm-Jan De Kluiver, 'Towards a Simpler and More Flexible Law of Private Companies – A New Approach and the Dutch Experience' (2006) 3(1) Eur. Comp. & Fin. L. Rev. 11; Mette Neville in Mette Neville and Karsten Engsig Sørensen (eds), *Company Law and SMEs* (Thomson Reuters 2010) 247–91, and in the same book Joseph A. McCahery and Erik P. M. Vermeulen, 'Conflict Resolution and the Role of Courts: An Empirical Study' 207–47.

form of articles of association and/or shareholder agreements. However, there can be considerable differences in the level of freedom of contract depending on whether this relates to the regulation of the articles of association, or the regulation of shareholder agreements. Although it is beyond the scope of this chapter to go into the question in depth, the following offers some indication of the differing levels of freedom of contract in different countries and their significance in relation to the use of suspension as a sanction in the articles of association and shareholder agreements.

Looking at private ordering in the form of articles of association, the perception in most countries, including Denmark, the Netherlands, Italy, Germany and Belgium, seems to be that the articles of association must not conflict with the mandatory provisions of company law. Nevertheless, there may be a considerable difference in the scope of the freedom of contract, partly due to the scope of mandatory regulation, and partly because the basis for the freedom of contract may differ.

In Denmark there is a general principle of freedom of contract in company law. This means that basically there is freedom to choose between different forms of incorporation and there is freedom to determine the contents of the company's contracts (for example the articles of association and shareholder agreements). Freedom of contract is limited only by the mandatory provisions of a company's legislation, general legal principles etc.[39] Thus, if a relationship is not exhaustively regulated, as a rule it is possible to supplement legislative regulation with a special sanction clause.

In Germany, there is also the possibility of supplementing the provisions of company law in the articles of association, but the freedom of contract for the shareholders of a public limited company is more limited than in Denmark. In accordance with the German Public Companies Act, § 23, subsection 5, the articles of association can only deviate from the provisions of the Act if the Act explicitly permits it (*Satzungsstrenge*).[40] Consequently, it is doubtful whether a suspension clause could be inserted into the articles of association under

---

[39] Martin Christian Kruhl, *Ejeraftaler* (Karnov Group 2011) 79; and Anders Ørgaard, Bernhard Gomard and Hans Viggo Godsk Pedersen, *Almindelig kontraktsret* (Jurist- og Økonomforbundets Forlag 2015) 15.

[40] Sebastian Mock, 'Shareholders' Agreements between Corporate and Contract Law' in Sebastian Mock, Kristian Csach and Bohumil Havel (eds), *International Handbook on Shareholders' Agreements* (De Gruyter 2018) 279. Certain tendencies to relax the rules for non-listed *Aktiengesellschaften* (AG – German public company) can be found in case law, cf. Mathias M. Siems, *Convergence in Shareholder Law* (Cambridge University Press 2008), and Susanne Kalss and Holger Fleischer, 'Neues zur Lockerung der Satzungsstrenge bei nicht börsennotierten Aktiengesellschaften' (2013) 19 Die Aktiengesellschaft 693–704.

German law. In contrast, German private limited companies are not bound by the *Satzungsstrenge* principle of the articles of association.

While the articles of association must not conflict with mandatory legislation, it is often assumed that shareholder agreements are not subject to the same limitation.[41] In Denmark it is assumed that shareholder agreements must not conflict with the mandatory provisions of company law.[42] Since company law does not prohibit supplementing the sanction provisions of the law, there seems to be nothing to prevent shareholders from inserting a suspension clause in the shareholder agreement. Greece seems to have an intermediate position with a high degree of freedom of contract. As regards the scope of the freedom of contract in shareholders' agreements, the starting point seems to be that the content may be contrary to what is termed 'simple mandatory rules' but it may not be incompatible with fundamental features of the corporate form involved.[43] As mentioned above, in Germany, there is a *Satzungsstrenge* principle in relation to the articles of association in public limited companies. In principle, this restriction only applies to the articles of association, but shareholders cannot replace the articles of association by a shareholder agreement. This means that if the shareholders address certain issues in a shareholder agreement which is supposed to be governed by the articles of association, the shareholder agreement has no binding effect among the existing shareholders. In that way, the *Satzungsstrenge* principle has a limiting effect on shareholders concluding shareholder agreements.[44]

2. The imposition of the sanction – *ex lege* or after legal examination?

If shareholders wish to incorporate suspension provisions in the articles of association or shareholder agreements, the question is how to impose the sanction. Does it come into force automatically at the point of sanctionable behaviour (*ex lege*), or must a decision be made to impose the provision, and if so, by whom? As mentioned in Section III.C, an *ex lege* approach is best suited for infringements that are more or less objectively identifiable. When applying a suspension provision in connection with violations that require a legal

---

[41] In Dutch theory, it is discussed whether this is the case or not, cf. Wino J. M. van Veen, 'The Netherlands' in Mock, Csach and Havel (eds) (n 40) 447f.

[42] Cf. The Danish Parliamentary Company Law Report 1498:2008. However, this has been questioned in legal theory, cf. Mette Neville, 'Denmark' in Mock, Csach and Havel (eds) (n 40) 222 with references.

[43] Cf. Georgios Psaroudakis, 'Greece' in Mock, Csach and Havel (eds) (n 40) 314f. As an example, the author mentions a general unanimity requirement within the voting consortium, which may lead to paralysis in the functioning of the corporation itself, and it is fundamentally incompatible with the majority principle in public corporations and the efficiency principle underlying it.

[44] Mock (n 40).

assessment, the question is who should conduct this assessment. The logical solution is to leave the decision as to whether to suspend voting rights to one of the corporate bodies, such as the board of directors or the general meeting. However, such corporate bodies may not be objective nor may they have sufficient legal expertise to decide whether the behaviour is of such nature that it warrants such a serious sanction. Thus, the solution may only be appropriate if there is a 'clear' case.[45] In other cases the assessment should be conducted by a body that has sufficient legal expertise. This may be a court, which would be a protracted and expensive process. In some countries like Denmark, there is also a tradition for allowing corporate conflicts to be solved by way of private arbitration. This ensures a quicker legal process and decision. In return, there is no opportunity for appeal.

3. The effect of suspension

When designing the suspension the following should be considered: which voting rights should be suspended and within which timeframe? These issues are discussed in Section III.B.2, but it is worth contemplating whether it is possible to go a bit further in enhancing the sanction when it is included in the articles of association or a shareholder agreement.

If the sanction is used to ensure that the shareholder will not influence decisions in the company, it should be ensured that the suspension does not leave the shareholder with rights that allow such influence. For instance, a shareholder may have a veto right which is linked to the status as a shareholder and it may be necessary to ensure that these rights are also suspended. In addition, is should be made clear whether the suspended shares are counted as being 'represented' at the general meeting even though they lack voting rights. If they are counted as represented shares, they may de facto count as 'No' votes where a simple or qualified majority of the represented shares is required to carry a decision. This effect can be avoided by making it clear in the articles that suspended votes should not be counted as being represented at a general meeting.[46] Finally, it may be prudent to cancel the offending shareholder's rights to attend the general meeting to ensure that the shareholder may not use this right to create further conflicts in the company.

If the suspension aims to curb the influence of the shareholder, it may be considered necessary also to restrict the managerial influence which the offending shareholder may have if he or she is an appointed director in the

---

[45] Seibt (n 29) 797–803.

[46] This solution has also been adopted as part of the regulation of suspension under the major shareholding regimes in Sweden, Finland and Germany, see Swedish Financial Instruments Trading Act, ch. 6, 3o §; and the Finnish Securities Act, ch. 17, 1a §, and for Germany, MüKoAktG/Bayer WpHG § 28, para 21.

company. It does not seem possible to suspend a director's exercise of voting rights on the board as this would make him or her unable to perform his or her function as a director. Therefore, if it is necessary to curb shareholders' influence as directors, it should be ensured by forcing the offending shareholder to give up his or her position as a director, allowing for the appointment of a different director.

V. CONCLUSIONS

Suspension of the exercise of voting rights as a sanction is already in use, and after the recent change to the Transparency Directive it will be used even more. It is potentially a very effective sanction against shareholders who value the influence they can gain using their voting rights. Therefore, using this sanction should be considered in a wider range of situations for both infringements of shareholder duties laid down by the law and for duties agreed among shareholders.

However, this sanction is far from suitable for all types of infringements. It is very difficult to construct a procedure that allows the sanction to be introduced with sufficient speed and therefore it seems to work best if it is imposed *ex lege* or automatically according to the terms agreed among the shareholders. Such a solution will, however, only work optimally for infringements that are fairly easy to ascertain, whereas more complicated duties need to be decided by either an official body, a court or the board of directors. If the decision needs to be left to an official body, a court or the board, there may still be some (preventive) effect in applying the sanction, but since it is likely that the sanction will be imposed too late, the sanction of suspension should probably be combined with other sanctions. This could include the possibility of annulling decisions taken in the time between the infringement being committed and the suspension being decided.

The most promising area for applying the sanction is in private ordering between shareholders. To our knowledge, the sanction is seldom used but our examination shows that there are situations where the sanction may have merits. However, in this area, it may also prove complicated to draft the sanction in an efficient manner as company law in some countries may make it impossible to use the sanction or may make it difficult to enforce. Therefore, drafters need to carefully consider how and when they can introduce this sanction.

9. Financial sanctions for breach of shareholders' duties

Jennifer Payne and Elizabeth Howell

I. INTRODUCTION

The focus in company law has traditionally been on shareholders' rights rather than shareholders' duties. While some forms of shareholders' duties have existed for many years, this is an issue that has come to greater prominence recently. This is due to a number of factors, including a growing recognition of the need to hold institutional investors accountable to their underlying investors, a trend that is evident in recent amendments to the Shareholder Rights Directive,[1] and also a recognition that corporations, and by extension their shareholders, should be held more accountable for the effect they have on societal issues such as environmental matters.[2] A discussion of shareholders' duties is therefore emerging in the rhetoric of academics, practitioners and regulators.

It is increasingly understood that any discussion of law on the books needs to be coupled with an analysis of the law in action. Issues of enforcement are therefore key to any consideration of the shape and nature of shareholders' duties. This chapter will consider one particular aspect of such enforcement, namely the imposition of financial sanctions as and when shareholders' duties are breached. The term 'financial sanctions' is not a term of art and requires some explanation. It is used here to mean sums required to be paid by a shareholder for breach of its duties qua shareholder. We include all forms of civil sanctions giving rise to such a payment, including damages for breach of contract and payments by way of compensation, but we do not include discussion of financial sanctions imposed following criminal proceedings (fines), as this has not, to date, been a significant means by which shareholder duties have been enforced.

---

1 Directive 2017/828/EU of the European Parliament and of the Council of 17 May 2017 amending Directive 2007/36/EC as regards the encouragement of long-term shareholder engagement.

2 See, e.g., Colin Mayer, *Firm Commitment* (Oxford University Press 2013).

Whether financial sanctions are imposed will depend on a number of factors. One of the key issues will be the nature of the breach and this depends in large part on how the duty arises. Sections II to IV of this chapter therefore consider the three different ways in which shareholders' duties can arise, namely by contractual agreement between the parties (shareholders' agreements) (Section II); by way of the company's constitution, generally the articles of association (Section III); and by imposition of law (Section IV). In each case the role and function of financial sanctions in enforcing the duties is considered. There are, however, other factors that will affect this issue, which do not map exactly onto these categories, including the nature of the company, the identities of the claimant and defendant, whether claims also exist for other claimants, most notably the company, and the availability of other remedies. These issues are therefore discussed as relevant throughout the chapter.

In Section V we draw together the threads of the arguments raised in the previous sections and we argue that financial sanctions can have the potential to play a valuable function with respect to enforcing shareholders' duties. That role will vary, however, depending on the way that the duty arises, as well as the wrongdoing in question. Specifically, where such duties are imposed via agreement, via the articles, or imposed by law in order to regulate the intra-shareholder relationship, then financial sanctions appear to have a relatively small role to play. This can be for a number of reasons, not least that it may be very difficult for parties to prove that a loss has been suffered due to a breach of duty, and that an alternative remedy may be preferable for the parties, such as the ability for a shareholder in a private company to exit the company at a fair price. In contrast, financial sanctions have the potential to play a greater role in enforcing shareholders' duties in publicly traded companies, particularly where duties are imposed to pursue broader societal goals, such as strengthening and supporting the European capital markets.

II. FINANCIAL SANCTIONS FOR BREACH OF DUTIES ARISING VIA A SHAREHOLDERS' AGREEMENT

In simple terms, shareholders' agreements are governed by the ordinary rules of contract, and such agreements have the ability to play a valuable, if supplemental, role to a company's constitution. Such agreements can offer a number of benefits over the company's constitution, not least privacy, meaning they can be advantageous for the inclusion of more delicate matters, such as a firm's dividend policy, and the remuneration of directors. In general terms, in addition to the members agreeing to adhere to the agreement, the company itself may also be joined as a party; however jurisdictions can vary on this, and there are dangers, including that the company can risk being seen to be contracting out of its statutory powers.[3]

Although such agreements commonly include shareholders' rights, they can be less effective for the imposition of duties. First, under the doctrine of privity, only those shareholders who are the parties to the contract are bound and so it will not automatically bind new members or transferees. Although incoming members can be required to execute a deed of adherence to the agreement, this quickly becomes impractical in companies where the identity of the members is frequently changing.[4] Accordingly, shareholders' agreements are only of limited use in larger companies. Next, as shareholders' agreements adhere to classical contractual law principles, the consent of all the parties will be necessary to form, and vary, the contract and to agree to the creation, and alteration, of rights and the imposition of duties. This means it may not be useful for the imposition of duties in the first place as a member could simply refuse to enter the contract.[5] As a result, shareholders' agreements have their greatest relevance, in practice, for small companies with a stable shareholder base, and in situations where the contractual rights and obligations are those to which the members wish to subscribe.

A. Enforcement: Overview

At the enforcement level, in general terms, contractual obligations are enforceable by the parties as of right. Claimants seeking to enforce a breach of duty will also not be constrained by the additional rules of company law, which can, for instance, require that claims be brought by members in their capacity as members (see further Section III). Accordingly, in principle, shareholders, and/or the company itself (if a party and not seen to be fettering its powers) can bring a claim, or be held to account, for breaches of duty arising from a shareholders' agreement.

Before considering contractual enforcement, it should first be observed, however, that a shareholders' agreement may provide for its own resolution mechanisms. Especially keeping in mind the private nature of a shareholders'

---

[3] E.g., *Russell v Northern Bank Development Corp Ltd* [1992] 1 WLR 588 (HL). Severance may be possible but, if not, the validity of the whole contract could be jeopardised, see Eilis Ferran, 'The Decision of the House of Lords in Russell v. Northern Bank Development Corporation Limited' (1994) 53 Cambridge L.J. 343.

[4] It can also be tricky to make adherence arrangements completely watertight, see Paul Davies and Sarah Worthington (eds), *Gower Principles of Modern Company Law*, (10th edn, Sweet & Maxwell 2016) ch 19, para 19.28.

[5] Jennifer Payne, 'Contractual Aspects of Shareholders' Duties' in Hanne S. Birkmose (ed), *Shareholders' Duties* (Kluwer Law International 2017) ch 6, §6.03.

agreement, the terms may specify, for instance, that any dispute be escalated to an independent third party for resolution, or the agreement may require that disputes be referred to binding arbitration. Alternative dispute resolution procedures can offer a number of benefits, especially keeping in mind the costs and related downsides of litigation, and arbitration proceedings will also have the advantage of being confidential.[6]

Aside from this, in principle, a range of contractual remedies is available, the aim being (broadly) to protect the injured party's right to contractual performance. In general terms, contractual remedies can be divided into three broad categories: compensatory financial damages (in practice the most common remedy on a breach of contract claim); non-compensatory financial remedies (where other aims, such as preventing a defendant profiting from a breach, are relevant); and specific remedies (which impose duties on the contract-breaker, such as providing that a sum is payable on breach of contract).[7] With respect to this third category, granting an equitable remedy (such as an award of specific performance or an injunction) may also be preferable to a member, rather than a damages award. Such remedies are attractive as they can compel a shareholder to comply with the agreement and/or to perform or refrain from specific acts. For example, in *Puddephatt v Leith*, an undertaking by a member to vote their shares in a particular way, as directed by another person, was enforceable by a mandatory injunction.[8] In many civilian legal systems (and in Scotland), some specific remedies may be relatively easily accessible in principle: for instance, a plaintiff is prima facie entitled to an award of specific performance.[9] In contrast, however, the English courts have been relatively reluctant to make such awards.

B. Damages

Turning to financial remedies, a breach of duty under a shareholders' agreement can give rise to a compensatory financial damages award. Nonetheless a shareholder claiming this remedy faces a number of hurdles. First, a common law claim for contractual damages will confine a claimant to recovering the

---

[6] E.g., *Fulham Football Club (1987) Ltd v Richards & Another* [2011] EWCA Civ 855.

[7] See further Ewan McKendrick, *Contract Law: Text, Cases and Materials* (7th edn, Oxford University Press 2016); Janet O'Sullivan, *The Law of Contract* (7th edn, Oxford University Press 2016).

[8] *Puddephatt v Leith* [1916] 1 Ch 200.

[9] Note, however, that there is considerable overlap between the situations in which different jurisdictions would refuse such an order (i.e., including where performance of the contract would expose a defendant to severe hardship).

actual loss suffered as a result of the breach, and the loss suffered by a breach of duty may be tricky to prove or to quantify. Such issues will depend on the nature of the breach in question but, for instance, it could be difficult to prove or quantify the loss suffered by the breach of a duty of disclosure. Next, shareholders may be barred from claiming damages if the loss flows to the company (the 'reflective loss' principle). Broadly, in most jurisdictions, the basic principle is that, where the company suffers loss caused by a breach of duty owed to it, only the company may sue in respect of that loss. No action lies with the shareholder where the shareholder's loss merely reflects that suffered by the company.[10] Exceptions do exist, so for instance where, by reason of the wrong done to it, it is impossible for the company to sue, then a member may be able to recover personal losses arising from the wrongdoing.[11] Further, in some jurisdictions, including the Netherlands and England, a member can have an independent cause of action if a separate legal duty towards the shareholder has been violated.[12] Nonetheless, in practice, it is not necessarily easy to distinguish between reflective and independent losses. Taken together, although it has been stated that there is 'surprisingly little authority' on shareholders' agreements and the breach thereof,[13] when one bears in mind these obstacles (and that the outcome of any arbitration procedures will be confidential) this may be less remarkable than at first glance.

With this in mind, the availability of an alternative, if exceptional, form of compensatory damages is worthy of consideration. This has been considered with respect to breaches of non-compete obligations in a shareholders' agreement in the English Court of Appeal case of *Morris-Garner v One Step (Support) Ltd.*[14] Here, the seller of shares in a joint venture company deliberately breached non-compete and non-solicitation obligations covertly. It was difficult for the claimants to identify the financial loss it had suffered by the defendants' breaches, and the damages awarded were assessed not on the normal measure, but as a sum it would have been reasonable for the party in breach to pay for the hypothetical release of the covenants immediately before the breach (sometimes referred to as '*Wrotham Park*' or 'negotiating' damag-

---

10 E.g., *Johnson v Gove Wood and Co* [2002] 2 AC 1 (HL). A number of rationales are put forward for the rule, including the prevention of double recovery and the protection of creditors.

11 *Giles v Rhind* [2002] EWCA Civ 1428.

12 See Bas J. de Jong, 'Shareholders' Claims for Reflective Loss: A Comparative Legal Analysis' (2013) 14 E.B.O.R. 97.

13 Robin Hollington, *Hollington on Shareholders' Rights* (8th edn, Sweet & Maxwell 2016) ch. 3, 3–59.

14 *Morris-Garner v One Step (Support) Ltd* [2016] EWCA Civ 180.

es).[15] Undoubtedly, the greater availability of such awards could help tackle some of the difficulties parties have when faced with the 'normal' contractual basis. Nonetheless, this approach has not been universally welcomed.[16] Indeed, the Supreme Court recently overturned the Court of Appeal ruling holding that negotiating damages is not a means of side-stepping the primary approach for measuring contractual damages.[17] The Supreme Court ruling signals a return to a more orthodox approach to awards for breach of contract claims; it narrows the scope of *Wrotham Park* damages, and rejects the notion that such damages could be simply available when the court considers them to be a 'just' response.[18] In light of this, it remains the case that *Wrotham Park* damages are certainly the exception and not the rule.

C. Agreed Damages Clauses

In light of these various issues, one alternative is to insert an agreed damages clause into the agreement, providing that a specific amount is payable in the case of breach.[19] Such a clause requires the defaulting party to pay a fixed sum regardless of the loss that is actually suffered. These types of terms can provide benefits to both parties: they can avoid court involvement and can enable parties to set out in advance the amount payable in the event of a breach. Nonetheless, under all major systems of law, there is a long-standing rule enabling courts to strike down terms that are, in fact, punitive penalties. In England, the retention of this penalty clause jurisdiction has been a topic of much debate, not least because in the case of sophisticated market participants of roughly equal bargaining power, there are powerful arguments to the effect that the principle of freedom of contract should prevail.[20] Such parties are gen-

---

15 See *Wrotham Park Estate Co Ltd v Parkside Homes Ltd* [1974] 1 WLR 798 where a reasonable sum was awarded when the defendant had breached his duty to the claimant by building houses in breach of a restrictive covenant.

16 E.g., in the context of breach of duties of confidence under contracts of employment, the High Court in *Marathon Asset Management Llp v Seddon* [2017] EWHC 300 (Comm) cast doubt on the availability of *Wrotham Park* damages.

17 *Morris-Garner v One Step (Support) Ltd* [2018] UKSC 20 (Supreme Court).

18 Ibid at para 81.

19 The insertion of such clauses is common in many jurisdictions. For instance, in Denmark, although the Danish Company Act (Act No 322 of 11 April 2011) provides that shareholders' agreements are binding neither on the company nor on decisions taken by the general assembly, agreed damages clauses tend to be inserted in shareholders' agreements to prevent or to remedy breach.

20 E.g., Sarah Worthington, 'Common Law Values: The Role of Party Autonomy in Private Law' in Andrew Robertson and Michael Tilbury (eds), *The Common Law of Obligations: Divergence and Unity* (Hart Publishing 2015) ch 14, 26.

erally capable of protecting their own interests, and it should not be possible for them to be relieved of their obligations simply because an agreement turns out to be a bad bargain.[21]

The recent English Supreme Court decision of *Cavendish Square Holdings BV v Talal El Makdessi*[22] is therefore pertinent for consideration for two reasons: first, to the disappointment of many commentators, the court refused to abolish the penalty clause jurisdiction; but secondly, it identified that financial compensation may not necessarily be the only legitimate interest an innocent party has in including such a clause.[23] In general terms, the case concerned a clause in a share sale agreement designed to protect goodwill in the company, where, if the seller breached the non-compete restrictive covenants, the seller lost the right to receive the final two instalments of the price (approximately 44 million dollars). The seller breached this duty by competing with the business, the purchaser withheld these payments, and the seller argued this was a penalty. The Court of Appeal held the clause to be a penalty and unenforceable, largely due to the fact that, according to the court, the payment strayed beyond the function of compensation and entered the territory of deterrence.[24] In Christopher Clarke LJ's view, the agreement prescribed a type of double jeopardy for the seller: the buyer would have remedies under the clause for breach of the restrictive covenant, and the seller would still remain liable to the company.[25]

The Supreme Court, however, held that the clause was not a penalty. In particular, the court stated that there was no simple distinction between clauses focused on compensation, and those focused on deterrence, stating that 'a deterrent provision in a contract is simply one species of provision designed to influence the conduct of the party potentially affected'.[26] Further, although recognising that in straightforward cases, the innocent party's interests will rarely extend beyond compensation, it acknowledged that this was not neces-

---

[21] With respect to concerns that such clauses could adversely affect consumer contracts, specific regulations are in place (via unfair terms provisions) to protect consumers.

[22] *Cavendish Square Holdings BV v Talal El Makdessi* [2015] UKSC 67.

[23] Jonathan Morgan, 'The Penalty Clause Doctrine: Unlovable but Untouchable' (2016) 75 Cambridge L.J. 11.

[24] The traditional view was that clauses designed to deter breach were penal and unenforceable, see *Dunlop Pneumatic Tyre Co Ltd v New Garage and Motor Co Ltd* [1915] AC 79.

[25] Accordingly, as the company had suffered a small loss, the reflective loss principle was engaged and the buyer was unable to recover, *Talal El Makdessi v Cavendish Square Holdings BV and Another* [2013] EWCA Civ 1539 at paras 106, 120–21 See also Janet O'Sullivan, 'Lost on Penalties' (2014) 73 Cambridge L.J. 480.

[26] Per Lords Sumption and Neuberger at para 31.

sarily a party's only legitimate interest, and that such clauses would only be struck down where 'unconscionable' or 'extravagant'.[27]

Regardless of one's stance on whether or not the penalty jurisdiction serves a valuable purpose, the Supreme Court's focus on the issues of compensation and deterrence is significant. Although an innocent party should not have an interest in punishing a contract-breaker, a carefully drafted clause should, in principle, be capable of both operating as a deterrent (in an attempt to secure performance), and also providing a means of obtaining compensation in the event of breach. Perhaps this is all the more vital in the arena of company law, given that shareholders could otherwise be barred from recovering damages due to the reflective loss principle.

D. Enforcement: the Company

The enforcement situation is more complex where the company is a party to the agreement. First, where the contract contains terms that fetter the company's exercise of its statutory powers, such terms will be unenforceable (although these may be enforceable against the shareholders if the company's obligation is severable).[28] But this limitation does not necessarily mean that, for instance, a company cannot bring a claim for breach, or that a claim cannot be brought against the company for breach of a prior contract. Nevertheless, even if damages are available in principle, in line with earlier observations, these may prove difficult to quantify. For example, in *Cullen Investments Ltd v Brown and Others*,[29] the company, which was party to a joint venture agreement, was in principle entitled to an award for damages arising from the other party's breach of their contractual duty of disclosure. Justice Barling commented that this may be of little more than academic interest, however, as it was not clear the company had suffered any loss due to the breach. Although alternative bases, including a non-compensatory disgorgement of profits, were considered, there was an absence of detailed submissions by the parties. Further, given that the company succeeded on its primary case of breach of directors' duties, the likely outcome was an account of profits that would render the contractual claim otiose.

---

[27] Ibid paras 31–32. Interestingly, the Supreme Court also considered that in principle (in the absence of reflective loss issues) a claim for common law damages could also remain open to the buyer (if they had suffered any loss), and left open whether or not the existence of such a contractual clause would abate any such loss recoverable by the party, see paras 76, 277.

[28] *Russell v Northern Bank Development Corp Ltd* [1992] 1 WLR 588.

[29] *Cullen Investments Ltd v Brown and Others* [2017] EWHC 1586 (Ch).

Drawing this section together, it is clear that financial sanctions for breach of duty are available to shareholders as a matter of general contract law. In practice, however, it can be difficult for parties to prove a loss has been suffered due to such a breach; and shareholders may also be barred from bringing a claim due to the reflective loss principle. Although alternative bases for calculating damages exist that can hold a shareholder accountable (such as *Wrotham Park* damages), these remain controversial and have, until recently, had relatively limited applicability to breaches of shareholder agreements. Rather, the alternative of including an agreed damages clause providing for a quantified sum payable on a breach of duty may offer more protection to the parties. Such a clause can seek to secure performance in the first place and provide a privately agreed financial sanction in the event of breach.[30]

III. FINANCIAL SANCTIONS FOR BREACH OF DUTIES ARISING VIA A BREACH OF THE ARTICLES

A. Overview

In addition to shareholders' agreements, shareholders' duties can also be created from the company's constitution, usually via the articles of association. To some extent the constitution is a type of contract; so, for instance, in England, section 33 of the Companies Act 2006 deems the constitution to be a contract between the company and each of the members: a 'multi-party' contract. This means, in line with Section II, that the provisions are, in theory, enforceable by one party against another and can be engaged where there is a breach or threatened breach of duty. At the same time, it is also commonplace to observe that the articles differ from a conventional contract; in particular, as the constitution is a public document (unlike a shareholders' agreement), the courts consider that contract law should apply with qualifications.[31] For example, to ensure the protection of third parties who rely on publicly available documents, the English courts have held they have no jurisdiction to rectify the articles.[32]

From the point of view of imposing duties on members, unlike a shareholders' agreement, the articles automatically bind new members to the company. This helpfully circumvents the obstacles observed in trying to seek the adherence of new shareholders joining the company and suggests that the

[30] See Worthington (n 20) ch 14, 21, who observes that contract law is exclusively concerned with agreed 'private financial sanctions', including agreed remedies.

[31] This is also a requirement of EU law, see Directive 2009/101/EC, art. 2(a).

[32] E.g., *Scott v Frank F Scott (London) Ltd* [1940] Ch 794 (CA).

articles may be a useful vehicle for the imposition of duties. Yet, on the other hand, as the articles can generally be altered by majority vote, it may be tricky to impose a new duty in the face of opposition from the majority.[33] Hence, although duties can be imposed on shareholders via the articles, it is not that common an occurrence in practice.

B. Enforcement: Overview

At the enforcement stage (and in comparison with obligations in a shareholders' agreement that are enforceable as of right) there are a number of challenges for aggrieved members. Specifically, there are an 'odd medley' of company law principles that can hamper the bringing of a claim under the articles.[34] For instance, English courts require members to bring actions in their capacity as a member (the 'qua member' rule) and not in some other capacity.[35] Further, if the court regards the wrong in question as merely an internal irregularity, capable of simple ratification by the majority, no personal remedy will be available for the member.[36]

With respect to the remedies available for breach of the articles, most company law remedies are discretionary and, in England, the imposition of a financial sanction for breach of the articles is rare. In part this is due to the fact that, prior to legislative intervention in the 1980s, it was not possible for shareholders to claim damages against a company for breach of the statutory contract.[37] The rationale for this particular restriction was never entirely clear and the current law now provides that being a member does not preclude a claim for damages.[38] Aside from this, the rarity of actions resulting in a financial remedy is also likely due to issues considered in Section II; a shareholder may struggle to prove the loss suffered by the breach; and/or the company may be regarded as the proper claimant. Accordingly, in practice the alternative of an unfair prejudice petition may provide a more straightforward avenue for an

---

[33] See further Payne (n 5) ch 6, §6 04.

[34] Sarah Worthington, *Sealy and Worthington's Text, Cases, and Materials in Company Law* (11th edn, Oxford University Press 2016) ch 4.

[35] *Hickman v Kent or Romney Marsh Sheep-Breeders' Association* [1915] 1 Ch 881. In practice this principle can often be worked around but it nonetheless remains an enforcement constraint.

[36] *MacDougall v Gardiner* (1875) 1 Ch D 13; cf. *Pender v Lushington* (1877) 1 Ch D 13.

[37] *Houldsworth v City of Glasgow Bank* (1880) 5 App Cas 317 (HL); *Re Addlestone Linoleum Co* (1887) 37 Ch D 191 (CA).

[38] Worthington (n 34) ch 4. Change occurred via the Companies Act 1985, s 111A, see now Companies Act 2006, s 655.

aggrieved member faced with a breach of duty than attempting to bring a claim for breach of the articles.[39]

C. Who Can Enforce the Statutory Contract?

In line with Section II, the starting point is that it is the parties to the contract who are capable of bringing a claim,[40] meaning the company can enforce the articles against the members, the members can enforce *inter se*, and the members can enforce against the company. The first two categories are relatively straightforward and, although not resulting in a financial sanction, there are some illustrations concerning enforcement for breaches of duty under the articles. For example, the English case of *Hickman v Kent or Romney Marsh Sheep-Breeders' Association*[41] concerned a breach of a member's obligation to submit disputes to arbitration. The company could enforce the statutory contract on the member, and a stay of legal proceedings was awarded. Equally, with respect to a member enforcing the articles *inter se*, in *Rayfield v Hands*[42] the articles provided that where a member wished to transfer his shares, the member could oblige the directors (who were also members) to take the shares. The court allowed the member to enforce the duty-imposing provision, ordering the purchase of the shares.

The third category of enforcement, namely against the company, is the most problematic, although more tangentially related to the issue of shareholders' duties. Nevertheless, the challenges facing members in such situations may also have a knock-on impact with respect to the likelihood of a member trying to enforce the statutory contract in other situations. In general terms, the English courts take a particularly restrictive approach to claims brought against the company. This is linked to earlier observations that breach of such obligations may be held to relate merely to an internal irregularity on the company's part, rather than the infringement of a personal right. More generally, even if a claim is actionable, the likely (or preferable) remedy may be a specific remedy such as an injunction, rather than the imposition of a financial sanction.[43]

An alternative approach to tackling the question of enforcement under the articles has been mooted. This would involve a default rule providing that all obligations are capable of enforcement contractually by members, both against other members and the company (unless the breach was trivial or the remedy fruitless;

---

39 See, e.g., Law Commission, *Shareholder Remedies* (Report No 246, 1997) part 7.

40 Note that third parties (certainly in England) have no rights to enforce the articles, see the Contracts (Rights of Third Parties) Act 1999, s 6(2).

41 [1915] 1 Ch 881.

42 *Rayfield v Hands* [1960] Ch 1.

43 See, e.g., *Pender v Lushington* (1877) 1 Ch D 13.

or unless the contrary was stated in the constitution).[44] Damages would then be an available remedy if the shareholder personally (as opposed to the company) suffered loss by the breach. This proposition comes with its own issues, not least practical concerns, including likely litigation levels and the impact it could have on the length and complexity of a company's articles. Nevertheless, it has much to commend it, including enabling financial sanctions (and their threat) to potentially play a bigger role in the event of a breach of duty arising. Indeed, in England, the proposition was strongly supported as part of the proposed revisions to the companies legislation but was not embraced in the 2006 Act.

Taken together, what is evident is that although the constitution can be used as a vehicle for imposing duties on members, this occurs only rarely in practice. Next, the various stumbling blocks a member must overcome in order to bring a successful claim means actions for breach of the articles are relatively uncommon. Finally, and in line with Section II, aggrieved shareholders seeking a financial remedy may struggle to prove and quantify the loss suffered by a breach.

IV. FINANCIAL SANCTIONS FOR BREACH OF DUTIES IMPOSED BY LAW

The law has intervened in the shareholders' bargain and introduced various duties upon the shareholders. These duties may be imposed by statute, case law, regulation and even, potentially, as a result of soft law norms. There are various reasons why the law may seek to impose duties on shareholders[45] but the most common are where the intervention is designed to provide minority shareholders with protection from the majority, i.e. to regulate the intra-shareholder relationship, and where the intervention is designed to protect other stakeholders, whether this is the employees, creditors or investors in the capital markets more generally. An example of the first is the obligation imposed on shareholders by the English courts to vote bona fide in the interests of the company as a whole when altering the articles of association.[46] Some jurisdictions go further and impose a duty of loyalty on shareholders.[47] An example of the second is the

---

[44] K. W. Wedderburn, 'Shareholders' Rights and the Rule in Foss v. Harbottle' (1957) 15 Cambridge L.J. 194; Company Law Review Steering Group, *Modern Company Law for a Competitive Economy: Final Report* (2001) ch 7, 7.34.

[45] See Payne (n 5) §6.05.

[46] *Allen v Gold Reefs of West Africa Ltd* [1900] 1 Ch 656; *Citco Banking Corp NV v Pusser's Ltd* [2007] UKPC 13; *Re Charterhouse Capital Ltd* [2015] EWCA Civ 536.

[47] For discussion see Andreas Cahn, 'The Shareholders' Fiduciary Duty in German Company Law' in Hanne S. Birkmose (ed), *Shareholders' Duties* (Kluwer Law International 2017).

duty imposed on institutional shareholders by the revised Shareholder Rights Directive to develop a policy on shareholder engagement and to disclose that policy.[48] This is intended to tackle concerns about short-termism in the financial markets and concerns about a lack of institutional shareholder engagement more generally, and thus to benefit investors generally.

Given that the law creates these duties, the nature of the remedy when the duty is breached is also determined by the law, rather than by the agreement of the parties. The law does not always make financial sanctions available for breach. Whether they are depends on a number of factors, including the nature of the wrong, the identity of the defendant, and, ultimately, on what the remedy is intended to achieve.

A. Intra-shareholder Duties

The structure of companies varies enormously on a spectrum from widely dispersed shareholding structures to single-person companies. It is very common, however, to see structures in which one shareholder, or a small group of shareholders, exercises control. Most jurisdictions support majority control, allowing a specified percentage of the shareholders short of 100 per cent to pass resolutions and to act as and for the company. This is necessary for the effective operation of companies but it leaves the minority exposed to the risk of abuse. The law will not step in to support minority shareholders in all scenarios, however. The fact that the minority is unhappy with the business policy determined by the majority is unlikely to prompt intervention, but other actions, for example the expropriation of the minority's shares, may do so.

To understand the remedies made available in this context, it is necessary to understand the reason for the law's intervention. It is notable that in many jurisdictions the law will intervene in the bargain between shareholders in order to provide minority shareholders with remedies in the event that they are treated unfairly by the majority. The concept of unfairness is one which requires some clarification if it is to be meaningfully applied in this context. The justification for the law's intervention rests on the fact that the shareholders strike a bargain when they enter a company, sometimes an explicit one via a shareholders' agreement, but more often the bargain is based on the company's constitution. As discussed in Section III, this is a peculiar form of contract, not least because it can be amended without a minority shareholder's consent. For shareholders in a private company, without a ready market for their shares, this means that

[48] Directive 2017/828/EU of the European Parliament and of the Council of 17 May 2017 amending Directive 2007/36/EC as regards the encouragement of long-term shareholder engagement, Art. 1(3) inserting new Art. 3g into Directive 2007/36/EC.

they may be effectively locked into a company that is materially different to the one in which they acquired shares. If a legal system wishes to incentivise investors to continue to take minority positions then some form of intervention is likely to be needed. This may take the form of rights but can also involve duties imposed on the majority.

Unfair treatment of the minority often arises from decisions taken in the general meeting and so attention in this area can provide the minority with protection. The law generally provides rules to govern this issue, such as determining the size of the majority required to pass certain decisions. This may also include setting out certain decisions that the majority are simply not permitted to take, such as increasing the size of a shareholder's investment in the company without their consent[49] or specifying circumstances in which controllers are excluded from voting on particular issues. The law may go further, however, and impose duties on shareholders regarding how they may exercise their power to pass shareholder resolutions. For example, in English law the courts have implied a requirement that shareholders act in a particular way when voting to alter the articles of the company. In *Allen v Gold Reefs of West Africa Ltd*[50] the Court of Appeal held that the power to alter the articles must be exercised 'not only in the manner required by law, but also bona fide for the benefit of the company as a whole, and must not be exceeded. These conditions are always implied, and are seldom, if ever expressed.'[51]

If the majority breach this duty, it is for the minority to bring a claim, not a regulator. If the claim succeeds, the remedy provided is not a payment to the shareholder, but (potentially) a reversal of the majority decision. In voting to amend the articles, the shareholders are, collectively, acting as the company. If the majority act improperly (however that is defined)[52] in voting to alter the articles, the principle set out in *Allen v Gold Reefs of West Africa Ltd* enables a minority shareholder to assert that the amendment is improper and should be set aside. Effectively, the claim is that the appropriate procedure has not been followed, and the amendment is thus invalid. Consequently, it is unsurprising that, if the court agrees that the decision is improperly taken, the remedy is to nullify the decision rather than to award a financial remedy. These cases effectively allow the minority a general right of appeal regarding the validity

---

[49] Companies Act 2006, s 25(1). Similar provisions are found in other jurisdictions, e.g. AktG §180 in Germany.

[50] [1900] 1 Ch 656.

[51] Ibid 671. See, e.g., *Citco Banking Corp NV v Pusser's Ltd* [2007] UKPC 13; *Re Charterhouse Capital Ltd* [2015] EWCA Civ 536.

[52] The 'best interests of the company' test is unclear and has been the subject of much judicial and academic discussion. For discussion see Davies and Worthington (eds) (n 4) 19-4–19-11.

of shareholder resolutions. It will then be for the court to determine how interventionist it is prepared to be.

One form of protection that the law can provide to the minority is therefore to ensure that the majority sticks to the rules provided by the law, whether those rules are explicitly or implicitly expressed. This addresses the point that the rules governing the company may be changed after the minority shareholder enters the company, i.e. the bargain entered into by the shareholder may change, but only in specified ways that either the shareholder can determine in advance or in circumstances where the shareholder can appeal to the court regarding the fairness of the alteration *ex post*.

Another form of protection is to provide the minority shareholder with a more direct form of redress. In particular, as set out above, the concern for the minority shareholder in a private company may be being locked in to a company which differs substantially from that which the shareholder joined. Some jurisdictions therefore provide the minority with appraisal rights, that is the right to exit the company at a fair price if certain decisions with which they disagree are taken by the majority. Crucially, they comprise not simply the right to exit the company, but to exit at a fair price, and as such they may also provide benefit to shareholders in a listed company. In English law, appraisal rights following specific decisions are relatively uncommon, reflecting the view that their use can place potentially significant hurdles in the path of the decisions that trigger those rights.[53] However, minority shareholders have a more general remedy under English law that can be utilised in this scenario, namely an unfair prejudice petition under sections 994–996 Companies Act 2006. The most common remedy provided is a buy-out of a successful petitioner's shares at a fair price.[54] This can be a useful alternative to a claim that the decision-making contained a procedural defect. The prospect of a more direct remedy may also be attractive. The court has a wide remedial discretion to 'make such order as it thinks fit for giving relief in respect of the matters complained of'[55] and so is not limited to the buy-out order.

Financial compensation is one possibility but this poses a number of difficulties. First, it would be necessary for the petitioning shareholder to demonstrate that financial compensation is the appropriate remedy. In general, these cases involve small quasi-partnership companies and the fact of disagreement and litigation between the parties makes it unlikely that they will be able to

[53] See, e.g., Insolvency Act 1986, ss 110–11 (triggered by a decision to reorganise the company). The sell-out right held by minority shareholders following the acquisition of a controlling block by a bidder (Companies Act 2006, s 983) is similar but is triggered by a control shift rather than a corporate decision.

[54] See *Re Bird Precision Bellows Ltd* [1984] Ch 419.

[55] Companies Act 2006, s 996(1).

work together in the future.[56] A remedy which enables a 'clean break' is often the most appropriate outcome. Where the petitioner does request payment of some kind, it will generally be for specific unpaid sums, such as dividends that have not been declared in favour of the petitioning shareholder.[57] Second, the shareholder would presumably need to demonstrate that the breach of duty had caused them loss, something which may not be straightforward, as discussed in Section II. Third, any such order raises the possibility that the payment may fall foul of the reflective loss principle set out in Section II. The relevance of the reflective loss principle to unfair prejudice claims has not been discussed often by the English courts, in part because financial compensation is rarely a remedy sought by petitioning shareholders.[58] This principle is potentially problematic for petitioning shareholders in the scenario in which the shareholder is basing the petition on a breach of the articles, or a breach of the duty to pass a shareholders' resolution in the correct manner, since this is a wrong both to the company and to the shareholder. As a minimum, any court considering the payment of financial compensation would need to ensure that there is no possibility of double recovery by the shareholder.

In summary, financial sanctions appear to have relatively little part to play in enforcing any of the intra-shareholder duties examined in this section. Instead, the law appears to focus on providing more pragmatic remedies, whether that is the reversal of an improperly taken majority decision, or facilitating the exit of the minority from the company at a fair price.

---

[56] It is possible for shareholders in publicly traded companies to petition under ss 994–96 Companies Act 2006 but such claims are rare, in part because shareholders have the ability to exit the company without the aid of the court by selling their shares on the market, see, e.g., *Re Astec (BSR) plc* [1998] 2 BCLC 556.

[57] Claims for unpaid dividends will fail, absent any special circumstances, as shareholders generally have no legitimate expectations to receive them. However, a claim may succeed where the petitioner can demonstrate some special arrangement, such as an agreement that the profits of the company would be taken out in a particular way (e.g. by the payment of dividends), that was subsequently breached: *Re Sam Weller & Sons Ltd* [1990] BCLC 80; *Re J&S Insurance & Financial Consultants Ltd* [2014] EWHC 2206 (Ch).

[58] The issue did arise in *Atlasview Ltd v Brightview Ltd* [2004] EWHC 1056 (Ch), where the judge felt that the reflective loss principle did not apply, but there are reasons to doubt the judge's decision in that case, see Jennifer Payne, 'Sections 459–61 Companies Act 1985 in Flux The Future of Shareholder Protection' (2005) 64 Cambridge L.J. 647, 667–74.

B. Duties to Other Stakeholders

By way of contrast, financial penalties seem to have a potentially more significant role where the duties are intended to benefit a group other than the shareholders. In addition, the means of enforcement of such duties may be located not with the shareholders, or at least not with the shareholders alone, but in some external body. In particular, where the duty is intended to benefit the market as a whole, the means of enforcement may well be placed in the hands of the regulator. There are a number of benefits to having the regulator as enforcer, including a potentially more nuanced view to remedies, since a regulator can take account of both deterrence and compensation when determining the size of any award.[59] As regards the latter, the UK regulator has the option of imposing a restitution order if it feels that compensation should be made available to particular individuals.[60] The recent restitution order imposed against Tesco by the Financial Conduct Authority (FCA) is notable, not least because the FCA has only rarely had recourse to restitution orders in the past. Accordingly, it could hint at the start of a wider shift by the regulator towards seeking to compensate those who have suffered a loss.[61] On the other hand, it remains clear that there are a number of potential downsides to actions brought by regulators; for example, a regulator has only limited resources, which may limit the number of actions brought, and such a regime also raises issues of regulatory capture.[62]

A good illustration of a duty imposed in this context is the obligation on shareholders under the Transparency Directive to disclose their shareholdings when they cross various thresholds,[63] an obligation which is, in part, intended to benefit those outside the company and the market more generally.[64] In line with a growing recognition that harmonisation at EU level requires a focus on supervision as well as on the rules, the Transparency Directive provides guidance to Member States as to how they should enforce the obligations set out in the Directive, while leaving to Member States the actual task of supervision. Member States are required to 'lay down rules on administrative measures and sanctions applicable to breaches of the national provisions adopted in

---

59 For further discussion see Chapter 6.

60 Financial Services and Markets Act 2000 ('FSMA') s 384.

61 See, e.g., FCA, Final Notice to Tesco plc and Tesco Stores Ltd, 28 March 2017.

62 The UK regulator has been criticised for the low level of its enforcement actions in the past (see, e.g., John C. Coffee, 'Law and the Market: The Impact of Enforcement' (2007) 156 U. Pa. L. Rev. 229, and this is something which it has sought to address in recent years.

63 Directive 2004/109/EC as amended by Directive 2013/50/EU, Art. 9(1).

64 Ibid, Recital 18.

transposition of this Directive and shall take all measures necessary to ensure that they are implemented. Those administrative measures and sanctions shall be effective, proportionate and dissuasive.'[65] The Directive details the factors that should be taken into account when determining the appropriate sanction.[66] Crucially, it also sets out the sanctions that should be available to competent authorities, and financial sanctions are one of the powers specified, alongside the issuing of a public statement of the person responsible for the breach and the nature of the breach, and an order for that person to cease the conduct constituting the breach.[67] The Directive sets out different sanctions for legal entities and natural persons and in each case specifies that the competent authority should have the power to impose a sanction of a specified amount (up to EUR 2,000,000 for natural persons, and, for legal entities, EUR 10,000,000 or up to 5 per cent of the total annual turnover according to the last available annual accounts approved by the management body) or up to twice the amount of the profits gained or losses avoided because of the breach, where those can be determined, whichever is the highest.

In the UK, this obligation is enforced by the FCA.[68] The FCA has a range of powers available to it where a shareholder is found to have breached this duty, including the power to fine shareholders that are in breach, but also the power to apply to court for an order suspending a shareholder's voting rights.[69] The UK financial regulator has exercised this power, although on only one occasion to date. In 2011 the Financial Services Authority (FSA) (the predecessor of the FCA) exercised this power, issuing a fine of £210,000 to Sir Ken Morrison for failing to disclose his reduced shareholding and voting rights in Morrison Supermarkets Plc (Morrison).[70] Between 2009 and 2010 he failed to notify the company on four separate occasions when his voting rights fell below the rele-

---

[65] Ibid, Art. 28(1).

[66] Ibid, Art. 28c.

[67] Ibid, Art. 28b.

[68] In the UK, shareholders have a statutory right to bring a claim for fraudulent misstatements in secondary market disclosures but this claim can only be brought against the company: FSMA, s 90A. In addition, they have a right at common law to bring a claim regarding negligent misstatements in secondary market disclosures where the purpose of the statement is to benefit the shareholders, and the maker of the statement is aware that it may be relied on by that group: *Caparo Industries plc v Dickman* [1990] 2 AC 605. This claim remains intact after the introduction of s 90A FSMA (FSMA, Sch 10A, para 7(3)(a)(v)). This claim is rarely brought and its parameters are unclear. It is theoretically possible that such a claim might arise regarding a shareholder's obligation to disclose under the Transparency Directive but it would require a special set of circumstances.

[69] See the Transparency Regulations 2015 (SI 2015/1755). For further discussion of this issue see Chapter 8.

[70] FSA, Final Notice, Sir Ken Morrison, 16 August 2011.

vant thresholds imposed by the UK Disclosure and Transparency Rules.[71] While he did not financially benefit from these breaches, his failure to notify Morrison of the changes to his shareholding resulted in Morrison not being in a position to update the market in accordance with the UK's disclosure rules. This resulted in the market being misled as to the ownership of voting rights in Morrison.

It is clear that financial sanctions can play an important role in this context. As the sanctions set out in the Directive make clear, there are a number of elements potentially present in the imposition of these penalties, including the removal of any advantage acquired by breaching the provisions, i.e. profits gained or losses avoided, and the need for the penalty to act as an effective deterrent. This is also clear from the FSA's decision to fine Sir Ken Morrison. The FSA applied careful and detailed criteria in order to determine the size of the appropriate penalty.[72] It considered that although he had not either made a profit or avoided a loss as a result of his failure to disclose, a penalty was nevertheless required in order to provide a deterrent: there was 'a clear need to impose a meaningful penalty to achieve deterrence',[73] particularly in view of his wealth and prominent position in the industry.

V. CONCLUDING REMARKS

In light of the foregoing analysis, and in order to judge the role and effectiveness of financial sanctions in enforcing shareholders' duties, the aims of enforcement must be considered. Very broadly, enforcement regimes tend to focus on one or both of two issues: deterrence and compensation. Deterrence aims to prevent a particular behaviour from occurring, and compensation is designed to provide a remedy to those who suffer loss or harm as a result of breach of shareholders' duties. Keeping such aims in mind, what becomes evident is that financial sanctions can be a valuable tool for shareholders (particularly when balanced against other remedies) but that the precise role such sanctions can play will vary depending on the different ways that shareholders' duties arise, as well as the wrongdoing in question. Equally, with respect to effectiveness, the actual levels of enforcement activity, and the size of any sanction imposed, will be important.

Specifically, with respect to a breach of shareholders' duties arising via contract, via the articles, or where imposed by law to moderate the

71 The disclosure triggers in the UK are located in the FCA Handbook, DTR 5.1 and are more onerous than those required by Directive 2004/109/EC, as amended.

72 Set out in the FCA's DEPP (Decision Procedure and Penalties Manual).

73 FSA, Final Notice, Sir Ken Morrison, 16 August 2011, para 30(b). The figure agreed on was £300,000, but this was reduced by 30% in view of the fact that Sir Ken Morrison had agreed to settle at an early stage in the FSA's investigation.

intra-shareholder relationship, the award of a remedy will generally be part of a wider attempt to try and regulate the bargain as agreed between the parties. In such instances, the enforcement aims of compensation and deterrence may have less significance than simply enforcing the terms agreed by the parties, explicitly or implicitly. Equally, although financial sanctions can be a useful tool in such situations, the chapter illustrates that it can be extremely difficult for parties to succeed with such a claim. Moreover, alternatives such as granting an injunction requiring a shareholder to vote their shares in a particular way, or awarding a buy-out, may provide more pragmatic remedies. Such awards may be preferable not only for a shareholder who can, for instance, exit a company in the case of an irretrievable breakdown of relations, but also for the courts, who can bypass having to make difficult decisions for a company by basing their rulings on the premise that they are enforcing the parties' bargain.

In contrast, with respect to the enforcement of shareholders' duties via an external party such as a regulator, financial sanctions may have a more valuable role to play in practice. In this regard, one should also keep in mind the type of companies at which such sanctions will be directed. These are not small, quasi-partnership companies; rather, these are publicly traded firms in which the public's pension pots may be invested, and where duties are placed on institutional shareholders in order to benefit their underlying investors and to benefit the market more generally. In such situations, the regulator is not attempting to manage or mediate the intra-shareholder relationship; rather the aim is to protect other stakeholders, including those that are investing in the securities markets. Accordingly, the regulator's intervention in the event of a shareholder's breach of duty can be justified here, both in order to hold those in breach accountable, and on the broader grounds of ensuring the effective and smooth functioning of the capital markets.

In light of this, the chapter demonstrates that the main function of the regulator imposing a financial sanction in such a scenario is to remove any profit obtained by the breach and to act as a deterrent. Nonetheless, in this regard, the broader development concerning the Tesco restitution order should be kept in mind, as this could hint at the start of a move towards seeking to compensate investors who have suffered a loss. Aside from this, however, deterrence remains key. Yet, if this is a major driver behind the imposition of a financial sanction, and if there could be greater use of financial sanctions by regulators to enforce breaches of shareholders' duty going forward, then the regulator needs to fully embrace its use of such enforcement powers in practice. Further, it must ensure the penalty imposed is high enough to act as a credible deterrent and not be merely just a cost of doing business for the party in breach. Accordingly, it may be that there are limits to the impact the civil law can have in this area. Specifically, the imposition of a civil sanction may have only a limited impact on sophisticated market players, and the greater threat of criminal law enforcement may be necessary in order to act as an effective deterrent. In this regard, the introduction of common minimum rules across the EU for the imposition of criminal sanctions in cases of market abuse may provide a valuable precedent.[74]

[74] See Ester Herlin-Karnell, 'White-Collar Crime and European Financial Crises: Getting Tough on EU Market Abuse' (2012) 37 Eur. L. Rev. 481. Note that the UK and Denmark did not opt in to the criminal sanctions regime. For the UK's approach, see, e.g., *Regina v Christopher McQuoid* [2009] EWCA Crim 1301, where Lord Judge Chief Justice held that there needed to be 'an element of deterrence' in such sentences.

10. The basis of shareholder liability for corporate wrongs

Christian A. Witting

I. INTRODUCTION

There is intense debate in the European Union and beyond about the current responsibilities and potential liabilities of shareholders.[1] This chapter argues for greater attention to be paid to the design of a liability regime that incentivises all participants in corporate endeavours to take appropriate measures to avoid the causation of personal injuries. The appropriate liability regime should incentivise shareholders to undertake their statutorily assigned roles in the governance of investee companies – namely, through making proper appointments to corporate boards and undertaking proper monitoring of corporate risk-imposition. The chapter argues that the only incentive that is likely to ensure that shareholders do their part is a residual personal liability for unsatisfied personal injury claims.

The chapter is structured as follows: first, the parameters of the discussion are set out. Second, the chapter examines rules of limited liability, which protect the personal assets of shareholders from claims by company creditors. Third, it argues that, in considering exceptions to limited liability, the problems of fault-based liability systems ought to be kept in mind. These problems open the way for greater reliance upon strict liability. Fourth, the chapter argues that the most appropriate liability system will exploit the enhanced 'deterrability' of companies. Deterrability arises because the company embodies a hierarchical structure, has formalised decision-making processes and can coordinate activity so that potentially harmful actions are constrained and wrongdoing avoided. Fifth, it is argued that, given their important functions in companies, shareholders constitute a key target group for the purposes of

1 A turning point in the debate was Henry Hansmann and Reinier Kraakman, 'Towards Unlimited Shareholder Liability for Corporate Torts' (1991) 100 Yale L.J. 1879.

achieving deterrence. Finally, the chapter sketches out a potential pro rata strict liability rule and considers the possible adverse consequences of such a rule for capital raising and economic growth.

II. PARAMETERS OF DISCUSSION

The basic problem with which we are concerned is that of corporate insolvency. The chapter assumes that a company has committed a wrong but cannot pay its tort victims in full. For reasons that will be explained, the focus will be upon the position of personal injury victims. In the premises, there is a need for recourse to individual participants involved in the company's endeavours. The chapter considers the strongest possible arguments that can be made in favour of the extended liability of shareholders – that is, where their liability derives from the wrongdoing of the company itself and not from their own personal wrongdoing.

In considering the design of an appropriate liability regime, the accepted goals of tort liability ought to be kept in mind. Courts have been consistent in holding that tort liability has the twin goals of compensation and deterrence.[2] Tort law is supposed to compensate tort claimants for losses that they have suffered and to deter persons from engaging in wrongful conduct. In certain types of insolvency situation, personal injury claimants have been unable to obtain full compensation from injuring companies. Typically, this is because those companies have engaged in physically risky processes, or supplied defective goods, over a long duration before injuries have started to manifest themselves. When claims finally arise, the assets of these companies prove to be inadequate. Cases falling into this category have included the supply of asbestos products[3] and defective pharmaceuticals.[4] In such situations, recourse to directors, senior officers and other individual wrongdoers is unlikely to be adequate; their resources will be dwarfed by the size and number of claims made. Therefore, personal injury claimants will likely have to fall back upon publicly funded health systems in order to facilitate their recovery – unless liability can be extended to shareholders, who typically will be high-net-worth individuals and/or present in sufficient numbers so as to be a viable avenue of recourse.

As to the second of the goals of tort liability, there is much scepticism in the private law literature about courts' ability to deter wrongful conduct through the imposition of liability rules. To some extent, the scepticism is

---

2 E.g., *E v English Province of Our Lady of Charity* [2013] QB 722, [47].

3 See, e.g., Jock McCulloch and Geoffrey Tweedale, *Defending the Indefensible: The Global Asbestos Industry and its Fight for Survival* (Oxford University Press 2008).

4 See, e.g., Christian A. Witting, *Liability of Corporate Groups and Networks* (Cambridge University Press 2018) 122–37.

warranted. The drunken driver rarely has deterrence imperatives on his or her mind. However, the contention will be that scepticism about deterrence is not warranted in the present context of insolvent companies. The deterrence potential here is real, the issue being how to exploit this potential by designing appropriate incentives to guide conduct. Again, much of the existing law focuses on directors and senior officers. Their susceptibility to personal liability is both important and well established. Such persons have the day-to-day control of the company and must be made accountable for the powers of the company that they exercise. The susceptibility of directors and senior officers to personal liability through the directors' duties owed to the company and other liability rules probably ensures that companies are – in most cases – run competently and that much potential wrongdoing is avoided. However, there is concern that, where wrongdoing does occur, directors and senior officers rarely end up making significant contributions to compensatory awards.[5]

In seeking to overcome the problem of corporate insolvency, this chapter argues that shareholders occupy a key position in the corporate governance hierarchy and that their potential liability for personal injury claims would be an important development in creating an effective company liability regime. The objective is not to turn all shareholders into full-time monitors, or to create another level of management in the corporate governance hierarchy – because such developments would have their own costs to the company and its ability to compete.[6] The objective, rather, is to place proper incentives upon shareholders so that they take responsibility for ensuring that their investee companies avoid wrongdoing that leads to the causation of personal injury. In many cases, as adumbrated, the optimal response to the prospect of shareholder liability will be to ensure that the company is in the hands of the right directors and senior managers[7] and otherwise to monitor major risks that affect company value either personally or through proxy advisory services.[8]

III. LIMITED LIABILITY

Discussions of shareholder liability frequently begin with observations about the basic building blocks of company and insolvency law that give shareholders a protected status. First, we recognise that companies are separate legal

---

5 Peter Conti-Brown, 'Elective Shareholder Liability' (2012) 64 Stan. L. Rev. 409, 453–54.

6 See Zohar Goshen and Richard Squire, 'Principal Costs: A New Theory for Corporate Law and Governance' (2017) 117 Colum. L. Rev. 767, 771.

7 Ibid 779.

8 See Paul H. Edelman, Randall S. Thomas and Robert B. Thompson, 'Shareholder Voting in an Age of Intermediary Capitalism' (2014) 87 S Cal. L. Rev. 1359, 1366.

persons with their own rights and responsibilities. These are different from the rights and responsibilities of shareholders, directors, and employees. Second, the introduction of the corporate veil facilitates the partitioning of assets.[9] This means, for example, that company assets are owned by the company and that shareholders have no claims to them. Third, limited liability introduces a special rule that prevents company creditors from reaching into shareholders' personal assets in order to satisfy liability claims that the company cannot fulfil. The rule of limited liability makes it clear that the default position is that shareholders are not responsible for those debts.

Nineteenth-century legislators saw limited liability as crucial to achieving many social and business objectives, including:[10] the desire to facilitate 'freedom of association' in business; demands for a suitable form of investment vehicle for middle- and lower-class savers; the need to ensure that entrepreneurs are not lost to competing jurisdictions which protect shareholders; and pressures to facilitate the raising of capital in large amounts in order to fund infrastructure.[11] Yet limited liability occasionally presents a barrier to tort claimants seeking compensation for their losses. In this way, it is appropriate that we should reassess whether it represents an appropriate policy stance. It is arguable that much has changed since the nineteenth century. Today, we live in a world of over-production and ever-increasing concerns about the water supply, air quality, and the natural environment. Greater attention is being paid to the prospect of life in a 'post-growth' world. Moreover, we live in a world which places great emphasis upon human rights – including rights to life and bodily integrity.[12] It is in this context that the position of shareholders needs to be reconsidered.

Although we are conditioned to its existence, limited liability is not immutable. Indeed, there is a considerable literature which doubts its continued economic necessity. The arguments against limited liability are strongest with respect to parent companies. Companies are not risk averse in the way that individuals are and do not need to be spared the role of monitoring management in their subsidiaries.[13] However, this chapter considers the suitability of a wider type of shareholder liability that would encompass individuals too.

---

9 Hansmann and Kraakman (n 1).

10 See Rob McQueen, *A Social History of Company Law* (Ashgate 2009) 24–27, 32–33, 58–63, 71, 74, 82, 110 and 123.

11 See also Andrew Muscat, *The Liability of the Holding Company for the Debts of its Insolvent Subsidiaries* (Dartmouth 1996) 163.

12 E.g., Convention for the Protection of Human Rights and Fundamental Freedoms, Arts 2 and 5.

13 E.g., Ian Ramsay, 'Allocating Liability in Corporate Groups: An Australian Perspective' (1999) 13 Conn. J. Int'l L. 329, 343.

Here it is conceded that there *seems* to be a reasonable prima facie case for protecting individual shareholders from investee company debts.[14] But, even when we allow for this, it is not the only important matter to take into consideration in the design of an appropriate liability regime.

Considerable justification exists for reducing the scope of current rules of limited liability. There are two initial matters to consider in making this argument. First, it is understood that tort claimants are less able to protect themselves from company wrongdoing than are contract creditors. Whereas contract creditors (typically) can seek security over assets[15] and personal guarantees of debts,[16] or else examine the creditworthiness of counterparties, usually this is not possible for tort claimants.[17] Most tort claims arise from negligent wrongdoing or 'accidents' that are not predictable by tort claimants in advance. Although Bainbridge and Henderson argue that they can protect themselves by taking out insurance,[18] there is a question as to why the onus should be upon them to protect themselves from risk when it is the law's role to prevent activities that injure from occurring by setting appropriate standards of interaction between persons engaged in commercial activities and those potentially affected by them.[19] Indeed, Bainbridge and Henderson disregard an important point. The ability to externalise costs reduces companies' incentives to take care in the conduct of their activities. More persons are injured than otherwise would be.[20] It is clear, therefore, that significant legal protection of tort claimants is required against corporate wrongdoers.

Second, we need to consider whether any exception to limited liability should operate in favour of tort claimants generally or be restricted to more important protected interests in physical integrity. Limited liability results in a world of mutual risk-imposition by companies on other companies and on

---

14 See Stephen M. Bainbridge and M. Todd Henderson, *Limited Liability: A Legal and Economic Analysis* (Edward Elgar Publishing 2016) esp. ch. 3.

15 See, e.g., Paul L. Davies, *Introduction to Company Law* (Oxford University Press 2002) 70–71.

16 Reinier Kraakman, John Armour, Paul Davies, Luca Enriques, Henry Hansmann, Gerard Hertig, Klaus Hopt, Hideki Kanda and Edward Rock, *The Anatomy of Corporate Law* (2nd edn, Oxford University Press 2009) 99.

17 Where, in theory, it might be possible for creditors to seek credit reports about counterparties or demand security for debts, this is not always practicable: Helen Anderson, 'Veil Piercing and Corporate Groups – An Australian Perspective' (2010) N.Z. L. Rev. 1, 12–13.

18 Bainbridge and Henderson (n 14) 69.

19 Christian Witting, *Street on Torts* (15th edn, Oxford University Press 2018) 9–10.

20 See, e.g., Timothy P. Glynn, 'Beyond "Unlimiting" Shareholder Liability: Vicarious Tort Liability for Corporate Officers' (2004) 57 Vand. L. Rev. 329, 371.

individuals. Generally, it is defensible insofar as it protects shareholders from liability for financial losses. Although Hansmann and Kraakman and other proponents of exceptions to limited liability make no distinction between types of tort claim,[21] this chapter argues that any exception should prioritise the protection of bodily interests. Tort theory suggests that claimants' interests in their physical person are worthy of greater protection than shareholders' financial interests.[22] Tort law protects interests in the body to a high degree[23] because these are the most basic interests required for human survival. The point is that, for 'corporate defendants, the cost of accidents is simply that – an economic cost and calculation. For [injured] plaintiffs, the costs of accidents are much more personal, physical and irremediable ... [M]onetary compensation does not alter, even if it cushions the physical effects of their injuries.'[24] Moreover, the 'victim of a major tort suffers damage to a large part of his wealth and probably to his future earning capacity'.[25] Shareholders are likely to be in a better position than personal injury victims to cope when residual losses represented by the shortfall in company assets are imposed on them because they can diversify against financial losses.[26] When taken together, these points establish the basic defensibility of a system of extended liability which prioritises the personal injury claims of tort victims over the financial interests of shareholders. The exception should be as narrow as is consistent with proper protection of fundamental personal interests.

IV. EXCEPTIONS TO LIMITED LIABILITY

Having made a basic argument for considering whether there ought to be an exception to limited liability in cases involving unsatisfied personal injury claims, we need to return to current rules of limited liability. At the moment, assorted statutory exceptions to limited liability exist[27] but they would not easily accommodate recovery in the cases to which this chapter applies.[28] Given this position under statute, it is unsurprising that courts in many jurisdictions prefer a narrow doctrine of 'veil-piercing', which in the UK is focussed

---

21 See Hansmann and Kraakman (n 1).

22 William Lucy, *Philosophy of Private Law* (Oxford University Press 2007) 216ff.

23 Peter Cane, *Responsibility in Law and Morality* (Hart 2002) 130.

24 Allan C. Hutchinson, 'Out of the Black Hole: Toward a Fresh Approach to Tort Causation' (2016) 39 Dalhousie L.J. 651, 677.

25 Ben Pettet, 'Limited Liability – A Principle for the 21st Century?' (1995) 48 CLP 125, 154.

26 Ibid.

27 E.g., Pensions Act 2004 (UK) ss 38 and 43.

28 See Witting (n 4) 266–7.

upon the use of companies in order to evade prior obligations.[29] The position is more open in the United States, where the Model Business Corporation Act, section 6.22(b) provides: 'Unless otherwise provided in the articles of incorporation, a shareholder of a corporation is not personally liable for the acts or debts of the corporation except that he may become personally liable by reason of his own acts or conduct.' Where the shareholder has done more than simply provide capital, where he or she has engaged in relevant acts or conduct that cause injury to others, he or she can be held responsible. This opens the ways for a court to ask questions such as: '[D]id the defendant-shareholder do anything for which he or she should be held directly liable? Did the shareholder commit fraud, which led a creditor to forego contractual protections? Did the shareholder use fraudulent transfers or insider preferences to siphon funds out of the corporation?'[30] In the view of Bainbridge and Henderson, these are indeed pertinent questions to ask of shareholders.[31] But the present writer does not believe this to be satisfactory. There is a real issue as to whether shareholders ought to be held liable for company debts only when they have acted in ways that transform them from passive investors into fault-based wrongdoers. This chapter argues that limiting the potential for extended shareholder liability to historic wrongs based on identified fault is too narrow and – more importantly – that such a liability regime fails to unlock shareholders' capacity to guide their companies so that they avoid causing personal injuries.

V. THE FAULT SYSTEM

A key argument to be made in advocating a liability regime that permits recourse to shareholders is that fault-based liability is problematic. Problems with the fault system are of three kinds. First, there is an issue about whether the preoccupation with fault as the basis for tortious liability is rational. Second, there is the question of what constitutes the 'fault' in a fault-based regime of liability. Third, there is the difficulty experienced in proving fault in the corporate context. The problems related to fault and its proof make it easier to argue for a regime of *strict* shareholder liability.

The first issue is whether the insistence on fault-based liability is rational. The preoccupation with fault derives from Kantian-inspired will theory. The general idea is that acts cannot be judged as good or bad, right or wrong, without

---

29 *Prest v Petrodel Resources Ltd* [2013] 2 AC 415.

30 Bainbridge and Henderson (n 14) 18.

31 Neither Bainbridge nor Henderson would be in favour of a veil-piercing doctrine which travels beyond fault-based liability.

determining whether they were intended.[32] If tort law were able to focus exclusively upon the moral qualities of defendants' past conduct, will theory would appear to be a sound basis for fault-based liability rules. However, tort law is concerned also with the position of claimants and with the kinds of loss they suffer. In some cases, the claimant will have no alternative recourse other than the particular defendant whom he or she sues. Where the claimant has suffered personal injury, it becomes especially clear that will theory might need to give way to a more pragmatic balancing of the parties' interests. It is this kind of pragmatism inhering in tort law that has led Cane to observe that tort embodies a 'two-sided relation' and that the focus is just as much upon injured claimants as it is upon the moral qualities of defendant actions.[33]

The second issue is what constitutes 'fault' in a fault-based system of responsibility. Even if we were to subscribe to the will theory of tort law, we would find it difficult to defend current tort rules by reference to it. There are significant elements of strict liability in the current system. Indeed, strict liability typically is found with respect to the activities of companies and other collectives. Thus, for example, UK law has been moving steadily away from traditional conceptions of vicarious liability based upon narrow employment relationships.[34] Organisations are being made strictly liable for the wrongs of a wide range of persons who act on their behalf where relationships between organisations and individual actors are 'akin' to employment.

Of course, the main kind of fault-based liability in tort law is for *negligent* conduct. Yet this type of liability cannot be justified on the basis of will theory for a number of reasons. Negligent conduct is not necessarily the result of morally significant intentional acts. Even where it is, negligence liability arises from a mere failure to reach objectively set standards of care. This standard of care applies whether the actual defendant was capable of meeting it or not. As Honoré has explained, the tort of negligence can operate in a manner similar to strict liability where the defendant did not have the capability of reaching the nominated standard.[35] These are cases of 'short-comers', with respect to which the imposition of liability is justified by reference to the need for common and readily observable standards of care.

The third issue of relevance to assessment of the fault system concerns the difficulty experienced in proving fault in the corporate context. Here we need to remember that fault doctrines have been designed with individuals in mind and that they stem from old ideas about the importance of moral wrongdoing

---

[32] John Finnis, 'Intention in Tort Law' in David G. Owen (ed), *Philosophical Foundations of Tort Law* (Oxford University Press 1995) 229–30, 239 and 243–47.

[33] Cane (n 23) 99.

[34] E.g., *Various Claimants v Catholic Child Welfare Society* [2013] 2 AC 1.

[35] Tony Honoré, *Responsibility and Fault* (Hart 2002) esp. ch. 2.

in punishment regimes. They were not devised for modern organisations such as companies. Indeed, there are several reasons why it is artificial to look for moral wrongness in individuals taking part in corporate actions.[36] Here we touch upon two of them.

Decision-making and action in the corporate context are frequently collective in nature. Thus, important decisions are made by the board of directors, by a sub-set of the board and/or after a process of consultation with specialist advisors. Decisions made by these collectives need not represent the decisions that would have been taken by any of the individuals involved when acting alone.[37] This might be for various reasons, including the continuation of past company policies and the need for compromise in doing what is thought best for the company as a whole. Courts have proven reluctant to impose liability upon individuals who make decisions as part of their 'constitutional function' (especially when voting in formal company settings, such as the board of directors) for their injurious consequences.[38] Even if it is sensible to look for fault within the company, this might not be very easy to either find or prove when the injured claimant is an outsider. Outside claimants wishing to bring actions against individuals based upon identified wrongdoing are confronted not only by decisions that do not reflect the intentions of particular individuals, but also by the disaggregation of corporate operations between different company departments in accordance with normal divisions of labour and specialisations of function.[39]

The outsider starts with a huge disadvantage in not knowing how the company works, who is responsible for decisions, who has acted inappropriately, how this has impacted upon his or her situation, and so on. These are matters that will need to be subject to evidence and proof, and which might be obscured by company employees unwilling to assist claimants suing their employer companies. Under the fault system, individual decision makers and employees effectively might be 'immunised' from personal liability. In these ways, the search for an effective (and just) regime of collective liability in the corporate context ought not to be based on backward-looking concepts of fault[40] but on forward-looking incentives that will help companies make better decisions and lower the personal injury 'body count'. It is here that law-makers

---

36 See Tracy Isaacs, *Moral Responsibility in Collective Contexts* (Oxford University Press 2011) 55.

37 Ibid 30.

38 *MCA Records v Charly* [2002] BCC 650, [49].

39 See Alfred D. Chandler, *Scale and Scope: The Dynamics of Industrial Capitalism* (Harvard University Press 1990).

40 Note, however, that some fault-based tort doctrines might have a role to play in binding together individual wrongdoers and making them joint tortfeasors: see Witting (n 4) chs 11 and 12.

might prefer a strict liability regime – that is, where liability arises on the basis of unwanted outcomes and irrespective of the proof of fault. Existing examples of such regimes include the European Union's product liability regime[41] and domestic laws on vicarious liability.[42]

VI. STRICT LIABILITY IN THE ORGANISATIONAL CONTEXT

A different approach is required in designing the optimal company liability regime. Whereas we might hesitate to make individuals liable when they are not at fault, fault would appear to be less important in moral terms when organisations act and cause harm – because they are groups of persons with an inherently greater capacity to harm than individuals have. This has been evident in any number of examples – such as the BP oil spill of 2010 and the Bhopal toxic leak of 1984. Individuals acting alone could have brought about neither of these events nor their destructive consequences.[43] BP and Union Carbide (respectively) were large corporate groups conducting highly risky operations involving thousands of employees. The disasters for which they were responsible indicate that real attention needs to be paid to the adverse societal and personal *effects* of organisational activities because of their great potential to harm.

The preferable liability rules would ensure that responsibility for preventing personal injuries is placed upon companies and other organisations *before* they begin risky activities. This cannot be done very effectively under a fault-based liability regime. Where liability is in doubt (as it always is when fault must be proved), those potentially subject to it will discount (to a greater or lesser extent) its relevance to their decision-making. Unlike fault-based liability, strict liability has a forward-looking nature. It is of real use in creating incentives in potentially liable parties to act to avoid the future causation of harm. Strict liability provides strong incentives for those made responsible either to cease the conduct of particularly risky activities,[44] or to put in place policies and procedures that actually work in preventing the occurrence of injury. The suggestion is that we need to use the corporate governance, decision-making, and other company structures in a forward-looking manner in order to reform the way that they operate. The argument will be that this is a coherent strategy because companies are *deterrable* actors.

---

41 See Jane Stapleton, *Product Liability* (Butterworths 1994).

42 See, e.g., Witting (n 4) 396–405.

43 See Charles Perrow, *The Next Catastrophe* (Princeton University Press 2007).

44 Cane (n 23) 84.

VII. THE COMPANY AS A DETERRABLE ACTOR

Recall that our discussion assumes that we are considering the design of a liability regime for companies that engage in physical processes or which have physical outputs with the potential to cause personal injury. Good management means implementing proper processes and procedures to deal with risks. And there is every reason to think that companies should be able to do this effectively. Medium-size and larger organisations are characterised by hierarchical structures, formalised decision-making, and coordination of activities. Companies are able to plan in various ways to avoid the future causation of personal injuries. Their plans are transmitted through the organisation by way of policies, routines, and organisational culture. These constrain the actions of individuals, encouraging them to act in conformity with company objectives. The result is that companies are *deterrable* and will act to avoid risks when provided with appropriate incentives to do so.[45]

The argument begins by noting that, in corporate settings, personal relations and mutual cooperation among participants give way to hierarchy and structure. This entails high-level, long-term, and strategic decision-making at the top,[46] decisions which run down the chain of command, and an organisational chart that indicates where individuals are placed within the decision-making and command structure.[47] Hierarchy and structure help to specify how decisions should be made and tasks allocated.[48] They also facilitate formalised decision-making. At higher- and middle-management levels, decision-making is deliberative, being undertaken by the board of directors or subcommittees thereof. Effective committees take advantage of the combined knowledge of their members and of diverse points of view.[49] They produce solutions to problems that no single individual would be capable of.[50] At lower organisational levels, tasks are undertaken according to written procedures or established routines.[51] These procedures 'greatly reduce the discretion of most participants so that they make few [risky] choices and are circumscribed in the choices

---

45 Bridget M. Hutter and Michael Powers (eds), *Organizational Encounters with Risk* (Cambridge University Press 2005) 9.

46 Paul R. Lawrence and Jay W. Lorsch, 'High-Performing Organizations in Three Environments' in Derek S. Pugh (ed), *Organization Theory: Selected Classic Readings* (5th edn, Penguin 2007) 120.

47 Mary J. Hatch, *Organization Theory: Modern, Symbolic, and Postmodern Views* (3rd edn, Oxford University Press 2013) 92–93 and 242.

48 Ibid 93.

49 Christian List and Philip Pettit, *Group Agency: The Possibility, Design and Status of Corporate Agents* (Oxford University Press 2011) 86.

50 Cass Sunstein, *Infotopia* (Oxford University Press 2006) 54–55.

51 Hatch (n 47) 151.

they do make'.[52] Written procedures and established routines facilitate uniform and measurable outcomes, which permit monitoring of work and detection of wrongdoing and other deviations.[53] Procedures and routines create efficiencies also in training and in passing on knowledge. More informal norms or expectations further assist in constraining conduct. These features permit participants 'to know what is expected of them in a wide variety of situations, including how to coordinate their behavior with that of others in acts of organizing'.[54]

Medium-size and larger companies are likely to be structured along functional lines,[55] meaning that discrete teams of persons, or 'branching hierarchies', undertake specialised activities.[56] Decision-making powers in each functional unit are delegated to middle managers.[57] Middle managers have oversight of specified numbers of individuals, and their main responsibility is to coordinate work.[58] Individuals working within each functional unit are likely to specialise in their tasks. They understand the work that others within their team are doing and can coordinate activities with them. Branching hierarchies facilitate collective learning and memorisation. The company has the benefit not only of what has been learned by teams and individual team members, but also 'the awareness of who knows what'.[59] Branching hierarchies facilitate learning from mistakes and adoption of corrective procedures. The successful implementation of new practices in one part of the company can infiltrate others and bring about larger organisational change.[60]

The key to the deterrability of companies is the way in which court decisions can impact upon them and make use of their structures so that precautions are taken on a wider scale than would be possible as regards individuals acting alone. Deterrability results from the forward-looking nature of organisational decision-making, the structures through which decisions are implemented, the ability to compel participants to comply with decisions reached higher in the organisational hierarchy, and the ability to create uniform standards of conduct

---

52 William Richard Scott, *Institutions and Organizations: Ideas, Interests and Identities* (4th edn, Sage 2014) 24.

53 Ibid 59.

54 Hatch (n 47) 170.

55 Chandler (n 39) 230.

56 Hatch (n 47) 91–92.

57 Derek S. Pugh, 'Does Context Determine Form?' in Pugh (ed) (n 46) 34.

58 Stephen Bainbridge, 'Why a Board? Group Decisionmaking in Corporate Governance' (2002) 55 Vand. L. Rev. 1, 7.

59 Ibid 20.

60 Hatch (n 47) 309.

and consistent norms of behaviour. All of these things mean that organisations can bring about change that 'reverberates through the system'.[61]

Again, we can drill down further in looking at how courts can deter wrongdoing by using these structures. Two points will be made. First, courts have a significant role in developing standards of interaction between legal persons because they determine disputes on a case-by-case basis and receive evidence as to the actual workings of organisations. When applying *fault*-based tort rules at least, judicial decisions about organisational failures outline the appropriate standards of interaction which should be achieved and have a signalling effect. The organisation is likely to have an enhanced capacity to interpret and learn from tort judgments and the norms of conduct that they promote. This is because organisations are advised by lawyers and have the technical expertise to determine proper responses to the imposition of liability. Ideally, organisations will want to learn from court judgments against them so that they are seen as good corporate citizens worthy of continuing custom and respect.[62] In cases of strict liability, there is a sense in which organisations are delegated the task of determining themselves what the appropriate standards of interaction are and precautions to be taken. However, the simple fact that they are held liable is itself a signal that standards must be higher.

Second, while there is debate about the deterrability of individual wrongdoers, companies are well placed to respond constructively to tort liability decisions. They have the capability to make proper decisions about precautions to avoid harm in their interactions with others.[63] This capacity arises from their ability to respond to legal directives through processes of sense-making,[64] risk assessment, and forward planning.

> Sanctioning the corporation involves direct deterrence when we envisage the sanction, in impersonal terms, as a 'disturbing event' in the corporation's environment which serves to alert its decision making process to the existence of a certain dysfunction, triggering some standard operating procedure into taking remedial action consisting in some structural, or systemic change.[65]

---

61 Meir Dan-Cohen, *Rights, Persons, and Organizations: Legal Theory for Bureaucratic Society* (University of California Press 1992) 130.

62 Peter A. French, *Collective and Corporate Responsibility* (Columbia University Press 1984) 40, 162; Brent Fisse and John Braithwaite, *Corporations, Crime and Accountability* (Cambridge University Press 1993) 40.

63 Dan-Cohen (n 61) 134.

64 Scott (n 52) 237–38.

65 Meir Dan-Cohen, 'Sanctioning Corporations' (2010) 19 J.L. & Pol'y 15, 29–30.

Managers take the information they have about such disturbing events and formulate strategic responses with the assistance of advisors.[66] Companies can take action by taking expert advice, devising appropriate systems and procedures, investing in infrastructure and safety devices, determining which functional units and individuals shall undertake tasks, properly training managers and employees, monitoring performance, and terminating relationships with those employee/agents unable to perform adequately.[67]

VIII. THE ROLE OF SHAREHOLDERS

So, what has this discussion about the deterrability of companies got to do with shareholders? The argument is that shareholders do not play some incidental part in the lives of their investee companies. They have a definite, although diffuse, responsibility for their conduct. They have statutorily assigned roles to play in the management and operation of companies, which can help unlock the company processes just described and reduce undesired outcomes so as to achieve tort law's deterrence goal.[68]

The first relevant function is that shareholders arm companies with the funds required in order to undertake corporate activities. The very point of the shareholders is their provision of funding to get a business up and running and to help it to expand over time.[69] The latter is true especially of companies of real size.[70] 'As companies become larger, equity finance as a source of capital

---

[66] Michael T. Hannan and John H. Freeman, 'The Population Ecology of Organizations' in Pugh (ed) (n 46) 184–85.

[67] Jennifer Arlen and William Bentley MacLeod, 'Beyond Master-Servant: A Critique of Vicarious Liability' in Murdaugh Stuart Madden (ed), *Exploring Tort Law* (Cambridge University Press 2005) 120.

[68] See Frank H. Easterbrook and Daniel R. Fischel, 'Limited Liability and the Corporation' (1985) 52 U. Chi. L. Rev. 89, 94.

[69] When the original owners of shares sell them, their rights and responsibilities are transferred to new owners. These successor shareholders can be assumed to have factored potential company liabilities into the prices that they pay for their shares. What is more, these successors may be seen to 'contribute to capital' when profits which are potentially payable to them are retained for corporate uses: see John Armour, Dan Awrey, Paul Davies, Luca Enriques, Jeffrey N Gordon, Colin Mayer and Jennifer Payne, *Principles of Financial Regulation* (Oxford University Press 2016) 25–26 and 41. As such, they can be treated as candidates for liability in the same way as the original shareholders.

[70] Frequently, this is not apparent in smaller companies. Indeed, it is not so in 'the majority of limited companies' which rarely attract outside capital: Andrew Hicks, 'Corporate Form: Questioning the Unsung Hero' (1997) J. Bus. L. 306, 306 and 328–29. These sorts of companies are also less likely (individually) to be significant in

is likely to become more significant.'[71] There are likely to be large numbers of shareholders and the funds that they supply become company assets.[72] As such, shareholders have a continuing *financial* interest in the company's operations, reputation, and success, given that both the value of their shares and their dividend income depends upon the success of the company. This financial interest is the basis for management accountability to shareholders.

The second relevant function of shareholders is that they assume a place right at the top of the hierarchy in the corporate governance of their investee companies. Whether the investee company is large or small, the role played by shareholders in corporate governance has attached to it various powers by which collectively they can control its destiny. Collectively, the shareholders can do such things as: issue directions to the directors by special resolution;[73] alter the articles of the company;[74] appoint and dismiss directors who under-perform or who do not comply with their demands;[75] vote on fundamental corporate actions, such as proposals to restructure;[76] and so on. As such, the general meeting and the board of directors can be seen to 'share between them the most important corporate functions'.[77]

The powers given to shareholders are such as to give them a great potential to influence the business direction set by the directors. The important role that shareholders can – and should – play in the corporate governance function has been acknowledged in the literature and in corporate governance practice. Much of the focus has been upon engaging institutional shareholders. Institutional shareholders such as pension funds and insurance companies have amassed very significant holdings in public listed companies: 'The rise of institutional investors has led to increased concentration of equity ownership, with most public corporations now having a substantial proportion of their shares held by a small number of institutional investors.'[78] Given their large stakes, institutional shareholders often are 'locked in' to their holdings, and

---

the infliction of uncompensated personal injury and thus, to some extent, are ignored in this chapter.

[71] Louise Gullifer and Jennifer Payne, *Corporate Finance: Principles and Policy* (2nd edn, Hart 2015) 14.

[72] See Companies Act 2006, ss 658ff.

[73] Model Articles for Public Companies, Art. 4. Cf. *Automatic Self-Cleansing Filter Syndicate Co Ltd v Cunninghame* [1906] 2 Ch 34.

[74] Companies Act 2006 (UK) s 21.

[75] Companies Act 2006 (UK) s 168.

[76] Companies Act 2006 (UK) Part 26.

[77] Sarah Worthington, *Sealy and Worthington's Text, Cases and Materials in Company Law* (11th edn, Oxford University Press 2016) 188.

[78] Lucian A. Bebchuk, Alma Cohen and Scott Hirst, 'The Agency Problems of Institutional Investors' (Draft Paper, June 2017) 1 and 3–4. Cf. Brian R. Cheffins,

have added financial incentives to improve corporate governance in investee companies in order to better their returns.[79]

Institutional shareholders not only have significant shareholdings in medium-size and larger companies, but they have several attributes which make them ideal monitors of directors and managers. They are professional investors, often with large resources and the ability both to undertake a monitoring role and to strengthen corporate governance regimes[80] through the 'non-negligible effect' of their votes on the outcomes of general meetings.[81] Such investors might establish their own voting policies,[82] which even without the exercise of their powers in general meetings can be used to influence investee company attitudes towards corporate issues. Often this engagement is 'beneficial to the management of companies pointing towards issues or shortcomings which management itself has not been able to settle'.[83] Engagement in monitoring of risk contributes to 'financial performance by reducing the cost of future liabilities due to enforcement actions, legal claims, and other negative risk events'.[84] When an institutional investor believes that corporate performance has been substandard, it can lobby for change either with a public challenge to management, or by engaging in dialogue behind the scenes.[85] Where management is resistant, institutional shareholders either can take the lead in seeking change,[86] or else join with other investors through campaigns orchestrated by corporate advisory firms.[87] '[P]roxy advisory firms help to solve the monitoring problem by offering a low-cost way for institutional investors to inform themselves about issues on the corporate ballot and in some

---

Corporate Ownership and Control: British Business Transformed (Oxford University Press 2008) 391.

[79] Jill Solomon and Aris Solomon, *Corporate Governance and Accountability* (Wiley and Sons 2004) 95 and 113.

[80] Ibid 112.

[81] Bebchuk, Cohen and Hirst (n 78) 5.

[82] Solomon and Solomon (n 79) 100.

[83] Peter Böckli et al., 'Shareholder Engagement and Identification' (European Company Law Experts, 2015) https://europeancompanylawexperts.wordpress.com/papers-of-the-ecle/shareholder-engagement-and-identification-february-2015/.

[84] V Harper Ho, 'Risk-Related Activism: The Business Case for Monitoring Nonfinancial Risk' (2016) 41 J. Corp. L. 647, 664.

[85] Brian R. Cheffins and John Armour, 'The Past, Present, and Future of Shareholder Activism by Hedge Funds' (2011) 37 J. Corp. L. 51, 56.

[86] Solomon and Solomon (n 79) 105–06. There is a danger in some jurisdictions that this will mean 'acting in concert' such as to activate takeover rules: see, e.g., UK Panel on Takeovers and Mergers, *Takeover Code* (2016) Rule 9.1, Note 2.

[87] Jonathan Eley, 'Be heard by companies whose shares you own' *FT Money* (4–5 May 2013) 11.

cases to cast votes for institutions.'[88] Proxy advisory firms recommend voting against directors who fail adequately to address governance risks.[89]

Following the Global Financial Crisis, the general desire of governments and industry associations has been that institutional shareholders adopt a pro-active stance as company 'stewards'.[90] This means engaging in management issues affecting the company, taking a position on these, and helping to guide the company towards better governance and operating outcomes.[91] Indeed, there is evidence of increasing institutional shareholder participation in corporate management,[92] which in turn is associated with increases in corporate valuations.[93] However, institutional shareholders have yet fully to embrace the challenges of 'stewardship'. Reasons for this include: the free-rider problem and the consequent lack of incentives in fund managers to do more than track the market;[94] the difficulty faced by foreign institutions in engaging in domestic activism;[95] the difficulty of engaging in the corporate governance of large numbers of investee companies; and various negative signals that activism might send to the market.[96] Most fund managers will not initiate proxy contests within investee companies – although they might support activist hedge funds.[97] The result is that institutional shareholders typically expend 'negligible resources ... beyond what is required to comply with regulations' on governance matters.[98]

In this way, extra incentives are needed in order to encourage institutions and other shareholders to play their part in the governance role.[99] The

---

[88] Edelman, Thomas and Thompson (n 8) 1425.

[89] Harper Ho (n 84) 680–1.

[90] See, e.g., EU Directive 2007/36/EC as regards the encouragement of long-term shareholder engagement, Art. 3g.

[91] EU Directive 2017/828/EU amending Directive 2007/36/EC as regards the encouragement of long-term shareholder engagement, Recital 14.

[92] E.g., Edelman, Thomas and Thompson (n 8) 1365.

[93] See ibid 1410.

[94] Bebchuk, Cohen and Hirst (n 78) 13ff.

[95] Cheffins (n 78) 392.

[96] See Jeffrey G. MacIntosh, 'Institutional Shareholders and Corporate Governance in Canada' (1996) 26 Can. Bus. L.J. 145, 158–71.

[97] Ronald J. Gilson and Jeffrey N. Gordon, 'The Agency Costs of Agency Capitalism: Activist Investors and the Revaluation of Governance Rights' (2013) 113 Colum. L. Rev. 863, 868–89.

[98] Bebchuk, Cohen and Hirst (n 78) 18. Activist hedge funds comprise a well-known exception: ibid 24ff. But they 'are focused on actions that will immediately increase shareholder value' and prefer to lobby about matters such as capital structure and deployment of resources rather than operational risks: Edelman, Thomas and Thompson (n 8) 1423; Cheffins and Armour (n 85) 68–69.

[99] Harper Ho (n 84) 662.

Shareholder Rights Directive has been amended to try to encourage engagement through a comply-or-explain approach.[100] This entails institutional shareholders providing minimum information to their own investors about policies on engagement and explanations where they could, but do not, engage with investee companies about their material medium- to long-term risks.[101] Such legislation might have a positive effect in increasing monitoring and improving operational outcomes.[102] However, it is almost certain that it will be inadequate. Limited liability has too many inbuilt incentives to externalise costs onto involuntary creditors. Because of the absolute importance of reducing the extent to which companies engaging in risky physical processes and selling risky products cause personal injuries, it is arguable that an appropriate incentive has to be found in *liability* rules.

IX. OUTLINE OF SHAREHOLDER LIABILITY REGIME

The current corporate governance framework typical of advanced economies is *dependent* upon shareholders undertaking their collective function. That governance function belongs to them and to no one else. Shareholders who do not take part in the execution of that function might be accused of a type of neglect. Such neglect could provide a basis for their legal responsibility for unsatisfied company debts. Indeed, this has been *recognised by the legislature* in its decision to grant shareholders the privilege of limited liability. In creating rules which limit shareholders' liability, legislatures have both recognised the potential for shareholder liability based on the roles that they play within their investee companies[103] *and* determined for policy reasons that shareholders ought to be protected from this prospect. For the reasons that have been given in this chapter, the full extent of shareholder limited liability is no longer defensible.

In other works, the present author has outlined the broad contours of a potential shareholder liability regime.[104] In brief, the proposal is for a regime of pro rata strict liability to attach at the point in time that the company knows of pending personal injury claims. Pro rata strict liability would avoid problems of wealthier shareholders having to monitor their fellow shareholders'

---

[100] See Financial Reporting Council, *The Stewardship Code* (2012).

[101] Directive 2017/828/EU of the European Parliament of the Council of 17 May 2017 amending Directive 2007/36/EC as regards the encouragement of long-term shareholder engagement, Recitals 17 and 20.

[102] But see Bebchuk, Cohen and Hirst (n 78) 31.

[103] There is historical precedent for shareholder liability in their former vulnerability to the imposition of leviations: see Bainbridge and Henderson (n 14) 30.

[104] E.g., Witting (n 4) 287–303.

ability to pay out.[105] And pinning liability to the point when knowledge of pending claims arises would prevent existing shareholders from seeking to sell their shares and to offload liability. These are features which the present author's proposal shares with that of Hansmann and Kraakman.[106] However, the proposals differ because the present author would provide for an exception to limited liability in cases of personal injury claims only. There is the potential for such an exception to limited liability to encompass property damage claims as well. In either case, the exception to limited liability would need to be accompanied by alteration to present rules about the priority of payments on a winding up of an insolvent company. The problems that exist at present are that: secured creditors rank ahead of general creditors;[107] and the claims of personal injury victims are lumped in with other general creditor claims.[108]

Holding shareholders strictly liable for company debts would be directly contrary to statutory limited liability because of its automatic attachment. A statutory amendment to limited liability laws would be needed both to create the relevant exception and to ensure that judges observe the new rules.

X. CONSEQUENCES OF SHAREHOLDER LIABILITY

There is an undoubted need to consider the potential consequences and policy issues to which a regime of pro rata strict liability for personal injuries would give rise. In doing so, it is as well to keep in mind the narrowness of the exception argued for in this chapter – which would attach to unsatisfied personal injury claims only. Shareholders would be called on to pay out only if large personal injury claims threatened the investee company, any shareholder with 'parent company status' refused to inject capital into the investee company, insurance was inadequate to meet shortfalls, the investee company thus became insolvent, and the claimants decided to sue shareholders for recovery. These circumstances would arise on rare occasions but the law must be ready to deal with them (hence the current proposals).

We start by considering the consequences of an exception to limited liability upon capital-raising and economic performance. The first point is that 'exposure to unlimited liability would not be a phenomenon of a completely

---

105 See, e.g., Timo H. Kaisanlahti, 'Extended Liability of Shareholders?' (2006) 6 J. Corp. L. Stud. 139, 143.

106 Hansmann and Kraakman (n 1).

107 Fixed security does not fall within the insolvent estate at all: Roy Goode, *Principles of Corporate Insolvency Law* (4th edn, Sweet & Maxwell 2011) 275. Floating charges are paid before general creditors minus the prescribed part set aside for unsecured creditors: Insolvency Act 1986 (UK) s 176A.

108 Insolvency (England and Wales) Rules 2016 (SI 2016/1024), r 14.2.

new order'.[109] Indeed, under the current liability regime, shareholders must accept a significant degree of financial responsibility for wrongdoing in their investee companies. Ultimately, they pay for fines and compensation orders made against investee companies through reduced profits and lower company valuations. In this way, shareholders are impacted by a kind of strict liability for wrongdoing by investee companies because there is no inquiry into their personal fault. The question is whether they should assume a further, direct liability to injured claimants.

Second, investors make their decisions looking forward in time, after assessing potential risks and expected returns on investments. They make their calculations on the basis of projects' net present values (NPVs). Businesses have every incentive to invest in projects with positive NPVs. As Presser observes: 'One invests in the belief that one will derive a profit ... One selects one's investments after having concluded that the investment is one that will make money, not lose it.'[110] By contrast, investors do not make their decisions in hindsight, with the certainty that tort claims will arise. Indeed, we would hope that such claims are avoidable with proper planning and precaution-taking. In this way, it is likely that investors will continue to invest in all but the riskiest projects. It is possible that those projects, if socially desirable, would need to attract government backing. However, this is not a foregone conclusion. Some individuals, perhaps 'high-rollers', would be attracted to the new risk propositions created by a rule of pro rata strict liability for personal injury debts because of the potential for higher returns on risky investments.[111]

Shareholders who are concerned about their potential exposure to pro rata strict liability will have several options for protecting their positions. The most important of these arises from the derivatives market, which permits persons to 'manage and distribute their risks more effectively and efficiently, be it for hedging or speculative purposes. A firm [or individual] can use derivatives to take the risks it wants to take, and to lay off to others the risks it does not want to take.'[112] The most obviously suitable derivative is the credit default swap, which can be used to pay out on a liability in the event of corporate insolvency impacting upon shareholders personally. In exchange for a premium proportionate to the ostensible risk faced, the shareholder obtains a form of insurance

---

[109] David W. Leebron, 'Limited Liability, Tort Victims, and Creditors' (1991) 91 Colum. L. Rev. 1565, 1574–75.

[110] Stephen B. Presser, 'Thwarting the Killing of the Corporation: Limited Liability, Democracy, and Economics' (1992) 87 Nw. U.L. Rev. 148, 159.

[111] Ibid 159.

[112] Clive Briault, 'Risk Society and Financial Risk' in Bridget M. Hutter (ed), *Anticipating Risks and Organising Risk Regulation* (Cambridge University Press 2010) 29.

which permits payment of pro rata liabilities attached to their shares arising on corporate insolvency.[113]

Other options available to concerned shareholders would be to either: (a) take proper advice, or undertake adequate research, about the risks of pro rata shareholder liability presented by their investee companies and to invest accordingly; or (b) move out of risky investments into 'safer' ones, whether these be in the shares of companies that do not undertake physically risky processes or into other types of asset class such as bonds and Real Estate Investment Trusts (REITs). Given that these escape options are open, notice that shareholders would have a *greater* range of investment choices with a rule of pro rata unlimited liability rather than a narrower one. However, they would need to exercise greater discretion in making their choices.

Bainbridge and Henderson worry that any exception to limited liability would entail a large number of expensive law suits in order for injured claimants to collect from individual shareholders their pro rata liability contributions.[114] Costs of collection might be a problem in the United States because the normal rule is that each party pays their own legal costs. But even there, the problem of collection appears to be overstated because investors are used to paying out on losing bets on calculated risk-taking.[115] In any case, the rule as to costs in jurisdictions outside the United States typically is that the winner recoups their costs. This means that, where strict liability attaches to shares for unsatisfied personal injuries caused by investee companies, shareholders who resist claims made against them would be faced with the prospect of paying the costs of lawsuits brought successfully against them. This would greatly alleviate their temptation to hold out. In case this is not a sufficient disincentive (although it should be), Conti-Brown has proposed that shareholders who are ordered to pay their pro rata liabilities after unsuccessfully defending lawsuits could be landed with a penalty – such as treble damages.[116]

A final potential consequence of a rule of pro rata unlimited liability for personal injury claims is raised by Kaisanlahti.[117] Such a rule might cause difficulties for securities markets should they be unable to price the risks presented by affected shares. If this were the case, it could mean that affected shares were less transferrable and more difficult for investors to sell. In such circumstances, the legislature might have to impose a notional upper limit on shareholder liability so that it would become a *capped* pro rata liability. The legislature could impose a cap on liability that is both generous to unsatisfied personal injury

[113] Conti-Brown (n 5) 439–40.
[114] Bainbridge and Henderson (n 14) 62–63 and 70–71.
[115] Conti-Brown (n 5) 465.
[116] Ibid 435.
[117] Kaisanlahti (n 105), 152–57.

claimants, and that would allow better pricing of shares – for example, 20 times the value (in real terms) of capital contributed. If necessary, a further rule could be imposed that created a time limit on shareholder liability – which might be important in an era of automated share trading (although the present writer does not feel any particular concern for hedge funds and the like!).[118]

XI. CONCLUSIONS

This chapter has considered the reasons why shareholders might be made liable for certain of the unsatisfied debts of their investee companies. Given the cogency of limited liability rules with respect to unsatisfied claims for financial losses, the chapter has argued for an exception for unsatisfied personal injury claims only. Shareholders can provide a pool of funds for payment of compensation to personal injury victims. Perhaps more importantly, shareholders have a role to play in a system of deterrence of future wrongdoing. They occupy a place at the top of the corporate governance hierarchy. As such, they are in a good position to monitor directors and managers, consult with them about operational risks, and replace them if need be. As such, shareholders have the ability to make the corporate governance system work. This can help in the achievement of deterrence of wrongdoing. Deterrability arises from the facts that the company embodies a hierarchical structure, has formalised decision-making processes, and can coordinate activity so that behaviour is constrained and wrongdoing avoided.

[118] See Conti-Brown (n 5) 433–34.

PART IV

Barriers to enforcement

11. Barriers to shareholder identification and entitlement

Matteo Gargantini[1]

I. STEWARDSHIP AND (OTHER) SHAREHOLDER DUTIES: THE ROLE OF SHAREHOLDER IDENTIFICATION

The most recent developments in the legal framework for corporate governance increasingly focus on the monitoring role of shareholders and, more specifically, on their engagement with investee companies. These developments aim at reducing agency problems along the investment chain by enhancing equity investors' oversight and asset managers' accountability.

Shareholder engagement typically relies on a wide array of strategies. Within the activist investor toolbox, voting at the general meeting retains a prominent role. To be sure, voting at the general meeting may be just a last-resort device for activist investors but this is by no means a limitation to its ability to hold managers accountable. Whether cast or not, voting rights can support other engagement techniques when they represent a credible threat. As a consequence, higher voting costs likely result in reduced shareholder ability to effectively monitor companies' management.

Voting at the general meeting inevitably requires, however, a safe and reliable system for shareholder entitlement. Issuers' ability to locate and identify their shareholders is a prerequisite for proper corporate action management, and voting is no exception. However, locating shareholders has traditionally proven difficult within the EU, especially when the identification involves the flow of the relevant information across the borders.

Mindful of the persistent hindrances to cross-border voting, EU law has striven to ease shareholder voice at the general meeting. The 2007 Directive

[1] The opinions expressed are personal and do not represent those of the organizations the author belongs to.

on shareholder rights[2] introduced a first set of measures that defined some common basic rights for equity investors of EU listed companies and set minimum harmonisation rules on some key features of the voting process – including a record date system for shareholder entitlement – that are essential to enabling the exercise of those rights. In 2017, the Directive on the encouragement of long-term shareholder engagement[3] brought the project forward by introducing additional harmonisation measures concerning shareholder identification, together with obligations aimed at strengthening issuers' accountability and reducing agency problems along the investment chain.

This chapter addresses some of the main obstacles to cross-border shareholder identification and voting within the EU and assesses whether the consolidated Directive on Shareholder Rights (SRD) can solve them. The analysis rests on the assumption that the SRD's effectiveness in tackling those obstacles is a crucial factor in the definition of asset managers' engagement practices, an exercise that underpins shareholder stewardship and that is likely to play an even more important role among shareholder duties in the future.[4] Particularly relevant in this respect is the disclosure of the institutional investors' and asset managers' engagement policies and their implementation under Article 3g SRD.

Beneficiaries should evaluate asset managers that make limited recourse to general meeting participation in their engagement strategies – or in their actual behaviour vis-à-vis specific companies – in the light of the costs of voting. While participation will always be convenient in some circumstances, and always inefficient in others, the costs of voting in marginal cases will be a key determinant for an efficient decision in terms of investment returns. For the same reason, a wise policymaker should carefully factor these (and other[5]) variables in before coming to the conclusion that engagement policies or reports displaying small recourse to general meeting vote demonstrate the need for a stricter enforcement of asset managers' or institutional investors' duties.

On a partially different note, barriers to shareholder identification play a more direct role in limiting the enforceability of other shareholder duties. This role rests on the intuitive fact that enforcement requires, by definition, the identification of the natural or legal person that bears the legal responsibility

---

[2] Directive 2007/36/EC on the exercise of certain rights of shareholders in listed companies.

[3] Directive 2017/828/EU amending Directive 2007/36/EC as regards the encouragement of long-term shareholder engagement.

[4] Iris H-Y. Chiu and Dionysia Katelouzou, 'From Shareholder Stewardship to Shareholder Duties: Is the Time Ripe?' in Hanne S. Birkmose (ed), *Shareholders' Duties* (Wolters Kluwer 2017) 131ff.

[5] Brian Cheffins, 'The Stewardship Code's Achilles' Heel' (2010) Mod. L. Rev. 1004.

for a breach. To the extent that such responsibility lies with the shareholder (or the final accountholder, as the case may be), any restriction in the possibility of identifying the responsible person will result in an equivalent restriction in the possibility of enforcing the violated duty. Rules and procedures on shareholder identification may therefore play a key role in calibrating issuer ability to identify possible violations and to react to them. The same applies whenever the power to detect and enforce rests, under the applicable law, with other entities, such as supervisors or other shareholders.

The chapter proceeds as follows. Section II describes the legal and operational techniques for securities holding, as these are the main source of the barriers to shareholder identification and entitlement. Section III addresses the company law requirements for shareholder entitlement, while Section IV shows that shareholder entitlement procedures may uneasily interact with those requirements. Section V submits some proposals to address the residual barriers to shareholder entitlement. Section VI analyses the mechanisms of shareholder identification in the light of the new SRD measures. Section VII concludes.

II. SECURITIES HOLDING SYSTEMS

From a functional perspective, managing a corporate action that relates to a general meeting involves the transmission of information from the issuer to the person in charge of the decision to vote and vice versa. This in turn requires, as for the first (downstream) information flow, that issuers be able to reach, directly or indirectly, their shareholders – and, if different, those determining the direction of the vote. Some of this information is easily accessible because issuers disseminate it under the applicable rules, as is the case with the notice convening the general meeting under Article 5 SRD or with other documents necessary to enable shareholders to exercise their rights (Article 17(2) Transparency Directive). However, certain investors prefer to receive such documents from the holding chain and would not actively look for them through other systems, such as an officially appointed mechanism for central storage of regulated information (Article 21 Transparency Directive).

Symmetrically, information that needs to flow upstream to enable the general meeting management concerns the identity of shareholders, the number of shares they own, and the direction of their vote. Local rules often require additional information, such as early communication of the intention to take part in the meeting.[6] The greatest hurdles to cross-border voting currently stem from the complex procedures adopted for the management of these information flows.

---

6 See Section III for examples.

In most jurisdictions, intermediaries providing securities holding services interpose themselves between issuers and their investors (Section B of Annex I, point (1) Directive 2014/65/EU – MiFID II). Such services involve the maintenance of securities accounts where securities are kept in book-entry form. Normally, the same security is registered in a number of hierarchically coordinated accounts, each kept by an intermediary forming part of a holding chain. At issuance, listed companies register their shares at the central securities depository (CSD), which is responsible for maintaining the top-tier account, where shares are credited to intermediaries participating in the CSD account systems (Article 3 Regulation (EU) No 909/2014).

On the investor side of the CSD, the platform takes the form of a complex network of intermediaries that connects final accountholders to the settlement system. Intermediaries participating in the CSD settlement system – thus holding accounts in the CSD system that registers the securities – maintain in their turn other accounts where the same securities are credited to their respective accountholders. These can be investors in the simplest case but will more often be intermediaries performing a similar service to their own customers, which may be intermediaries in their turn, and so on down the holding chain. When issuers and final account holders are located in different countries, the holding chain may comprise a number of intermediaries and may be particularly complex.[7] Efficiency reasons induce intermediaries to pool the securities they hold for their customers into accounts kept by other intermediaries. These accounts are often referred to as 'omnibus accounts'.

An omnibus account typically commingles securities belonging to various customers of the same intermediary, which opens the account in its name – but on behalf of those customers – at the upper-tier intermediary in the custody chain. Therefore, the upper-tier custodian that keeps the omnibus account is not aware of the actual identity of the investors (or of the sub-custodians) on whose behalf the account-holding intermediary is registering the securities. One of the main reasons why securities holding systems often rely on omnibus accounts is that this reduces the number of entries custodians have to modify when transferring securities.

On the flipside of the coin, broad recourse to omnibus accounts prevents upper-tier intermediaries, and consequently issuers themselves, from knowing who holds securities at lower-tier levels and, therefore, from easily identifying investors. Reciprocally, investors often need to take action if they want to be identified and, therefore, to exercise their rights towards their companies. To

[7] Philip Paech, 'Market Needs as Paradigm – Breaking Up the Thinking on EU Securities Law' in Pierre-Henri Conac, Ulrich Segna and Luc Thévenoz (eds), *Intermediated Securities* (Cambridge University Press 2013) 29.

be sure, in some jurisdictions the national holding systems enable easy access to investors' identities, either because they do not resort to omnibus accounts, or because ad hoc communications ensure a regular and timely updating of the register of members. However, these systems do not normally work on a cross-border basis so that shareholder identification is normally more complex when investors and issuers are domiciled in different countries.

Although securities holding systems often hinder a smooth voting procedure even between countries whose legal regimes are comparable, the obstacles to cross-border voting are exacerbated when issuers and voters are domiciled in countries belonging to different legal traditions. Take, for instance, the case of an investor based in a continental European country that wishes to vote at the general meeting of an issuer having its registered office in the UK.[8] Custodians in common law countries often rely on trusts when holding their clients' securities, so that the holding system is in this case (not only intermediated, but also) indirect.[9] Consequently, final investors normally have the quality of (mere) beneficial owners, while intermediaries participating in the CSD settlement system retain the status of shareholders. On top of this, the CSD participants, the beneficial owner and the final investors are often unknown to each other, so that proxies and voting instructions can hardly circulate without involving some further intermediaries.

This complex architecture is an additional obstacle to the creation of a direct communication system between issuers and final account holders – a system where information can flow with no intermediation from the company to its investors and vice versa. Against this backdrop, casting votes on a cross-border basis becomes a more complex activity. Voting at the general meeting can, in fact, become a work-intensive procedure, at best, while during the procedure votes may, at worst, get lost along the holding chain or may not reach the issuer in due time.[10]

III. THE ROLE OF COMPANY LAW

How complex shareholder entitlement can be depends not only on the technicalities of the securities holding systems, but also on the legal requirements national company laws set for admitting shareholders to vote at the general meeting. As the analysis will demonstrate, harmonisation is still low in this

---

8 A similar analysis can equally apply, *mutatis mutandis*, to Ireland.

9 I use the terms 'intermediated' to refer to systems where investors hold securities through intermediaries, and 'indirect' to refer to systems where investors do not typically enjoy the legal ownership (or co-ownership) of those securities. Like any taxonomy, this classification is subject to simplifications: see Paech (n 7) 50f.

10 See recently Eva Micheler, 'Building a Capital Markets Union: Improving the Market Infrastructure' (2016) Eur. Bus. Organ. L. Rev. 481.

respect, which makes general meeting participation more expensive for cross-border investors with diversified portfolios. These investors may in fact have to comply with a different set of rules for each of the countries – and sometimes for each of the companies – they have invested in.

In Germany, the exercise of rights conferred by bearer shares requires a certification by the custodian (para 123(4) AktG [Stock Corporation Act]). While the record date for the general meeting vote is set as the 21st day preceding the general meeting (para 123(4) Abs. 2 AktG), the confirmation needs to reach the issuer at least six days prior to the general meeting, unless the bylaws provide for a shorter term. To cast their vote, holders of bearer shares may also need to send a notice of participation, if the bylaws so require. This message also has to reach the company at least six days prior to the general meeting, once again unless the bylaws provide for a shorter term (para 123(2) AktG).

Companies may require a notice of participation, to be notified within the same deadlines, also for registered shares. However, the very nature of registered shares makes the entry of the investor names in the register of members (*Aktienregister*) a precondition for being considered as shareholders (para 67(2) AktG) and to vote at the general meeting. For this reason, the depositary banks are under an obligation to provide issuers with the information they need to fill in the register (para 67(4) AktG).[11] This leads to a permanent information flow from banks to issuers,[12] which, however, does not necessarily result, after the trade is made, in the registration of the buyer's name, absent an autonomous request by the latter, because purchases and sales may be communicated with separate messages.

Consequently, German companies often enter nominees in the register of members, a practice that seems especially popular for non-resident shareholders because these are not identified on a regular basis by the national identification systems.[13] When the custodian is registered as nominee and is entitled as

[11] Michael Gruson, 'Global Shares of German Corporations and Their Dual Listings on the Frankfurt and New York Stock Exchange' (2001) U. Pa. J. Int'l L. 185, 216ff. Issuers must pay adequate compensation to the banks for this service.

[12] Ulrich Noack, 'Anlegerrechte bei mittelbar gehaltenen Wertpapieren. Bemerkungen zu dem Dreieck aus Emittent – Intermediär – Aktionär' in Theodor Baums and Andreas Cahn (eds), *Die Zukunft des Clearing und Settlement* (De Gruyter 2006) 73ff. See also Uwe Schneider, 'Azionisti non iscritti nel libro dei soci: la loro "sicura identificazione" tra norma ed effettività' in Paola Balzarini, Giuseppe Carcano and Marco Ventoruzzo (eds), *La società per azioni oggi. Tradizione, attualità e prospettive* (Milan 2007) 694.

[13] Noack (n 12) 71 ss. More recently, Konrad von Nussbaum, 'Präsenzsteigerung bei Namensaktien' (2014) HV-Magazin 24.

a shareholder, it will have the right to vote upon authorisation by the investor (para 135(6) AktG).[14]

Unlike bearer shares, registered shares do not formally rely on a pure record date system for the determination of the entitlement to vote. However, even in the absence of express provisions in the law, practical reasons determine an outcome that is in many respects comparable, albeit not identical,[15] to that of a record date. Simplification of the general meeting process has determined the practice, which is reportedly widespread among German listed companies,[16] of blocking entries in and cancellations from the *Aktienregister* during the week preceding the general meeting.

For bearer shares, shareholders may therefore need a double communication – one to notify their intention to participate in the general meeting, the other one to certify the possession of a certain number of shares as at the record date. These communications are equally mandatory for national shareholders, but cross-border investors may not be familiar with these technicalities, so that the risk of their votes being rejected for not having sent the double communication is higher. The same applies to registered shares because foreign investors may have to ask their intermediaries to send the issuer an ad hoc request if they want to have their name registered in the share register, which is a precondition to voting. This request for registration does not replace the need to send the notice of participation.

To the contrary, a feature of the German system that seems particularly friendly to non-resident investors is the possibility, granted to the custodian banks, to send directly to the issuers, rather than through the custodian chain, the communications needed to have standing to vote.

Casting votes on a cross-border basis may be more difficult than doing so on a purely national basis also for French companies. In principle, national investors holding registered shares do not need to actively seek registration in the share register as this occurs automatically. The settlement system generates, in fact, ad hoc daily messages (*bordereau de référence nominative* – BRN) that allow issuers to keep their registers of members up to date.

The circulation of BRNs relies on electronic communications that are still grounded on the national clearing and settlement system. Therefore, BRNs only cover shareholders having their account at a French custodian, while foreign custodians are not subject to the obligation to issue BRNs towards the French CSD. To cope with this issue, foreign investors normally rely on

---

14 Schneider (n 12) 710; Gruson (n 11) 213 and 267.

15 See, for instance, Hanno Merkt, 'Kommentar sub. para 67 AktG' in Klaus J. Hopt and Herbert Wiedemann (eds), *Großkommentar zum Aktiengesetz*, II (De Gruyter 2008), 40f.

16 Cf. Schneider (n 12) 699.

nominee accounts (*compte intermédié*) as per express law provision (Art. L 228-1(7) *Code de commerce*). In this manner, the intermediary appears as a shareholder in the register of members and maintains, vis-à-vis the issuer, the entitlement to participate and vote at the general meeting.[17]

The relevant record date for the identification of the shareholders having the right to vote is the second day preceding the general meeting (*date d'enregistrement*; Art. R. 225-85 *Code de commerce*). The time span between the record date and the general meeting therefore has the same length as the settlement period for the transactions executed on a trading venue (T+2, as per Article 5(2) Regulation (EU) No 909/2014 on Central Securities Depositories).

In Italy, shares are issued – with some limited exceptions – only in registered form.[18] However, the register of members does not play any role in entitling shareholders to vote at the general meeting of listed companies (Article 2355 Civil Code). To the contrary, shareholder entitlement relies exclusively on a confirmation released by the last intermediary (Article 83-V Consolidated Law on Finance). Shareholders wishing to attend or to vote at the general meeting, in person or by proxy, need to request from their custodian banks a confirmation of entitlement as of the record date, which in Italy falls at the end of the seventh business day preceding the general meeting (Article 83-VI Consolidated Law on Finance). The custodian banks send the required information up the holding chain because only CSD participants can release certification of entitlements having legal value before listed companies (Article 27 Consob-Bank of Italy Joint Regulation on Post-Trading).

At the same time, the law harmonises both the cut-off dates for the last intermediaries and the issuer deadlines. In particular, intermediaries are duty-bound to accept requests of entitlement until the end of the second business day after the record date (Article 22 Consob-Bank of Italy Joint Regulation on Post-Trading). The confirmation must reach the issuer by the end of the third business day preceding the general meeting. Although late confirmations can still entitle the shareholders if delivered by the opening of the general meeting, delays may lead to administrative sanctions for the custodians that could not meet the issuer deadline (Articles 83-VI(4), 83-IX(1)(c) and 190.1(2)(a) Consolidated Law on Finance). This leaves intermediaries only two days to deliver the confirmation of entitlement; as the analysis in Section IV will show, this short time span may not always be sufficient, though.

---

[17] Jean-Paul Valuet, 'Les dispositions du décret du 3 mai 2002 relatives à l'identification et au vote des actionnaires non-résidents des sociétés cotées' (2002) Revue des sociétés 450.

[18] Art. 1 R.D.L. 25 October 1941, No 1148.

Finally, some hurdles in the way of a smooth cross-border exercise of voting rights may stem from divergent legal qualification of the holding techniques adopted by the jurisdictions involved in the voting process. The most striking example is of course the United Kingdom, as a consequence of the widespread recourse to trusts in the custody of investments.[19] The separation between the investors' equitable ownership and the custodians' legal ownership has a deep influence on the corporate action process that leads to the general meeting. It is in fact the custodian participating in the CSD settlement system that has its name registered in the issuer's register of members, thus having the entitlement to vote.[20] In the UK, each issuer determines the record date for the general meeting by reference to the register of members as at a time that is no more than 48 hours before the time for the holding of the meeting (s 360B(2) Companies Act 2006).[21]

Because they are not formally recognised as shareholders, investors at the end of the holding chain need to instruct the custodians registered in the register of members before these – or the proxy holders – can vote, or they need to be appointed as proxies if they want to directly participate in the meeting. For foreign investors, knowing the identity of the pertinent custodian at the top of the holding chain may prove impossible, however, so that the voting instructions may need to go through the whole series of custodians before they reach their destination.

IV. SECURITIES HOLDING AND COMPANY LAW: EAST IS EAST AND WEST IS WEST?

Directive 2007/36/EC helped remove most of the restrictions to the national and cross-border exercise of voting rights based on company law rules. Directive 2017/828/EU has expanded the scope of harmonisation so as to include some key elements of the securities holding systems. This section addresses some remaining obstacles to the (cross-border) exercise of shareholder rights, with a specific focus on general meeting voting, and provides a preliminary assessment of the expected impact of the new EU provisions, yet to be transposed in most jurisdictions as at the time of writing. All in all, the new provisions are likely to further facilitate shareholder voting but they do not seem able

19 Joanna Benjamin, *Interest in Securities* (Oxford University Press 2001) para 2.01ff; Eva Micheler, *Property in Securities – A Comparative Study* (Cambridge University Press 2007) 119ff.

20 See, however, s 145 Companies Act 2006, enabling a member to nominate another person as entitled to enjoy or exercise shareholder rights.

21 See also European Commission, *List of days provided for according to Article 15 of Directive 2007/36/EC* (2010/C 285/01) 5. Only working days are taken into account.

to remove all the existing hindrances. Voting, especially on a cross-border basis, will plausibly remain a complex exercise for many reasons, chief among them the costs investors still incur in ascertaining different rules and practices for voting and, then, in routing their instructions in a timely fashion across a complex intermediation system. From a policy perspective, this persistent complexity justifies some scepticism on any attempt to tighten enforcement of shareholder duties that involve the exercise of voting.

A. Confirmation of Entitlement and Notice of Participation

The analysis developed in the previous sections shows that transmitting information along the custodian chain is not without costs for various reasons, mainly attributable to the techniques adopted to maintain securities accounts and to divergent national rules concerning the legal quality of custodians and of their customers. As long as the costs of sharing information are not negligible, the more frequent the circulation of such information, the more expensive the system for the parties involved.

In this respect, a source of complexity comes from the need to enter the name of the shareholder in the register of members as a prerequisite to attending the general meeting and casting a vote. By the same token, the need to inform the company in advance of the intention to participate in the voting procedure, even if only in absentia, may easily increase the number of communications required.

In a system that facilitates remote voting, the requirement to give advance notice of the intention to vote does not always seem justified. Companies may have an interest in receiving this information when they arrange the meeting venue or set up real-time electronic communication systems that enable shareholder remote participation (Article 8(1)(b) SRD). Conversely, electronic systems that merely enable votes to be cast in absentia and without the appointment of a proxy holder (Article 8(1)(c) SRD) would not seem to require early notifications because a broad idea of the number of votes that the electronic system should be able to support and process would suffice in this case.

Other communications may not be equally easy to remove. In countries where the register of members is the main legal source for the entitlement to vote, keeping registrations as a prerequisite to participating in the general meeting reduces the risk of issuers being involved in disputes among investors – or between investors and intermediaries – concerning share ownership or the exercise of voting rights.[22] In this case, adequate corporate action procedures

22 Richard Nolan, 'Indirect Investors: A Greater Say in the Company?' (2003) J. Corp. L. Stud. 73, 78–79.

could reduce the burden upon investors. The possibility of aggregating multiple communications in a single message would be an important step in this respect. For instance, absent a real-time shareholder identification system – as is normally the case when issuers and investors are located in different countries – a single communication should be deemed sufficient both to request registration in the register of members and to announce the intention to vote at the general meeting. The draft SRD implementing act, under consultation at the time of writing, contemplates the possibility of a link between the notice of participation and the confirmation of entitlement (Article 6(2)). Under the proposed rule, if the notice includes a reference to the entitled position, the last intermediary in the holding chain is responsible for ensuring that this information is accurate, and in the event the notice is transmitted ahead of the record date, the same account keeper is in charge of updating the notice.

A more intrusive, but at the same time more effective, solution would be one that curbed issuer ability to establish different deadlines for participation notices and confirmations of entitlement, so that the two messages could always go hand in hand. As the next subsection shows, harmonisation of record dates across the EU would also bring further benefits. This way, homogeneous issuer and market deadlines for both notice of participation and confirmation of entitlement would greatly reduce the indirect costs of voting.

B. Record Date Entitlement and Enduring Share-blocking Practices

Another source of complexity investors have to face when exercising their voting rights stems from the often complex route the information has to go through before reaching issuers. As the messages conveying shareholder entitlement have to travel across a number of intermediaries, proving entitlement or having voting instructions delivered may require a considerable amount of time. This section shows that such a lengthy procedure may even have indirect consequences for investors' ability to sell their shares in the proximity of the general meetings they participate in. In less extreme scenarios, time-consuming procedures may make voting more difficult when the required information (including voting instructions) does not reach its destination in time.

The complex route this information has to follow depends in part on legal requirements and in part on practical needs. Some jurisdictions directly or indirectly mandate the involvement of one or more intermediaries forming the holding chain in the pre-meeting shareholder identification process. For instance, in common law countries where custodians – rather than final accountholders – qualify as shareholders, intermediaries at the top of the holding chain inevitably play a role in the voting procedure. In other countries, express provisions may require that the information flow concerning the final accountholder, who qualifies as a shareholder, also involves intermediaries other than those keeping the final account.[23]

According to some surveys, when messages go through the custodian chain, the time needed for confirmations of entitlement or notices of participation to reach the issuer can amount to up to two days for each intermediary involved.[24] Procedures seem to be even slower when market practices combine the circulation of the certifications of entitlement with voting instructions,[25] due to reduced harmonisation of the corresponding messages.[26]

As mentioned, the excessive length of the corporate action processing in the context of a general meeting may occasionally lead to restrictions in the investors' ability to sell their shares after confirmations of entitlement and voting instructions are sent. If the time elapsing between the record date and the issuer deadline (which may in its turn fall well ahead of the general meeting: see Section III) is shorter than the time needed for the message to reach the issuer, the last intermediary will need to set a cut-off date for receiving its customer's requests that falls before the record date.[27] When this is the case, the market deadline for the exercise of the vote may precede the ex-date – however this is defined at national level.[28] The draft SRD implementing measures may help reduce the time required for the entitlement to reach the issuer as they set tight deadlines intermediaries have to comply with when transmitting the information regarding shareholder actions to the issuer concerned (Article 9(4) draft Implementing Regulation). The same provision, however, enables cut-off dates that fall three business days or less prior to the issuer deadline or record date.

---

[23] See for Italy Art. 27 Consob-Bank of Italy Joint Regulation on Post-Trading.

[24] Christiane Hölz, *Barriers to Shareholder Engagement. Report on Cross-Border Voting* (2012) 11, http://betterfinance.eu.

[25] See recently Micheler (n 10) 484 (deadlines for processing voting instructions, which may lead to share blocking, fall 7–10 days before the meeting). See also Hölz (n 24) 11 (mentioning Belgium); Francesco Chiappetta, *Diritto del governo societario* (Cedam 2010) 103 (reporting that investors often send out cross-border voting instructions concerning Italian companies between 22 and 19 days before the general meeting date).

[26] Manifest, Cross-border Proxy Voting in Europe (2008) 21, 24–55, 70, http://www.cscs.org. See also ECSDA, Issuer services (2008) 2, 9 and 17, https://www.ecb.europa.eu (reporting lower compliance of voting instruction formats with SWIFT ISO standards).

[27] Manifest (n 26) 78ff; Hölz (n 24) 11.

[28] There is apparently widespread uncertainty as to the identification of the ex-date across the EU: ESMA, *Report on Shareholder Identification and Communication Systems* (ESMA 31-54-435) 5 April 2017, 13, 28 (also reporting divergent applicable rules).

Cut-off dates falling before the record date may result in two equally suboptimal scenarios.[29] First, buyers may not be able to effectively exercise their votes, even if the shares traded cum, whenever the last intermediary would not send out confirmations of entitlement after the cut-off date.[30] To avoid this consequence, investors that already own shares at the cut-off dates may request their intermediaries to send the confirmation of entitlement in advance of the record date.[31] This leads to the second suboptimal outcome as a result of the risk that the entitlement changes before the record date and no update can reach the issuer before the applicable deadline or the general meeting, as the case may be (Article 5(2) draft Implementing Regulation). To ensure consistency between certifications of entitlement, voting instructions and actual entitled positions as of the record date, some custodians reportedly prevent account holders from selling their shares once the confirmation of entitlement is sent.[32]

There are of course two possible remedies, not necessarily alternative, that could enable cut-off dates to fall after the record date. The first one is to make the current communication systems smoother and quicker. The second one is to set the record date at an earlier moment. The next section deals with these aspects, on the assumption that straight-through processing represents the first-best solution, and that a better identification of the voting record date can stand in as a second-best when this is not possible.

V. ADRESSING THE BARRIERS TO SHAREHOLDER ENTITLEMENT

It is a rather common statement, especially among practitioners, that the involvement of upper-tier intermediaries in the circulation of data concerning the final accountholder increases legal certainty in the communication of information, which is crucial to the proper management of general meetings.

---

29 Art. 9(4) draft Implementing Regulation seems to be aware of such risks: 'The last intermediary may caution the shareholder as regards the risks attached to changes in the entitled position close to the record date.'

30 See Hölz (n 24) 11–12. Better Finance, 'Shareholders Rights Directive Implementing Acts Last Chance to Ensure Rights of Individual Shareholders Taken Into Account', 18 April 2018, http://betterfinance.eu.

31 See the consultation document that preceded the adoption of the general meeting standards by the Joint Working Group on General Meeting, *Private Sector Response to the Giovannini Reports (Barrier 3 – Corporate Actions)* (2010), http://www.ecsda.eu.

32 Sources reporting persisting share-blocking practices are manifold. See, for instance, Micheler (n 10) 484; Manifest (n 26) 20; Hölz (n 24) 10–12; Fabio Bianconi and Sergio Carbonara, 'Evoluzione degli assetti proprietari ed attivismo assembleare delle minoranze: l'indagine empirica' in Luiss Ceradi and Georgeson (eds), *FTSE MIB. Proxy Season 2010* (Rome 2011) 27.

It is submitted here that, while this belief may make sense *de lege lata*, there is no reason not to rely more extensively on a direct communication system for the general meeting management.[33] Section V.A contends that conveying pre-meeting messages through the holding chain (indirect communication system) is a necessary evil for the time being, but there seems to be no compelling reason, *de lege ferenda*, to maintain this burdensome and time-consuming approach unless exceptional reasons so require. Section V.B provides some examples of those reasons and suggests, in line with the previous analysis, that a minimum time span between the record date and the general meeting – or the issuer deadline, if any – may contribute to reducing the impact of the residual obstacles to shareholder entitlement.

A. Fostering Direct Communication

None of the reasons normally invoked to justify the current widespread recourse to indirect communication systems seems to bear close scrutiny. The most credible rationale lies perhaps with the obstacles intermediaries would face if required to prepare and send out communications according to (potentially) 28 different standards. This statement is undoubtedly an accurate snapshot of the current situation but an adequate legal framework could contribute to facilitating direct communications. The SRD, as recently amended, makes important steps in this direction as it fosters harmonisation of some key elements of the information flowing from issuers to investors and vice versa. It in fact delegates the Commission to adopt implementing acts (Treaty on the Functioning of the European Union (TFEU) Article 291) to specify some minimum requirements of the messages circulating along the chain of intermediaries – including their contents, their format and the applicable deadlines – so as to ensure security and interoperability (see Articles 3a(8), 3b(6) and 3c(3) SRD).[34]

Another frequently mentioned reason not to adopt a system that relies on direct communications between lower-tier intermediaries and issuers refers to the need for intermediaries at each level of the holding chain to verify that the

---

[33] See Carmine Di Noia, Matteo Gargantini and Salvatore Lo Giudice, 'General Meeting-Related Processes in Italy: the Role of Listed Companies, Intermediaries and Central Securities Depositories in the Light of Some Recent EU Developments' (2008) 1(2) J. Securities Operations & Custody 195; Christian Strenger and Dirk Zetzsche, 'Corporate Governance, Cross-Border Voting and the (Draft) Principles of the European Securities Law Legislation – Enhancing Investor Engagement Through Standardization' (2013) 2 J. Corp. L. Stud. 503, 515–17.

[34] See in this direction already European Commission, *Legislation on Legal Certainty of Securities Holding and Dispositions* (DG Markt G2 MET/OT/acg D(2010) 768690) 29.

messages are accurate. This view stresses that, absent such additional control, incorrect messages could lead to over-voting.[35] However, the reconciliation measures that the securities settlement system as a whole performs on a daily basis to verify that the number of issued securities registered at the CSD is equal to the sum of securities recorded in the intermediaries accounts (Central Securities Depositories Regulation (CSDR) Article 37) would seem to suffice in this respect.[36]

Whether the SRD and its implementing measures can facilitate the establishment of a direct communication system between lower-tier intermediaries and issuers will crucially depend on the way they are transposed and interpreted. Two conditions seem to be key in this respect. The first one is that rules that still allow indirect communication systems be narrowly interpreted. The second condition requires mutual recognition of custodians' communications.

Unlike the Commission's original proposal,[37] Directive 2017/828/EU seems to consider direct contacts between ultimate intermediaries and issuers as the preferential solution for upstream communication of information. As for generic shareholder identification, Article 3a(3) SRD specifies that intermediaries who hold the required information should transmit it 'directly to the company', or to the CSD in the event the company asks this latter to collect and consolidate the data. Information concerning shareholders and related to the exercise of their rights 'shall be transmitted between intermediaries' but only 'unless the information can be directly transmitted by the intermediary to the company' (Article 3b(5) SRD). It seems, therefore, that the SRD considers direct communications as the default mechanism for upstream transmission of information. Because Article 3b(4) refers to election decisions in the context of corporate actions in general, there seems to be no reason not to apply this rule – including its related implementing measures – both to voting instructions and to communication requiring registration in the register of members or participation in the general meeting, even though in combination with the more specific rules on facilitations of the exercise of shareholder rights under Article 3c.

The draft Implementing Regulation – under consultation at the time of writing – does not take an open position as to the preferential communication systems the intermediaries should adopt when managing general

---

[35] Reconciliation after the (voting) record date is also regarded as a best practice in Joint Working Group on General Meetings (n 31) 18ff.

[36] See Matteo Gargantini, *Identificazione dell'azionista e legittimazione all'esercizio del voto nelle S.p.A. quotate* (Giappichelli 2012) 189–90, 209–10; Strenger and Zetzsche (n 33) 525.

[37] Art. 3b(4) of the proposal stated: 'Where there is more than one intermediary in a holding chain, information … shall be transmitted between intermediaries without undue delay'.

meeting-related corporate actions. While measures implementing Article 3a(3) SRD on generic shareholder identification simply omit to address the point (perhaps because the SRD provision is quite clear on its own), rules on confirmation of entitlement and notice of participation in general meetings seem to consider direct and indirect transmission of information as equivalent systems, perhaps with a slight preference for the latter.

As for the confirmation of entitlement to exercise voting rights, the main responsibility for the communication lies in principle with the CSD (or any equivalent entity – Article 5 draft Implementing Regulation). Furthermore, the implementing measure specifies that the last intermediary is responsible for confirming the entitled position 'to the shareholder', but only unless the position is known to the issuer and the CSD 'or is transmitted to the issuer and first intermediary through the chain of intermediaries'. At the same time, the proposed rule stresses that 'the entitled positions shall be reflected in the records of all intermediaries in the chain', which leaves the questions whether this requires an ad hoc reconciliation or not. These rules would seem to prevail over the general statement that intermediaries shall transmit information regarding shareholder action 'to the issuer' (Article 9(4)) because even intermediated transmissions are eventually addressed to the issuer.

Overall, the draft Commission Implementing Regulation does not take an unambiguous stance in favour of a direct communication system. To facilitate straight-through processing of general meeting-related corporate actions, and to simplify shareholder voting by removing the residual share-blocking practices described in the previous section, it is of the utmost importance to interpret the SRD as enabling direct communication in all circumstances. Indirect transmissions should be limited to cases where the quality of shareholder lies with intermediaries that are not in direct contact with final account holders.

When the holding system allows direct communications, a precondition for a smooth cross-border exercise of voting rights seems to be a mutual recognition of the messages prepared and sent by the last intermediaries. Only some jurisdictions clearly enable custodians based in other EU countries to release communications giving full evidence, vis-à-vis the issuer, of the shareholder entitlement.[38] The SRD final implementing measures should adopt this approach so as to clarify that intermediaries defined under Articles 1(5) and

---

[38] For instance, this is hardly the case with Italy, where only intermediaries maintaining national accounts may qualify as 'last intermediaries' and may, therefore, be the recipient of the request to release a confirmation of entitlement (see Art. 1(1)(jj) Consob-Bank of Italy Joint Regulation on Post-Trading). At least one Italian intermediary and one CSD participant (see n 23 and accompanying text) have therefore to take part in the entitlement process.

2(d) SRD, which are authorised to perform custody services according to EU law,[39] have the ability to release communications having such legal effects.

B. Identifying Adequate Record Dates

As anticipated, the legal framework for securities holding does not always facilitate a direct communication between the final account keeper and the relevant issuer. This is mainly the case when the holding chain involves trusts (indirect holding models[40]). The reason is that, absent a uniform definition of 'shareholder' in the SRD, when the final account holder does not enjoy the quality of shareholder under the applicable company law, the entitlement procedure may require the involvement of the intermediary having, instead, such a quality. This is not exclusive to common law jurisdictions, because civil law countries also sometimes employ trust-like systems, especially when the holding chain involves some foreign elements. An example is the holding technique Austrian banks can adopt for foreign shares, which they normally hold as nominees while granting their customer only a claim for delivery of securities (*Wertpapierrechnung*).[41] In such a scheme, the bank operates as a trustee and is usually regarded as the shareholder vis-à-vis the company. The ultimate account holder retains a (mere) contractual claim against the bank, whereby she bears all the legal and economic risks and enjoys all the rights flowing from the shares.

Other examples are the above-mentioned German and French nominee accounts in use for non-resident investors.[42] As these investors are not recognised as shareholders, they need to send their voting instructions to the custodian, or ask for an ad hoc validation of their identity and number of shares that they can use before the issuer in case they want to vote as proxy holders.[43]

In circumstances where, for any reasons, the messages conveying confirmations of entitlement or notices of participation (or any similar corporate action-related information) cannot be delivered before the issuer deadline, the ultimate account holders may lose their votes, unless the last intermediary

---

[39] See in particular Annex I, No 12, Directive 2013/36/EU (Capital Requirements Directive (CRD IV); Annex I, Section B, No 1, Directive 2014/65/EU (Market Financial Instruments Directive (MiFID) II).

[40] See n 19 and accompanying text.

[41] See CJEU, Case C-375/13, *Harald Kolassa v Barclays Bank plc*, 28 January 2015, ECLI:EU:C:2015:37. See also Matteo Gargantini, 'Jurisdictional Issues In The Circulation and Holding of (Intermediated) Securities' (2014) Rivista di diritto internazionale privato e processuale 1095.

[42] See nn 13 and 17, and accompanying text.

[43] ANSA, *Proxy Voting Reform In France: A Guide For Non-Resident Shareholders* (2003) 44–55, http://www.ansa.fr.

sends those messages sufficiently in advance. As explained above, the only realistic way to avoid adverse consequences for investors is to set the record date sufficiently in advance of the general meeting so as to ensure that the last intermediary's cut-off date does not fall before the ex-date or the record date.[44]

VI. SHAREHOLDER IDENTIFICATION AND OTHER SHAREHOLDER DUTIES

As anticipated, rules and procedures on shareholder identification may be crucial in determining the effectiveness of enforcement of some shareholder duties. Sometimes identification measures will be in place but they might not deliver the desired results for various reasons. First, they may simply be unable to map investors with a sufficient level of detail. Second, even when the identification systems can effectively spot investors, legal restrictions may prevent this information from reaching those – including fellow shareholders – who are in charge of, or have an interest in, the enforcement of shareholder duties.

Shareholder identification mechanisms are in place in about half of the EU Member States.[45] However, the effectiveness of these systems on a cross-border basis has often proven limited. For this reason, the SRD has introduced some common rules aimed at facilitating identification also when issuers and investors are located in different countries. For the time being, issuers having their registered office in a country that allows shareholder identification carry out such an exercise with variable frequency.[46] Sometimes, the inquiry is also accessible to minority shareholders, either via the issuer[47] or directly.[48]

As with any other corporate actions, shareholder identification relies on information flows that convey the relevant information along the holding chain. By and large, this process may take one of two forms, depending on how much the identification process is centralised. In some jurisdictions (such as the UK and Germany) issuers – or their delegate entities – take part in every step of the process. In particular, the inquiry usually starts from the registered

---

[44] Gargantini (n 36) 179ff and 210ff; Hölz (n 24) 11 (mentioning France and the UK as jurisdictions where the record date is too close to the general meeting); Better Finance (n 30).

[45] The European Securities and Markets Authority (ESMA) (n 28) 10.

[46] According to the available data, the higher rate is found in the UK (12 times per company per year, on average): see European Commission, *Review of the operation of directive 2004/109/EC: emerging issues* (2010) 90, available at www.europa.eu.

[47] This is the case in the UK (s 804 Companies Act 2006) and Italy (Art. 83-XII Consolidated Law on Finance).

[48] In Italy, those promoting a proxy solicitation may access the CSD and other intermediaries in order to ascertain the identity of shareholders (see Art. 134 Consob Issuers Regulation).

holders. When the record holder is the CSD, issuers first require a list of CSD participants holding shares either on their own behalf or on behalf of shareholders. Thereafter, the issuers repeat the inquiry by sending a similar request to the CSD participants that hold shares on behalf of investors and to the other depositories that are subsequently identified during the search.[49] The process continues until it reaches the ultimate account holders. As each custodian has exclusive access to its clients' identities, it could in theory charge issuers to access information at a potentially unlimited price. The applicable laws therefore sometimes provide for some form of tariff regulation.[50]

In other jurisdictions, the law facilitates issuers' access to shareholders' data by setting a higher level of centralisation for the identification process. For instance, the CSD may sometimes operate as a single entry point for the issuers' requests to identify their shareholders. The CSD then forwards the requests along the holding chain and the identification proceeds with no further issuer intervention (such is the case in Italy[51]). At a higher level of efficiency, shareholder identification mechanisms operate automatically, as is the case in France with the above-mentioned BRN system.

As shareholder identification systems already in place in some EU countries display a variety of technical features, the SRD adapts to this variety by granting Member States some optional choices. The 'centralised' system will be the mandatory mechanism for shareholder identification to which all European issuers will have access (Article 3a(3) SRD). On top of this, Member States will also have the possibility of allowing a 'decentralised' search along the model currently prevailing in some countries.

It is of course too early to tell whether cross-border identification mechanisms will overcome the current limitations and will be more effective in the future. Some regulatory choices seem to go in the right direction, at least as long as one assumes that fostering shareholder identification is a policy worth pursuing.[52] For instance, centralised shareholder identification – the preferential choice of the SRD – can be less time consuming than its alternative. At the same time, this system does not leave issuers any flexibility in the selection of the intermediaries to contact, which prevents confining the inquiry to those custodians that may offer a lower cost per identified client. However, Member States' ability to

[49] In the UK, the request is known as 'Section 793 Notice' (formerly 'Section 212 Notice'): s 793 Companies Act 2006. For a similar provision in Germany see para 67(4) AktG.

[50] For the UK, see ss 793–95 Companies Act 2006. For Germany, see para 67(4) AktG.

[51] See Art. 83-XII Consolidated Law on Finance.

[52] For an analysis see Luca Enriques, Matteo Gargantini and Valerio Novembre, 'Mandatory and Contract-Based Ownership Disclosure' (2010) Uniform L. Rev. 713.

regulate the custodians' fees might reduce the side-effects of centralised identification systems (Article 3d SRD). Keeping charges low will be a crucial factor in making these procedures an efficient enforcement system because shareholder identification can only be of help if its benefits exceed its costs.[53]

One may doubt, instead, that the inquiry may be cheaper if limited to shareholders holding more than 0.5 per cent of shares or voting rights, as the Directive allows (Article 3a(1) SRD). To avoid easy circumventions of the identification process, the limit is based on the total shareholding, as opposed to the holding registered on each account. However, to make the calculation of the threshold a viable exercise, it seems that a centralised entity – such as a CSD – will in any case have to collect the information concerning all the account holders. This is likely to offset potential cost savings.[54]

A more substantial restriction to the effectiveness of the SRD identification mechanism may rather come from its limitation to 'shareholders' alone. In the absence of a common definition of what a 'shareholder' is,[55] investors that do not qualify as shareholders but have beneficial ownership of shares (or another qualified interest in shares[56]) may easily fall outside the scope of the inquiry.

Finally, the SRD identification system will not, in and of itself, help enforcement of duties that shareholders owe to their fellow shareholders or to other constituencies. Major jurisdictions show a wide spectrum of solutions in this respect. In the UK and in Italy, investors may access the information gathered by their issuers with limited (or no) restrictions.[57] Tighter rules apply in France, where shareholders may only access the register of members during the short term of 15 days preceding the general meeting,[58] and in Germany, where no right of access is granted.[59] Similarly, the right to start an inquiry is granted to qualified minorities only in some countries, such as the UK[60] and Italy.[61] No such right is granted in France or Germany instead. Because broader shareholder access to identification mechanisms seems to be compatible with Article

53 At the same time, banning fees would result in cross-subsidisation of issuers at the expense of all the intermediaries' customers.

54 A more convincing rationale for the 0.5 per cent threshold may therefore be the protection of the right to create a relatively small toehold without being spotted by a potential target: see in general Enriques et al. (n 52).

55 Article 2(b) SRD refers to national applicable laws when defining shareholders.

56 See 793 Companies Act 2006 (UK).

57 See ss 117 and 807–11 Companies Act 2006 (UK) as well as Art. 83-XII Consolidated Law on Finance and Art. 2422 Civil Code (Italy).

58 See Arts L225-116 and R225-90 *Code de commerce*.

59 See para 67(6) AktG.

60 See s 804 Companies Act 2006.

61 See Art. 83-XII Consolidated Law on Finance.

3 SRD, rules will likely remain uneven in this respect, as will the mechanisms' ability to facilitate enforcement of shareholder duties by other shareholders.

VII. CONCLUSION

The SRD, together with it recent amendments and the draft Commission Implementing Regulation, has remarkably facilitated shareholder identification and entitlement and will likely deliver positive results in the near future. There are areas, however, where nothing is achieved until everything is achieved. No matter how many steps are taken in the right direction, just a few remaining obstacles may suffice to hinder cross-border identification and voting, or to make them less effective.

Persistent imperfections in the identification and entitlement process that directly and indirectly affect institutional shareholders' engagement with their investee companies can still make the costs of voting non-negligible, and suggest a careful approach when assessing shareholder compliance with stewardship best practices.[62] This approach should apply to any form of enforcement, whether formal or informal, and whether performed by supervisors, investors or other stakeholders, in line with the general rule that management companies should decide their voting strategy on the basis of the fund's exclusive interest (Article 21 Directive 2010/43/EU; Article 37 Reg. (EU) No 231/2013) and this may also lead, in some circumstances, to a rational decision not to vote (Recital 16 Directive 2010/43/EU).

As for the issuers' ability to enforce (other) shareholder duties, shareholder identification mechanisms remain an imperfect tool and the SRD will leave some of the current limitations in place. However, it is questionable that the benefits of implementing tighter identification systems will exceed the ensuing overall costs.

On a final note, this chapter has addressed the legal and operational problems that affect shareholder identification and entitlement in the current technological context. Things may change, however, in the near future. While developments – such as the Target 2 Securities project – that still rely on the current framework of the post-trading industry are in this respect deemed insufficient,[63] expectations are high that a major shift in the way securities are dematerialised will come from the blockchain technology.[64] If the distributed

---

[62] On the calibration of hard and soft approaches in the enforcement of best practices see, in general, Konstantinos Sergakis, 'EU Corporate Governance: A New Supervisory Mechanism for the "Comply or Explain" Principle?' (2013) European Council on Foreign Relations (ECFR) 394.

[63] Micheler (n 10) 492–93.

[64] Eva Micheler, 'Custody Chains and Asset Values: Why Crypto-Securities are Worth Contemplating' (2015) Cambridge L.J. 505; Anne Lafarre and Christoph

ledger technology keeps its promises, this chapter will most probably have to be rewritten to take into account future developments that may deeply affect the securities holding and transfer techniques.

Van der Elst, 'Blockchain Technology for Corporate Governance and Shareholder Activism' (2018) ECGI Working Paper No 390.

12. Barriers to the enforcement of shareholders' duties flowing from primary EU law

Christoph Teichmann and Lothar Wolff

I. INTRODUCTION

Shareholders are to a large extent investing in companies that are not governed by their own jurisdiction. Consequently, the enforcement of shareholders' duties arising from national law frequently involves a cross-border element. This means that within the European Union, state measures regulating and enforcing shareholder duties will have to be assessed in the light of primary EU law, which affects practically all transnational economic activities in the Common Market.

The most important yardstick for the compatibility of state measures with the idea of an integrated market are the fundamental freedoms. Shareholders investing cross-border may rely upon the free movement of capital and on the freedom of establishment. Consequently, this chapter will first assess the general framework of primary EU law (Section II) and then explore to what extent shareholders' duties may constitute an obstacle to cross-border investment (Section III) and corporate mobility (Section IV). The findings will be summarized in a final conclusion (Section V).

II. THE FRAMEWORK OF PRIMARY EU LAW

In this chapter we will first describe the effect of primary EU law with regard to national law (Section II.A). We will then focus on the fundamental freedoms, which are perhaps the most important cornerstones for the integration of the Common Market.[1] In the case of shareholders' duties, free movement of capital (Section II.B) and freedom of establishment may be invoked. The latter may be applied to shareholder duties imposed by national law (Section II.C).

[1] For a general overview, see Catherine Barnard, *The Substantive Law of the EU: The Four Freedoms* (5th edn, Oxford University Press 2016).

It also has an indirect effect insofar as it grants corporate mobility (Section II.D). We finally look at the approach of the European Court of Justice (ECJ) to restrictions and their justification (Section II.E).

A. The Primacy and Direct Effect of Primary Law

In order to fully understand the normative effects of primary EU law it must be borne in mind that the law of the European Union has primacy over the law of its Member States.[2] Although EU law does not render conflicting national law null and void, the latter becomes inapplicable (*primacy of application*). As such, the Treaties confer directly enforceable rights on individual citizens of the EU Member States, in particular the fundamental freedoms.[3] This *direct effect*, together with the primacy of application, renders any cross-border transaction in the Common Market ultimately assessable against the background of primary EU law.[4]

According to Art. 267 of the Treaty on the Functioning of the European Union (TFEU), the role of interpreting primary law lies with the ECJ.[5] Member States' courts may request a ruling of the ECJ on questions regarding the interpretation of the Treaties, and are obliged to do so if there is no more judicial remedy against the decision under national law. In that regard, the ECJ's interpretation of the Treaties serves as a judicial review of shareholders' duties imposed by national law. In case of incompatibility, EU law demands primacy of application and thereby hinders the enforcement of the respective duty.

B. Free Movement of Capital (Article 63 TFEU)

Article 63, para (1) TFEU protects the free movement of capital, with para (2) prohibiting restrictions on payments as an 'addendum'. The scope of the provision corresponds to Annex I of the Capital Directive of 1988.[6] Free movement of capital therefore covers any cross-border investment scenario. This includes both 'direct investments' in a company with the intention to actively partici-

---

2 ECJ, Case 6/64 *Costa v E.N.E.L.*, ECLI:EU:C:1964:66.

3 ECJ, Case 26/62 *van Gend en Loos v Netherlands Inland Revenue Administration*, ECLI:EU:C:1963:1.

4 See Stefan Grundmann, *European Company Law* (2nd edn, Intersentia 2011) 83f.

5 This role, according to Art. 344 TFEU, also constitutes a monopoly of the ECJ on dispute settlement in Treaty-related questions, see in particular Opinion 2/13 of the Court, 18 December 2014, paras 201ff.

6 ECJ, Case C-222/97 *Trummer and Mayer*, ECLI:EU:C:1999:143, paras 20f; Case C-112/05 *Commission v Germany*, ECLI:EU:C:2007:623, para 18.

pate in the management and control of the company, as well as the acquisition of shares for purely financial reasons, so-called 'portfolio investments'.[7] Since both active and passive investment behaviour are covered, the distinction is without practical relevance.

Some have instead argued in favour of a clear distinction that has direct investments only protected by freedom of establishment and limits the scope of Art. 63, para (1) TFEU to portfolio investments[8] but the ECJ has never followed this approach. This is appropriate if we consider that the value of a passive investment in a share lies not only in the perspective of a financial dividend, but also in the controlling and voting rights attached to it, which make it a *potential* active investment and therefore an attractive object of speculation. A passive investment can at any moment, in particular in the context of a takeover, turn into an active one.[9] The coverage of direct investments necessarily leads to an overlap with the scope of Art. 49 TFEU, which will be described in more detail below.

An important feature distinguishing Art. 63 TFEU from the other fundamental freedoms, and in particular Art. 49 TFEU, is its territorial scope. Free movement of capital is guaranteed not only between EU Member States, but also from and to third countries. While breaches of freedom of establishment may only be claimed by nationals of a Member State, investors from third countries can nevertheless rely upon free movement of capital when faced with a restrictive duty.[10]

C. Freedom of Establishment (Article 49 TFEU)

Article 49, para. (1) TFEU prohibits restrictions on the freedom of establishment of nationals of a Member State in the territory of another Member State. This describes cases in which the main establishment, i.e. the registered office or headquarters, is set up on the territory of another Member State (so-called *primary establishment*). The rule then extends this prohibition to restrictions on the setting-up of agencies, branches or subsidiaries by nationals of any

[7] Cf. ECJ, Case C-222/97 *Trummer and Mayer*, ECLI:EU:C:1999:143, para 21; Case C-483/99 *Commission v France*, ECLI:EU:C:2002:327, paras 36f; Case C-98/01 *Commission v United Kingdom*, ECLI:EU:C:2003:273, paras 39f.

[8] AG Colomer Opinion on Cases C-463/00 and C-98/01, ECLI:EU:C:2003:71, para 36.

[9] Jonathan Rickford, 'Protectionism, Capital Freedom, and the Internal Market' in Ulf Bernitz and Wolf-Georg Ringe (eds), *Company Law and Economic Protectionism* (Oxford University Press 2010) 54, 59 at n 11.

[10] See Wolfgang Schön, 'Free Movement of Capital and Freedom of Establishment' (2016) 17(3) Eur. Bus. Org. L. Rev. 229, 232.

Member State established in the territory of another Member State, commonly called *secondary establishment*.

The scope of protected activities is described in para (2). They include taking up and pursuing activities as self-employed persons as well as setting up and managing undertakings, in particular companies or firms, under the conditions laid down for its own nationals by the law of the country of establishment. As with free movement of capital, there must be a cross-border element present in order for the provision to apply. Unlike Art. 63 TFEU, however, a purely financial investment in a company is not covered by freedom of establishment. As the latter protects the management of undertakings, the investment must give the shareholder definite influence over the company's decisions and allow them to determine its activities in order to fall within the scope of Art. 49 TFEU.[11]

As already indicated, there is an overlap in the scope of application between Art. 63 and Art. 49 TFEU with regard to direct investments. When assessing the compatibility of national provisions restricting direct investments with primary EU law, the ECJ sometimes relies on both freedoms complementarily. In other decisions, the Court has not examined freedom of establishment separately as possible restrictions would be 'a direct consequence of the obstacles to the free movement of capital ... to which they are inextricably linked'.[12] This is in line with the Court's statement in *Casati* that 'freedom to move certain types of capital is, in practice, a pre-condition for the exercise of other freedoms guaranteed by the Treaty, in particular the right of establishment'.[13]

D. Corporate Mobility (Article 54 TFEU)

Article 54, para (1) TFEU stipulates that companies or firms formed in accordance with the law of a Member State and having their registered office, central administration or principal place of business within the Union shall be treated in the same way as natural persons. This extends the scope of application of Art. 49 TFEU towards companies incorporated within the EU. These companies exercise freedom of establishment in their own right, without having to rely upon their shareholders. In particular, even if Member State nationals use a company incorporated in another Member State solely for economic activities within their home Member State, the cross-border element is present in the foreign 'nationality' of the company.[14]

---

11 ECJ, Case C-251/98 *Baars*, ECLI:EU:C:2000:205, para 22; Case C-436/00 *X and Y*, ECLI:EU:C:2002:704, para 37.

12 ECJ, Case C-463/00 *Commission v Spain*, ECLI:EU:C:2003:272, para 86; Cases C-282/04 and C-283/04 *Commission v Netherlands*, ECLI:EU:C:2006:608, para 43.

13 ECJ, Case 203/80 *Casati*, ECLI:EU:C:1981:261, para 8.

14 ECJ, Case C-212/97 *Centros*, ECLI:EU:C:1999:126.

Since a company does not have 'nationality' in the same sense as natural persons, the connecting factor to a particular Member State lies in the fact that the company has been 'formed in accordance with the law' of a particular Member State. Once a company exists under the law of a Member State it will be protected by the freedom of establishment and may create an establishment in another Member State even if this establishment represents the only economic activity of the company. Consequently, the activity of the so-called *pseudo-foreign company* is protected by freedom of establishment since it is a company formed in accordance with the law of a Member State as required by Art. 54, para (1) TFEU.[15]

E. Restrictions and Their Justifications

Both freedom of establishment and free movement of capital go beyond a prohibition of direct or indirect discrimination. Instead, they cover all types of restrictions and subject them to scrutiny by the ECJ. For freedom of establishment, this effect was first stated in the decisions in *Kraus* and *Gebhard* in which the Court held that it precludes any national measure which – even though applicable without discrimination on grounds of nationality – is liable to hinder or make the exercise of the fundamental freedom less attractive.[16]

This wide interpretation of the fundamental freedoms obviously creates a tension between the idea of the Internal Market and the sovereignty of the Member States.[17] In the absence of secondary law, the Member States generally are competent to regulate a particular matter by national law. In order to balance the Member States' competences and the inherent necessities of the fundamental freedoms, the Court stated that national measures being qualified as restrictions may nevertheless be justified if they fulfil four conditions: (1) they must be applied in a non-discriminatory manner, (2) they must be justified by imperative requirements in the general interest, (3) they must be suitable for securing the attainment of the objective which they pursue, and (4) they must not go beyond what is necessary in order to attain it.

Beyond the written grounds of justification stipulated in Art. 52 and Art. 65 TFEU respectively, the Court has thus developed a general proportionality test for the justification of non-discriminatory measures.

---

[15] See in detail Christoph Teichmann in Martin Gebauer and Christoph Teichmann, *Enzyklopädie Europarecht* (Nomos 2016) at para 6, mn. 33f.

[16] ECJ, Case C-19/92 *Kraus*, ECLI:EU:C:1993:125, para 32; Case C-55/94 *Gebhard*, ECLI:EU:C:1995:411, para 37.

[17] See Christoph Teichmann, *Binnenmarktkonformes Gesellschaftsrecht* (De Gruyter 2006) 147f.

F. Primary EU Law as a Barrier to the Enforcement of Shareholders' Duties

When assessing how primary EU law can be a barrier to the enforcement of shareholders' duties, we may distinguish between the shareholder exercising a fundamental freedom (freedom of establishment and/or free movement of capital), and the company exercising it, namely its own freedom of establishment as granted by Art. 54 para (1) TFEU. The first perspective stresses the shareholder's role as an *investor* that might be deterred from making a cross-border investment, while the second perspective focuses on the legal framework governing the shareholder's position vis-à-vis the company, sometimes described as being a *member* in an association.[18] As we have already seen, both positions are protected by the Treaties.[19] Thus, the enforcement of duties imposed upon the shareholder in either capacity must obey the requirements stipulated by primary law.

III. SHAREHOLDERS' DUTIES AS OBSTACLES TO CROSS-BORDER INVESTMENT

The existence of shareholders' duties that might prevent or deter foreign investors from investing in a company is of particular relevance in large companies where shareholders are unable to negotiate their position towards the company in any other way than refraining from the investment.[20] Shareholders' duties that are relevant in that regard may have their source in tax law[21] or capital markets law, or serve to protect other public interests.[22] That includes, for example, restrictions on the investment in sports clubs, like the German '50+1' rule, which stipulates that only less than 50 per cent of shares in football clubs may be offered to external investors and thus prevents these investors from

[18] Cf. the 'ideal types of shareholders' described by Mathias M. Siems, 'With Great Power Comes Great Responsibility' in Hanne S. Birkmose (ed), *Shareholders' Duties* (Kluwer Law International 2017) 69, 70f.

[19] With a similar differentiation, Florian Möslein, *Grenzen unternehmerischer Leitungsmacht im marktoffenen Verband* (De Gruyter 2007) 193; see also Wolfgang Schön, 'The Concept of the Shareholder in European Company Law' (2000) 1 Eur. Bus. Org. L. Rev. 3.

[20] Florian Möslein, 'Europäisierung der Haftungsbeschränkung' (2011) NZG 174, 175.

[21] For a comparative overview on shareholders' liability for tax debts see Michael Stöber, 'Kapitalverkehrsfreiheit und persönliche Gesellschafterhaftung im europäischen Kapitalgesellschaftsrecht' (2014) 113 ZVglRWiss 57, 79ff.

[22] Cf. Hanne S. Birkmose and Florian Möslein, 'Introduction: Mapping Shareholders' Duties' in Birkmose (ed) (n 18) 1, 11ff.

acquiring a majority.[23] We have also seen case law on provisions that 'pierced the corporate veil' in a way that held shareholders liable for misconduct of the company (Section III.A) and the famous 'golden shares' cases (Section III.B) that raise the question as to whether any provision having a deterrent effect may be subject to scrutiny under free movement of capital (Section III.B).

A. The *Idrima Tipou* Case

1. Facts and background to the case

The ECJ had to decide on a shareholders' duty with a deterrent effect towards investors in the *Idrima Tipou* case,[24] which dealt with Greek rules regarding television companies. The Greek Law No. 2328/1995 allowed for fines where a television channel violated, *inter alia*, the rules of good conduct. These fines could be imposed jointly and severally on the company, on the management board, and on all its shareholders with a holding of over 2.5 per cent. According to the Greek legislator, the joint liability served the purpose of creating an incentive for shareholders to form alliances and exert their influence on the company's management in order to ensure compliance with good practice.[25] In other words, the liability regime was intended as a corporate governance instrument and stimulus for shareholder activism.[26]

In the case, a news programme had infringed the obligation to respect the character, honour, reputation, family life and presumption of innocence of two singers and a fashion designer. The Greek courts asked the ECJ to decide whether the rule stipulating shareholders' liability for administrative penalties was in accordance with the First Directive[27] and with the Treaties, in particular with freedom of establishment and free movement of capital.

2. The Advocate General's opinion

Like some scholars,[28] Advocate General Trstenjak held that EU law contained an unwritten principle of limited liability. This would imply that sharehold-

---

[23] For a critical approach, cf. Michael Stöber, 'Das Verbot von Mehrheitsbeteiligungen an Fußball-Kapitalgesellschaften und seine europarechtliche Bewertung' (2015) BB 962.

[24] ECJ, Case C-81/09 *Idrima Tipou*, ECLI:EU:C:2010:622; see Möslein (*supra* n 20); Stöber (n 21); Thomas Papadopoulos, 'Case C-81/09, Idrima Tipou' (2012) 49 Common Mkt. L. Rev. 401.

[25] ECJ, Case C-81/09 *Idrima Tipou*, ECLI:EU:C:2010:622, paras 40, 41.

[26] On shareholder activism as a corporate governance mechanism see Mette Neville, 'Shareholder Activism: The Dubious Shareholder Revisited' in Birkmose (ed) (n 18) 175.

[27] Directive 68/151/EEC, now consolidated in Directive 2017/1132/EU.

[28] Grundmann (n 4) 144f.

ers of a company usually must not be held liable either for the debts of the company or for the misbehaviour of the company. This principle may, in particular, be derived from the First Directive on disclosure of limited liability companies and from the Twelfth Directive[29] on single-member limited liability companies. Albeit limited liability was not stated explicitly in these directives, the Advocate General argued that a separation between corporate assets and shareholders' assets was implicitly recognized in various provisions.[30] Moreover, the fact that the Twelfth Directive recognizes the single-member company as the most problematic scenario of asset separation is used as an argument *a fortiori* for a general principle of limited liability.[31] One may also refer to the Directive on Annual Financial Statements, which in its recitals expressly justifies the importance of coordinating national rules in this area by the fact that companies subject to the directive offer no safeguards to third parties beyond the amount of their net assets.[32]

3. The decision of the Court

The ECJ, however, denied that the First Directive contained an unwritten principle of limited liability. It argued that the directive 'does not prescribe what a company limited by shares or otherwise having limited liability must be, but merely lays down rules which must be applied to certain types of companies [*scil.* under national law] identified by the European legislature as companies limited by shares or otherwise having limited liability'.[33] Thus, limited liability is not granted by secondary law itself, but rather by the company law of the Member States. This approach may be seen in the light of the overall reluctance of the ECJ to derive general principles from secondary law as had already been shown previously by the ECJ in the *Audiolux* judgment, where the Court declined to acknowledge a general principle of equal treatment of shareholders.[34]

Instead of secondary law, the ECJ relied upon Arts 49 and 63 TFEU. National legislation imposing fines jointly and severally upon a company's shareholders may have a deterrent effect for foreign investors and must therefore comply with the justification standard developed by the ECJ. As in many other cases, the ECJ is not restrictive at all when it comes to accepting legitimate objec-

---

29 Directive 89/667/EWG, now regulated in Directive 2009/102/EG.

30 AG Trstenjak Opinion on Case C-81/09 *Idrima Tipou*, ECLI:EU:C:2010:304, para 39.

31 Grundmann (n 4) 189; Möslein (n 20).

32 Recital 3, Directive 2013/34/EU.

33 ECJ, Case C-81/09 *Idrima Tipou*, ECLI:EU:C:2010:622, para 41.

34 ECJ, Case C-101/08 *Audiolux*, ECLI:EU:C:2009:626, paras 34ff.

tives in the public interest brought forward by Member States.[35] This may be attributed to the fact that the cases refer to areas which basically fall into the legislative competence of the Member States. Hence, in the *Idrima Tipou* case, securing compliance by television companies with legislation and rules of professional conduct was considered undoubtedly a legitimate objective.

The measure at hand, however, in the view of the ECJ, went beyond what was necessary to attain the objective. The Court questioned the rationale behind the rule of motivating shareholders to influence the company's operative activity. In particular, the Court dismissed the Greek argument that shareholders in television companies were typically journalists and held that other measures such as personal penalties for the journalists would be more suitable to create incentives for good practice.[36] Strict liability based merely on shareholding, on the other hand, goes beyond what is necessary to achieve the objective. The rule has a particularly deterrent effect towards foreign investors as they are less capable of forming alliances with other shareholders and often seek to diversify their portfolio without the intention to influence the management and control of the undertaking.[37]

In the light of these arguments, the Court ruled that the liability regime was incompatible with freedom of establishment and considered the general assumption of shareholders having to be activist shareholders 'the very negation of free movement of capital'.[38]

B. The Cases on Golden Shares

1. Over-proportional power of control

An investor-centred perspective is also the basis for the ECJ decisions on so-called golden shares. Golden shares are special rights used by states to retain control over privatized companies in strategic sectors.[39] These rights do not usually correspond to the state's nominal share in the companies' capital. For example, the state might reserve veto rights, blocking powers, or rights to nominate directors or members of the supervisory board. These rights may be adopted by using the mechanisms of company law, i.e. in the company's statutes, or they may be foreseen by specific legislative acts. By retaining a power

---

[35] See Astrid Epinay, 'Gemeinwohlinteressen und Grundfreiheiten' in Cordula Stumpf, Friedemann Kainer and Christian Baldus (eds), *Festschrift Müller-Graff* (Nomos 2015) 467.

[36] ECJ, Case C-81/09 *Idrima Tipou*, ECLI:EU:C:2010:622, para 64f.

[37] Ibid paras 59 and 69.

[38] Ibid para 69f.

[39] Tomas Papadopoulos, 'Shareholders' Duties in Case of State Ownership' in Birkmose (ed) (n 18) 255.

of control over the company which is over-proportional in relation to their investment, the states seek to prevent takeovers and corporate restructurings as well as to safeguard the provision of services in essential (and therefore formerly public) business sectors.[40] The rights vested in golden shares might therefore be considered to serve external, public interest-driven duties imposed upon the state as a shareholder, which have their source in the respective legislation.[41] Conversely, one could argue that golden shares also impose upon the other investing shareholders the duty to endure the state's preferential influence over the company's management.

2. Case law

The protectionism inherent in golden shares[42] makes them obvious candidates for hindering cross-border investment. Since 2002, the ECJ has had to decide on a number of cases involving golden shares.[43] The European Commission had considered the special rights various Member States retained in privatized companies to have a deterrent effect for foreign investors and therefore to unduly restrict freedom of establishment as well as free movement of capital.[44] The Court for the most part followed this assessment and held that Art. 63, para (1) TFEU prohibits all restrictions of the free movement of capital between Member States, both as direct as well as portfolio investments. Beyond open or indirect discrimination against foreign investors, each state measure that may potentially block the acquisition of shares in companies or may dissuade investors from other Member States from investing in companies restricts the free movement of capital.[45]

The only case in which the Court accepted the golden share legislation as justified on the grounds of public interest is *Commission v Belgium*. Not only was the objective of the Belgian legislation – to guarantee energy supplies in the event of a crisis – considered a legitimate public interest, what allowed the justification was the fact that the Belgian rule only catered for a ministerial intervention in the event of an objective threat to this public interest. It thus

---

[40] See in detail ibid 256.

[41] For a general duty to protect the public interest in case of state ownership, see ibid 258f.

[42] See Rickford (n 9) 56ff.

[43] ECJ, Case C-367/98 *Commission v Portugal*, ECLI:EU:C:2002:326; Case C-483/99 *Commission v France*, ECLI:EU:C:2002:327; Case C-503/99 *Commission v Belgium*, ECLI:EU:C:2002:328.

[44] Communication of the Commission on certain legal aspects concerning intra EU-investments [1997] OJ C220, 15.

[45] See, e.g., ECJ, Case C-483/99 *Commission v France*, ECLI:EU:C:2002:327, para 41; Cases C-282/04 and C-283/04 *Commission v Netherlands*, ECLI:EU:C:2006:608, para 20; Case C-112/05 *Commission v Germany*, ECLI:EU:C:2007:623, para 19.

did not constitute a general state influence over the company's management, but instead only applied in certain well-defined and sufficiently transparent situations subject to judicial review.[46]

In later decisions, the ECJ stressed that golden shares had a deterrent effect precisely because they constituted a disproportionality between the share of capital and the influence or control over the company. Both the right to approve (or veto) certain decisions[47] as well as the capping of voting rights and special appointment rights[48] break with this correlation. The ECJ decisions on golden shares have therefore prompted some authors to assume a general proportionality principle ('one share, one vote') in European company law. According to this opinion, investors may legitimately expect that the acquisition of shares in a company will grant voting rights proportional to the investment.[49]

3. Obstacles based upon party autonomy

The question thus arises whether *any* legal rule that deviates from the 'one share, one vote' principle constitutes a restriction of freedom of establishment and free movement of capital. If this were true, the criteria from the golden shares cases would have to be applied also to general company and capital markets law that provides shareholders with instruments to deviate from the proportionality principle. In particular, many Member States allow for voting caps or the creation of multiple voting right shares in the statutes.[50]

One may object that the use of these legal instruments is based upon autonomous decisions of private agents, i.e. the shareholders. But the ECJ has already endorsed the concept of *horizontal application*, i.e. the application between private parties, for other fundamental freedoms, in particular for the free move-

---

46 ECJ, Case C-503/99 *Commission v Belgium*, ECLI:EU:C:2002:328, paras 49ff; cf. Papadopoulos (n 39) 270ff.; Johannes Adolff, 'Turn of the Tide: The "Golden Share" Judgements of the European Court of Justice and the Liberalization of the European Capital Markets' (2002) 3 Germ. L.J. 46, para 35f.

47 See ECJ, Cases C-282/04 and C-283/04 *Commission v Netherlands*, ECLI:EU:C:2006:608, para 43.

48 ECJ, Case C-112/05 *Commission v Germany*, ECLI:EU:C:2007:623.

49 Michael Stöber, 'Goldene Aktien und Kapitalverkehrsfreiheit in Europa' (2010) NZG 977, 978.

50 See in detail the *Study on the Proportionality Between Ownership and Control in EU Listed Companies* commissioned by the European Commission, http://ec.europa.eu/internal_market/company/docs/shareholders/study/final_report_en.pdf; cf. also Stefan Grundmann and Florian Möslein, 'Die Goldene Aktie und der Markt für Unternehmenskontrolle im Rechtsvergleich' (2003) 102 ZVglRWiss 289.

ment of workers but also for freedom of establishment.[51] Likewise, Advocate General Maduro argued that

> the question should be raised as to whether legislation which enables some shareholders to obtain certain special rights in order to shield them from the market process, may itself constitute a restriction on the free movement of capital. Legislation of this type may restrict access to capital in the national market by protecting the position of certain operators who have acquired a stronghold in that market. Such operators, moreover, are likely to be domestic shareholders. Legislation of this kind may therefore hinder access to the national market for investors established in other Member States.[52]

The Court, however, seems to take a different stance. Both in *Volkswagen*[53] and in *Portugal Telecom*[54] the Member States had argued that their privileges derived from general company law and could be inserted into any company's articles of association by the autonomous will of the shareholders. The Court stressed, however, that 'there is a difference between a power made available to shareholders, who are free to decide whether or not they wish to use it, and a specific obligation imposed on shareholders by way of legislation, without giving them the possibility to derogate from it'.[55] Even if the creation of golden shares were based purely on private law – as seems to have been the case in *Portugal Telecom* – the provisions were only inserted into the articles of association by the Member State exercising its voting power, which makes them attributable to state authority and therefore problematic from an investor's perspective.[56] We thus find that the Court limits the scope of review to shareholders' duties created through the Member State's influence and for its own benefit.[57] Deviations from the proportionality principle adopted through

---

[51] See to this effect ECJ, Case 36-74 *Walrave and Koch*, ECLI:EU:C:1974:140, para 18; Case C-415/93 *Bosman*, ECLI:EU:C:1995:463, para 83; Case C-281/98 *Angonese*, ECLI:EU:C:2000:296, para 32; Case C-438/05 *Viking Lines*, ECLI:EU:C:2007:772, para 57.

[52] AG Maduro Opinion on Cases C-282/04 and C-283/04 *Commission v Netherlands*, ECLI:EU:C:2006:234, para 24.

[53] ECJ, Case C-112/05 *Commission v Germany*, ECLI:EU:C:2007:623, paras 38 and 45.

[54] ECJ, Case C-171/08 *Commission v Portugal*, ECLI:EU:C:2010:412, para 41; see also Cases C-282/04 and C-283/04 *Commission v Netherlands*, ECLI:EU:C:2006:608, para 22.

[55] ECJ, Case C-171/08 *Commission v Portugal*, ECLI:EU:C:2010:412, para 40.

[56] Stöber (n 49) 979.

[57] See also Jaron van Bekkum, Joost Kloosterman and Jaap Winter, 'Golden Shares and European Company Law: the Implications of Volkswagen' (2008) Eur. Comp. L. 5.

autonomous shareholders' decision do not fall under the 'investor deterrence test' developed by the Court.[58]

C. Conclusion

From an investor's perspective, shareholders' duties are liable to have a deterrent effect on cross-border investment. Although the ECJ is reluctant to rely upon general principles of company law, the deterrent effect is in practice determined by a foreign investor's reasonable expectations towards shareholding. Duties are restrictions attributable to a Member State if the duty is imposed by legislation serving public interests, or if the state uses a private law instrument which would not have been employed without state influence. When applying the proportionality test, the ECJ seems to be disinclined to accept duties that are solely attached to shareholding as they go beyond what is necessary to protect legitimate public interests. Situative, well-focused duties are more likely to be justified in terms of investor deterrence.

IV. SHAREHOLDERS' DUTIES AS OBSTACLES TO CORPORATE MOBILITY

Looking at barriers imposed by Art. 54 TFEU, which offers cross-border mobility to companies, implies a shift in perspective from investment to membership (Section IV.A). Shareholders' duties may be based on the *lex societatis* of the company (Section IV.B) or may be imposed by the host Member State applying national rules overriding the *lex societatis* (Section IV.C).

A. From Investment to Membership

Shareholders' duties can also be problematic from the perspective of the company's freedom of establishment. Beyond the investor-centric view, shareholders can be considered in their capacity as members of the organizational structure which is the company. Company law provides a legal framework for this organizational structure and for the legal relations between the parties concerned. The shareholders' legal position vis-à-vis the company is often described as a position of *membership*.[59] Most scholars believe that

---

[58] Christoph Teichmann and Elisabeth Heise, 'Das VW-Urteil des EuGH und seine Folgen' (2007) BB 2577, 2581; Jan Lieder, 'Staatliche Sonderrechte in Aktiengesellschaften' (2008) 172 ZHR 306, 339; Stöber (n 49) 979.

[59] Cf. Andreas Cahn, 'The Shareholders' Fiduciary Duty in German Company Law' in Birkmose (ed) (n 18) 347f; Andreas Cahn and David C. Donald, *Comparative Company Law* (Cambridge University Press 2010) 469ff.

the company as an organizational framework is ultimately contractual in nature, albeit contractual freedom might be constrained to a certain degree by mandatory rules.[60] The rights and duties of membership in the company are in consequence determined by the voluntary or mandatory content of the 'corporate contract'.[61]

B. Shareholders' Duties as Part of the *Lex Societatis*

1. Establishment by companies incorporated in another Member State

In a series of landmark decisions,[62] the ECJ has opened the Internal Market for companies incorporated in another Member State, even if they do not have any economic activity in the state of incorporation. This case law has considerably strengthened the conflict-of-laws approach that determines the *lex societatis* by the place of incorporation (the so-called *incorporation theory*).[63] It has been argued that thereby the incorporation of a pseudo-foreign company is to be considered to be a legitimate business activity that falls within the scope of Arts 49 and 54 TFEU.[64] But this is not entirely correct: the incorporation of a pseudo-foreign company, first of all, is governed by the national law of incorporation. The application of Arts 49 and 54 TFEU is triggered by the fact that this company, in a second step, actually creates an establishment

---

[60] See Jeffrey N. Gordon, 'The Mandatory Structure of Corporate Law' (1989) 89 Colum. L. Rev. 1549, 1555; John Armour, Henry Hansmann, Reinier Kraakman and Mariana Pargendler, 'What Is Corporate Law?' in Reinier Kraakman, John Armour, Paul Davies, Luca Enriques, Henry Hansmann, Gerard Hertig, Klaus J. Hopt, Hideki Kanda, Mariana Pargendler, Wolf-Georg Ringe and Edward Rock (eds), *The Anatomy of Corporate Law* (3rd edn, Oxford University Press 2017) 17f.

[61] Jennifer Payne, 'Contractual Aspects of Shareholders' Duties' in Birkmose (ed) (n 18) 347; for the concept of the 'corporate contract' see in particular Frank H. Easterbrook and Daniel R. Fischel, 'The Corporate Contract' (1989) 89 Colum. L. Rev. 1416.

[62] ECJ, Case C-212/97 *Centros*, ECLI:EU:C:1999:126; Case C-208/00 *Überseering*, ECLI:EU:C:2002:632; Case C-167/01 *Inspire Art*, ECLI:EU:C:2003:512.

[63] As to the opposing theories (real seat theory and incorporation theory) see Vanessa Edwards, *EC Company Law* (Oxford University Press 1999) 334f; Elvin R. Latty, 'Pseudo-Foreign Corporations' (1955) 65 Yale L.J. 137; Stephan Rammeloo, *Corporations in Private International Law* (Oxford University Press 2001) 9f.

[64] See Otto Sandrock and Jean J. du Plessis, 'The Impact of European Developments on German Codetermination' in Jean J. du Plessis, Claus Luttermann, Otto Sandrock, Bernhard Großfeld, Ingo Saenger and Matthias Casper (eds), *German Corporate Governance in International and European Context* (2nd edn, Springer 2012) 204.

in another Member State which perfectly fulfils the requirements of Art. 49 TFEU, being an establishment in the sense of a long-term economic activity.[65]

2. Indirect protection of the shareholders' choice of company law

The discussion of these cases has mainly focused on the rights of the company itself. However, there are also strong, albeit indirect, implications for the enforcement of shareholders' duties. As we have seen, membership-related duties have their source in the company's legal framework. For this purpose, it may be useful to understand the company as a 'set' of terms determining the legal relations.[66] Incorporating a company thus also creates a certain 'set' or 'package' of shareholders' duties, beginning with the pre-incorporation duty of raising capital[67] but continuing throughout the company's entire lifecycle. The scope and content of this framework, and thereby the scope and content of shareholders' duties, is first and foremost determined by the company's personal statute, i.e. the applicable company law regime. This regime decides which legal forms are available and what rights and duties they offer.[68] It also sets the boundaries of possible contractual modifications of these rights and duties by deciding whether company law rules are mandatory or default rules.

Member States, in principle, have to recognize (pseudo-)foreign companies under the law of the Member State in which they have been incorporated.[69] Articles 49 and 54 TFEU thereby clearly limit the possibility of Member States to impose additional burdens upon EU-foreign companies. Many Member States have therefore changed their conflict-of-laws approach and now determine the *lex societatis* of EU-foreign companies based on the statute of incorporation. As a matter of fact, Arts 49 and 54 TFEU thus protect the party autonomy of the (future) shareholders when they set up a company. Through their corporate choice of law, they determine the content of their duties as shareholders.

According to the incorporation theory, all internal affairs of the company will be governed by this statute.[70] This includes, in particular, shareholders' duties towards the company itself or towards other shareholders. For example,

---

[65] See Christoph Teichmann, 'Gesellschaftsrecht im System der Niederlassungsfreiheit' (2011) ZGR 639, 669ff.

[66] Easterbrook and Fischel (n 61) 1444; Gordon (n 60) 1551.

[67] Cf. Melanie Döge, 'The Financial Obligations of the Shareholder' in Birkmose (ed) (n 18) 283.

[68] See, e.g., Larry E. Ribstein, 'Statutory Forms for Closely Held Firms: Theory and Evidence from LLCs' (1995) 73 Wash. U. L.Q. 365.

[69] Teichmann (n 15) para 6, mn. 33f; Sandrock and du Plessis (n 64) 204.

[70] This so-called 'internal affairs rule' is predominant in US corporate law, see US Supreme Court, *Edgar v MITE Corp.*, 457 US 624 (1982); in more detail Christian Kersting, 'Corporate Choice of Law – A Comparison of the United States and European Systems and a Proposal for a European Directive' (2002) 28 Brook. J. Int'l L. 1, 3.

the scope and content of the shareholders' duty of loyalty[71] or the general duty not to abuse rights[72] may vary considerably between jurisdictions. By choosing a certain state of incorporation, shareholders also agree at least implicitly on the shape of those 'fuzzier' rules that result from the complexity and duration of the corporate relationship.[73]

With regard to the enforcement of these duties, it should be noted that according to Art. 24 No. (2) of the Brussels Ia Regulation,[74] the courts of the company's seat shall have exclusive jurisdiction over the validity of the constitution, the nullity or the dissolution of companies and the validity of the decisions of the company's organs. Jurisdiction under this rule may also extend to disputes that are closely linked to the decision of a corporate organ, such as the review of the financial consideration paid in a squeeze-out.[75] As Art. 24 No. (2) is exclusive, shareholders may not choose a different jurisdiction in the articles.[76]

3. Regulatory competition

The freedom of incorporation has sparked a regulatory competition in the Common Market over the most attractive company law. Many Member States opened their restrictive company law in order to keep up with the legal regimes that offer more flexibility.[77] The flexibility, however, has not been mandated by primary law; it is instead an autonomous development on the market for 'company law as a product'.[78] ECJ case law so far strongly suggests that Arts 49 and 54 TFEU cannot be invoked against the state of incorporation when it does not offer a more flexible corporate framework.[79] Being incorporated according to the law of a Member State is a necessary precondition for the

---

71 See Cahn (n 59) 347.

72 See Pierre-Henri Conac, 'The Shareholders' Duty Not to Abuse Rights' in Birkmose (ed) (n 18) 363.

73 On the 'incompleteness' of the corporate contract, see Gordon (n 60), 1573; Kraakman et al. (n 60) 19f.

74 Regulation (EU) No. 1215/2012, OJ L351/1.

75 See ECJ, Case C-560/16 E.ON Czech Holding AG, ECLI:EU:C:2018:167, para. 31 ff.; cf. ECJ, Case C-372/07 Hassett and Doherty, ECLI:EU:C:2008:534, para. 20 f.

76 See Bundesgerichtshof, 12 July 2011, II ZR 28/10, BGHZ 190, 242, for the case of a pseudo-foreign English limited company with its real seat in Germany.

77 See the contributions in A. Jorge Viera González and Christoph Teichmann (eds), *Private Company Law Reform in Europe: The Race for Flexibility* (Aranzadi 2015). See also Christoph Teichmann, 'Die GmbH im europäischen Wettbewerb der Rechtsordnungen' (2017) ZGR 543ff.

78 Cf. the famous article by Roberta Romano, 'Law as a Product: Some Pieces of the Incorporation Puzzle' (1985) 1 J. L. Econ. & Org. 225.

79 In this direction ECJ, Case 81/87 *Daily Mail*, ECLI:EU:C:1988:456; Case C-210/06 *Cartesio*, ECLI:EU:C:2008:723.

company to enjoy freedom of establishment under Arts 49 and 54.[80] Founders therefore have only the right to opt into the conditions of incorporation as they are offered (in a non-discriminatory way) by national company law. This approach to a certain extent protects the legislative competence of the Member States to create their own company law rules. It should be noted, however, that the possibility to incorporate in other Member States de facto reduces the possibility to impose comparatively stricter rules in one Member State than offered by other Member States.

C. Shareholders' Duties Overriding the *Lex Societatis*

The ECJ case law on the recognition of pseudo-foreign companies has raised the follow-up question under what circumstances EU-foreign companies may be made subject to the law of the host Member State, in particular if they exercise any or all of their economic activity there. Mandatory provisions that may prove particularly problematic when circumvented by employing a foreign legal form may be found in group law,[81] in insolvency law, and in particular labour law mechanisms such as workers' co-determination.[82]

1. Liability rules within a cross-border group of companies

One case that raises the question of shareholder-specific duties in a cross-border group scenario is the *Impacto Azul* decision.[83] Under Portuguese group law, the parent company of a wholly owned subsidiary is always liable for the subsidiary's debts. However, the provision is limited in its scope to groups in which both parent and subsidiary have their real seat in Portugal. Portuguese courts therefore saw no basis for holding a French parent company liable for the debts incurred by its Portuguese subsidiary. From the primary law perspective, the case is quite clear: the provisions constitute a discrimination – but towards Portuguese groups. As foreign companies are explicitly exempt from the liability, there is no restriction to cross-border establishment that would require justification.[84]

More interesting, however, is the opposite question: under what circumstances may Member States impose group-related shareholders' duties, and in particular parent liability, in a cross-border scenario? So far, no such case has ever reached the ECJ. We can, however, make a number of observations.

---

[80] ECJ, Case C-210/06 *Cartesio*, ECLI:EU:C:2008:723, para 109.

[81] Blanaid Clarke, 'The Duties of Parent Companies' in Birkmose (ed) (n 18) 229ff.

[82] Sandrock and du Plessis (n 64) 197ff.

[83] ECJ, Case C-186/12 *Impacto Azul*, ECLI:EU:C:2013:412; see Christoph Teichmann, 'Konzernrecht und Niederlassungsfreiheit' (2014) ZGR 45.

[84] ECJ, Case C-186/12 *Impacto Azul*, ECLI:EU:C:2013:412, para 36; Teichmann (n 82).

First, we could ask again whether there is a general principle of limited liability in European company law, in this case from the perspective of a shareholder-member actively influencing and directing the management of the company, rather than that of a passive shareholder-investor. The Twelfth Directive on the single-member company, which was previously used as an argument *a fortiori*,[85] contains in Art 2, para (2) an explicit exception for group cases, which would indicate that shareholders' duties could be enforced more easily in this area.[86] Parent duties towards the subsidiary, however, are also likely to make the exercise of freedom of establishment less attractive and therefore constitute a potential restriction.

In transnational group scenarios, we have to distinguish between two legal entities as bearers of the fundamental freedom: the subsidiary is exercising freedom of *primary* establishment, while the parent makes use of the right to *secondary* establishment. Article 49, para (1) TFEU explicitly protects secondary establishment by setting up branches or subsidiaries. Unlike the branch, the subsidiary has a separate legal personality.[87] When a parent company sets up a foreign subsidiary in a legal form that offers limited liability, it exercises freedom of secondary establishment.[88] In effect, Arts 49 and 54 TFEU thus recognize the cross-border group of companies as a legitimate form of economic activity.[89] While this does not mean that separation of assets in a group must be respected under all circumstances, it strongly suggests that a structural liability in groups, like the Portuguese approach, would be against primary law when applied in a cross-border context.[90]

2. Rules of conduct applied after market access (tort law, insolvency law)

The result is less clear in the case of duties that prescribe a certain conduct while acting in a foreign market. As this type of duty would only apply to the shareholder *after* the company has accessed the market and is even approaching insolvency, some scholars have argued that it would not be within the

[85] See Section III.A.

[86] See Grundmann (n 4) 196ff.

[87] ECJ, Case 270/83 *Commission v France*, ECLI:EU:C:1986:37, para 22; see also Wolfgang Schön, 'The Free Choice between the Right to Establish a Branch and to Set-up a Subsidiary – A Principle of European Business Law' (2001) 2 Eur. Bus. Org. L. Rev. 339, 344.

[88] Christoph Teichmann, 'Corporate Groups within the Legal Framework of the European Union' (2015) Eur. Comp. Fin. L. Rev. 202, 214ff.

[89] Schön (n 86) 354; Teichmann (n 87) 214ff; Christoph Teichmann, 'Die grenzüberschreitende Unternehmensgruppe im Compliance-Zeitalter' (2017) ZGR 485, 496.

[90] Teichmann (n 82) 67f; Schön (n 19) 24.

scope of freedom of establishment.[91] In essence, this line of argumentation tries to transfer the concept of 'selling arrangements' developed for free movement of goods in the *Keck & Mithouard* case to freedom of establishment.[92]

Although previously reluctant to apply the *Keck* concept to other fundamental freedoms, the Court has recently shown an inclination towards the approach in the *Kornhaas* decision.[93] The German Bundesgerichtshof wanted to impose liability for the reimbursement of payments which the director made before the opening of the insolvency proceedings but after the company had become insolvent to the director of a pseudo-foreign English limited company. This liability is stipulated in § 64 of the German Limited Liability Companies Act (GmbHG) and thus *prima facie* only applies to companies incorporated as German *GmbHs*. Nevertheless, the Bundesgerichtshof favoured the qualification of § 64 GmbHG as an insolvency law provision and therefore applicable to all companies under an insolvency proceeding in Germany. According to Art. 4 of the European Insolvency Regulation, the applicable insolvency law is determined by the *lex fori concursus*, which is in turn determined by the company's 'centre of main interest' (i.e. its real seat).

The Court held that § 64 GmbHG could indeed be qualified as an insolvency law provision. Regarding its compatibility with freedom of establishment, the ECJ stated that the application of § 64 GmbHG

> in no way concerns the formation of a company in a given Member State or its subsequent establishment in another Member State, to the extent that that provision of national law is applicable only after that company has been formed, in connection with its business, and more specifically, ... from the time when it must be considered, pursuant to the national law applicable ... to be insolvent.[94]

The judgment could therefore be read in the sense that Art. 49 TFEU only imposes strict requirements for the initial act of establishment in a Member State, and that provisions which are applicable after market access has already been granted will be outside the scope of freedom of establishment or at least may have a lower threshold for justification.[95]

---

[91] Teichmann (n 65) 653ff.

[92] ECJ, Case C-267/91 *Keck & Mithouard*, ECLI:EU:C:1993:905; Aaron Khan, 'Corporate Mobility, Market Access and the Internal Market' (2015) 40 Eur. L. Rev. 371, 389.

[93] ECJ, Case C-594/14 *Kornhaas*, ECLI:EU:C:2015:806; see Wolf-Georg Ringe, 'Kornhaas and the Challenge of Applying Keck in Establishment' (2017) 42 Eur. L. Rev. 270.

[94] ECJ, Case C-594/14 *Kornhaas*, ECLI:EU:C:2015:806, para 28.

[95] Ringe (n 92) 275f; Teichmann (n 65) 646ff.

This reasoning would leave room also for the enforcement of shareholders' duties that apply only after the company has already entered the market. In particular, it would allow for a general shareholders' duty to respect the existence of the company as a separate pool of assets. Such a duty could be considered as being rooted in either tort law or insolvency law and thereby be separated from the applicable *lex societatis*. For example, under German law, there is a liability of shareholders who destroyed the very existence of the company (i.e. caused insolvency) by unduly depriving it of essential assets (*existenzvernichtender Eingriff*).[96] This concept functions in a similar way as group-related veil piercing.[97]

The normative basis of such liability lies in general tort law, the duty is therefore independent of the statute of incorporation. Based on the Rome II Regulation, tort law is governed by the law of the country in which the damage occurs.[98] The same place determines jurisdiction of national courts.[99] This leads to the question of where the harmful event occurs in a case where the plaintiff intends to 'pierce the corporate veil'. According to the ECJ, where the plaintiff was seeking to hold liable a member of the board and a shareholder for the debts of the company, because they had carried on business of an undercapitalized company,[100] the place where the harmful event occurred was the place to which the activities carried out by the company were connected.[101] Welcome back, real seat theory!

D. Shareholders' Duties and Cross-border Transfer of the Statutory Seat

A topic that has received considerable interest over recent years is corporate mobility through cross-border transformations, i.e. cross-border mergers, cross-border divisions, and in particular, cross-border conversions.[102] In a line

---

96 Bundesgerichtshof, 16 July 2007, II ZR 3/04, BGHZ 173, 246; Adriaan Dorresteijn, Christoph Teichmann, Erik Werlauff, Tiago Monteiro and Nadia Pocher, *European Corporate Law* (3rd edn, Kluwer 2017) 337; with regard to implications from the *Kornhaas* decision, see Ringe (n 92) 278.

97 Dorresteijn et al. (n 95) 350ff; for a common law perspective on group-related duties, cf. Clarke (n 80) 229ff.

98 Art. 4(1) Regulation (EC) No. 864/2007.

99 Art. 7(2) Regulation (EU) No. 1215/2015.

100 ECJ, Case C-147/12 *ÖFAB*, ECLI:EU:C:2013:490, para 42.

101 Ibid para 55.

102 For an overview of cross-border conversions registered by German commercial registers, see Christoph Teichmann, 'Cross-border Conversions after Vale – The German Experience' in Harold Koster, Frans Pennings and Catalin Rusu (eds), *Essays on Private and Business Law – A Tribute to Professor Adriaan Dorresteijn* (Eleven International Publishing 2017) 249ff.

of decisions, the ECJ has held that cross-border transformations form an integral part of a company's freedom of establishment.[103] In particular, the two most recent cases, *VALE* and *Polbud*, deal with companies converting their respective legal form into that of another Member State. Under the incorporation theory, the *lex societatis* can be altered by changing the place of incorporation, i.e. the statutory seat. Cross-border conversions can thus be achieved through a transfer of the statutory seat to another Member State. According to the Court, freedom of establishment covers even the isolated transfer of statutory seat without any economic link to the Member State of destination, provided that is not an incorporation requirement in the latter.[104] With regard to shareholders, the procedure of seat transfer can be the source for specific, transfer-related duties. At the same time, it affects the already existing set of shareholders' duties by modifying the applicable company law.

In the *Polbud* case, a Polish *sp. z o.o.* wanted to transfer its statutory seat to Luxembourg in order to convert into a *Sàrl* under Luxembourg law. While the register in Luxembourg had already inscribed the resolution by the shareholders to that effect, the Polish register denied the deletion of the company on the grounds that Polish law demanded a full liquidation of the company prior to the transfer. The ECJ held, *inter alia*, that the requirement of prior liquidation violated the company's freedom of establishment as it created an obstacle that is liable to impede, if not prevent, the cross-border conversion of the company. With regard to a possible justification, mandatory liquidation goes beyond what is necessary to attain the legitimate objective of protecting the interests of creditors, minority shareholders, and employees.

While the Court mainly stressed the deterrent effect for the company that has to liquidate, we may view the case also from the perspective of shareholders' duties and conclude that they are prevented from taking the decision to choose a new *lex societatis* without winding up 'their' company first. According to Art. 270(2) of the Polish Companies Code, a resolution of the shareholders on the transfer of the registered office to a Member State other than Poland entails the winding-up of the company on the conclusion of a liquidation procedure.[105]

The duty is thus effectively hindering shareholders from re-exercising their contractual freedom with regard to the company's statute once it has been incorporated. The Court emphasizes that, since the act of initial incorporation is protected by freedom of establishment as stated in the *Centros* case, the act

[103] ECJ, Case C-411/03 *SEVIC Systems*, ECLI:EU:C:2005:762; Case C-210/06 *Cartesio*, ECLI:EU:C:2008:723; Case C-378/10 *VALE*, ECLI:EU:C:2012:440; Case C-106/16 *Polbud*, ECLI:EU:C:2017:804.

[104] ECJ, Case C-106/16 *Polbud*, ECLI:EU:C:2017:804, para 43.

[105] Ibid para 3.

of conversion which entails re-incorporation in a different Member State must likewise be protected.[106]

E. Conclusion

From a membership-oriented perspective, shareholders' duties and their possible enforcement may be influenced indirectly through the company's right to freedom of establishment. By choosing the applicable law and legal form for their company, shareholders are exercising contractual freedom which is protected in the company as a legal subject within the personal scope of Art. 49 TFEU. At the same time, they are opting into a certain set of membership-related duties. Enforcing shareholders' duties against this choice is therefore problematic with regard to primary law. Recent case law indicates that justification is possible for duties that have little or no effect on the company's access to the market. In the context of changes to the corporate framework and the respective set of duties through cross-border seat transfers, duties imposed upon shareholders likewise have to stand the proportionality test.

V. FINAL CONCLUSIONS

This chapter examined barriers to the enforcement of shareholder duties flowing from primary EU law. We assessed the framework of primary EU law based on the dogmatic structure of the Treaty. In this respect, the direct effect of primary law has to be taken into account. National law which is in conflict with primary law will no longer be applicable.

The provisions of the TFEU that may create barriers to the enforcement of shareholder duties refer to the free movement of capital and the freedom of establishment. The latter is important in two respects: the shareholders themselves may rely on freedom of establishment insofar as they acquire a participation in a foreign company that allows them to influence the company's decisions and determine its activities. Moreover, the shareholders indirectly benefit from the corporate mobility of the company itself, which is protected by Art. 54 TFEU. Generally, any infringement of the fundamental freedoms needs to be justified by applying the proportionality test developed by the ECJ in the *Gebhard* case.

A duty imposed on shareholders was assessed to be in breach of free movement of capital in the *Idryma Tipou* case. Even though the Court did not acknowledge a general EU principle of limited liability, it held that personal liability of shareholders for illegal conduct of the company had a deterrent

---

106 Ibid para 38.

effect for foreign investors and could not be justified. In the famous cases on golden shares, the Court qualified over-proportional power of control granted to the state as a restriction of free movement of capital that could only exceptionally be justified when applied in well-defined situations being subject to judicial review. These cases raised the question as to whether duties imposed on shareholders by the articles of association might constitute a restriction on the free movement of capital. We argue that usually party autonomy should prevail except for cases where the content of the articles is attributable to the state exercising control over the company.

Corporate mobility in the sense of the landmark cases *Centros*, *Überseering* and *Inspire Art* creates a situation where shareholders may choose their personal set of company law. They may even subsequently change the initially chosen company law by converting into the legal form of another Member State. By incorporation in a particular Member State the shareholders also opt for a particular set of rights and duties in their capacity as members of the company. This decision, in principle, is protected by primary law since any Member State has to recognize the legal personality of a company being formed in accordance with the law of another Member State. In the area of private international law, the judgments of the ECJ have led to a shift from the real seat theory to the incorporation theory. Recent developments show, however, that Member States may override the company law of the state of incorporation by applying their own tort law and insolvency law provisions. They thereby change the set of duties that the shareholders may have expected when creating their company in another jurisdiction. As a consequence, shareholders should carefully take into account the boundaries between company law, tort law and insolvency law when doing business cross-border with their company.

13. Jurisdictional barriers to enforcement

Justin Borg-Barthet

I. INTRODUCTION

The substantive weaknesses discussed in other chapters of this book point to a lack of clarity concerning the nature and extent of shareholders' duties, and ambiguous legal provision for the domestic enforcement of such obligations as do exist. The weaknesses in national substantive laws are exacerbated by the present state of transnational harmonisation. There is a lack of focused attention on specific problems arising from the corporate form, particularly insofar as the negative externalities of limited liability and separate legal personality are concerned.[1] Coupled with intrinsic risks and costs of transnational litigation, this renders cross-border enforcement a costly and uncertain route for the attainment of justice. Essentially, the law fails to address the full spectrum of relationships arising from the corporate form in a coherent fashion, or to view significant market failures as much more than an 'unfortunate wrinkle in the economic perfection of the law'.[2]

Regulatory shortcomings include a lack of tailor-made systems of judicial and administrative cooperation which would enable stakeholders to exact claims against shareholders in a cost-effective fashion. Indeed, existing jurisdictional rules, and the practice of transnational litigation, enable shareholders to deploy litigation strategies which render transnational justice prohibitively expensive to the injured party. Shareholders can therefore use multinational corporate structures to insulate themselves from claims through a jurisdictional veil, which reinforces the corporate veil itself.[3]

---

1 For theoretical discussion of risk-transfer, see Susan E. Woodward, 'Limited Liability in the Theory of the Firm' in Donald A. Wittman (ed), *Economic Analysis of the Law. Selected Readings* (Blackwell Press 2003) 153.

2 David W. Leebron, 'Limited Liability, Tort Victims and Creditors' (1991) Colum. L. Rev. 1565, 1601.

3 See generally Peter Muchlinski, 'Corporations in International Litigation: Problems of Jurisdiction and the United Kingdom Asbestos Cases' (2001) Int'l & Comp. L.Q. 1.

A jurisdictional veil, coupled with multiple corporate veils, provides ultimate beneficial owners with a complex system of insulation from liability for potential harm caused to third parties.[4] Moreover, it creates further artificial ring-fencing within an economic entity, insulating the entity itself from its own harmful activities.[5] Indeed, it is commonplace for contemporary corporate group architecture to be designed to insulate parent companies from liabilities of their foreign subsidiaries, whether in tort or contract.[6] This is a far cry from the original conception of the limitation of liability whereby individual companies were expected to operate independently and deal with all third parties – including shareholders – at arm's length.[7] Insofar as the glitches of limited liability are concerned, the law has yet to catch up with the manner in which the market has deployed the facilities it provides. This is true of domestic systems, which, particularly in common law jurisdictions, continue to enforce an orthodox view of separate legal personality.[8] But the problem is especially accentuated in a transnational context, where the complexities of the private international law of companies are such that academic commentary often dares not tread;[9] that shyness is all the more apparent in the context of holistic transnational legislative intervention, or the conspicuous lack thereof.[10]

In the absence of legislative intervention, transnational corporate legal practice tolerates a significant degree of behaviour whereby wealth is transferred to shareholders to the detriment of vulnerable parties, often in situations where there is already significant economic disparity between parties and the states in which they are situated prior to the further transfer.[11] Whereas it is arguable, albeit qualifiedly, that contractual creditors are able to foresee the transfer of

---

4 See, e.g., Irit Mevorach, 'Appropriate Treatment of Corporate Groups in Insolvency: A Universal View' (2017) Eur. Bus. Org. L. Rev. 179.

5 Ibid.

6 Muchlinski (n 3) 16–17; Sandra K. Miller, 'Piercing the Corporate Veil Among Affiliated Companies in the European Community and in the US: A Comparative Analysis of US, German, and UK Veil-Piercing Approaches' (1998) Am. Bus. L.J. 73, 129–32.

7 Karl Hofstetter, 'Parent Responsibility for Subsidiary Corporations: Evaluating European Trends' (1990) Int'l & Comp. L.Q. 576.

8 See, e.g., Brenda Hannigan, 'Wedded to *Salomon*: Evasion, Concealment and Confusion on Piercing the Veil of the One-man Company' (2012) Irish Jurist 11–39.

9 Muchlinski (n 3) 1; Paul Beaumont and Jonathan Harris, 'Series Editors' Preface' in Justin Borg-Barthet, *The Governing Law of Companies in EU Law* (Hart/Bloomsbury 2012) vii.

10 See Justin Borg-Barthet, *The Governing Law of Companies in EU Law* (Hart/Bloomsbury 2012) 4–8 and the references therein.

11 For a well-rounded discussion of the extent of opportunistic risk transfer, contrast Leebron (n 2) 1565 and Henry Hansmann and Reinier Kraakman, 'Toward Unlimited Shareholder Liability for Corporate Torts' (1991) Yale L.J. 1879.

risk and to price this into agreements, the problem of risk transfer is especially accentuated for non-contractual stakeholders who, generally, could not foresee harm, still less deploy contractual mechanisms to guard against their bearing the risk of corporate activity.

Furthermore, the addition of a jurisdictional veil renders the rational apathy of shareholders ever more rational.[12] In the absence of the risk associated with transnational corporate activity operating as a commensurate cost for shareholders, monitoring the transnational activities of companies is often a poor investment of shareholders' time and resources.[13] Essentially, monitoring constitutes an opportunity cost which shareholders may find is disproportionate to the potential personal benefit.[14] It follows, then, that legal strategies are required which would make apathy less rational, albeit doing so in a manner which is proportionate to the overarching aims of the limitation of liability.

It is therefore argued hereunder that there is a need for international instruments to facilitate cross-border recovery of losses suffered due to shareholder acts or omissions. Ideally, this would be done on the basis of a holistic reform of both substantive and private international law, including relevant choice of law and jurisdictional rules.[15] The primary focus hereunder, however, is the manner in which litigation is costed beyond the means of would-be claimants as a consequence of a lack of tailor-made rules. It is submitted that reforming jurisdictional rules, and enhancing the role of the state in enforcement of obligations through cooperation between administrative authorities, could offset, to a degree, the financial and psychological barriers to cross-border litigation.

II. SEISING THE PROPER FORUM IN THE EU

The discussion hereunder proceeds on the basis that the imposition of obligations on shareholders presupposes that, in economic terms, they act as agents of other corporate stakeholders, as opposed to acting purely on the basis of self-interest, and that they should be held to account as such.[16] It is

---

[12] For discussion of the nature and geographic extent of shareholders' 'rational apathy' see, e.g., Mathias M. Siems, *Convergence in Shareholder Law* (Cambridge University Press 2011) 89–90, and the references therein.

[13] Hansmann and Kraakman (n 11) 1894.

[14] Ibid.

[15] This should, in principle, consider both *ex ante* and *ex post* measures, which would dissuade opportunistic behaviour and remedy it in the event of corporate insolvency. This chapter focuses in particular on core corporate law during the viable lifetime of companies. Cross-border insolvency regulation merits fulsome analysis beyond the scope of the present work.

[16] For a more sophisticated account of the relationship between self-interest and agency theory, and applicability to shareholders as agents, see John Hendry, 'Beyond

the presumption of this economic agency relationship which justifies any liability to other stakeholders in corporations. It is noteworthy that the Brussels I Recast Regulation[17] does not rely on any such analysis and focuses instead on broad-brush distinctions between civil law classifications. It is beyond the scope of this chapter to consider the full spectrum of corporate legal theory and its implications for adequate jurisdictional design.[18] Suffice it to note, however, that corporate stakeholders affected by the acts or omissions of shareholders could include employees, creditors, the company itself, other shareholders and the public at large. Essentially, each stakeholder to whom it could be argued that a company owes obligations could in turn be owed obligations by shareholders as originators of the company, and as the stakeholders who exercise ultimate control over companies by virtue of their instruction rights, monitoring rights (and obligations), and their power to appoint officers exercising day-to-day control.

This section considers the ability of a stakeholder to bring an action through the prism of existing jurisdictional rules. What emerges from the analysis in an EU context is a highly integrated market in which remedies for market failures remain fragmented due to the sheer cost of cross-border litigation and potential for expensive contestation of jurisdiction. Furthermore, there is a lack of specific focus on the particular nature of the relationships arising from the corporate form, including the vulnerability of corporate stakeholders to corporate decision-makers. Potential remedies include the reframing of jurisdictional rules and the further involvement of states in monitoring and enforcement. These are considered in Section II.B. and Section IV.

Self-Interest: Agency Theory and the Board in a Satisficing World' (2005) British J. Management 55, 56.

[17] Regulation (EU) No. 1215/2012 of the European Parliament and of the Council of 12 December 2012 on jurisdiction and the recognition and enforcement of judgments in civil and commercial matters (recast) [2012] OJ L351/1 (Hereinafter 'Brussels I Recast').

[18] For an account of the spectrum of theories of the firm and their potential deployment in company law, see, for example, John Paterson, 'The Company Law Review in the UK and the Question of Scope: Theoretical Concerns, Practical Constraints and Possible New Directions' in Robert Cobbaut and Jacques Lenoble (eds), *Corporate Governance. An Institutional Approach* (Kluwer 2003) 141, 141–79; Janet Dine, *The Governance of Corporate Groups* (Cambridge University Press 2000) 1–36; Alice Belcher, 'The Boundaries of the Firm: The Theories of Coase, Knight and Weitzman' (1997) Legal Studies 22, 22–39.

A. Current Jurisdictional Rules for Private Enforcement in the EU

The current jurisdictional design under the Brussels I Recast provides a number of avenues for courts to be seised of claims regarding shareholder liability. In the absence of exclusive grounds of jurisdiction,[19] which are discussed in Section II.A.1, the first port of call to determine which courts should exercise jurisdiction is consideration of whether there is a choice-of-court agreement between the parties. If so, that agreement will usually be upheld by the courts of the Member States.[20] The operation of choice-of-court agreements is typically sound although it is not free from criticism.[21] The analysis here focuses, however, on the rules concerning jurisdiction in the absence of choice by the parties since, as noted above, the primary concern in actions against shareholders is situations in which potential harm could not be foreseen and priced by the plaintiff, still less could a choice-of-court agreement have been concluded in advance of the events requiring litigation. Relevant provisions of the Regulation include the default rules concerning jurisdiction based on the domicile of the defendant,[22] special grounds of jurisdiction in tort and contract,[23] and exclusive jurisdiction over the internal affairs of a company.[24] It is pertinent to note also the possibility of suing co-defendants in a single court in which one of them is domiciled,[25] which offers employees and consumers additional potential litigation venues as against shareholders.[26]

While the multiplicity of potential grounds of jurisdiction appears at first blush to favour the plaintiff, a lack of specific rules for the shareholder–stakeholder relationship, coupled with occasional lack of clear definition of key concepts, is problematic in that it reduces predictability and consequently increases costs of litigation. Jurisdictional wrangling where several grounds of jurisdiction are available is known to result in legal costs amounting to hundreds of thousands of euros, and sometimes in excess of 1 million euros, before substantive litigation has commenced.[27] These costs are in sharp contrast to the

---

19 Brussels I Recast (n 17) Art. 24.

20 Ibid Art. 25.

21 See, e.g., Zheng Sophia Tang, 'Cross-border Contract Litigation in the EU' in Paul Beuamont, Mihail Danov, Katarina Trimmings and Burcu Yüksel (eds), *Cross-Border Litigation in Europe* (Hart/Bloomsbury 2017) 624–27.

22 Brussels I Recast (n 17) Arts 4 and 63.

23 Ibid Art. 7.

24 Ibid Art. 24(2).

25 Ibid Art. 8.

26 Ibid ss 4–5.

27 See, e.g., the following family law cases: *V v V* [2011] EWHC 1190 (Fam) [61]: 'The overall bill to the family, now standing at £925,000, will no doubt top £1 million if next month's hearing about the children goes ahead. It should be recalled that this level

disposable income available to most individuals. The OECD average in 2017 was $30,563 (or €24,792 at the time of writing), which is dwarfed by the costs well-capitalised litigants are able to impose on litigation.[28]

Furthermore, Beaumont et al. observe that jurisdictional challenges arise in 84.4 per cent of British cases concerning EU private international law instruments, often regardless of whether the defendant has any realistic prospect of persuading the court that it should not exercise jurisdiction.[29] Of those challenges to jurisdiction, the vast majority are unsuccessful and appear to be primarily tactical, although it is worth noting – for the sake of completeness – that successful challenges indicate a degree of abusive attempts to ground jurisdiction by the plaintiff.[30] In any event, qualitative data corroborates the intuitive understanding that jurisdictional challenges are often deployed tactically in order to delay proceedings and increase costs with a view to exacting advantage over plaintiffs.[31] In these circumstances, a well-capitalised shareholder is at liberty to price litigation beyond the reach of the aggrieved party simply by contesting the jurisdiction of the court seised. The mere potential to do so could act as a disincentive to a would-be litigant seeking to enforce rights in cross-border cases, or as an incentive to reach extrajudicial settlements at values which they might not otherwise accept.

In the context of suits in which the respondent shareholder is a legal person, an attempt to seise a court of the state of the defendant's domicile is particularly susceptible to preliminary pleading contesting the jurisdiction of the court. The general rule that a defendant may be sued in the Member State of his domicile must be read in conjunction with Article 63(1) of Brussels I Recast, which defines domicile of a legal person. That article provides three potential

---

of expense has been incurred without a basis of jurisdiction having been established'; *W Husband v W Wife* [2010] EWHC 1843 (Fam): legal costs to determine jurisdiction amounted to £120,000; *JKN v KCN* [2010] EWHC 843 (Fam) [7]: the combined legal cost to determine jurisdiction amounted to £900,000 at the preliminary stage. In civil and commercial matters, similar costs have been observed; e.g. in *Kolden Holdings Ltd v Rodette Commerce Ltd and Anor.* [2008] EWCA Civ. 10, the court lamented the expenditure of £400,000 on a spurious challenge to jurisdiction.

[28] OECD Better Life Index, 'Income' (2017), http://www.oecdbetterlifeindex.org/topics/income/ (accessed 22 March 2018).

[29] Paul Beaumont, Mihail Danov, Katarina Trimmings and Burcu Yüksel, 'Great Britain' in Beaumont et al. (eds) (n 21) 84.

[30] Mihail Danov and Paul Beaumont, 'Effective Remedies in Cross-border Civil and Commercial Disputes: A Case for an Institutional Reform at EU Level' in Beaumont et al. (eds) (n 21) 612.

[31] Beaumont, Danov, Trimmings and Yüksel (n 29) 84–85.

venues in which to bring an action, namely the '(a) statutory seat; (b) central administration; or (c) principal place of business' of the legal person.[32]

The default rule grounding jurisdiction in the place of the domicile of the defendant is designed to provide clarity and to prevent the plaintiff from shopping for jurisdictional advantage.[33] Nevertheless, there remains a measure of choice as a consequence of multiple potential venues in which a legal person could be domiciled; it is not necessarily the case that the three connecting factors are to be found in the same jurisdiction. Indeed, the jurisprudence of the Court of Justice of the European Union (CJEU) on freedom of establishment of companies has restricted the ability of states to require the coincidence of the statutory seat and central administration of a company,[34] and market actors have increasingly taken advantage of the freedom to separate the location of the connecting factors with a view to benefiting from accommodating corporate law and fiscal regimes.[35]

Whereas the place of the company's statutory seat is readily identifiable with reference to requisite documentation,[36] where the court seised is that of the central administration or principal place of business, there is significant room for strategic preliminary pleading in which this factual connection is contested.[37] Unlike the statutory seat, which is a formal connecting factor for

---

32 For Cyprus, Ireland and the United Kingdom, a further definition is included to clarify the meaning of statutory seat in respect of these common law jurisdictions for which the concept is somewhat alien: 'For the purposes of Ireland, Cyprus and the United Kingdom, "statutory seat" means the registered office or, where there is no such office anywhere, the place of incorporation or, where there is no such place anywhere, the place under the law of which the formation took place' (Brussels I Recast (n 17) Art. 63(2)).

33 See Ibid Recital 15.

34 Case C-212/97 *Centros Ltd v Erhvervs-og Selskabsstyrelsen* [1999] ECR I-01459; Case C-208/00 *Überseering BV v Nordic Construction Company Baumanagement GmbH (NCC)* [2002] ECR I-9919 Case C-378/10 *VALE Építési kft* [2012] ECR 00000.

35 For empirical evidence, as well as analysis of the motivations for this phenomenon, see Mathias Siems, Edmund Schuster, Federico Mucciarelli and Carsten Gerner-Beuerle, 'Why Do Businesses Incorporate in other EU Member States? An Empirical Analysis of the Role of Conflict of Laws Rules' (2017) ECGI – Law Working paper No. 61/2017, SSRN: https://ssrn.com/abstract=3012139; Mario Becht, Colin Mayer and Hannes F Wagner, 'Where Do Firms Incorporate?' (2008) 14(3) J. Corp. Fin. 241.

36 See by analogy, Dagmar Coester-Waltjen, 'German Conflict Rules and the Multinational Enterprise' (1976) Georgia J. Int'l & Comp. L. 197, 204–05.

37 Much of the literature criticising the real-seat theory as an unpredictable system for the determination of the governing law can be transposed to a discussion concerning jurisdiction. See, in particular, Stephan Rammeloo, *Corporations in Private International Law. A European Perspective* (Oxford University Press 2001) 11–20; Borg-Barthet (n 10) 41–46.

which evidence in writing is publicly accessible, the place of a company's central administration or principal place of business are not determined simply by identifying relevant documentation providing evidence of a legal formality. Rather, litigants may be required to adduce evidence that decisions are taken in a particular place in the case of the central administration, or that business activity is centred in a particular location in the case of the principal place of business.[38] Factual connections are certainly useful in respect of the determination of the governing law of a company in that they provide an indicator of where interests are primarily located, and where therefore governance should, arguably, be centred.[39] By the same measure, these connecting factors are potentially sound in respect of jurisdiction in the location of the company's main interests, which is more likely to coincide with the place in which creditors are situated.[40] Essentially, then, they provide connecting factors which in most cases would centre a dispute in a convenient court for the plaintiff, and one which is predictable for the respondent. Nevertheless, factual connecting factors are susceptible to criticism in that they are not readily determinable.[41] In the context of problems of potential strategic jurisdictional challenges, it is clear that opportunities have multiplied as a consequence of the *Centros* line of judgments, which has resulted in far greater incidence of separation of the place of incorporation from the other connecting factors which could determine a company's domicile.[42] It follows, therefore, that where a plaintiff sues a shareholder in the place of its central administration or principal place of business, the likely advantage of that place being situated conveniently for the plaintiff is offset somewhat by the susceptibility of relevant connecting factors to strategic jurisdictional wrangling.

Special grounds of jurisdiction, which a plaintiff may opt to deploy in place of the general grounds based on the defendant's domicile, raise similar concerns regarding vexatious jurisdictional challenges. This is most especially evident where it is arguable that a claim could be framed as both a breach of contract and a tort. In contractual matters, an action may be brought in the place of the performance of the contract.[43] The contractual place of performance and the place in which the harmful event giving rise to a non-contractual obligation are often not the same, of course. It follows that facts which could be argued to straddle contract and tort may, in principle, be subject to the jurisdiction of

---

[38] See *Owners of Cargo Lately Laden on Board the Rewia v Caribbean Liners (Caribtainer) Ltd* [1991] 1 Lloyd's Rep 69.

[39] Coester-Waltjen (n 36) 206.

[40] Ibid 207.

[41] Rammeloo (n 37) 14–15.

[42] See Siems, Schuster, Mucciarelli and Gerner-Beuerle (n 35).

[43] Brussels I Recast (n 17) Art. 7(1).

a plurality of courts. The CJEU has offered some clarity on the demarcation between contract and tort: a case is classified as contractual for the purposes of jurisdiction where there exists 'an obligation freely assumed by one party towards another'.[44] There remains, however, ample room for litigants to argue that courts have been seised incorrectly, particularly since the judgment in *Granarolo*, in which the Court of Justice obfuscated the meaning of contract by extending it to situations in which there is a 'tacit' contractual relationship.[45] The precise circumstances in which there is a tacit contractual relationship are, of course, a matter of fact to be determined by a court on the basis of 'a body of consistent evidence'.[46] It follows that any attempt to seise a court on the basis of jurisdiction in non-contractual matters is susceptible to contestation on the grounds that there is a tacit contractual relationship. Equally, if a plaintiff argues that there is a tacit contractual relationship, the respondent is at liberty to make the opposite argument. In either case, the need to adduce evidence, and the susceptibility of a claim to contestation, again provide litigants with significant room to prolong proceedings and multiply costs.[47]

Furthermore, whether jurisdiction in tort or contract is contested on grounds of incorrect classification, there is further room for jurisdictional challenge once the broad classification is determined. In particular, in non-contractual matters there is ample opportunity for strategic contestation of jurisdiction based on the location of the tort, in addition to a seemingly inexorable need for clarification of concepts from the CJEU.[48] Article 7(2) of the Regulation provides that, in matters relating to tort, delict or quasi-delict, an action may be raised in the courts of the place where the harmful event occurred. It is, of course, open to the shareholder to contest the assertion that an alleged harmful event did in fact occur in a particular place with a view to prolonging litigation or signalling an ability to cost it prohibitively. Similar issues arise in respect of contractual litigation, where further classification as a contract for the provision of services or sale of goods is required.[49] In the context of the present regulatory scheme, this is arguably unavoidable, save to the extent that defi-

---

[44] Case C-26/91 *Handte* [1992] ECR I-03967, para 15.

[45] Case C-196/15 *Granarolo SpA v Ambrosi Emmi France SA* EU:C:2016:559, paras 23–28. For academic commentary, see Michael Wilderspin, 'Cross-border Non-contractual Disputes: The Legislative Framework and Court Practice' in Beaumont et al. (eds (n 21) 641–42.

[46] *Granorolo* (n 45) para 26.

[47] See Uglješa Grušić, 'Long-Term Business Relationships and Implicit Contracts in European Private Law' (2016) Eur. Rev. Cont. L. 395, 397; Wilderspin (n 45) 641.

[48] Wilderspin (n 45) 640–41.

[49] Brussels I Recast (n 17) Art. 7(1).

ciencies in national procedural systems which allow room for prolongment of proceedings could be curtailed through supranational legislative intervention.[50]

Bespoke jurisdictional rules concerning employees[51] and consumers[52] provide some remedy to the cost of establishing jurisdiction in a convenient location for the more vulnerable party in a shareholder–stakeholder relationship. Exceptions to the default rule concerning jurisdiction in the place of the domicile of the defendant are to be interpreted narrowly, however.[53] It follows that an attempt to seise the court of the place of a consumer's domicile, or the place where an employee habitually works, would require a direct contractual relationship with the respondent. An attempt to sue a shareholder using these jurisdictional grounds, therefore, would fail unless the company itself was also sued with the shareholder due to the proximity of the claims against the company and the shareholder.[54] Here too, of course, a lack of tailor-made rules allows the shareholder to contest the joinder of proceedings. In particular, the plaintiff is required to show that there is a risk of irreconcilable judgments; the onus is on the plaintiff to show that the claim has not been brought against both the company and the shareholder 'for the sole purpose of removing one of them from the jurisdiction of the courts of the Member State in which that defendant is domiciled'.[55]

In addition to the expense arising from protractive strategies deployed in jurisdictional disputes, the need to litigate in a foreign jurisdiction could be prohibitive in and of itself.[56] By way of example, engaging lawyers in a foreign jurisdiction in addition to one's own multiplies costs, where a plaintiff is placed at further disadvantage due to potential disparities in cost arising from economic asymmetries between jurisdictions. Moreover, potential costs of translation, travel and other unavoidable logistical barriers and opportunity costs operate as a further disincentive.[57] This is before the potential litigant

---

[50] Danov and Beaumont (n 30) 605.

[51] Brussels I Recast (n 17) s 5.

[52] Ibid s 4.

[53] Case C-168/02 *Kronhofer* [2004] ECR I-6009, para 14.

[54] Brussels I Recast (n 17) Art. 8.

[55] Case C-103/05 *Reisch-Montage AG v Kiesel Baumaschinen Handels GmbH* [2006] ECR I-6827, para 32.

[56] Louis Visscher, 'A Law and Economics View on Harmonisation of Procedural Law' in Xandra E. Kramer and C. H. van Rhee (eds), *Civil Litigation in a Globalising World* (Springer 2012) 82–84.

[57] See generally Jean Albert et al., *Study on the Transparency of Costs of Civil Judicial Proceedings in the European Union* (European Commission Directorate-General 2007) https://e-justice.europa.eu/fileDownload.do?id=99bdd781-aa3d-49ed-b9ee-beb7eb04e3ce; Adriani Dori and Vincent Richard, 'Litigation Costs and Procedural Cultures – New Avenues for Research in Procedural Law' in Burkhard

has even paused to consider a lack of substantive harmonisation, resulting in additional cost arising from the need to appoint court experts to prove foreign law and potential disputes as to the meaning of foreign law.[58]

1. Minority shareholders and exclusive jurisdiction

In addition to the jurisdictional grounds noted above, it is pertinent to consider the rules on exclusive jurisdiction in matters pertaining to the internal affairs of a company. Article 24(2) provides that the following matters shall be within the exclusive jurisdiction of the state of the company's seat:

> in proceedings which have as their object the validity of the constitution, the nullity or the dissolution of companies or other legal persons or associations of natural or legal persons, or the validity of the decisions of their organs, the courts of the Member State in which the company, legal person or association has its seat. In order to determine that seat, the court shall apply its rules of private international law.

The first hurdle to consider here is the scope of exclusive jurisdiction. Article 24(2) is particularly relevant to minority shareholders insofar as they might seek to impugn acts of the company. In this respect, it is uncontroversial that Article 24(2) would apply. Accordingly, where a minority shareholder contests a decision of other shareholders taken via the company's general meeting, for example, this would be subject to the jurisdiction of the court of the company's seat. Not necessarily so, however, shareholder obligations *inter se*. The CJEU has affirmed repeatedly that Article 24(2) is to be interpreted narrowly and addresses only the validity of decisions of a company, as opposed to matters which in some way are linked to decisions of the company.[59] An unfair prejudice claim resulting from a decision of the controlling shareholders in the company would not necessarily, it seems, be governed by the rules on exclusive jurisdiction save if it sought to impugn the decision itself or an aspect thereof.[60] Nor is it clear whether a failure to act would equally be governed by Article 24(2). In such cases there is no decision to impugn, unless it can be shown that the company had deliberately decided not to act.

Hess and Xandra E. Kramer (eds), *From Common Rules to Best Practices in European Civil Procedure* (Nomos 2018) 303–52.

[58] See Visscher (n 56) 82–84.

[59] Case C-327/07 *Hassett and Doherty* ECLI:EU:C:2008:534, paras 22–26; Case C-302/13 *flyLAL-Lithuanian Airlines* ECLI:EU:C:2014:2319; Case C-560/16 *E.ON Czech Holding AG v Michael Dědouch and Others* ECLI:EU:C:2018:167, para 33. For academic commentary concerning earlier cases, see Paul Beaumont and Burcu Yüksel, 'Cross-Border Civil and Commercial Disputes Before the Court of Justice of the European Union' in Beaumont et al. (eds) (n 21) 557–58.

[60] *Dědouch* (n 59) paras 34–43.

In any event, where a claim is governed by Article 24(2), a shareholder would be required to bring an action in the courts of the Member State in which the company's seat is situated, and every other state must refuse jurisdiction. When determining the seat, however, Article 24(2) refers back to the private international law of the Member States. Notwithstanding judicial intervention in respect of cross-border recognition of companies, and indeed partly due to a lack of consistency in that respect,[61] the Member States retain diverse rules on the meaning of the seat of a company. Several Member States continue to rely on factual connecting factors to determine the seat.[62] This disconnect between choice of law and jurisdictional rules presents further potential for contestation of jurisdiction for the reasons noted above in respect of factual connecting factors for domicile of legal persons.[63]

Moreover, the rule in Article 24(2) is problematic to the extent that a minority shareholder is not necessarily entitled to choose a court which is conveniently located or indeed which is well suited to address the relevant matters expeditiously. The cost of protracted litigation, for example, might render the potential benefit too distant or uncertain. Still, there is an irresistible logic to grounding jurisdiction in the state of incorporation or the company's seat given the likely fluency of that court in relevant substantive law.[64] Furthermore, the majority shareholder bearing responsibility for corporate decisions may change from time to time, and it would therefore be cumbersome to allow jurisdiction to float when the matter at hand is closely connected to a specific jurisdiction in which proceedings might have already begun.[65] To these justifications, it is worth adding an overarching principle that shareholders have a contractual relationship with one another and it is therefore perfectly tenable to argue that, in principle, the act of incorporation is comparable to a prorogation clause whereby shareholders agree to submit a defined class of disputes to the exclusive jurisdiction of defined courts.[66]

That irresistible logic is dented, somewhat, in respect of a company which has transferred its seat or changed its governing law. The judgment of the CJEU in *Vale* enables a company to change its place of incorporation as a consequence of the Court's interpretation of the contractual nature of corporate

---

[61] See Justin Borg-Barthet, 'Free at Last? Choice of Corporate Law in the EU Following the Judgment in *VALE*' (2013) Int'l & Comp. L.Q. 503–12.

[62] Ibid.

[63] See Section II.A.

[64] *Dědouch* (n 59) para 30.

[65] Ibid para 44.

[66] See by analogy Case C-214/89 *Powell Duffryn plc v Wolfgang Petereit* [1992] ECR I-01745.

law in the context of freedom of establishment.[67] Unlike cross-border mergers, which are now governed by the Cross-Border Merger Directive,[68] seat transfers operate in a legislative vacuum so far as minority shareholder protections are concerned. It follows that the decisions of the company regarding the place of incorporation need not necessarily be endorsed by all shareholders, save to the extent that shareholders accept the fluidity of the corporate contract intrinsically. A minority shareholder may therefore be subjected to a change in the governing law – and consequently a change in the fora in which suit may be brought – without having consented or having been provided with opportunities to compensate for a lack of consent by way of termination of their membership of the company.[69] Here too there is a need for legislative intervention with a view to addressing remaining lacunae in the regulation of cross-border corporate mobility.[70]

B. Alternative Classifications of Shareholder Obligations

If existing and future regulation of shareholders' obligations within core company law and liability for certain acts of a company are to be enforced fully by relevant stakeholders, it may be necessary to make specific provision to classify the nature of the breach of those obligations for the purposes of the exercise of jurisdiction. At present, it is not entirely clear which heads of jurisdiction would apply to such obligations since they could variously be classified

---

67 Case C-378/10 *VALE Építési kft* [2012] ECR 00000. For academic commentary see Oliver Mörsdorf, 'The Legal Mobility of Companies Within the European Union Through Cross-border Conversion' (2012) C.M.L. Rev. 629–70; Borg-Barthet (n 61); Stephan Rammeloo, 'Freedom of Establishment: Cross-border Transfer of Company "Seat" – The Last Piece of the Puzzle?' (2012) Maastricht J. Eur. & Comp. L. 563–88.

68 Directive 2005/56/EC of the European Parliament and of the Council of 26 October 2005 on cross-border mergers of limited liability companies [2005] OJ L310/1.

69 See, e.g., Roberta Panizza, *Cross-Border Transfer of Company Seats* (European Parliament Policy Department for Citizens' Rights and Constitutional Affairs 2017: PE 583.143) 2, http://www.europarl.europa.eu/RegData/etudes/BRIE/2017/583143/IPOL_BRI(2017)583143_EN.pdf.

70 See, e.g., Conseil allemand pour le droit international privé, 'Proposition du Deustcher Rat für Internationales Privatrecht en vue de l'adoption d'une réglementation du droit international des sociétés au niveau européen/national' (2006) Révue Critique 712, 712–34; Eva-Maria Kieninger, 'The Law Applicable to Corporations in the EC' (2009) 73 RabelsZ 607, 619–20; Christian Timmermans, 'Impact of EU Law on International Company Law' (2010) 18(3) Eur. Rev. Priv. L. 549, 556; Paul Beaumont and Peter McEleavy, *Anton's Private International Law* (3rd edn, SULI/W. Green 2011) 25.31; Anneloes Bart, 'Crossing Borders: Exploring the Need for a Fourteenth EU Company Law Directive on the Transfer of the Registered Office' (2015) 26(4) Eur. Bus. L. Rev. 581–612.

as pertaining to the internal affairs of the company, arising from tort, or contractual obligations. As noted above, the law affords ample room for litigation concerning jurisdiction in these circumstances. Indeed, in *Dědouch* Advocate General Melchior Wathelet laments a lack of dedicated jurisdictional grounds to address matters arising from corporate relationships.[71] There is, essentially, a failure to view the firm as a distinct market.[72]

So far as exclusive jurisdiction over internal affairs of companies is concerned, Article 24(2) of Brussels I Recast is framed with reference to a restricted list of acts of the company in cases in which the validity of those acts is contested. Barriers to enforcement of obligations to minority shareholders could be remedied by inserting text to the following effect:

> in proceedings which have as their object the liability of a shareholder to another shareholder for the acts of a company in which they hold shares or for the acts of shareholders in their capacity as shareholders of that company, the courts of the state in which the company is incorporated or, in proceedings concerning such liability arising from changes in the governing law of the company, the state in which the company is incorporated or the state in which the company was incorporated at the time of the relevant acts.

This would be consistent with the contractual view of the relationship between shareholders, albeit with adjustments to allow the plaintiff the option of capturing the contractual choice of law at the relevant time in the event that this is changed. Importantly, it would also do away with multiple factual definitions of a company's seat with a view to reducing opportunities for strategic contestation of jurisdiction.

Other claims concerning the liability of shareholders could, in principle, continue to be governed by one of the other heads of jurisdiction, particularly tort, and occasionally contract. Nevertheless, common classification of claims against shareholders by non-shareholder constituencies would be beneficial insofar as it would limit room for preliminary pleas concerning jurisdiction, thereby removing hurdles to substantive claims. This could be achieved by way of a recital to clarify which rules to apply, and how to determine the relevant jurisdiction in each case. Alternatively, a clear classification of shareholder liability by way of tailor-made rules recognising the vulnerability of defined non-shareholder constituencies and situating jurisdiction in the courts of the plaintiff's domicile would leave little room for doubt or strategic pleading to dissuade potential litigants. Private international law instruments do, of course,

---

[71] Advocate General Melchior Wathelet in Case C-560/16 *E.ON Czech Holding AG v Michael Dědouch and Others* (n 59) para 23.

[72] See Ronald H. Coase, 'The Nature of the Firm' (1937) 4 *Economica* 386, 386–405.

recognise that disparity between the parties should, in some circumstances, be redressed by way of exception to the general rules.[73] Indeed, the current jurisdictional rules concerning tort, employees, consumers, and the general rule on the domicile of a company are intrinsically designed with a view to providing the plaintiff with the option to sue in the court of their own domicile since this is the likely location of the company's real seat or the place in which a harmful act could be argued to have taken place. Providing a clear and explicit rule to this effect in respect of shareholders' obligations would, in principle, limit the possibility of strategic contestation of jurisdiction. In the case of shareholders in groups of companies in particular, it would also provide clear recognition of the vulnerability of third parties to the risk transfer arising from shareholders' ring-fencing of liabilities.

These measures could not, however, eliminate the problem of private international law litigation altogether. It is submitted, therefore, that states are required to exercise a more active role in the cross-border enforcement of obligations. How this could be achieved is explored further in Section IV, following brief consideration of the effects of lack of global harmonisation.

III. LACK OF A GLOBAL INSTRUMENT ON JURISDICTION, RECOGNITION AND ENFORCEMENT

The barriers highlighted above in respect of the European Union pale in comparison to the situation pertaining in cases connected to states outwith the European judicial area. Globally, there is no universal instrument on jurisdiction and recognition and enforcement of judgments. The Hague Choice of Court Convention provides some remedy, but given that its scope is limited to business-to-business cases in which there is a choice of court agreement,[74] it is usually of no consequence to a claimant seeking to enforce shareholder obligations. Litigants are left to contend with the vagaries of divergent private international law rules concerning both jurisdiction and enforcement, including ample room for contestation of jurisdiction, available most especially in common law jurisdictions.[75] Jurisdictional rules concerning the extent to which national courts are suited to address transnational claims are not necessarily applied consistently and provide further room for litigants to prolong proceedings through reliance on unclear and conflicting precedent.[76] Nor is there

---

[73] See, e.g., Brussels I Recast (n 17) Recital 14.

[74] Hague Convention of Choice of Court Agreements 2005, Arts 1–2.

[75] See, e.g., Muchlinski (n 3).

[76] Cassandra Burke Robertson, 'Transnational Litigation and Institutional Choice' (2010) B.C. L. Rev. 1081, 1107–13.

any instrument coordinating choice of law rules, including the demarcation between substance and procedure, which would make substantive outcomes predictable. Still less has there been any successful effort to coordinate private international law rules concerning companies or corporate groups with a view to addressing the market failures arising from the entity doctrine.

Several high-profile cases in which it was argued that shareholders bore responsibility for a company's activity highlight the barriers arising from a lack of international harmonisation. The facts of cases like *Bhopal*,[77] *Lubbe v Cape*[78] and *Shell*[79] illustrate the gravity of the substantive abuses which transnational corporate architecture is capable of shielding. These cases concern allegations of human rights abuses and significant environmental harm by corporations for which it was claimed that shareholders – parent companies specifically – were responsible. But it is the procedural lengths to which the shareholders were willing and able to go that are most troubling for present purposes, particularly when considered in the context of the fact that these cases were remarkable in that claimants were sufficiently organised and well resourced to bring actions in the first place. In each of these cases, as in many others before and since, a lack of predictable rules allowed shareholders to contest jurisdiction on *forum non conveniens* grounds and to appeal decisions on the exercise of jurisdiction to higher courts in a G7 state. When considered in the context of mass torts arising from activities in materially poorer communities in less developed countries, the full import of jurisdictional wrangling is especially stark.

Moreover, where a *forum non conveniens* claim is upheld by a court, it follows that claimants are required to bring fresh proceedings in another state and, if they have the resources to do so and are successful despite potential inequality of arms, to then seek to enforce the judgment in the courts of other states. In cases such as *Cape*, a decision to stay proceedings in favour of a South African court would have further exacerbated inequality of arms due to the unavailability of legal aid for the claimants.[80] When considered in the context of multinational entities such as Shell, composed of some '1367 different companies which are located in 101 different countries', claimants are

---

[77] *In Re Union Carbide Corporation Gas Plant Disaster at Bhopal India in December 1984* 634 F. Supp. 842 (S.D.N.Y. 1986).

[78] *Lubbe v Cape Plc* [2000] 1 WLR 1545.

[79] *His Royal Highness Okpabi v Royal Dutch Shell Plc* [2017] EWHC 89 (TCC). It is noteworthy in this case that Shell sought a stay on grounds of *forum non conveniens* notwithstanding the clear prohibition of the application of that doctrine in the CJEU judgment in Case C-281/02 *Andrew Owusu v N.B. Jackson* EU:C:2005:120.

[80] Muchlinski (n 3) 6.

truly faced with a veritable jurisdiction and enforcement maze in the absence of predictable jurisdictional rules and systems of administrative cooperation.[81]

These cases highlight the considerable room for the planning of corporate architecture with a view to transfer of risk to non-shareholder constituencies where the facts of cases do not fall within both (i) substantively, the narrow factual exceptions to limited liability carved out by the courts,[82] and (ii) procedurally, the defences to a claim of *forum non conveniens*.[83] Strategic design of group structure therefore continues to enable multinational entities to ring-fence risky activities, thereby ensuring that assets and liabilities are kept as separate as possible. That the mass torts considered in this section persisted over a significant period of time, and continue to present shareholders with a considerable armoury of litigious techniques, must surely give international regulators pause for thought. Here too there is a need for the intervention of states, and the coordination of their interventions, with a view to limiting the transfer of risk to poor risk-bearers.

IV. LOCATING THE STATE

Given that the very existence of companies, including the conferral of special legal features and the recognition of those features on a cross-border basis, is contingent on concessions of states, it is arguable that shareholder obligations are owed to states by way of quid pro quo. This is borne out in the practice of all states' corporate laws.[84] On some accounts of the emergence of the corporate form, the state endows a company with separate legal personality and limits the liability of shareholders with a view to attaining particular ends.[85] It follows that states are owed obligations in exchange for the conferral of these special legal features.[86] This is relatively uncontroversial. Even the United Kingdom – a jurisdiction which is otherwise permissive of contractual freedom of shareholders – imposes monitoring obligations on institutional shareholders in listed companies in such a manner as to render those obligations indirectly

---

81 *Opkabi v Shell* (n 79) [82]. For academic commentary, see Mihail Danov, 'Cross-Border Litigation in England and Wales: Pre-Brexit Data and Post-Brexit Implications' (2017) Exeter Centre for International Law Working Paper Series 2017/3, 32, http://socialsciences.exeter.ac.uk/media/universityofexeter/collegeofsocialsciencesandinternationalstudies/lawimages/research/Danov_-_Cross-Border_Litigation_in_England_and_Wales_-_ECIL_WPS_2017-3.pdf.

82 *Opkabi v Shell* (n 79) [70]–[80].

83 See Muchlinski (n 3) and Burke Robertson (n 76).

84 See Borg-Barthet (n 10) 57.

85 See Dine (n 18) 1–36.

86 Ibid.

owed to the state.[87] Moreover, it is arguable that the state's conferral of special legal features which result in risk transfer to third parties requires the state to exercise a policing function as a consequence of the state's own agency relationship with natural persons subject to its jurisdiction. Indeed, the governance of companies is, arguably, an exercise in the outsourcing of state functions to the shareholders in the first place, and to the company by extension.[88]

That obligations could be owed by shareholders to the state is therefore broadly accepted. But the matter of which state (or states) is owed obligations and can therefore enforce those obligations inspires little consensus.[89] The question of enforcement cannot fully be separated from that of the governing law of companies. Essentially, disagreement concerning which state is responsible for the organisation of a company's internal affairs has knock-on effects in respect of the question of which state is to enforce obligations of a company and its constituents. During the ordinary course of a solvent company's lifetime, it is only the state which has control over the internal affairs, including the life and death of a company, which can exact effective measures to police the observance of obligations of corporate constituents.[90]

The core problem in respect of the determination of the governing law relates to the extent to which corporate decision-makers – shareholders in particular – should be free to order the internal affairs of a company, including the delimitation of matters which are subject to corporate law, such as obligations which may be owed by the shareholders.[91] The contractual school of thought, referred to as the incorporation theory, takes the view that promoters

---

87 See Financial Reporting Council, UK Stewardship Code 2012, https://www.frc.org.uk/getattachment/d67933f9-ca38-4233-b603-3d24b2f62c5f/UK-Stewardship-Code-(September-2012).pdf.

88 See Janet McLean, 'The Transnational Corporation in History: Lessons for Today?' (2004) Ind. L.J. 363, 363–72; Dine (n 18) 114–16. For an account of the introduction of limited liability in its historical context, see Donna Loftus, 'Capital and Community: Limited Liability and Attempts to Democratize the Market in Mid-Nineteenth-Century England' (2002) 45 Victorian Studies 93, 93–120.

89 For an overview of relevant theoretical disagreements, see Rammeloo (n 37) 11–20; Ernst Rabel, *The Conflict of Laws: A Comparative Study. Vol. 2* (2nd edn, University of Michigan 1960) 31–46; Francisco J. Garcimartín Alférez, 'Cross-Border Listed Companies' (2007) 328 Recueil des Cours de l'Académie de Droit International 13, 48–55.

90 See Case C-167/01 *Kamer van Koophandel en Fabrieken voor Amsterdam v Inspire Art Ltd* [2003] ECR I-10155, para 105.

91 Werner F. Ebke, 'The European Conflict-of-Corporate-Laws Revolution: Überseering, Inspire Art and Beyond' (2004) 38 The International Lawyer 813, 817–18; Eric Stein, 'Conflict-of-Laws Rules by Treaty: Recognition of Companies in a Regional Market' (1970) 68 Mich. L. Rev. 1327, 1333; Florence Guillaume, 'The Law Governing Companies in Swiss Private International Law' (2004) Y.B. Priv. Int'l

of companies should be free to choose the most efficient law.[92] In contrast, the concessionary view has it that companies are creatures of national law and that they should be subject to the laws of the state with which they are most closely connected because this is where the most affected polity is located.[93]

Latterly, there has been significant global movement towards the adoption of a contractual view of choice of law. In this construct, the legal system which is empowered to regulate a company is the system in which corporate decision-makers have chosen to incorporate the company, or indeed to reincorporate it.[94] This may or may not be a legal and administrative system with which the company has a strong factual connection.[95] It follows, then, that the state which is empowered to regulate the relationship between shareholders and other corporate stakeholders is not necessarily one which has a real interest in the effects of corporate activity, save to the extent that the company is in good stead insofar as the formalities of incorporation are concerned.[96]

Freedom of incorporation often results in that state having little political interest in the effects of shareholder activity or inactivity. Indeed, there is compelling evidence to support the view that it drives states to lower substantive protections, and arguably enforcement standards, with a view to accommodating shareholders as the primary drivers of incorporation choices.[97] One solution is for the question of the governing law to be revisited with a view to facilitating control by the most closely connected state.[98] This would offer significant advantages for state enforcement of obligations, including relatively uncomplicated routes to the imposition of penalties by corporate registries. An ancillary benefit would be greater familiarity with the governing law among all stakeholders, which in turn would reduce costs of discovery of rights and obligations.[99] It would not, however, resolve all cross-border

---

L. 251, 257; Andrew Johnston and Phil Syrpis, 'Regulatory Competition in European Company Law after *Cartesio*' (2009) 34 Eur. L. Rev. 378, 389–90.

92 Stefano Lombardo, 'Conflict of Law Rules in Company Law after *Überseering*: An Economic and Comparative Analysis of the Allocation of Policy Competence in the European Union' (2003) 3 Eur. Bus. Org. L. Rev. 301, 314–22; Michael J. Whincop, 'Conflicts in the Cathedral: Towards a Theory of Property Rights in Private International Law' (2000) 50 U. Toronto L.J. 41, 52–54; Edward M. Iacobucci, 'Toward a Signaling Explanation of the Private Choice of Corporate Law' (2004) 6 Am. L. & Econ. Rev. 319, 319–20.

93 Coester-Waltjen (n 36) 206.

94 See Rammeloo (n 37) 11–20; Rabel (n 89) 31–46; Garcimartín Alférez (n 89) 48–55.

95 Ibid.

96 Coester-Waltjen (n 36) 205–06.

97 See Borg-Barthet (n 10) 63–64.

98 Ibid 142–70.

99 Coester-Waltjen (n 36) 206.

matters since cross-border activity would subsist regardless, and cross-border shareholder obligations would therefore arise too. Nor is it especially likely to be a palatable solution to regulators and commentators who view freedom of choice as a central plank of the emergence of integrated international markets.[100] Regardless of any resolution of the governing law problem, therefore, there will remain multiple states to which it is arguable that shareholders owe obligations. It follows that there is a need for coordination of state activities by way of administrative and judicial cooperation.

A. Administrative Cooperation

The question of enforcement by the state raises difficult conceptual questions concerning legal mechanisms to be deployed to this end. A traditional private international law approach would exclude acts *iure imperii* from the scope of cross-border recognition and enforcement of judgments and administrative decisions.[101] In other words, where the state exercises a regulatory function to police the activities of shareholders, there is not a predicable system of cross-border enforcement to facilitate this since public acts are beyond the scope of relevant private international law instruments.[102] It follows that, in the absence of systems of cross-border administrative cooperation between authorities, the possibility of enforcement of obligations on a cross-border basis is constrained to a significant extent by the vagaries of international politics rather than law.

The flaws of a strict demarcation between public and private acts are recognised in a growing number of private international law instruments, most notably in family law instruments of the Hague Conference and the European Union.[103] In particular, it is recognised that a less-capitalised litigant often requires the assistance of state entities in order to enforce a claim in other states.[104] Accordingly, where artificial legal distinctions between public and private aspects of the same set of facts operate as a shield against the enforce-

---

[100] See, e.g., Tito Ballarino, 'From *Centros* to *Überseering*: EC Right of Establishment and the Conflict of Laws' (2002) Y.B. Priv. Int'l L. 203, 208.

[101] See Borg-Barthet (n 10) 18–19.

[102] Brussels I Recast (n 17) Art. 1.

[103] See, e.g., Hague Convention on the International Recovery of Child Support and Other Forms of Family Maintenance 2007 (Hereinafter 'Hague Maintenance Convention 2007') ch. II; Hague Convention on the Civil Aspects of International Child Abduction 1980, ch. II; Council Regulation (EC) No. 2201/2003 concerning jurisdiction and the recognition and enforcement of judgments in matrimonial matters and the matters of parental responsibility, repealing Regulation (EC) No. 1347/2000 [2003] OJ L338/1, ch. IV.

[104] Hague Maintenance Convention 2007, Arts. 15–16.

ment of obligations, private international law has now subsumed functions which are more properly characterised as public.

In this vein, a future instrument addressing the cross-border enforcement of shareholder duties could, in principle, include provision for authorities in different states to cooperate with a view to enabling stakeholders to enforce claims through state action on their behalf. Enabling states to enforce obligations through a system of cross-border cooperation would provide numerous advantages over private enforcement alone. First, state authorities could act *ex officio* to bring breaches of shareholder duties to the attention of authorities in other states, or to request the enforcement of their decisions elsewhere. This would be in keeping with the obligation of states to fulfil their fiduciary function towards natural or legal persons affected by decisions to establish companies or recognise those established elsewhere.[105] Secondly, administrative cooperation could be particularly efficacious insofar as it would supplement traditional private international mechanisms and limit cost for complainants who lack the means to contend with the attrition of protracted procedural and substantive litigation.[106] In particular, a system could be envisaged in which a state in receipt of a complaint could, if it judged the complaint to be prima facie tenable, communicate the breach to authorities in the state of incorporation with a view to the latter state deploying administrative measures to remedy the breach. This could have multiple benefits in terms of reduction of litigation costs and would shift the onus to the putative recalcitrant shareholder to disprove a prima facie tenable complaint.

Proportionality could be ensured by way of the prima facie evaluation of a complaint, which would limit the possibility of vexatious abuse of the mechanism by having impartial public authorities act as gatekeepers. Furthermore, the deployment of any such system could, if necessary, be circumscribed through means-testing of complainants, and the limitation of complaints to natural persons only as against legal persons only.[107] The risk of abuse of such a system could be further limited by deploying modest administrative charges to reduce the incentive to use the system for minor or weak complaints, and through the possibility of recovery of administrative costs where a complaint proves to be manifestly untenable. In sum, then, if the view is taken that shareholders owe fiduciary obligations to states and/or that the state owes policing obligations to corporate stakeholders, a system of administrative cooperation between states would go some way to supplement a system of private enforcement both

---

105 See Dine (n 18) 1–36.

106 See Danov and Beaumont (n 30) 612.

107 See Hague Maintenance Convention 2007, Art. 16.

through *ex officio* state action and through private complaints, which could be limited to instances in which state assistance is merited and proportionate.

V. CONCLUSIONS: A NEED TO DEDICATE ATTENTION TO PRIVATE INTERNATIONAL LAW OF COMPANIES IN THE ROUND

As noted above, there exist numerous routes to enforce claims against shareholders on a cross-border basis. The difficulties posed by jurisdictional rules are not to be found in a dearth of routes to enforcement. Rather, a lack of specific focus on market failures arising from the corporate form results in private international law rules which enable shareholders to deploy litigation strategies which price enforcement prohibitively. A lack of predictability as a consequence of diverse legal routes and outcomes therefore operates as a barrier in and of itself. Consequently, litigants are less likely to pursue claims against shareholders who are better equipped to deal with the attrition resulting from protracted legal proceedings with uncertain outcomes. Indeed, whether in the European judicial area or elsewhere, well-capitalised respondents are empowered under current rules to raise pleas which ensure that there is indeed a great deal of attrition and thereby to render litigation less affordable and attractive for the injured party.

Solutions to weaknesses in cross-border enforcement mechanisms are not to be found solely in a jurisdictional scheme which renders the exercise of jurisdiction and the enforcement of judgments more attractive to claimants. Revisiting questions concerning the substantive harmonisation of shareholder liability should be accompanied by a root and branch overview of private international law rules with a view to enhancing the role of states in the transnational protection of vulnerable parties. The scenarios noted above suggest that, notwithstanding the degree of complexity, there is a pressing need for administrative cooperation to facilitate the enforcement of shareholders' obligations.

Index